The Excel® Analyst's
Guide to Access®

The Excel® Analyst's Guide to Access®

Michael Alexander

Wiley Publishing, Inc.

The Excel® Analyst's Guide to Access®

Published by
Wiley Publishing, Inc.
10475 Crosspoint Boulevard
Indianapolis, IN 46256
www.wiley.com

Copyright © 2010 by Wiley Publishing, Inc., Indianapolis, Indiana

Published simultaneously in Canada

ISBN: 978-0-470-56701-2

This is dedicated to the fans of DataPigTechnologies.com . . .
all 12 of you.

About the Author

Mike Alexander is a Microsoft Certified Application Developer (MCAD) and author of several books on advanced business analysis with Microsoft Access and Excel. He has more than 15 years experience consulting and developing Office solutions. Michael has been named a Microsoft MVP for his ongoing contributions to the Excel community.

In his spare time he runs a free tutorial site, www.datapigtechnologies.com, where he shares basic Access and Excel tips to the Office community.

Credits

Executive Editor
Carol Long

Project Editor
Maureen Spears

Technical Editor
Dick Kusleika

Production Editor
Kathleen Wisor

Copy Editor
C.M. Jones

Editorial Director
Robyn B. Siesky

Editorial Manager
Mary Beth Wakefield

Marketing Manager
Ashley Zurcher

Production Manager
Tim Tate

Vice President and Executive Group Publisher
Richard Swadley

Vice President and Executive Publisher
Barry Pruett

Associate Publisher
Jim Minatel

Project Coordinator, Cover
Lynsey Stanford

Proofreader
Sheilah Ledwidge, Word One

Indexer
Robert Swanson

Cover Designer
Ryan Sneed

Acknowledgments

My deepest thanks to Carol Long and Maureen Spears, for all the hours of work put into bringing this book to life. Thanks also to Dick Kusleika (one of the best tech editors I've worked with) for suggesting numerous improvements to the examples and text in this book. Finally, a special thank you goes out to the wife and kids for putting up with all the time spent locked away on this project.

Contents at a Glance

Contents

Introduction

If you were to ask a random sampling of people what data analysis is, most would say that it is the process of calculating and summarizing data to get an answer to a question. In one sense, they are correct. However, the actions they are describing represent only a small part of the process known as data analysis.

For example, if you were asked to analyze how much revenue in sales your company made last month, what would you have to do in order to complete that analysis? You would just calculate and summarize the sales for the month, right? Well, where would you get the sales data? Where would you store the data? Would you have to clean up the data when you got it? How would you present your analysis: by week, by day, by location? The point being made here is that the process of data analysis is made up of more than just calculating and summarizing data.

A more representative definition of data analysis is the process of systematically collecting, transforming, and analyzing data in order to present meaningful conclusions. To better understand this concept, think of data analysis as a process that encapsulates four fundamental actions: collection, transformation, analysis, and presentation.

- **Collection.** Collection encompasses the gathering and storing of data—that is, where you obtain your data, how you will receive your data, how you will store your data, and how you will access your data when it comes time to perform some analysis.

- **Transformation.** Transformation is the process of ensuring your data is uniform in structure, free from redundancy, and stable. This generally entails things like establishing a table structure, cleaning text, removing blanks, and standardizing data fields.

■ **Analysis.** Analysis is the investigation of the component parts of your data and their relationships to your data source as a whole. You are analyzing your data when you are calculating, summarizing, categorizing, comparing, contrasting, examining, or testing your data.

■ **Presentation.** In the context of data analysis, presentation deals with how you make the content of your analysis available to a certain audience. That is, how you choose to display your results. Some considerations that go along with presentation of your analysis include the platform you will use, the levels of visibility you will provide, and the freedom you will give your audience to change their view.

As you think about these four fundamental actions, think about this reality: most analysts are severely limited to one tool—Excel. This means that all of the complex actions involved in each of these fundamentals are mostly being done with and in Excel. What's the problem with that? Well, Excel is not designed to do many of these actions. However, many analysts are so limited in their toolsets that they often go into hand-to-hand combat with their data, creating complex workarounds and inefficient processes.

What this book highlights is that there are powerful functionalities in Access that can help you go beyond your one dimensional spreadsheet and liberate you from the daily grind of managing and maintaining redundant analytical processes. Indeed, using Access for your data analysis needs can help you streamline your analytical processes, increase your productivity, and analyze the larger datasets that have reached Excel's limitations.

Throughout this book, you will come to realize that Access is not the dry database program used only for storing data and building departmental applications. Access possesses strong data analysis functionalities that are easy to learn and certainly applicable to many types of organizations and data systems.

What to Expect from This Book

After reading the first three chapters, you will be able to demonstrate proficiency in Access, executing powerful analysis on large datasets that have long since reached Excel's limitations. After the first nine chapters, you'll be able to add depth and dimension to your analysis with advanced Access functions, building complex analytical processes with ease. By the end of the book, you'll be creating your own custom functions, performing batch analysis, and developing automated procedures that essentially run on their own. You'll also you will be able to analyze large amounts of data in a meaningful way, quickly slice data into various views on the fly, automate redundant analysis, save time, and increase productivity.

What Not to Expect from This Book

It's important to note that there are aspects of Access and data analysis that are out of the scope of this book.

While this book does cover the fundamentals of Access, it is always in the light of data analysis and it is written from a data analyst's point of view. This is not meant to be an all-encompassing book on Access. That being said, if you are a first-time user of Access, you can feel confident that this book will provide you with a solid introduction to Access that will leave you with valuable skills you can use in your daily operations.

This book is not meant to be a book on data management theory and best practices. Nor is it meant to expound on high-level business intelligence concepts. This is more of a "technician's" book, providing hands-on instruction that introduces Access as an analytical tool that can provide powerful solutions to common analytical scenarios and issues.

Finally, while this book does contain a chapter that demonstrates various techniques to perform a whole range of statistical analysis, it is important to note that this book does not cover statistics theory, methodology, or best practices.

Skills Required for This Book

In order to get the most out of this book, it's best that you have certain skills before diving into the topics highlighted in this book. The ideal candidate for this book will have:

- Some experience working with data and familiarity with the basic concepts of data analysis such as working with tables, aggregating data, and performing calculations
- Experience using Excel with a strong grasp of concepts such as table structures, filtering, sorting and using formulas
- Some basic knowledge of Access; enough to know it exists and to have opened a database once or twice

How This Book is Organized

The following sections discuss this books structure and what it has to offer.

Part I: Fundamentals of Data Analysis in Access

Part I, which includes Chapters 1 , 2 and 3, provides a condensed introduction to Access. Here, you will learn some of the basic fundamentals of Access, along with the essential query skills required throughout the rest of the book. Topics covered in this part are: relational database concepts, query basics, using aggregate queries, action queries, and Crosstab queries.

Part II: Basic Analysis Techniques

Part II introduces you to some of the basic analytical tools and techniques available in Access. Chapter 4 covers data transformation, providing examples of how to clean and shape raw data into staging areas. Chapter 5 provides in-depth instruction on how to create and utilize custom calculations in analysis. Chapter 5 also shows you how to work with dates, using them in simple date calculations. Chapter 6 introduces you to some conditional analysis techniques that allow for the addition of business logic into analytical processes.

Part III: Advanced Analysis Techniques

Part III demonstrates many of the advanced techniques that truly bring data analysis to the next level. Chapter 7 introduces you to powerful subquery and domain aggregate functionality. Chapter 8 demonstrates many of the advanced statistical analysis that can be performed using subqueries and domain aggregate functions. Chapter 9 provides you with an in-depth look at Access macros and how to schedule batch data processing. Chapter 10 not only shows you how to use SQL and VBA to run data analysis without queries, but also how to create your own custom functions.

Part IV: Reports, Dashboards and Visualizations in Access

Part IV focuses on building reports and visualizations using Access. In Chapter 11, you will cover the basics of turning data into a slick-looking PDF-style Access reports. The chapter also talks about creating charts in Access to enhance the look and feel of Access reports. Chapter 12 discusses the real-world benefits of using the built-in PivotTable and PivotChart functionality found in Access. Chapter 13 demonstrates some of the innovative ways you can implement dashboard-style visualizations in your Access Queries and Reports.

Part V: Advanced Excel and Access Integration Techniques

Part V turns your attention to automation and integration, showing you how your reporting mechanisms can be enhanced by leveraging other programs and platforms. Chapter 14 discusses the various ways to move data between Excel and Access using VBA and ADO. Chapter 15 focuses on using Excel and Access automation to manage the inevitable need to show parts of your reporting through Excel. In Chapter 16, you're introduced to the automation techniques, which allow Excel and Access to take control of one another, resulting in some interesting reporting options. In Chapter 17, you get a thorough introduction to XML including a detailed explanation of how XML can collect and transfer data. You conclude with Chapter 18, where you'll get a taste of some of the techniques you can use to integrate Excel and other applications in the Microsoft Office suite. Here, you will be shown how to perform the most common tasks in more efficient ways through integration.

Part VI: Appendixes

Part VI includes useful reference materials that will assist you in your everyday dealings with Access. Appendix A provides a high-level overview of VBA for those users who are new to the world of Access programming. Appendix B introduces SQL, offering a concise tutorial on SQL syntax and usage. Appendix C offers ideas on how to avoid performance and corruption issues when working with Access databases. Appendix D details many of the built-in Access functions that are available to data analysts.

Conventions

To help you get the most from the text and keep track of what's happening, we've used a number of conventions throughout the book.

> **TRICKS OF THE TRADE**
>
> These features give you in-depth information on how to handle specific problems you might encounter when working with Access.

WARNING These hold important, not-to-be forgotten information that is directly relevant to the surrounding text.

NOTE Notes, tips, hints, tricks, and asides to the current discussion are presented like this.

As for styles in the text:
We *highlight* new terms and important words when we introduce them.

- We show keyboard strokes like this: Ctrl+A.

- We show file names, URLs, and code within the text like so: `persistence.properties`.

- We present code as follows:

```
We use a monofont type for code examples.
```

Companion Database

The examples demonstrated throughout this book can be found in the companion database. This sample database is located at `www.wiley.com/go/excelanalystguide`.

Fundamentals of Data Analysis in Access

In This Part

The Case for Data Analysis in Access

When you ask most people which software tool they use for their daily data analysis, the answer you most often get is Excel. Indeed, if you were to enter the key words *data analysis* in an Amazon.com search, you would get a plethora of books on how to analyze your data with Excel. Well if so many people seem to agree that using Excel to analyze data is the way to go, why bother using Access for data analysis? The honest answer: to avoid the limitations and issues that plague Excel.

This is not meant to disparage Excel. Many people across varying industries have used Excel for years, considering it the tool of choice for performing and presenting data analysis. Anyone who does not understand Excel in today's business world is undoubtedly hiding that shameful fact. The interactive, impromptu analysis that Excel can perform makes it truly unique in the industry.

However, Excel is not without its limitations, as you will see in the following section.

Where Data Analysis with Excel Can Go Wrong

Years of consulting experience have brought me face to face with managers, accountants, and analysts who all have had to accept one simple fact: Their analytical needs had outgrown Excel. They all met with fundamental issues that stemmed from one or more of Excel's three problem areas: scalability, transparency of analytical processes, and separation of data and presentation.

Scalability

Scalability is the ability of an application to develop flexibly to meet growth and complexity requirements. In the context of this chapter, scalability refers to Excel's ability to handle ever-increasing volumes of data. Most Excel aficionados will be quick to point out that as of Excel 2007, you can place 1,048,576 rows of data into a single Excel worksheet. This is an overwhelming increase from the limitation of 65,536 rows imposed by previous versions of Excel. However, this increase in capacity does not solve all of the scalability issues that inundate Excel.

Imagine that you are working in a small company and you are using Excel to analyze your daily transactions. As time goes on, you build a robust process complete with all the formulas, pivot tables, and macros you need to analyze the data stored in your neatly maintained worksheet.

As your data grows, you will first notice performance issues. Your spreadsheet will become slow to load and then slow to calculate. Why will this happen? It has to do with the way Excel handles memory. When an Excel file is loaded, the entire file is loaded into memory. Excel does this to allow for quick data processing and access. The drawback to this behavior is that each time something changes in your spreadsheet, Excel has to reload the entire spreadsheet into memory. The net result in a large spreadsheet is that it takes a great deal of memory to process even the smallest change in your spreadsheet. Eventually, each action you take in your gigantic worksheet will become an excruciating wait.

Your pivot tables will require bigger pivot caches, almost doubling your Excel workbook's file size. Eventually, your workbook will be too big to distribute easily. You may even consider breaking down the workbook into smaller workbooks (possibly one for each region). This causes you to duplicate your work. Not to mention the extra time and effort it would take should you want to recombine those workbooks.

In time, you may eventually reach the 1,048,576-row limit of your worksheet. What happens then? Do you start a new worksheet? How do you analyze two datasets on two different worksheets as one entity? Are your formulas still good? Will you have to write new macros?

These are all issues you need to deal with.

Of course, you will have the Excel power-users, who will find various clever ways to work around these limitations. In the end, though, they will always be just workarounds. Eventually, even these power-users will begin to think less about the most effective way to perform and present analysis of their data and more about how to make something "fit" into Excel without breaking their formulas and functions. Excel is flexible enough that a proficient user can make most things *fit* into Excel just fine. However, when users think only in terms of Excel, they are undoubtedly limiting themselves, albeit in an incredibly functional way.

In addition, these capacity limitations often force Excel users to have the data prepared for them. That is, someone else extracts large chunks of data from a large database and then aggregates and shapes the data for use in Excel. Should the serious analyst always be dependent on someone else for his or her data needs? What if an analyst could be given the tools to access vast quantities of data without being reliant on others to provide data? Could that analyst be more valuable to the organization? Could that analyst focus on the accuracy of the analysis and the quality of the presentation, instead of routing Excel data maintenance?

Access is an excellent (many would say logical) next step for the analyst who faces an ever-increasing data pool. Since an Access table takes very few performance hits with larger datasets and has no predetermined row limitations, an analyst can handle larger datasets without requiring the data to be summarized or prepared to fit into Excel. Since many tasks can be duplicated in both Excel and Access, an analyst proficient at both will be prepared for any situation. The alternative is telling everyone, "Sorry, it is not in Excel."

Also, if ever a process becomes more crucial to the organization and needs to be tracked in a more enterprise-acceptable environment, it will be easier to upgrade and scale up if that process is already in Access.

NOTE An Access table is limited to 256 columns but has no row limitation. This is not to say that Access has unlimited data storage capabilities. Every bit of data causes the Access database to grow in file size. An Access database has a file-size limitation of 2 gigabytes.

Transparency of Analytical Processes

One of Excel's most attractive features is its flexibility. Each cell can contain text, a number, a formula, or practically anything else the user defines. Indeed, this is one of the fundamental reasons Excel is such an effective tool for data analysis. Users can use named ranges, formulas, and macros to create an intricate system of interlocking calculations, linked cells, and formatted summaries that work together to create a final analysis.

So what is the problem with that? The problem is that there is no transparency of analytical processes. Thus, it is extremely difficult to determine what is actually going on in a spreadsheet. Anyone who has had to work with a spreadsheet created by someone else knows all too well the frustration that comes with deciphering the various gyrations of calculations and links being used to perform some analysis. Small spreadsheets performing modest analysis are painful to decipher, while large, elaborate, multi-worksheet workbooks are virtually impossible to decode, often leaving you to start from scratch.

Even auditing tools available with most Excel add-in packages provide little relief. Figure 1-1 shows the results of a formula auditing tool run on an actual workbook used by a real company. It's a list of all the formulas in this workbook. The idea is to use this list to find and make sense of existing formulas. Notice that line one shows that there are 156 formulas. Yeah, this list helps a lot; good luck.

Number of formulas: 156

Address	Row	Column	Formula
AF9	9	32	='Customer Input'!AK$10
D15	15	4	='Customer Input'!AK$12
D17	17	4	='RFQ Input'!$I23
D18	18	4	='RFQ Input'!$I13
D19	19	4	='RFQ Input'!$I15
D20	20	4	=CONCATENATE('RFQ Input'!$I17,", ",'RFQ Input'!$I19," ",'RFQ Input'!$I21)
I24	24	9	='Customer Input'!AK$10
D27	27	4	=CONCATENATE("Dear ",$D17,":")
D57	57	4	=IF('RFQ Input'!$AA$47="TPM Project Mgr",'Customer Input'!$J$12,'Customer Input'!$J$24)
D58	58	4	=IF('RFQ Input'!$AA$47="TPM Project Mgr","TPM Project Manager",'Customer Input'!$J$26)
G60	60	7	=CONCATENATE('Customer Input'!$J$16)
AF65	65	32	='Customer Input'!AK$10
D65	65	4	=$D18
D66	66	4	=$D15
D71	71	4	='RFQ Input'!$B52
AF71	71	32	=IF(OR($T71=0,$AB71=0),0,$T71*$AB71)
AF86	86	32	=IF(SUM(AF71:AJ85)<0.1,0,SUM($AF71:$AJ85))
AF89	89	32	=IF(OR($T89=0,$AB89=0),0,$T89*$AB89)
AF94	94	32	=IF(SUM(AF89:AJ93)<0.1,0,SUM($AF89:$AJ93))
D97	97	4	='RFQ Input'!$B78
T	97	20	='RFQ Input'!$R78
W97	97	23	='RFQ Input'!$U78

Figure 1-1: Formula auditing tools don't help much in deciphering spreadsheets.

Compared to Excel, Access might seem rigid, strict, and unwavering in its rules. No, you can't put formulas directly into data fields. No, you can't link a data field to another table. To many users, Excel is the cool gym teacher who lets you do anything, while Access is the cantankerous librarian who has nothing but error messages for you. All this rigidity comes with a benefit, however.

Since only certain actions are allowable, you can more easily come to understand what is being done with a set of data in Access. If a dataset is being edited, a number is being calculated, or if any portion of the dataset is being affected as a part of an analytical process, you will readily see that action. This is not to say that users can't do foolish and confusing things in Access. However, you definitely will not encounter hidden steps in an analytical process such as hidden formulas, hidden cells, or named ranges in dead worksheets.

Separation of Data and Presentation

Data should be separate from presentation; you do not want the data to become too tied to any particular way of presenting it. For example, when you receive an invoice from a company, you don't assume that the financial data on that invoice is the true source of your data. Rather, it is a presentation of your data. It can be presented to you in other manners and styles on charts or on Web sites, but such representations are never the actual source of data. This sounds obvious, but it becomes an important distinction when you study an approach of using Access and Excel together for data analysis.

What exactly does this concept have to do with Excel? People who perform data analysis with Excel, more often than not, tend to fuse the data, the analysis, and the presentation together. For example, you will often see an Excel Workbook that has 12 worksheets, each representing a month. On each worksheet, data for that month is listed along with formulas, pivot tables, and summaries. What happens when you are asked to provide a summary by quarter? Do you add more formulas and worksheets to consolidate the data on each of the month worksheets? The fundamental problem in this scenario is that the worksheets actually represent data values that are fused into the presentation of your analysis. The point here is that data should not be tied to a particular presentation, no matter how apparently logical or useful it may be. However, in Excel, it happens all the time.

In addition, as previously discussed, because all manners and phases of analysis can be done directly within a spreadsheet, Excel cannot effectively provide adequate transparency to the analysis. Each cell has the potential of holding formulas, becoming hidden, and containing links to other cells. In Excel, this blurs the line between analysis and data, which makes it difficult to determine exactly what is going on in a spreadsheet. Moreover, it takes a great deal of effort in the way of manual maintenance to ensure that edits and unforeseen changes don't affect previous analyses.

Access inherently separates its analytical components into tables, queries, and reports. By separating these elements, Access makes data less sensitive to changes and creates a data analysis environment where you can easily respond to new requests for analysis without destroying previous analyses.

Many who use Excel will find themselves manipulating its functionalities to approximate this database behavior. If you find yourself in this situation, you must consider that if you are using Excel's functionality to make it behave like a database application, perhaps the real thing just might have something to offer. Utilizing Access for data storage and analytical needs would enhance overall data analysis and would allow the Excel power-user to focus on the presentation in his or her spreadsheets.

In the future, there will be more data, not less. Likewise, there will be more demands for complex data analysis, not fewer. Power-users are going to need to add some tools to their repertoire in order to get away from being simply spreadsheet mechanics. Excel can be stretched to do just about anything, but maintaining such creative solutions can be a tedious manual task. You can be sure that the sexy part of data analysis is not in routine data management within Excel. Rather, it is in the creation of slick processes and utilities that will provide your clients with the best solution for any situation.

Deciding Whether to Use Access or Excel

After such a critical view of Excel, it is important to say that the key to your success in the sphere of data analysis will not come from discarding Excel altogether and exclusively using Access. Your success will come from proficiency with both applications and the ability to evaluate a project and determine the best platform to use for your analytical needs. Are there hard-and-fast rules you can follow to make this determination? The answer is no, but there are some key indicators in every project you can consider as guidelines to determine whether to use Access or Excel. These indicators are the size of the data; the data's structure; the potential for data evolution; the functional complexity of the analysis; and the potential for shared processing.

Size of Data

The size of your dataset is the most obvious consideration you will have to take into account. Although Excel can handle more data than in previous versions, it is generally a good rule to start considering Access if your dataset begins to approach 100,000 rows. The reason for this is the fundamental way Access and Excel handle data.

When you open an Excel file, the entire file is loaded into memory to ensure quick data processing and access. The drawback to this behavior is that Excel requires a great deal of memory to process even the smallest change in your spreadsheet. You may have noticed that when you try to perform an AutoFilter on a large formula-intensive dataset, Excel is slow to respond, giving you a Calculating indicator in the status bar. The larger your dataset is, the less efficient the data crunching in Excel will be.

Access, on the other hand, does not follow the same behavior as Excel. When you open an Access table, it may seem as though the whole table is opening for you, but in reality, Access is storing only a portion of data into memory at a time. This ensures the cost-effective use of memory and allows for more efficient data crunching on larger datasets. In addition, Access allows you to make use of Indexes that enable you to search, sort, filter, and query extremely large datasets very quickly.

Data Structure

If you are analyzing data that resides in a table that has no relationships with other tables, Excel is a fine choice for your analytical needs. However, if you have a series of tables that interact with each other (such as a Customers table, an Orders table, and an Invoices table), you should consider using Access. Access is a relational database, which means it is designed to handle the intricacies of interacting datasets. Some of these are the preservation of data integrity, the prevention of redundancy, and the efficient comparison and querying of data between the datasets. You will learn more about the concept of table relationships in Chapter 2.

Data Evolution

Excel is an ideal choice for quickly analyzing data used as a means to an end, such as a temporary dataset crunched to obtain a more valuable subset of data. The result of a pivot table is a perfect example of this kind of one-time data crunching. However, if you are building a long-term analytical process with data that has the potential of evolving and growing, Access is a better choice. Many analytical processes that start in Excel begin small and run fine, but as time passes these processes grow in both size and complexity until they reach the limits of Excel's capabilities. The message here is that you should use some foresight and consider future needs when determining which platform is best for your scenario.

Functional Complexity

There are far too many real-life examples of analytical projects where processes are forced into Excel even when Excel's limitations have been reached. How many times have you seen a workbook that contains an analytical process encapsulating multiple worksheets, macros, pivot tables, and formulas that add, average, count, look up, and link to other workbooks? The fact is that when Excel-based analytical processes become overly complex, they are difficult to manage, difficult to maintain, and difficult to translate to others. Consider using Access for projects that have complex, multiple-step analytical processes.

Shared Processing

Although it is possible to have multiple users work on one central Excel spreadsheet located on a network, ask anyone who has tried to coordinate and manage a central spreadsheet how difficult and restrictive it is. Data conflicts, loss of data, locked-out users, and poor data integrity are just a few examples of some of the problems you will encounter if you try to build a multiple-user process with Excel. Consider using Access for your shared processes. Access is better suited for a shared environment for many reasons, some of which are:

- The ability for users to concurrently enter and update data
- Inherent protection against data conflicts
- Prevention of data redundancy
- Protection against data entry errors

An Excel User's Guide to Access: Don't Panic!

Many seasoned managers, accountants, and analysts come to realize that just because something can be done in Excel does not necessarily mean Excel is the best way to do it. This is the point when they decide to open Access for the first time. When they do open Access, the first object that looks familiar to them is the Access table. In fact, Access tables look so similar to an Excel spreadsheet that most Excel users try to use tables just like a spreadsheet. However, when they realize that they can't type formulas directly into the table or duplicate most of Excel's behavior and functionality, most of them wonder just what exactly the point of using Access is.

When many Excel experts find out that Access does not behave or look like Excel, they write Access off as too difficult or as taking too much time to learn. However, the reality is that many of the concepts behind how data is stored and managed in Access are those with which the user is already familiar. Any Excel user has already learned such concepts in order to perform and present complex analysis. Investing a little time up front to see just how Access can be made to work for you can save a great deal of time in automating routine data processes.

Throughout this book, you will learn various techniques in which you can use Access to perform much of the data analysis you are now performing exclusively in Excel. This section is a brief introduction to Access from an Excel expert's point of view. Here, you will focus on the big-picture items in Access. If some of the Access terms mentioned here are new or not terribly familiar, be patient. They will be covered in detail as the book progresses.

Tables

What will undoubtedly look most familiar to you are Access tables. Tables appear almost identical to spreadsheets with familiar cells, rows, and columns. However, the first time you attempt to type a formula in one of the cells, you will see that Access tables do not possess Excel's flexible, multi-purpose nature that allows any cell to take on almost any responsibility or function.

The Access table is simply a place to store data, such as numbers and text. All of the analysis and number crunching happens somewhere else. This way, data will never be tied to any particular analysis or presentation. Data is in raw form, which leaves users to determine how they want to analyze or display it.

Chapter 2 will help you get started with a gentle introduction to Access basics.

Queries

You may have heard of Access queries but have never been able to relate to them.

Consider this: In Excel, when you use AutoFilter, a VLookup formula, or Subtotals, you are essentially running a query. A query is a question you pose against your data in order to get an answer or a result. The answer to a query can be a single data item, a Yes/No answer, or many rows of data. In Excel, the concept of querying data is a bit nebulous, as it can take the form of the different functionalities, such as formulas, AutoFilters, and PivotTables.

In Access, a query is an actual object that has its own functionalities. A query is separate from a table, ensuring that data is never tied to any particular analysis. You will cover queries extensively in subsequent chapters. Your success in using Microsoft Access to enhance your data analysis will depend on your ability to create all manners of both simple and complex queries.

Chapter 3 begins your full emersion into all the functionality you can get from Access queries.

Reports

Access reports are an incredibly powerful component of Microsoft Access, which allow data to be presented in a variety of styles. Access reports, in and of themselves, provide an excellent illustration of one of the main points of this book: Data should be separate from analysis and presentation. The report serves as the presentation layer for a database, displaying various views into the data within. Acting as the presentation layer for your database, reports are inherently disconnected from the way your data is stored and structured. As long as the report receives the data it requires in order to accurately and cleanly present its information, it will not care where the information comes from.

Access reports can have mixed reputations. On one hand, they can provide clean-looking PDF-esque reports that are ideal for invoices and form letters. On the other hand, Access reports are not ideal for showing the one-shot displays of data that Excel can provide. However, Access reports can easily be configured to prepare all manners of report styles, such as crosstabs, matrices, tabular layouts, and subtotaled layouts. You'll explore all the reporting options available to you starting in Chapter 11.

Macros and VBA

Just as Excel has macro and VBA functionality, Microsoft Access has its equivalents. This is where the true power and flexibility of Microsoft Access data analysis resides. Whether you are using them in custom functions, batch analysis, or automation, macros and VBA can add a customized flexibility that is hard to match using any other means. For example, you can use macros and VBA to automatically perform redundant analyses and recurring analytical processes, leaving you free to work on other tasks. Macros and VBA also allow you to reduce the chance of human error and to ensure that analyses are preformed the same way every time. Starting in Chapter 9, you will explore the benefits of macros and VBA and how you can leverage them to schedule and run batch analysis.

Summary

Although Excel is considered the premier tool for data analysis, Excel has some inherent characteristics that often lead to issues revolving around scalability, transparency of analytic processes, and confusion between data and presentation. Access has a suite of analytical tools that can help you avoid many of the issues that arise from Excel.

First, Access can handle very large datasets and has no predetermined row limitation. This allows for the management and analysis of large datasets without the scalability issues that plague Excel. Access also forces transparency—the separation of data and presentation by separating data into functional objects (that is, tables, queries, and reports) and by applying stringent rules that protect against bad processes and poor habits.

As you go through this book, it is important to remember that your goal is not to avoid Excel altogether but rather to broaden your toolset and to understand that, often, Access offers functionality that both enhances your analytical processes and makes your life easier.

Access Basics

When working with Access for the first time, it is tempting to start filling tables right away and querying data to get fast results, but it's important to understand the basics of the relational database concept before pounding away at data. A good understanding of how a relational database works will help you take full advantage of Access as a powerful data analysis solution. This chapter covers the fundamentals of Access and methods to bring data into the program.

Access Tables

Upon opening any existing Access database, you notice that the Database window, shown in Figure 2-1, contains a task pane on the left. Using the topmost dropdown box, change the navigation category to All Access Objects. You will get six sections. Each section represents one of the six database objects: Tables, Queries, Forms, Reports, Macros, and Modules. The Tables section is appropriately at the top of the list because it is the precise location where your data will be stored. All other database objects will refer to the tables in your database for data, whether asking questions of the data or creating reports based on the data. This section covers the basics to get you working with Access tables.

Table Basics

One way to think of a table is as a collection of data concerning a specific type of entity (such as customers, branches, transactions, products, and so on). You want each of these entities to have its own unique table. Among the many advantages to storing your data using this approach is eliminating or significantly decreasing duplicate information. Later in this chapter, you will learn about the dangers inherent in storing data with excessive duplications.

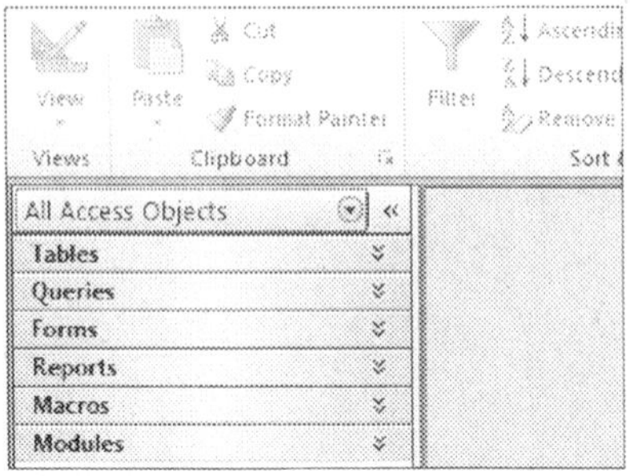

Figure 2-1: The navigation pane on the left allows you to navigate through the six types of database objects: Tables, Queries, Forms, Reports, Macros, and Modules.

Opening a Table in the Datasheet View

Open your sample database and go to the Tables section in the navigation pane. Double-click the Dim_Customers table. When the table opens, it is in the Datasheet view. In this view, you are able to directly view and edit the contents of the table. As you can see in Figure 2-2, the names of the columns are at the top.

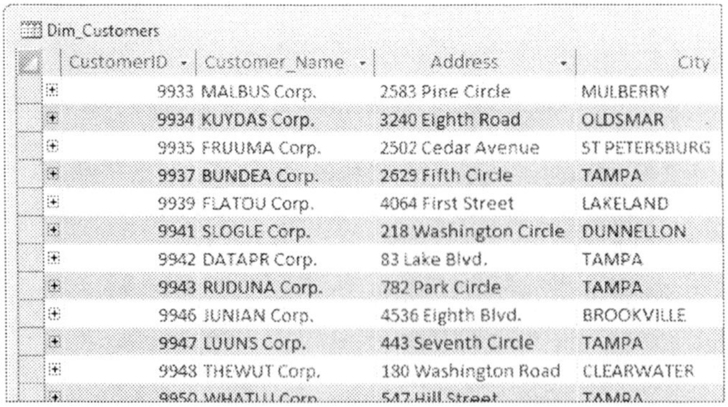
Dim_Customers

CustomerID	Customer_Name	Address	City
9933	MALBUS Corp.	2583 Pine Circle	MULBERRY
9934	KUYDAS Corp.	3240 Eighth Road	OLDSMAR
9935	FRUUMA Corp.	2502 Cedar Avenue	ST PETERSBURG
9937	BUNDEA Corp.	2629 Fifth Circle	TAMPA
9939	FLATOU Corp.	4064 First Street	LAKELAND
9941	SLOGLE Corp.	218 Washington Circle	DUNNELLON
9942	DATAPR Corp.	83 Lake Blvd.	TAMPA
9943	RUDUNA Corp.	782 Park Circle	TAMPA
9946	JUNIAN Corp.	4536 Eighth Blvd.	BROOKVILLE
9947	LUUNS Corp.	443 Seventh Circle	TAMPA
9948	THEWUT Corp.	180 Washington Road	CLEARWATER
9950	WHATUU Corp.	547 Hill Street	TAMPA

Figure 2-2: Opening the table in Datasheet view allows you to view and edit the data stored in the table.

Identifying Important Table Elements

A table is composed of rows, with each row representing an individual entity. In the Dim_Customers table, each row represents a single distinct customer. The proper database terminology for a row is *record*.

A table is also composed of columns, with each column representing a particular piece of information common to all instances of the table's entities.

In Dim_Customers, each column represents some attribute of the customer record. The proper database terminology for a column is *field*.

TIP The number of records in a table is visible at the bottom left of the Datasheet view, next to the record selectors.

Opening a Table in the Design View

Through the Design view of a table, you are able to set the field names and data types. To get to the Design view of the Dim_Customers table, go to the Home tab and select View ⇨ Design View, as demonstrated in Figure 2-3.

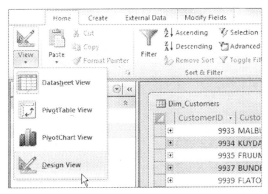

Figure 2-3: You can configure the structure of your table by switching to Design view.

As you can see in Figure 2-4, the Design view shows you the fields that compose the Dim_Customers table in an easy-to-manage view.

Note how each field has a Field Name and a Data Type. The *Field Name* is the descriptive text string given to that particular column of a table. It appears at the top of the table when it is in the Datasheet view. The *Data Type* of the field ensures that only a certain type of data is allowed in the field. If a data type is tagged as a Number, Access does not allow any text to be entered into that field. By setting the data type of each column, you go a long way toward ensuring the integrity and consistency of the data.

TIP It's good practice to avoid putting any spaces in your field names. When constructing queries or referring to tables in VBA code, spaces in the field names can lead to problems. If you need to indicate a space in your field name, use the underscore character. Keep in mind that your field names cannot include a period (.), an exclamation point (!), an accent grave ('), or brackets ([ ]).

Exploring Data Types

With the Design view of the Dim_Customers table open, select the Data type section of the first field and click the drop-down arrow. A list of predefined data type choices becomes visible. These data types are Text; Memo; Number; Date/Time; Currency; AutoNumber; Yes/No; OLE Object; Hyperlink; Attachment; and Calculated.

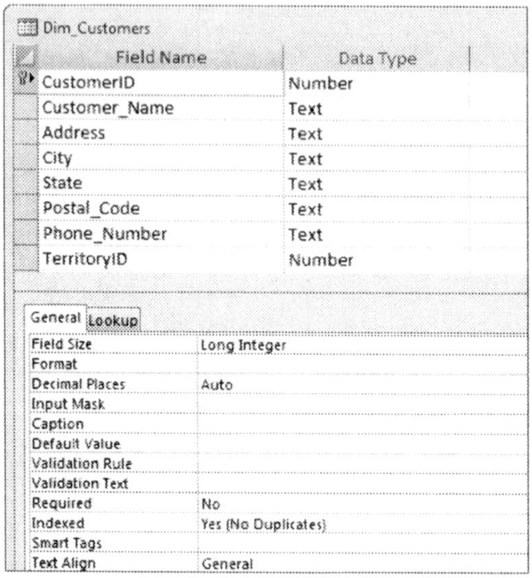

Figure 2-4: Opening the table in the Design view allows you to add field names or change existing ones.

NOTE When in Design View, you will also see a data type selection called Lookup Wizard. This selection is actually not a data type at all; it's a mechanism used to activate the Lookup Wizard in order to create lookup fields. The Lookup Wizard is beyond the scope of this book.

- **Text:** Any combination of letters, numbers, spaces, and characters is text. This is by far the most common data type. Although text can be a number, it should not be a number used in a calculation. Examples of common uses of the Text data type are customer names, customer numbers (using customer numbers in calculations would have no meaning), and addresses. The maximum number of characters allowed in a Text field is 255 characters.

- **Memo:** If you need to store text data that exceeds the 255-character limit of the Text field, the Memo field should be used. Long descriptions or notes about the record can be stored in fields of this type.

- **Number:** This type is for all numerical data used in calculations, except currency (which has its own data type). Actually, Number is several data types under one heading. When you select Number as a data type in the Design view of the table, you go to the Field Size field at the top of the General tab. When you select the drop-down arrow, you get the following options: Byte, Integer, Long Integer, Single, Double, Replication ID, and

Decimal. Probably the most commonly used field sizes of the Number data type are Long Integer and Double. Long Integer should be selected if the numbers are whole numbers that do not have any non-zeros to the right of the decimal point. Double should be selected if numbers with decimals need to be stored.

- **Date/Time:** Another data type often used in calculations is Date/Time. Recording the time that certain events occur is among the more important uses of this data type. Recording dates and times allows you to compare data by time durations, be it months, years, or whatever. In the business world, the date field can be crucial to analysis, especially in identifying seasonal trends or year-over-year comparisons.

- **Currency:** A special calculation data type, Currency is ideal for storing all data that represents amounts of money.

- **AutoNumber:** This data type is actually a Long Integer automatically and sequentially created for each new record added to a table. The AutoNumber can be one mechanism by which you can uniquely identify each record in a table. You will not enter data into this field.

- **Yes/No:** There are situations where the data that needs to be represented is in a simple Yes/No format. Although you could use the Text data type for creating a True/False field, it is much more intuitive to use Access's native data type for this purpose.

- **OLE Object:** This data type is not encountered very often in data analysis. It is used when the field must store a binary file, such as a picture or sound file.

- **Hyperlink:** When you need to store an address to a Web site, this is the preferred data type.

- **Attachment:** This data type was introduced with Access 2007. When you set a field to the Attachment type, you can attach images, spreadsheet files, documents, charts, and other types of supported files to the records in your database. You can also configure the field to view and edit attached files.

- **Calculated:** This data type is new to Access 2010. With Calculated type fields, you can build mathematical operations, textual evaluations, or any other calculation directly into your table.

Creating a Table from Scratch

Access provides several methods for creating a table. The ideal way to create a table in Access is with the Design view. Why? The Design view allows for a compact work area so you can add fields, reposition fields, and assign attributes easily.

Imagine that the human resources department asks you to create a simple list of employees in Access.

1. To create this table in the Design view, go to the application ribbon and select the Create tab and then the Table Design button. This opens an empty table called Table1 in Design view.

2. The idea here is to create a list of fields that describe employee attributes. Among the more common attributes in this situation are the following: EmployeeNumber, FirstName, LastName, Address, City, State, Zip, and HourlyWage. You begin by entering the names of the columns going down the list. When you have entered all of the required column names, your dialog box should look like Figure 2-5.

Field Name	Data Type
EmployeeNumber	Text
FirstName	Text
LastName	Text
Address	Text
City	Text
State	Text
Zip	Text
HourlyWage	Text

Figure 2-5: Enter the column names you want to see in your table.

3. As you enter the field names, the data types default to the most common data type, Text. You now want to set the data type for each field or at least change the data type of each non-text field. Choosing the correct data type for the first field, EmployeeNumber, may be initially confusing. With the word "Number" in the field, you might think that Number would be the logical choice for the data type. Actually, the rule of thumb is that if the field will not be used in a calculation, it is best to set its data type to Text. Because there is no logical reason to perform a calculation on an employee's EmployeeNumber, the EmployeeNumber data type should remain Text. Another reason for using the Text data type for the field EmployeeNumber is that there could be a need to use alphabetic or other characters in the field.

As you go through the field names, it should be fairly obvious that you will want to set all of the fields to Text, except for HourlyWage. This field will almost certainly be used in calculations, and it will represent a monetary value, so you should change the data type to Currency.

At this point, your Design view should look similar to Figure 2-6.

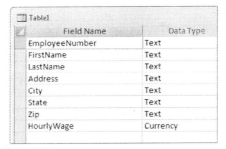

Figure 2-6: You have created your first table!

4. Now you can save and name your table. Click File on the application Ribbon and select Save As. If you are using Access 2007, click the Office Icon and select Save As. This opens the Save As dialog box where you will give your newly created table an appropriate name like "Employees" or "EmployeeMaster."

Keep in mind that at this point, this table has no data. You can begin entering employee information directly into the table through the Datasheet view. For tables with a small number of records, you can enter your records manually. However, most sets of data are quite large, so other techniques of bringing data into Access are introduced later in this chapter.

NOTE When you save a table, you may be prompted to set a primary key. Primary keys are explained later (see Setting Primary Keys in this chapter). In most cases, Access will try to choose one for you. It's generally good practice to accept Access' recommendation to create a primary key if you do not already have one on mind.

Working with Field Properties

When working with data in tables, you may encounter situations that require the data be restricted or to adhere to some default specifications in particular columns. You can define these requirements by using the field properties.

The field properties affect how the data is stored and presented, among other things. The list of field properties that are available to you is dependent on the data type chosen for that field. Some field properties are specific to Text fields, and others are specific to Number fields. The field properties can be found in the Design view, as illustrated in Figure 2-7. As you click on each field, you will see the field properties for that field.

Some of the most important field properties to note are:

▪ **Field Size:** You encountered the Field Size before, when working with the Number data type. This property also exists for the common Text data type. This property allows you to set a maximum size limit on data entered in that column. For the Text data type, size refers to the length (number of characters and spaces) of the Text data in that column. For example, looking at the Employees table, you see a field for State. Your firm tells you that the names of states should be recorded using their two-letter designation. If you set the field size to "2" for the State column, the user will be unable to type any text that is longer than two characters. So with Access, you are not only able to force a certain data type in a particular column, you can also customize that individual column to accept data only in the rigid format that you specify.

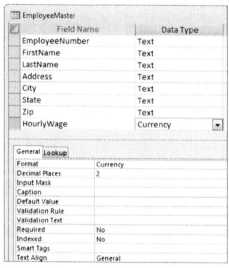

Figure 2-7: You can find the Field Properties in Design view beneath the field names.

- **Format:** This property allows you to set the precise manner in which Access displays or prints the data that is located in its Tables. As with Field Size, the format available to select will depend on the data type of that column. For example, with a Currency field, you can display the data in a form that uses a dollar sign, a Euro sign, or no sign at all. With these settings, the data itself does not change—just how it displays. Another very useful function of Format is with Date/Time data types. Whether you want to display data in the long format or short format, this property allows you to set that option.

- **Input Mask:** This feature can be useful in data entry situations. Where Format controls how data is displayed, Input Mask controls how data is entered into a particular field. Input mask is available for the following data types: Text, Number, Date/Time, and Currency. For example, if a user needs to enter a telephone number, the input mask can create the characters and structure with which you are all familiar. As the user types, the number automatically assumes a phone number format: (###) ###-####.

- **Decimal Places:** In number fields, you can set the number of decimal places to the right of the decimal point that will be recorded. There is an Auto setting, which defers to the Format setting to determine the correct number of places. Apart from Auto, you are able to select 0 to 15 for the number of decimal places.

- **Default Value:** An important database concept, the default value can help save time in the data entry process. The default value is automatically placed in that column every time a new record is added. Defaults can be overridden by simply entering data into the field.

- **Required:** Another important property, Required simply forces a user to enter some value, using the proper data type, in the designated field. The user cannot add a new record if the Required field is not properly filled. As with Input Mask, this property is an excellent mechanism for asserting more control over the data entry process.

Setting Primary Keys

In some tables, you will need to ensure the uniqueness of each record. This is typically achieved by including a field whose records will not have duplicate values. One example of this is a field for Social Security numbers. Each person has one and only one unique Social Security number. By definition, you cannot have a Social Security number that represents two people. This type of unique column is what you call a *primary key*.

You can identify a given field as the primary key for you table in Design view—by right clicking the chosen field and selecting Primary Key. When you save your table, Access determines whether your selected fields have any null (or blank) values or duplicate data (data duplicating in multiple records for a single field). If there are blanks or duplicates, Access informs you with an error message. You must fill in the blanks with unique values and remove any duplicates if that column is indeed to become the primary key for the table.

TIP Sometimes a table will have two or more fields that together uniquely identify a record. In these cases, you will need to create what is called a *compound key*. For example, imagine a table with both an invoice number and a product number. A sales representative may have sold multiple products to a customer on the same invoice. Therefore, when you look at each value separately, you'll find duplicate values of each field. By combining invoice and product number, however, you can create a compound primary key that is truly unique for each record. If you need a compound key, do the following:

1. Select the first field that will be included in your compound key by clicking on the grey square to the right of the Field Name. Then while holding down the Control key on your keyboard, click the grey square next to the second field to be included.

2. Right click on the Field Name (right clicking on the grey square will cause Access to forget your multiple selection).

3. Close the table and save your changes.

Importing Data into Access

Apart from creating a table from scratch and manually entering the data, you can import data, which essentially makes a copy of the data directly in your Access database. After importing, the data is disconnected from the source from which it was imported.

To get an idea of how Importing works, imagine that HR has passed you an Excel file containing their master employee table. You want to import that table into your database.

> **TIP** The ExcelMaster.xlsx file can be found within the sample files for this book, installed under C:\OffTheGrid.

1. Click the External Data tab and then click the Excel icon.

2. Browse for the file you wish to import and then select the "Import the source data into a new table ... " option. Figure 2-8 shows you what the wizard should look like.

3. Click the OK button to activate the Import Spreadsheet Wizard shown in Figure 2-9. The first dialog box in the Import Spreadsheet Wizard allows you to specify the worksheet or range you want to import. If your workbook has more than one worksheet, all worksheets are listed on this screen. In this case, there is only one worksheet. Select the target worksheet and click the Next button.

4. The next screen (Figure 2-10) allows you to select whether or not the source data has headings or column labels. As you can see, you will simply check the checkbox if your source data has headings. Click the Next button to move on.

5. The next screen (Figure 2-11) allows you to specify the data type for each field. This setting allows you to tell Access whether the given field is a number, text, currency, date, etc. The idea is to select each field and check to make sure the data type for that field is correct.

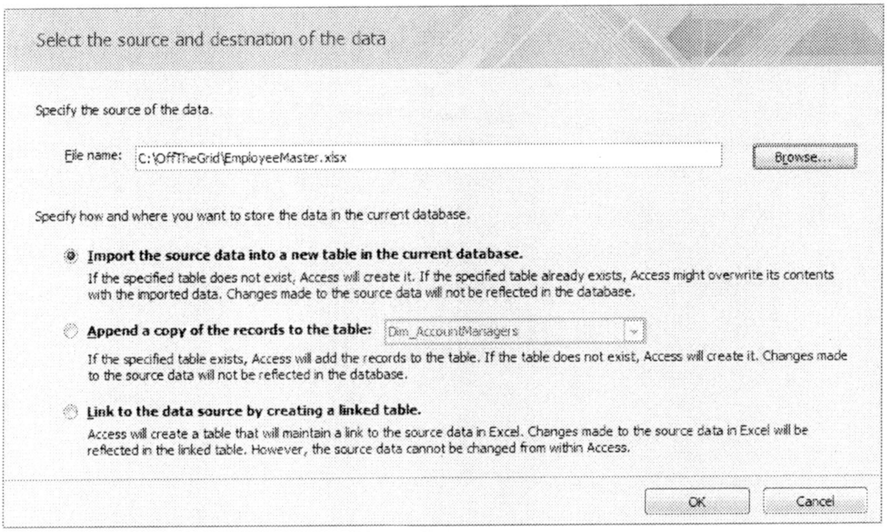

Figure 2-8: Select the data source and select the import option.

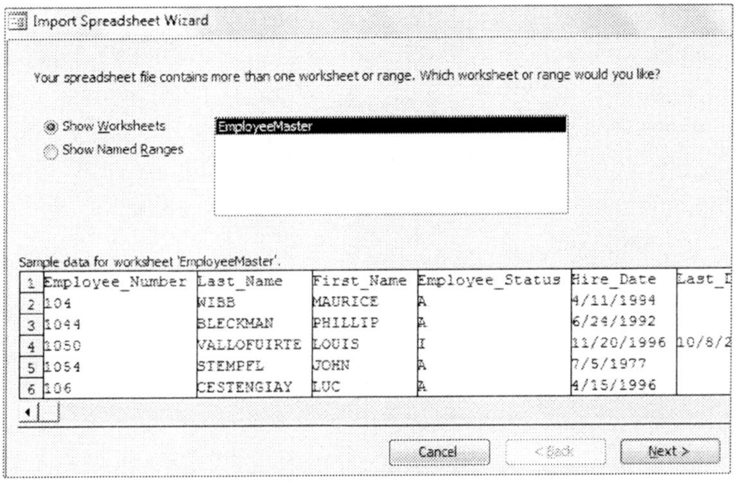

Figure 2-9: Identify the worksheet or range you want to import.

Also in this screen (Figure 2-11), you can specify whether any given field is to be indexed. When you index a field, Access creates a kind of organizational mapping of the field allowing for faster querying and grouping.

The best way to illustrate indexing is by an analogy. Imagine you had a file cabinet with 10,000 folders, each dedicated to a specific customer. Now imagine these files were in random order. To access the customer file for "Mike's Coffee House," you would have to search through every customer file until you found it. Now imagine finding the file if your customer folders were organized or "indexed" alphabetically. It would be a much faster task. When you sort or filter on a non-indexed field, Access will search every record until the correct record is found. Indexing a field in Access is conceptually identical to alphabetizing the file system. Indexing a field makes Access create an organizational scheme for that field such that it can be quickly searched when needed.

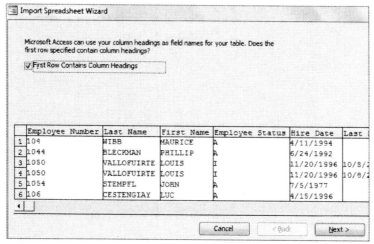

Figure 2-10: Specify whether your data source comes with headings.

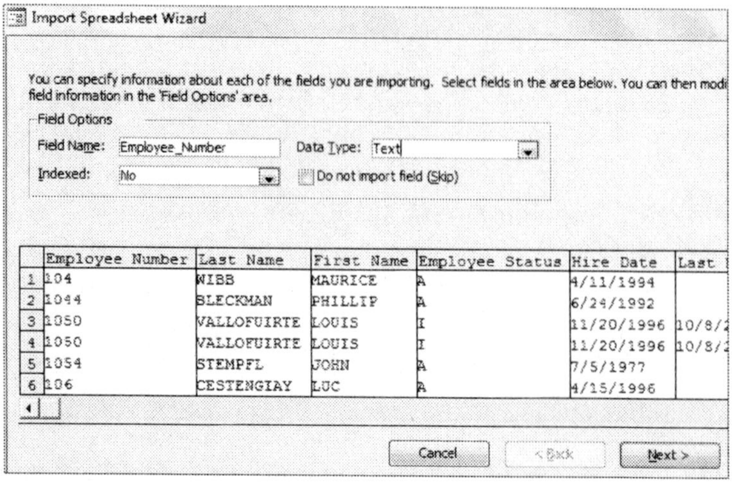

Figure 2-11: Apply data types and indexing to your fields.

NOTE You may wonder why you would not index all your fields. Wouldn't that make your queries run faster? The answer is an emphatic *no!* Indexing is a good idea on fields you expect to filter or join to another table. Indexing is not a good idea for fields you expect to perform calculations on. You should also be aware that while indexing can improve the performance for some types of analysis, other types could actually be slowed by using indexed fields.

6. Clicking Next will bring you to the screen shown in Figure 2-12. Here, you can choose the field to set as the primary key. In this case, the Employee_Number field will be primary key.

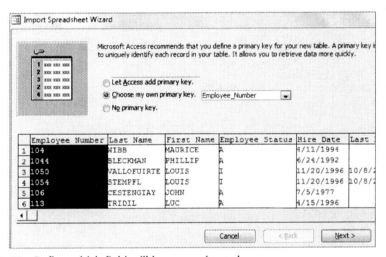

Figure 2-12: Define which field will be your primary key.

7. The last screen of the Import Spreadsheet Wizard (Figure 2-13) will ask to you name your new table. If you are importing an Excel worksheet, the new table name will default to the name of your imported worksheet. However, you can change the name to suit your needs. At this point, you can click the Finish button to start the import.

NOTE It's important to note that naming your import table the same name as an existing table in your database will cause Access to give you an overwrite warning. That is to say, Access will warn you that you are about to overwrite your existing table. Be careful that you do not inadvertently overwrite an existing table with a careless table name choice.

Once your data has been imported, an interesting dialog box activates (Figure 2-14). This dialog box asks if you want to save your import steps. This is a relatively new feature introduced in Access 2007, allowing you to save time when the same dataset must be routinely imported. As you can see in Figure 1-14, clicking the "Save import steps" option allows you to save your import steps as a named task that can be fired whenever you need. To recall a saved import task, simply click the Saved Imports command button under the External Data tab in the Access ribbon.

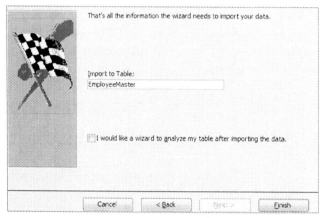

Figure 2-13: Name your imported table and Click the Finish button.

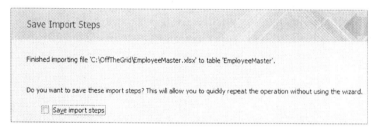

Figure 2-14: You now have the option of saving your import steps.

Importing Data from Text File

You may want to import and analyze non-Excel data and then send it to Excel after analysis in Access. One of the most common data types for import is text-delimited data. Delimited text is simply text where the individual fields in a record are separated by a specific character such as a tab, comma, or space.

Fortunately, Access recognizes delimited text and even allows you to choose the specific character that separates fields. To get delimited text into Access, simply choose Text File from the External Data ribbon and walk through the same process you would when importing or linking to an Excel file.

TRICKS OF THE TRADE: USING COMPACT AND REPAIR

As you bring data into Access, it's important to remember that Access does not let go of disk space on its own. This means that as time passes, all the file space taken up by the data you imported will be held by your Access file, regardless of whether the data is actually still there.

In that light, it's critical to that you perform a compact and repair operation on your Access database regularly to ensure that your database does not grow to an unmanageable size or, even worse, become corrupted.

To compact and repair your database in Access 2007, click the Office icon and select Manage ⇨ Compact and Repair Database.

To compact and repair your database in Access 2010, go to the application ribbon and select File ⇨ Info ⇨ Compact and Repair Database.

How often you perform this operation really depends on how frequently you add and then delete tables from your database. The best practice is to compact and repair your Access database at least every time you open or close it. You can automate this action by clicking Access Options ⇨ Current Database. Once in the Current Database Menu section, select the Compact on Close check box. This will ensure your database is compacted and repaired at least every time you close the application.

Linking an Excel Worksheet to Access

Sometimes, the data you want to incorporate into Access is going to change frequently. Does it make sense to import that data into a new Access table every time it changes? What if you do not know when it changes yet it is critical to have the most up-to-date information for your analysis? In these situations, it makes more sense to create a link to your data.

Linking data is different from importing data in that Access references the linked data in its original location. Importing data brings a local copy of the information into the Access database. Any changes made to the local copy in Access do not affect the original spreadsheet. Likewise, any changes made to the original spreadsheet after importing will not be reflected in the Access table.

Conversely, a linked Excel sheet exists in *real time*. Changes made to the sheet in the original Excel file will be reflected in Access upon refresh. However, you will not be able to make changes to the Excel data through Access. Linking is a one-way street of data flow.

To link to a data source, you would start by selecting the External Data tab and then select the Import Excel icon. This time, select the "Link to the data source by creating a linked table" option (see Figure 2-15).

From here, Access will walk you through steps similar to those taken when importing data.

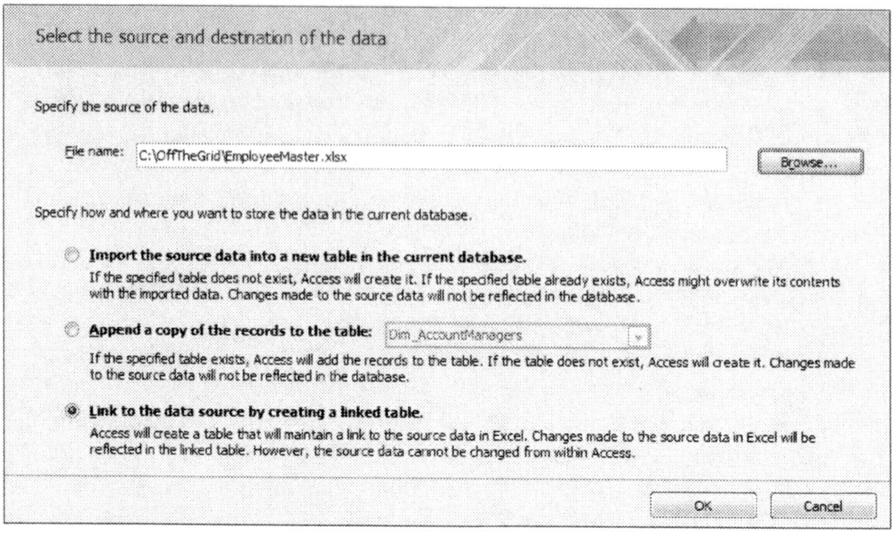

Figure 2-15: To link to a data source, select the Link option.

NOTE When linking to a data source, you will not be able to specify data types, indexing, or primary keys. Therefore, you will not see those selections in the Link Spreadsheet Wizard.

Understanding the Relational Database Concept

Now that you have covered tables and brought some data into the database, you can turn your focus to one of the more useful features of Access: relationships. Access relationships are the mechanisms by which separate tables are related to each other. The idea behind relationships is the Relational Database Concept. Before you begin to create relationships between Access tables, take a closer look at the concept behind relational database systems.

Why Is This Concept Important?

This concept is important because it is the theoretical framework from which most databases programs are designed. If you want to understand just how databases work, you need to understand this concept. You are learning Access, among other reasons, because the data storage and data manipulation capacity of Excel is insufficient for your analysis needs.

The concept that dictates just how data is stored and structured is the Relational Database Concept. Even though you may have no intention of becoming a database administrator, having some understanding of how the data that you would like to analyze has been stored and structured will increase your performance and productivity. It will also promote better communication between you and the IT department and the database administrator, since now you will be able to understand at least some of the vocabulary of the database language.

Excel and the Flat-File Format

Before you cover the proper techniques for storing data in Access, examine the common data storage scenario that led to the problems that the concept attempts to address. Even if they are not aware of the term flat-file format, most Excel users are very adept at working with data that has been stored in it. In fact, most people are familiar with the concept because it is used in so many things that they encounter every day. The flat-file, of course, organizes data into rows and columns.

There are data analysis scenarios that are not terribly complex, in which a flat-file representation of the data to be analyzed is adequate. However, most data-analysis scenarios require analyzing data that is much more multi-dimensional. One of the main reasons that the flat-file can prove inadequate is that it is two-dimensional. Real-world business data rarely falls into a convenient, two-dimensional format. Of course, it can be forced into that format by the Excel guru who wants all analysis to fit into the spreadsheet.

Take a look at a typical example of a flat-file; Figure 2-16 shows a typical flat-file list of orders.

Customer Name	Address	City	State	PONumber	OrderDate	Sales Amount
ACASCO Corp.	4470 View Blvd.	FONTANA	CA	53320	29-Aug-08	$107.00
ACASCO Corp.	4470 View Blvd.	FONTANA	CA	53833	05-Sep-08	$87.00
ACASCO Corp.	4470 View Blvd.	FONTANA	CA	62234	17-Jan-09	$59.00
ACECUL Corp.	1821 Sixth Circle	CLEARWATER	FL	45120	08-Jan-07	$4,637.00
ACECUL Corp.	1821 Sixth Circle	CLEARWATER	FL	54868	23-Sep-08	$4,255.00
ACECUL Corp.	1821 Sixth Circle	CLEARWATER	FL	60620	23-Dec-08	$1,759.00
ACECUL Corp.	1821 Sixth Circle	CLEARWATER	FL	62343	18-Jan-09	$4,120.00
ACEHUA Corp.	3162 Sixth Avenue	CHANDLER	AZ	48279	30-Nov-07	$1,578.00
ACEHUA Corp.	3162 Sixth Avenue	CHANDLER	AZ	50343	02-May-08	$3,735.00
ACEHUA Corp.	3162 Sixth Avenue	CHANDLER	AZ	59749	10-Dec-08	$3,782.00
ACOPUL Corp.	2765 Main Street	FONTANA	CA	45102	05-Jan-07	$4,637.00
ACOPUL Corp.	2765 Main Street	FONTANA	CA	48562	15-Dec-07	$3,735.00
ACOPUL Corp.	2765 Main Street	FONTANA	CA	60193	17-Dec-08	$878.00
ACOPUL Corp.	2765 Main Street	FONTANA	CA	67690	05-Apr-09	$940.00
ACORAR Corp.	1764 Third Street	ORLANDO	FL	51469	19-Jul-08	$3,876.00
ACORAR Corp.	1764 Third Street	ORLANDO	FL	56241	17-Oct-08	$85.00
ACORAR Corp.	1764 Third Street	ORLANDO	FL	70924	19-May-09	$789.00

Figure 2-16: Data is usually stored in an Excel spreadsheet using the flat-file format.

In order to get the customer information for each order, there are several fields for customer-specific information such as customer name, address, city, and so on. Because most firms sell to customers more than once, for each order the same customer information has to be repeated. Duplicate information is one of the main drawbacks of the flat-file format.

What is wrong with duplicate data? Initially, the duplicate data may not appear to be a potential source of future problems, but upon further examination, you discover the shortcomings:

- **File Size**. Duplicate data wastes space, both on the computer hard drive, where the file is stored, and in the computer's memory, where the data resides when it is being used. Although the enormous amount of memory that is standard with today's machines goes a long way to handling these demands, you are wasting valuable computer space and resources. The duplicate information is not valuable. In fact, it leads to problems.

- **Updating data:** One of the main problems that can arise from too much duplicate data occurs when that data needs to be updated.

In Figure 2-16, you can see there are several orders for ACASCO Corp. You can also see that you have to repeat the information **about the customer** for each instance of an order. Imagine a scenario where the customer information might change. For example, the **customer acquires** new office space, and you want to reflect this change of location in your data. You will have to update the change in several different places. You need to ensure that every order will correctly map back to its relevant customer information.

While there are excellent functions that find and replace data in Excel, there is still a danger that you might not make all of the updates correctly. Whenever you are changing duplicate information, there is always the risk of introducing unintentional errors.

Splitting Data into Separate Tables

Data must be consistent if analysis is to have any true value in the decision-making process. Duplicate data is the bane of consistent data. If an entity is changed in one place, it must be changed in every place. Would it not be more logical and efficient if you could create the name and information of a customer only once? Would it not be great simply to have some form of customer reference number instead of creating the same customer information repeatedly? Then that customer reference could send you to another list where the information is unique and written once.

This is the idea behind the relational database concept. You have separate, carefully designed, unique lists of data, and you relate them to each other by using their unique identifiers (primary keys).

In a relational database, customer details such as address, city, state, etc, would be listed only once in a master customer table. A transactions table using a primary key such as CustomerID would then reference that table (Figure 2-17). This way, if any of the details for a given customer were to change, edits would have to be applied only to that customer's one record in the master customer table.

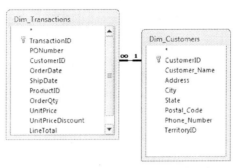

Figure 2-17: The relational data model for customers and orders.

Excel users may not realize it, but they often make great efforts to keep the data on their spreadsheets "relational." They use (or overuse) VLOOKUP or HLOOKUP to match data from separate lists that have some data field or key in common. While much is possible with these functions, they do have their limitations. The functions are not very intuitive and try to solve a problem that Access was designed, from the ground up, to address. When Excel users use functions like VLOOKUP and HLOOKUP to bring data from separate lists onto a single row, they are emulating a relationship of that data.

The problem for the analyst is that if there are relationships between the data that are consistent or even permanent, it is easier somehow to reflect this in a behind-the-scenes representation of the data. Some of the data relationships can be quite complex, which compels the analyst to remember and manually enforce all of them but also detracts from analysis and increases the possibility of mistakes.

Relationship Types

Three types of relationships can be set in a relational database:

- **One-to-one relationship:** For each record in one table, there is one and only one matching record in a different table. It is as if two tables have the exact same primary key. Typically, data from different tables in a one-to-one relationship are combined into one table.

- **One-to-many relationship:** For each record in one table, there may be 0, 1 or many records matching in a separate table. For example, you might have an invoice header table related to an invoice detail table. The invoice header table has a primary key, Invoice Number. The invoice detail table will use the Invoice Number for every record representing a detail of that particular invoice. This is certainly the most common type of relationship you will encounter.

▪ **Many-to-many relationship:** Used decidedly less often, this relationship cannot be defined in Access without the use of a mapping table. This relationship states that records in both tables can have any number of matching records in the other table.

In the sample database that came with this book, relationships have already been established between the tables. Take a look at some of these relationships to get a better idea of how you can set and change them.

▪ In Access 2007, go up to the application ribbon and select the Database Tools ⇨ Relationships.

▪ In Access 2010, go up to the application ribbon and select File ⇨ Info ⇨ Relationships.

As you can see in Figure 2-18, the tables are represented with lines between them. The lines signify the relationships.

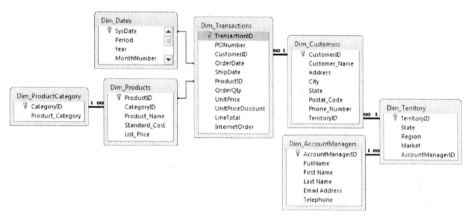

Figure 2-18: The one-to-many relationship between tables can be identified by the ∞ symbol on the line connecting the tables.

Query Basics

Once you have a fundamental understanding of tables and relationships in Access, you are ready to start analyzing data with queries. In this section, you are going to focus on what is perhaps the most common type of query: the select query. You will see the concept behind the query and a few examples that illustrate just how easy it is to create queries in Access.

What Is a Query?

By definition, a *query* is a question. For your purposes, it is a question about the data, which is stored in tables. Queries can be exceedingly simple, like asking what all of the data in a table is. Queries can also be quite complex, testing for different criteria, sorting in certain orders, and performing calculations. In Access, there are two main types of queries: select and action:

- **Select queries** are perhaps the most common type. This query simply asks a question of the data and returns the results. No changes are made to the data whatsoever. You can always run select queries and never worry that the actual data is being altered.

- **Action queries** actually manipulate and change the data in a table. The action query can add records, delete records, or change (update) information in existing records.

TRICKS OF THE TRADE: SORTING AND FILTERING FOR ON-THE-FLY ANALYSIS

There is inherent functionality within Access that allows you to sort and filter the contents of your tables on the fly: without queries. With this functionality, you can perform quick, impromptu data analysis with just a few clicks of the mouse.

This functionality definitely has an Excel feel to it. To get a sense of what this means, open a table in the Datasheet view and select the column you wish to sort or filter. Then click the dropdown arrow next to that column's field name.

For example, if you wanted to find any customer located in Aberdeen, you could click the dropdown arrow under the City field, select Text Filters, and then select Equals as demonstrated in Figure 2-19. This opens a Custom Filter dialog box where you can simply enter the name that you are filtering.

The resulting dataset, shown in Figure 2-20, has only the records for the filtered name.

To remove the filter, simply click the dropdown arrow next to the filtered column's field name and select Clear Filter from *x*, where *x* equals the field name.

(continued)

TRICKS OF THE TRADE: SORTING AND FILTERING FOR ON-THE-FLY ANALYSIS (continued)

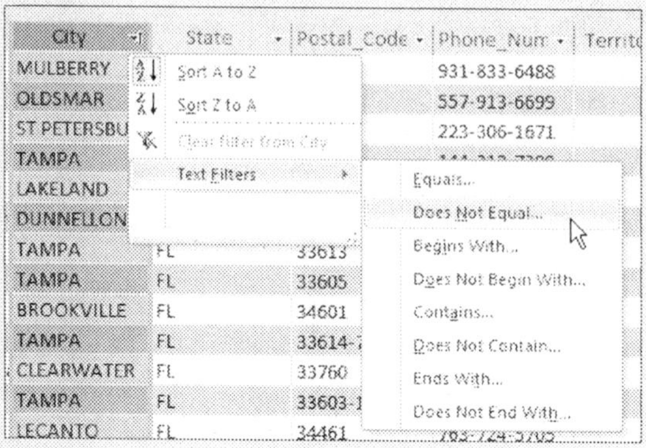

Figure 2-19: The dropdown arrow next to the field name will bring up the sorting and filtering menu.

Figure 2-20: There are two customers located in Aberdeen.

Creating Your First Select Query

Quite often, when you are working with or analyzing data, it is preferable to work with smaller sections of the data at a time. The tables contain all the records pertaining to a particular entity, but perhaps for your purposes you need to examine a subset of that data. Typically, the subsets are defined by categories or criteria. The select query allows you to determine exactly which records will be returned to you.

If you thought that creating queries required learning a programming language or some other technological hurdle, you are mistaken. While it is possible to create queries using the programming language of databases (SQL), Access provides a graphical interface that is easy to use and quite user-friendly. This graphical interface has been called the QBE (Query by Example) or QBD (Query by Design) in the past. Now Microsoft calls it the Query Design view. In the Query Design view, tables and columns are visually represented, making it easy to visualize the "question" you would like to ask of the data.

Follow these steps:

1. Go up to the application ribbon and select Create ⇨ Query Design. The Show Table dialog box now opens on top of a blank Query Design

interface, as shown in Figure 2-21. The white grid area you see in the Query Design view is often called the query grid.

When creating your "question" of the data, the first thing you must determine is from which tables you need to retrieve data. The Show Table dialog box allows the user to select one or more tables. As you can see in Figure 2-21, there are also tabs for Queries and Both. One of the wonderful features of queries is that you are not limited to just querying directly from the table. You can create queries of other queries.

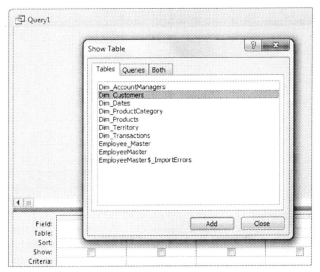

Figure 2-21: The Show Table dialog box allows you to select the tables or queries to add to the Query Design view.

2. For this first query, select the Dim_Customers table, either by selecting the table in the list and clicking Add or by double-clicking the table in the list. Now that you have selected the table from which you want to retrieve data, you can close the Show Table dialog box and select the fields of that table that you would like to retrieve.

The Query Design view is divided into two sections. The top half shows the tables or queries from which the query will retrieve data. The bottom half (often called the query grid) shows the fields from which the query will retrieve data. You will notice in Figure 2-22 that the Dim_Customers table shown at the top half of the Query Design view lists all the fields but has an asterisk at the top of the list. The asterisk is the traditional database symbol that means that all fields from that table will be in the output.

3. For this example, select the following three fields: Customer_Name, City, and State. To select fields, you can either double-click the field or click it

once and drag it down to the bottom half (the query grid). Each field that you add to the query grid will be included in the output of the query. Figure 2-23 shows you how your query should look after selecting the output fields.

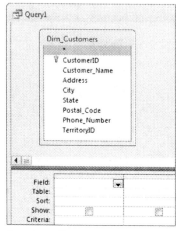

Figure 2-22: The Query Design view allows you to query all fields easily.

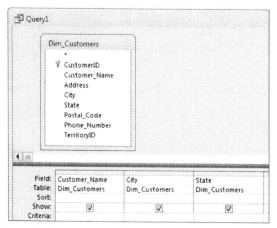

Figure 2-23: The lower half, or query grid, shows the output fields of the select query.

4. At this point, you have all you need to run the query. To run the query, click the Run button located on the Design tab. As you can see in Figure 2-24, the output from a query looks similar to a regular table after it is open.

NOTE To return to the Query Design view, simply click Home ⇨ View ⇨ Design View.

Customer_Name	City	State
MALBUS Corp.	MULBERRY	FL
KUYDAS Corp.	OLDSMAR	FL
FRUUMA Corp.	ST PETERSBURG	FL
BUNDEA Corp.	TAMPA	FL
FLATOU Corp.	LAKELAND	FL
SLOGLE Corp.	DUNNELLON	FL
DATAPR Corp.	TAMPA	FL
RUDUNA Corp.	TAMPA	FL
JUNIAN Corp.	BROOKVILLE	FL
LUUNS Corp.	TAMPA	FL
THEWUT Corp.	CLEARWATER	FL

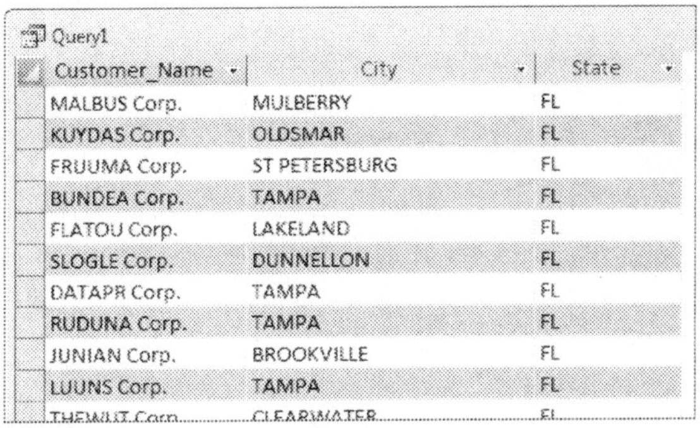

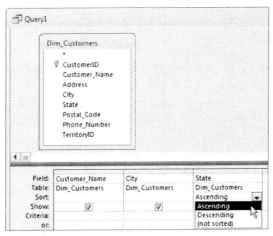

Figure 2-24: The Datasheet view of a query shows the results of the query.

Sorting Query Results

Now examine how you can sort the results of this query. Just as you sorted in Excel, you are going to select a column and choose between an ascending sort and a descending sort. In the query grid, notice the Sort row of the grid. This is where you can select either one or multiple sort columns. If you select multiple sort columns, the query will sort the results in order from left to right.

Go to the State column and click your mouse on the Sort section. As shown in Figure 2-25, a dropdown box appears, allowing you to select either Ascending or Descending for that particular column.

Figure 2-25: The sort order options for a column are provided by the Query Design view.

Select Ascending and rerun the query. When you ran the query before, the states were in no particular order. After setting the sort order of the State column to ascending, the query output simply looks better and more professionally formatted, as seen in Figure 2-26.

Query1		
Customer_Name ▾	City ▾	State ▾
CORTUK Corp.	SMITHS	AL
UDSPU Corp.	UNION SPRINGS	AL
GABBUN Corp.	PHENIX CITY	AL
LUUNOR Corp.	AUBURN	AL
SRMOGG Corp.	ALEXANDER CITY	AL
BLECKS Corp.	PHENIX CITY	AL
CALLUW Corp.	TUSKEGEE	AL
WJSUSR Corp.	TROY	AL
UPGLEA Corp.	AUBURN	AL
MULSUN Corp.	SALEM	AL

Figure 2-26: The results of the query are now sorted in ascending order by the State field.

Filtering Query Results

Next, you'll examine how you can filter the query output so that you retrieve only the specific records to analyze. As in Excel, in Access this filter is also called *Criteria*.

> **NOTE** You will notice a Criteria row in the query grid. This is where you enter the value or values for which you would like to query. When entering a value in the Criteria section, all records that match it are returned in the query output. When entering text, you must enclose the text string with quotation marks. You can either place them there yourself or type your text and click another part of the query grid. Access then automatically places quotation marks around your criteria if the field you are filtering is a text field.

In the example demonstrated in Figure 2-27, your manager wants to see the list of customers from California. Since California is designated by the abbreviation "CA" in the table, that is exactly what you will enter in the Criteria row of the State column.

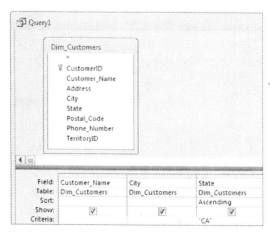

Figure 2-27: The Criteria section is where you type in a value for which you want to filter the data.

After you run the query, you will notice that fewer records are returned. This is obvious from looking at the Record Selector at the bottom of the query output window. A quick scan of the results verifies that indeed only records with "CA" in the State column were returned, as shown in Figure 2-28.

TIP **You can sort and filter query results just as if they were a Table. Simply click the dropdown arrow next to each of the column headings to activate the sorting and filtering context menu. Remember, this is only temporary and does not affect the underlying query.**

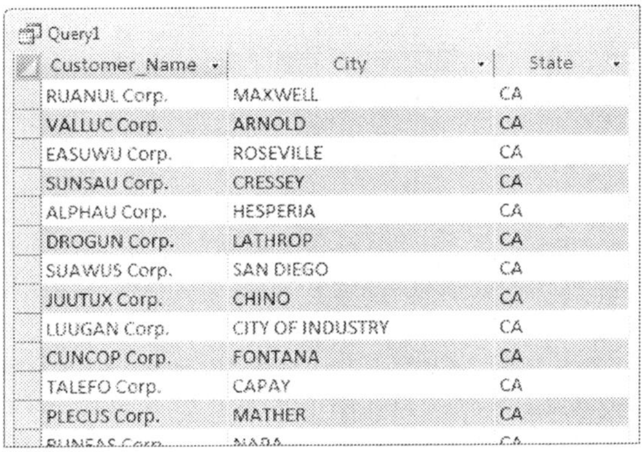
Query1

Customer_Name	City	State
RUANUL Corp.	MAXWELL	CA
VALLUC Corp.	ARNOLD	CA
EASUWU Corp.	ROSEVILLE	CA
SUNSAU Corp.	CRESSEY	CA
ALPHAU Corp.	HESPERIA	CA
DROGUN Corp.	LATHROP	CA
SUAWUS Corp.	SAN DIEGO	CA
JUUTUX Corp.	CHINO	CA
LUUGAN Corp.	CITY OF INDUSTRY	CA
CUNCOP Corp.	FONTANA	CA
TALEFO Corp.	CAPAY	CA
PLECUS Corp.	MATHER	CA

Figure 2-28: The results of the query will be all records that match the criteria.

Querying Multiple Tables

In this section you'll see how you can perform a query on multiple tables. Remember that you split your data into separate tables. You used Relationships to define the logical relationships between the data. Now you will query from the tables based on the relationships established.

For example, say you want to see the customer transactions from California. A quick examination of the Dim_Transactions table reveals that there is no State field on which you can filter. However, you see that there is a CustomerID field. Follow these steps:

1. In the query that you already have opened, add the Dim_Transactions table so you can include some fields from that table in your query output.
2. Right-click the top half of the Query Design view and select Show Table.
3. Double click the Dim_Transactions table to add it to the Query Design view. You will notice that the previously established relationship is automatically represented, as shown in Figure 2-29. You can see the one-to-many relationship, indicating possible multiple records in Dim_Transactions for each individual customer in the Dim_Customers table.

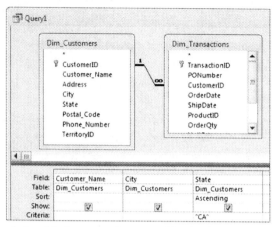

Figure 2-29: The relationship between the two tables is visually represented.

4. You must now select the fields from your newly added table, which you need to appear in the query output. Select the following three fields from the Dim_Transactions table: PONumber, OrderDate, LineTotal. As you can see in Figure 2-30, the field names from the two tables are brought together in the query grid.

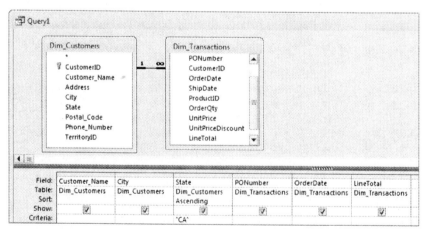

Figure 2-30: Fields from two tables are brought together to create a new dataset.

As you can see in Figure 2-31, you now have orders matched with the appropriate customer data. Although there is repeating data, as with the flat-file examples, there is a significant difference. The repeating data is being read from a single source, the Dim_Customer table. If a value were to change in the Dim_Customer table, that changed value would be repeated in your query results.

Query1

Customer_Name	City	State	PONumber	OrderDate	LineTotal
KUNSBA Corp.	DAVIS	CA	74065	6/29/2009	$81.00
RUDDAN Corp.	REDDING	CA	67988	4/10/2009	$6.00
BACKMO Corp.	SACRAMENTO	CA	73389	6/20/2009	$81.00
BACKMO Corp.	SACRAMENTO	CA	73389	6/20/2009	$6.00
BACKMO Corp.	SACRAMENTO	CA	73389	6/20/2009	$53.00
BACKMO Corp.	SACRAMENTO	CA	73389	6/20/2009	$1,759.00
BACKMO Corp.	SACRAMENTO	CA	60716	12/25/2008	$6.00
BACKMO Corp.	SACRAMENTO	CA	60716	12/25/2008	$13.00
GRUGUS Corp.	REDDING	CA	66135	3/13/2009	$53.00
DUNNUS Corp.	TRUCKEE	CA	72050	6/2/2009	$1,759.00
GRUGUS Corp.	REDDING	CA	58267	11/20/2008	$13.00
DUNNUS Corp.	TRUCKEE	CA	72405	6/7/2009	$806.00
KUNSBA Corp.	DAVIS	CA	74065	6/29/2009	$806.00

Figure 2-31: The results of the query have successfully brought together and have matched data from two separate tables.

Refining the Query

You can narrow your results even further by filtering the query results according to a certain date. As you can see, there are several rows of criteria cells. These allow you to enter multiple criteria from which to filter. One thing to keep in mind is that each separate criteria row functions as its own separate set of criteria. Take a look at how this works.

- **Single Criterion:** Click the Criteria cell in the OrderDate column and type **12/5/2008**. When you click out of that cell, you will notice that number signs (#) now surround the date, as shown in Figure 2-32. When running this query, only results matching the two criteria (State = CA and Invoice_Date = 12/5/2008) are returned.
- **Multiple Criteria:** Say you want to bring in orders for the data 3/8/2009 as well as 12/5/2008. You will want to add the new criteria line below the existing criteria. This will have the effect of testing the records for either one criteria or the other. Since you want to limit your query to only results from California, you must retype CA on your new Criteria line. If you do not do that, the Query will think that you want all orders from California on 12/5/2008 or orders from all states on 3/8/2009. The criteria lines will be evaluated individually. Add CA to the state column under the existing CA, as shown in Figure 2-33.

  After running the query, you can see your results have been refined even further. You have only those orders from California issued on March 9, 2009 and December 5, 2008.

Using Operators in Queries

To use multiple criteria in a query, you are not limited to using the separate criteria lines. By using operators, you can place your multiple criteria on the same line. That is to say, you can filter for multiple criteria on any given field by using operators.

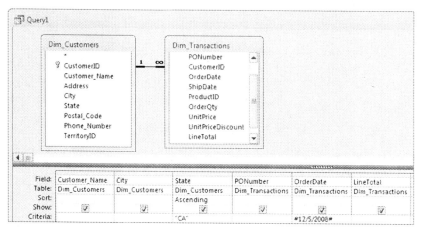

Figure 2-32: The number signs, which are surrounding the date, identify the criteria as being a Date/Time data type.

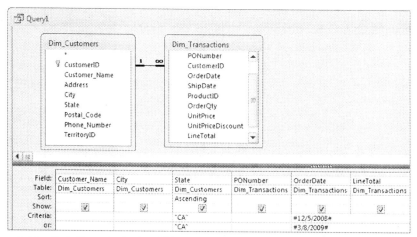

Figure 2-33: Each line of criteria will be evaluated separately.

The following operators allow you to combine multiple values in different logical contexts so you can create complex queries:

- **Or:** Either condition can be true. Multiple criteria values for one field can either be separated on different criteria lines or combined in one cell with the use of the Or operator. For example, using your query, you can filter for both California and Colorado by typing **CA or CO** in the Criteria field.

- **Between:** Tests for a range of values. For example, using your query, you can filter for all orders between 4/20/2009 and 11/19/2009 instead of testing just for those particular dates by typing **Between #4/20/2009# AND #11/19/2009#** in the Criteria field.

- **Like:** Tests for string expressions matching a pattern. For example, you can filter for all records with a customer ID that begins with the number 147 by typing **Like 147*** in the Criteria field. The asterisk is the wild card character, which can signify any character or combination of characters.

- **In:** Similar to or. Tests for all records that have values, which are contained in parentheses. For example, you can filter for both California and Colorado by typing **In ("CA", "CO")** in the Criteria field.

- **Not:** Opposite of writing a value in Criteria. All records not matching that value will be returned. For example, you can filter for all states except California by typing **Not "CA"** in the Criteria field.

- **Is Null:** Filters all records that have the database value Null in that field.

- **=, <, >, <=, >=, and <>:** The traditional mathematical operators allow you to construct complex criteria for fields used in calculations.

For example, suppose you want to further refine your query so that only order amounts over $200 will be returned in the results. As shown in Figure 2-34, use the greater-than operator to filter the LineTotal.

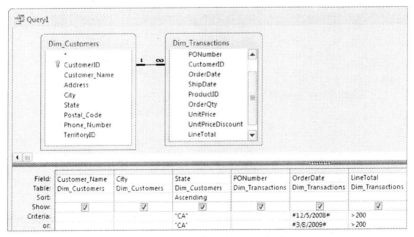

Figure 2-34: You can use operators to test for ranges of values.

After running the query, you can see that you narrowed your results down to just nine records. These are the only records that match the multiple criteria designated in the query grid. Figure 2-35 shows the query results.

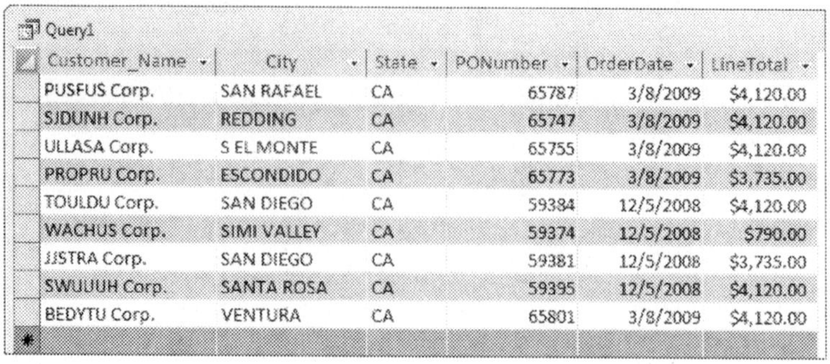

Query1

Customer_Name	City	State	PONumber	OrderDate	LineTotal
PUSFUS Corp.	SAN RAFAEL	CA	65787	3/8/2009	$4,120.00
SJDUNH Corp.	REDDING	CA	65747	3/8/2009	$4,120.00
ULLASA Corp.	S EL MONTE	CA	65755	3/8/2009	$4,120.00
PROPRU Corp.	ESCONDIDO	CA	65773	3/8/2009	$3,735.00
TOULDU Corp.	SAN DIEGO	CA	59384	12/5/2008	$4,120.00
WACHUS Corp.	SIMI VALLEY	CA	59374	12/5/2008	$790.00
JJSTRA Corp.	SAN DIEGO	CA	59381	12/5/2008	$3,735.00
SWUUUH Corp.	SANTA ROSA	CA	59395	12/5/2008	$4,120.00
BEDYTU Corp.	VENTURA	CA	65801	3/8/2009	$4,120.00

Figure 2-35: Here are your query results.

The Top Ten Query Errors

When starting to build analyses with Access, you will inevitably do something that makes Access throw up an error. In order to ease the confusion when first starting out, Table 2-1 and Table 2-2 list the ten most common errors new users are likely to encounter while working with queries. The tenth error deservers a table all of its own! Ironically, although these are the most common errors in a query environment, they are also the least descriptive. This leaves many new Access users scratching their heads.

Table 2-1: Top Nine Query Errors

ERROR	MESSAGE	MESSAGE MEANING
6	Overflow	The number you are using is outside the range of the data type you are assigning it to. In other words, the number you are using is either too big or too small for the data type.
7	Out of memory	The query or procedure you are running requires more memory than available on your system. Try closing any other applications you have open. You can also try breaking up the query or procedure in two steps.
11	Division by zero	When you divide a number by zero you get this message.
13	Type mismatch in Expression	You typically get this message when you are trying to join two fields with different data types; i.e. Text field and a Number field. Make sure any fields you are joining are the same data type.
16	Expression too complex	You have too many nested expressions or subqueries in your query. Try breaking up your query into steps.

ERROR	MESSAGE	MESSAGE MEANING
3001	Invalid Argument	Most often raised when your database has reached the 2 gigabyte limit. When this error is thrown, you should check the current size of the database. If your database has reached 2 gigabytes (or close to it), perform a Compact and Repair. This will resolve the error.
3060	Wrong data type for parameter `<Parameter Name>`	You are feeding a parameter the wrong type of data
3068	Not a valid alias name	You have either used a reserved word for your alias name, or your alias name contains invalid characters.

The error messages "Operation must use an updateable query" and "This Recordset is not updateable," are thrown when any of the queries in Table 2-2 are applied.

Table 2-2: Tenth Query Error, 3073 and 3326

QUERY	WORKAROUND
Your query is using a join to another query.	Create a temporary table that you can use instead of the joined query.
Your query is based on a crosstab query, an aggregate query, a union query, or a subquery that contains aggregate functions.	Workaround: Create a temporary table that you can use instead of the query.
Your query is based on three or more tables and there is a many-to-one-to-many relationship.	Create a temporary table that you can use without the relationship.
Your query is based on a table where the Unique Values property is set to Yes.	Set the Unique Values property of the table to No.
Your query is based on a table on which you do not have Update Data permissions, or is locked by another user.	Ensure you have permissions to update the table, and that the table is not in design view or locked by another user.
Your query is based on a table in a database that is open as read-only or is located on a read-only drive.	Obtain write access to the database or drive.
Your query is based on a linked ODBC table with no unique index or a Paradox table without a primary key.	Add a primary key or a unique index to the linked table.
Your query is based on a SQL pass-through query.	Create a temporary table that you can use instead of the query.

Summary

The fundamental tools in Access are tables and queries. A table is a collection of data concerning a specific types of entities such as customers, branches, transactions, and products. Access allows you to build relationships between your tables and enforce certain rules that guide these relationships. This reduces the chance for error and allows for easy analysis across multiple tables.

A query is a question about the data that is stored in tables. The results of a query are separate from the data. If the data in the table is changed and the query run again, you would most often get different results. The most common query is the select query. With a select query, you can extract a dataset or individual data items. You can also utilize the built-in operators to apply filters and sorting to your queries.

Beyond Select Queries

Retrieving and displaying specific records with a select query is indeed a fundamental task in analyzing data. However, it's just a small portion of what makes up data analysis. The scope of data analysis is broad and includes grouping and comparing data; updating and deleting data; performing calculations on data; and shaping and reporting data. Access has built in tools and functionality designed specifically to handle each one of these tasks.

In this chapter, you take an in-depth look at the various tools available to you in Access and how they can help you go beyond Select queries.

Aggregate Queries

An *aggregate query*, sometimes referred to as a *group-by query*, is a type of query you can build to help you quickly group and summarize your data. With a select query, you can only retrieve records as they appear in your data source. However, with an aggregate query, you can retrieve a summary snapshot of your data that will show you totals, averages, counts, and more.

Creating an Aggregate Query

To get a firm understanding of what an aggregate query does, take the following scenario as an example. You have just been asked to provide the sum of total revenue by period. In response to this request, start a query in Design view and bring in the Period and LineTotal fields, as shown in

Figure 3-1. If you run this query as is, you will get every record in your dataset instead of the summary you need.

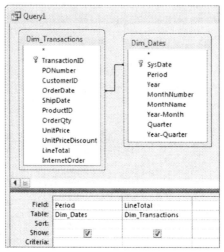

Figure 3-1: Running this query returns all the records in your dataset, not the summary you need.

> **TIP** Here's a quick reminder on how to start a query in Design view. Go to the application ribbon and select Create⇨ Query Design. The Show Table dialog box opens on top of a blank Query Design view. Select the table or tables with which you need to work and you're on your way. Feel free to refer to Chapter 2 for a quick refresher on the basics of Access Queries.

To get a summary of revenue by period, you need to activate Totals in your design grid. To do this, go up to the ribbon and select the Design tab and then click the Totals button. As you can see in Figure 3-2, after you have activated Totals in your design grid, you will see a new row in your grid called "Totals." The Totals row tells Access which aggregate function to use when performing aggregation on the specified fields.

Notice that the Totals row contains the words "group by" under each field in your grid. This means that all similar records in a field will be grouped to provide you with a unique data item. You will cover the different aggregate functions later in this chapter.

The idea here is to adjust the aggregate functions in the Totals row to correspond with the analysis you are trying perform. In this scenario, you need to group all the periods in your dataset and then sum the revenue in each period. Therefore, you will need to use the Group By aggregate function for the Period field and the Sum aggregate function for the LineTotal field.

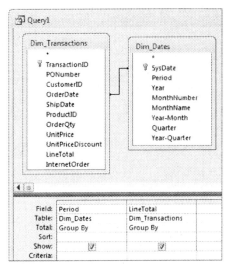

Figure 3-2: Activating Totals in your design grid adds a Totals row to your query grid that defaults to "Group By."

Since the default selection for Totals is the Group By function, no change is needed for the Period field. However, you need to change the aggregate function for the LineTotal field from Group By to Sum. This tells Access that you want to sum the revenue figures in the LineTotal field, not group them. To change the aggregate function, simply click the Totals dropdown and the LineTotal field, shown in Figure 3-3, and select Sum. At this point, you can run your query.

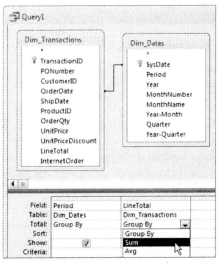

Figure 3-3: Change the aggregate function under the LineTotal field to Sum.

As you can see in Figure 3-4, the resulting table gives a summary of your dataset, showing total revenue by period.

Query1	
Period ▾	SumOfLineTotal ▾
200607	$1,282,530.35
200608	$3,008,547.90
200609	$2,333,985.05
200610	$1,982,360.35
200611	$4,338,025.75
200612	$3,457,253.40
200701	$1,928,725.30
200702	$3,712,032.10
200703	$3,109,211.70
200704	$2,224,498.50
200705	$4,308,999.75
200706	$3,227,812.65
200707	$1,604,596.00
200708	$6,327,232.40
200709	$4,853,215.95
200710	$3,009,334.25

Figure 3-4: After you run your query, you have a summary showing you total revenue by period.

TRICKS OF THE TRADE: CREATE ALIASES FOR YOUR COLUMN NAMES

Notice that in Figure 3-4, Access automatically changes the name of the Line-Total field to "SumOfLineTotal." This is a normal courtesy extended by Access to let you know that the figures you see here are a result of summing the Line-Total field. This may be convenient in some cases, but if you need to distribute these results to other people, you may want to give this field a more seemly name. This is where aliases come in handy.

■ An *alias* is an alternate name you can give to a field to make it easier to read the field's name in the query results. There are two methods for creating an alias for your field.

■ **Method 1:** The first method is to preface the field with the text you would like to see as the field name, followed by a colon. Figure 3-5 demonstrates how you would create aliases to ensure your query results have user-friendly column names. Running this query results in a dataset with a column call Period and column called Total Revenue.

■ **Method 2:** The second method is to right-click the field name and select Properties. This activates the Property Sheet dialog box for Field Properties. In this dialog box, simply enter the desired alias into the Caption input, as shown in Figure 3-6.

TRICKS OF THE TRADE: CREATE ALIASES FOR YOUR COLUMN NAMES

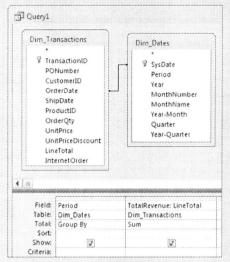

Figure 3-5: In this example, you are creating an alias called TotalRevenue.

Figure 3-6: Using the Property Sheet dialog box for field properties is an alternate way of defining an alias for your field.

WARNING Be aware that if you do use the Field Properties dialog box to define your alias, there will be no clear indication in your query's Design view or in your query's SQL string that you are using an alias. This may lead to some confusion for anyone using your queries. For this reason, it is generally better to use the first method to define an alias.

About Aggregate Functions

In the example shown in Figure 3-3, you select the Sum aggregate function from the Totals dropdown list. Obviously, you could select any of the 12 functions available. Indeed, you will undoubtedly come across analyses where you will have to use a few of the other functions available to you. In this light, it is important to know what each one of these aggregate functions implicates for your data analysis.

Group By

The Group By aggregate function aggregates all the records in the specified field into unique groups. Here are a few things to keep in mind when using the Group By aggregate function.

- **Access performs the** Group By **function in your aggregate query before any other aggregation.** If you are performing a Group By along with another aggregate function, the group by function will be performed first. The example shown in Figure 3-4 illustrates this concept. Access groups the Period field before summing the LineTotal field.

- **Access sorts each group by field in ascending order.** Unless otherwise specified, any field tagged as a group by field will be sorted in ascending order. If your query has multiple Group By fields, each field will be sorted in ascending order starting with the left-most field.

- **Access treats multiple Group By fields as one unique item.**

To illustrate the last bullet point, create a query that looks similar to the one shown in Figure 3-7. This query will count all the transactions logged in the "200701" Period.

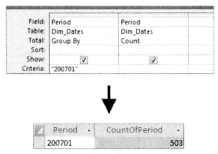

Figure 3-7: This query returns only one line showing total records for the 200701 period.

Now return to the Query Design view and add ProductID, as shown here in Figure 3-8. This time, Access treats each combination of Period and Product Number as a unique item. Each combination is grouped before the records in each group are counted. The benefit here is that you have added a dimension to your analysis. Not only do you know how many transactions per ProductID were logged in 200701, but if you add all the transactions, you will get an accurate count of the total number of transactions logged in 200701.

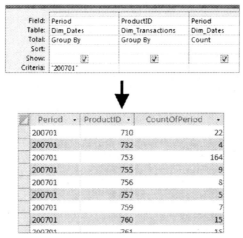

Figure 3-8: This query results in a few more records, but if you add the counts in each group, they will total to 503.

Sum, Avg, Count, StDev, Var

These aggregate functions all perform mathematical calculations against the records in your selected field. It is important to note that these functions exclude any records set to null. In other words, these aggregate functions ignore empty cells.

- ▪ Avg: Calculates the Average.

- ▪ Sum : Calculates the total value of all the records in the designated field or grouping. This function will only work with the following data types: AutoNumber, Currency, Date/Time, Yes/No, and Number.

- ▪ Avg: Calculates the Average of all the records in the designated field or grouping. This function will only work with the following data types: AutoNumber, Currency, Date/Time, Yes/No, and Number.

- ▪ Count: Simply counts the number of entries within the designated field or grouping. This function works with all data types.

- ▪ StDev: Calculates the standard deviation across all records within the designated field or grouping. This function will only work with the following data types: AutoNumber, Currency, Date/Time, and Number.

- ▪ Var: Calculates the amount by which all the values within the designated field or grouping vary from the average value of the group. This function will only work with the following data types: AutoNumber, Currency, Date/Time, and Number.

Min, Max, First, Last

Unlike other aggregate functions, these functions evaluate all the records in the designated field or grouping and return a single value from the group.

- Min: Returns the value of the record with the lowest value in the designated field or grouping. This function will only work with the following data types: AutoNumber, Currency, Date/Time, Number, and Text.

- Max: Returns the value of the record with the highest value in the designated field or grouping. This function will only work with the following data types: AutoNumber, Currency, Date/Time, Number, and Text.

- First: Returns the value of the first record in the designated field or grouping. This function works with all data types.

- Last: Returns the value of the last record in the designated field or grouping. This function works with all data types

Expression, Where

One of the steadfast rules of aggregate queries is that every field must have an aggregation performed against it. However, there will be situations where you will have to use a field as a utility. That is, use a field to simply perform a calculation or apply a filter. These fields are a means to get to the final analysis you are looking for, rather than part of the final analysis. In these situations, you will use the Expression function or the Where clause. The Expression function and the Where clause are unique in that they don't perform any grouping action per se.

The Expression Aggregate Function

This function is generally applied when you are utilizing custom calculations or other functions in an aggregate query. Expression tells Access to perform the designated custom calculation on each individual record or group separately.

To use this function, you create a query in Design view that looks like the one shown in Figure 3-9.

> **NOTE** Note that you are using two aliases in this query: "Revenue" for the LineTotal field and "Cost" for the custom calculation defined here. Using an alias of "Revenue" gives the sum of LineTotal a user-friendly name.

Now you can use [Revenue] to represent the sum of LineTotal in your custom calculation. The Expression aggregate function ties it all together by telling Access that [Revenue]*.33 will be performed against the resulting sum of LineTotal for each individual Period group. Running this query will return the total Revenue and Cost for each Period group.

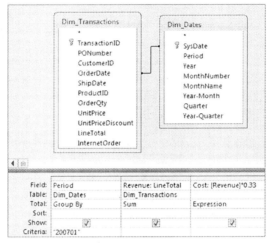

Figure 3-9: The `Expression` aggregate function allows you to perform the designated custom calculation on each Period group separately.

The Where Clause

The `Where` clause allows you to apply a criterion to a field that is not included in your aggregate query, effectively applying a filter to your analysis. To see the `Where` clause in action, create a query in Design view that looks like the one shown in Figure 3-10.

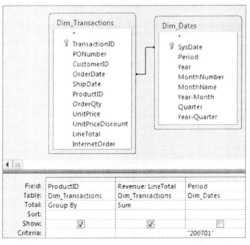

Figure 3-10: Running this query causes an error message because you have no aggregation defined for Period.

As you can see in the Total row, you are grouping ProductID and summing LineTotal. However, Period has no aggregation selected, because you only want to use it to filter out one specific period. You have entered "200701" in the criteria for Period. If you run this query as is, you will get the following error message: "You tried to execute a query that does not include the specified expression Dim.Dates.Period="200701" as part of an aggregate function."

To run this query successfully, click the Totals dropdown for the Period field and select "Where" from the selection list. At this point, your query should look similar to the one shown here in Figure 3-11. With the `Where` clause specified, you can successfully run this query.

NOTE Here is one final note about the `Where` clause. Notice in Figure 3-9 that the check box in the "Show" row has no check in it for the Period. This is because fields tagged with the `Where` clause cannot be shown in an aggregate query. Therefore, this checkbox must remain empty. If you place a check in the "Show" checkbox of a field with a `Where` clause, you will get an error message stating that you cannot display the field for which you entered `Where` in the Total row.

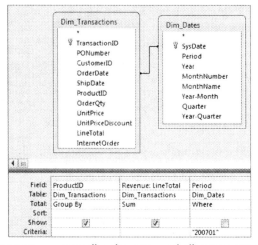

Figure 3-11: Adding a `Where` remedies the error and allows you to run the query.

Action Queries

You can think of an action query the same way you think of a select query. Like a select query, an action query extracts a dataset from a data source based on the definitions and criteria you pass to the query. The difference is that when an action query returns results, it does not display a dataset; instead, it performs some action on those results. The action it performs depends on its type.

NOTE Unlike select queries, you cannot use action queries as a datasource for a form or a report, as they do not return a dataset that can be read.

There are four types of action queries: Make-Table queries, delete queries, append queries, and updated queries. Each query type performs a unique action that you will cover in this section.

Why Use Action Queries?

As mentioned before, along with querying data, the scope of data analysis includes shaping data, changing data, deleting data and updating data. Access provides action queries as data analysis tools to help you with these tasks. Unfortunately, too many people do not make use of these tools; instead, opting to export small chunks of data to Excel in order to perform these tasks.

This may be fine if you are performing these tasks as a one-time analysis with a small dataset. However, what do you do when you have to carry out the same analysis on a weekly basis, or if the dataset you need to manipulate exceeds Excel's limits? In these situations, it would be impractical to routinely export data into Excel, manipulate the data, and then re-import the data back into Access. Using action queries, you can increase your productivity and reduce the chance of errors by carrying out all your analytical process within Access.

Make-Table Queries

A *Make-Table* query creates a new table consisting of data from an existing table. The table created consists of records that have met the definitions and criteria of the Make-Table query.

Why Use a Make-Table Query?

In simple terms, if you create a query and would like to capture the results of your query in its own table, you can use a Make-Table query to create a hard table with your query results. You can then use your new table in some other analytical process.

What Are the Hazards of Make-Table Queries?

When you build a Make-Table query, you must specify the name of the table that will be created when the Make-Table query is run. If you give the new table the same name as an existing table, the existing table will be overwritten. If you accidentally write over another table with a Make-Table query, you will not be able to recover the old table. Be sure that you name the tables created by your Make-Table queries carefully to avoid overwriting existing information.

The data in a table made by a Make-Table query is not linked to its source data. This means that the data in your new table is not updated when data in the original table is changed.

Creating a Make-Table Query

You have been asked to provide the marketing department with a list of customers along with information about each customer's sales history. To meet this task, follow these steps:

1. Create a query in the Query Design view that looks similar to the one shown here in Figure 3-12.

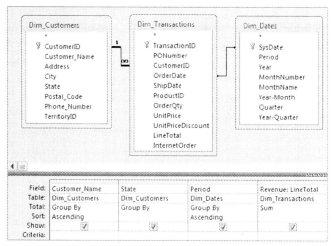

Figure 3-12: Create this query in Design view.

2. Go up to the ribbon, select Design ⇨ Make Table. The Make Table dialog box shown in Figure 3-13 will be activated.

Figure 3-13: Enter the name of your new table.

3. Enter the name you would like to give to your new table in the Table Name input box. For this example, type **SalesHistory**.

WARNING Be sure not to enter the name of a table that already exists in your database, as it will be overwritten.

4. Once you have entered the name, click the OK button to close the dialog box, and then run your query. At this point, Access will throw up the warning message shown in Figure 3-14 in order to make you aware that you will not be able to undo this action.

You are about to paste 23754 row(s) into a new table.

Once you click Yes, you can't use the Undo command to reverse the changes. Are you sure you want to create a new table with the selected records?

Yes   No

Figure 3-14: Click Yes to run your query.

5. Click Yes to confirm and create your new table.

When your query has completed running, you will find a new table called SalesHistory in your Table objects.

TRICKS OF THE TRADE: TURNING AGGREGATE QUERY RESULTS INTO HARD DATA

The results of aggregate queries are inherently not updatable. This means you will not be able to edit any of the records returned from an aggregate query. This is because the relationship between the aggregated data and the underlying data only goes one way. That is, changing the aggregated data will not change the underlying data.

However, you can change your aggregate query into a Make- Table query and create a static table with your aggregate query's results. With your new hard table, you will be able to edit at your heart's content.

To illustrate how this works, create the query shown in Figure 3-15 in design view. Then, change the query into a Make-Table query, enter a name for your new table, and run it.

(continued)

TRICKS OF THE TRADE: TURNING AGGREGATE QUERY RESULTS INTO HARD DATA *(continued)*

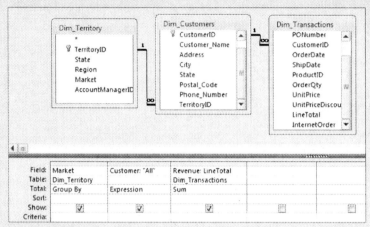

Figure 3-15: Running this query as a Make-Table will allow you to edit the aggregate query's results.

TIP Notice that in the previous figure you defined a column with an alias of Customer. After the alias, you simply entered All in quotes. When you run the query, you will notice that your new table has a column named Customer in which the value for every record is All. This example illustrates that when running a Make-Table query, you can create your own columns on the fly by simply creating an alias for the column and defining its contents after the colon.

Delete Queries

A *delete* query deletes records from a table based on the definitions and criteria you specify. That is, a delete query affects a group of records that meet a specified criterion that you apply.

Why Use a Delete Query?

Although you can delete records by hand, there are situations where using a delete query is more efficient. For example, if you have a very large dataset, a delete query will delete your records faster than a manual delete. In addition, if you want to delete certain records based on several complex criteria, you will want to utilize a delete query. Finally, if you need to delete records from one table based on a comparison with another table, a delete query is the way to go.

What Are the Hazards of Delete Queries?

As with all other action queries, you will not be able to undo the effects of a delete query. However, a delete query is much more dangerous than the other action queries because there is no way to remedy accidentally deleted data.

Given that deleted data cannot be recovered, you should get into the habit of taking one of the following actions to avoid a fatal error.

- Run a select query to display the records you are about to delete. Review the records to confirm that they are indeed the ones you want to delete, and then run the query as a delete query.

- Run a select query to display the records you are about to delete; then change the query into a Make-Table query. Run the Make-Table query to make a backup of the data you are about to delete. Finally, run the query again as a delete query to delete the records.

- Make a backup of your database before running your delete query.

Creating a Delete Query

The marketing department has informed you that the SalesHistory table you gave them includes records that they do not need. They want you to delete all history before the 200806 Period. To meet this demand, do the following:

1. Design a query based on the SalesHistory table you created a moment ago.

2. Bring in the Period field and enter <**200806** in the Criteria row. Your design grid should look like the one shown here in Figure 3-16.

Figure 3-16: This query selects all records with a Period earlier than 200806.

3. Perform a test by running the query. Review the records returned, and take note that 6418 records meet your criteria. You now know that 6418 will be deleted if you run a delete query based on these query definitions.

4. Return to the Design view. Go up to the ribbon and select Design⊙ Delete. Now run your query again. At this point, Access will throw up a message, as shown in Figure 3-17, telling you that you are about to delete 6418 rows of data and warning you that you will not be able to undo this action. This is the number you were expecting to see, as the test you ran earlier returned 6418 records.

Figure 3-17: Click Yes to continue with your delete action.

5. Since everything checks out, click Yes to confirm and delete the records.

NOTE If you are working with a very large dataset, Access may throw up a message telling you that the "undo command won't be available because the operation is too large or there isn't enough free memory."

Many people mistakenly interpret this message to mean that this operation can't be performed because there is not enough memory. This message simply tells you that Access will not be able to give the option of undoing this change if you choose to continue with the action.

This is applicable to delete queries, append queries, and update queries.

TRICKS OF THE TRADE: DELETING RECORDS FROM ONE TABLE BASED ON RECORDS FROM ANOTHER

You will encounter many analyses where you will have to delete records from one table based on records from another. This is relatively easy to do. However, many users get stuck on this because of one simple mistake.

The query in Figure 3-18 looks simple enough. It tells Access to delete all records from the Customer_ListA table if the customer is found in the Customer_ListB table.

If you run this query, Access throws up the message shown in Figure 3-19. This message asks you to specify which table contains the records you want to delete.

TRICKS OF THE TRADE: DELETING RECORDS FROM ONE TABLE BASED ON RECORDS FROM ANOTHER

This message stumps many Access users. Unfortunately, this message does not clearly state what you need to do to remedy the mistake. Nevertheless, the remedy is a simple one:

1. Clear the query grid by deleting the CustomerName field.

2. Double-click the asterisk (*) in the Customer_ListA table. This explicitly tells Access that the Customer_ListA table contains the records you want to delete. Figure 3-20 demonstrates the correct way to build this query.

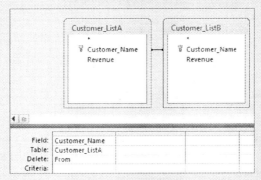

Figure 3-18: This delete query seems as though it should run fine, but there is something wrong.

Figure 3-19: Access does not know which table you want the records deleted from.

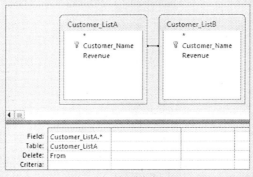

Figure 3-20: This is the correct way to build this query.

Append Queries

An *append* query appends records to a table based on the definitions and criteria you specify in your query. In other words, with an append query, you can add the results of your query to the end of a table, effectively adding rows to the table.

Why Use an Append Query?

With an append query, you are essentially copying records from one table or query and adding them to the end of another table. In that light, append queries come in handy when you need to transfer large datasets from one table to another. For example, if you have a table called Old Transactions where you archive your transaction records, you can add the latest batch of transactions from the New Transactions table by using an append query.

What Are the Hazards of Append Queries?

The primary hazard of an append query is losing records during the append process. That is, not all of the records you think you are appending to a table actually make it to your table. There are generally two reasons why records can get lost during an append process.

- **Type Conversion Failure:** This failure occurs when the character type of the source data does not match that of the destination table column. For example, imagine that you have a table with a field called Cost. Your Cost field is set as a TEXT character type because you have some entries that are tagged as "TBD" (to be determined), as you don't know the cost yet. If you try to append that field to another table whose Cost field is set as a NUMBER character type, all the entries that have "TBD" will be changed to Null, effectively deleting your TBD tag.

- **Key Violation:** This violation occurs when you are trying to append duplicate records to a field in the destination table that is set as a primary key or is indexed as No Duplicates. In other words, when you have a field that prohibits duplicates, Access will not allow you to append any record that is a duplicate of an existing record in that field.

Another hazard of an append query is that the query may simply fail to run. There are two reasons why an append query might fail:

- **Lock Violation:** This violation occurs when the destination table is open in Design view or is open by another user on the network.

- **Validation Rule Violation:** This violation occurs when a field in the destination table has one of the following properties settings:

- **Required Field is set to Yes:** If a field in the destination table has been set to Required Yes and you do not append data to this field, your append query will fail.

- **Allow Zero Length is set to No:** If a field in the destination table has been set to Zero Length No and you do not append data to this field, your append query will fail.

- **Validation Rule set to anything:** If a field in the destination table has a validation rule and you break the rule with your append query, your append query will fail. For example, if you have a validation rule for the Cost field in your destination table set to >0, you cannot append records with a quantity less than or equal to zero.

Luckily, Access will clearly warn you if you are about to cause any of these errors. Figure 3-21 demonstrates this warning message.

ZalexCorp Restaurant Equipment and Supply can't append all the records in the append query.

ZalexCorp Restaurant Equipment and Supply set 0 field(s) to Null due to a type conversion failure, and it didn't add 5979 record(s) to the table due to key violations, 0 record(s) due to lock violations, and 0 record(s) due to validation rule violations.
Do you want to run the action query anyway?
To ignore the error(s) and run the query, click Yes.
For an explanation of the causes of the violations, click Help.

Figure 3-21: The warning message tells you that you will lose records during the append process.

As you can see, this warning message tells you that you cannot append all the records due to errors. It goes on to tell you exactly how many records will not be appended because of each error. In this case, 5979 records will not be appended because of key violations. You have the option of clicking Yes or No. The Yes button ignores the warning and appends all records minus the two with the errors. The No button cancels the query, which means that no records will be appended.

Keep in mind that as with all other action queries, you will not be able to undo your append query once you have pulled the trigger.

TIP If you can identify the records you recently appended in your destination table, you can technically undo your append action by simply deleting the newly append records. This will obviously be contingent upon your providing yourself a method of identifying appended records. For example, you can create a field that contains some code or tag that identifies the appended records. This code can be anything from a date to a simple character.

Creating an Append Query

The marketing department contacts you and tells you that they made a mistake. They actually need all the sales history for the 2008 Fiscal year. So they need periods 200801 thru 200805 added back to the SalesHistory report.

To meet this demand:

1. Create a query in the Query Design view that looks similar to the one shown in Figure 3-22.

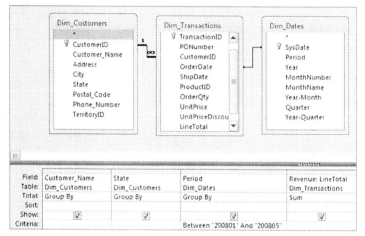

Figure 3-22: This query selects all records contained in Periods 200801 thru 200805.

2. Go to the ribbon and select Design ⇨ Append. The Append dialog box, shown in Figure 3-23, will be activated. In the Table Name input box, enter the name of the table to which you would like to append your query results. In this example, enter **SalesHistory**.

Figure 3-23: Enter the name of the table to which you would like to append your query results.

3. Once you have entered your destination table's name, click the OK button. You will notice that your query grid has a new row called "Append To" under the Sort row. Figure 3-24 shows this new row.

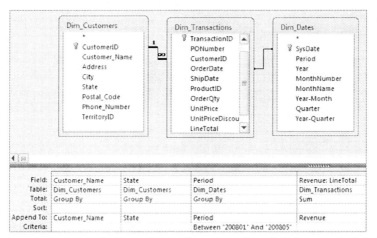

Figure 3-24: In the Append To row, select the name of the field in your destination table where you would like to append the information resulting from your query.

The idea is to select the name of the field in your destination table where you would like append the information resulting from your query. For example, the Append To row under the Period field shows the word "Period." This means that the data in the Period field of this query will be appended to the Period field in the SalesHistory table.

4. Now you can run your query. After you run your query, Access will throw up a message, as shown in Figure 3-25, telling you that you are about to append 1760 rows of data and warning you that you will not be able to undo this action. Click Yes to confirm and append the records.

Figure 3-25: Click Yes to continue with your append action.

TRICKS OF THE TRADE: ADDING A TOTALS ROW TO YOUR DATASET

Your manager wants you to create a revenue summary report that shows the total revenue for each account manager in each market. He also wants to see the total revenue for each market. Instead of giving your manager two separate reports, you can give him one table that has account manager details and market totals. This is a simple two-step process:

1. **Make an Account Manager Summary. Create a query in the Query Design view that looks similar to the one shown in the Figure 3-26. Note that you are creating an alias for the LineTotal field. Change the query into a Make-Table query and name your table RevenueSummary. Run this query.**

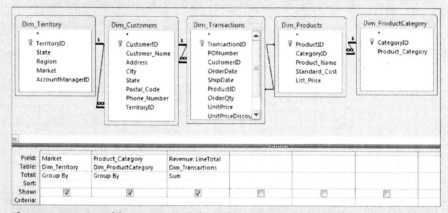

Figure 3-26: Run this query as a Make-Table query to make a table called Revenue-Summary.

2. **Append the Market Totals. Now use the RevenueSummary table you just created to summarize revenue by Market. To do this, create a query in the Query Design view that looks similar to the one shown in the Figure 3-27.**

3. **Take a moment and look at the query in the previous figure. You will notice that you are making a custom Product_Category field, filling it with the word "(Total)." This will ensure that the summary lines you append to the RevenueSummary table will be clearly identifiable, as they will have the word "Total" in the Product_Category field.**

4. **Change the query into an append query and append these results to the RevenueSummary table.**

TRICKS OF THE TRADE: ADDING A TOTALS ROW TO YOUR DATASET

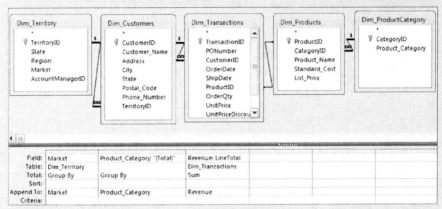

Field:	Market	Product_Category: "[Total]"	Revenue: LineTotal		
Table:	Dim_Territory		Dim_Transactions		
Total:	Group By	Group By	Sum		
Sort:					
Append To:	Market	Product_Category	Revenue		
Criteria:					

Figure 3-27: Run this market summary query as an append query and append it to the RevenueSummary table.

5. Now you can open the **RevenueSummary** table and sort by **Market** and **Product_Category**. As you can see in Figure 3-28, you have success-fully created a table that has a total revenue line for every product category and a total revenue line for each market, all in one table.

Market	Product_Category	Revenue
Baltimore	Warmers	$755.00
Baltimore	Refrigerators and Coolers	$10,730.00
Baltimore	Ovens and Ranges	$7,470.00
Baltimore	Fryers	$352.00
Baltimore	Bar Equipment	$80.00
Baltimore	(Total)	$19,387.00
Buffalo	Warmers	$1,009,447.95
Buffalo	Refrigerators and Coolers	$2,030,464.50
Buffalo	Ovens and Ranges	$1,654,376.65
Buffalo	Fryers	$127,287.70
Buffalo	Concession Equipment	$187,711.00
Buffalo	Commercial Appliances	$237,297.85
Buffalo	Bar Equipment	$37,397.90
Buffalo	(Total)	$5,283,983.55
California	Warmers	$1,699,423.65

Figure 3-28: Sort by market and product category.

Update Queries

An *update* query allows you to alter the records in a table based on the definitions and criteria you specify in your query. In other words, with an update query, you can change the values of many records at one time.

Why Use an Update Query?

The primary reason to use update queries is to save time. There is no easier way to edit large amounts of data at one time than with an update query. For example, imagine you have a Customers table that includes the customer's zip code. If the zip code 32750 has been changed to 32751, you can easily update your Customers table to replace 32750 with 32751.

What Are the Hazards of Update Queries?

As is the case with all other action queries, you must always take precautions to ensure that you are not in a situation where you cannot undo the effects of an update query. Get into the habit of taking one of the following actions in order to give yourself a way back to the original data in the event of a misstep.

- Run a select query to display, then change the query to a Make-Table query. Run the Make-Table query to make a backup of the data you are about to update. Finally, run the query again as an update query to delete the records.
- Make a backup of your database before running your update query.

Creating an Update Query

You have just received word that the zip code for all customers in the 33605 zip code has been changed to 33606. To keep your database accurate, you must update all the 33605 zip codes in your Dim_Customers table to 33606.

1. Create a query in the Query Design view that looks similar to the one shown in Figure 3-29.
2. Perform a test by running the query.
3. Review the records returned and take note that six records meet your criteria. You now know that six records will be updated if you run an update query based on these query definitions.
4. Return to the Design view. Go up to the Ribbon and select Design ⇨ Update. You will notice that your query grid has a new row called Update To. The idea is to enter the value to which you would like to

update the current data. In this scenario, shown in Figure 3-30, you want to update the zip code for the records you are selecting to 33606.

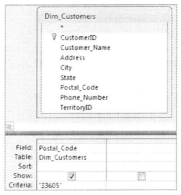

Figure 3-29: This query selects all customers in the 32750 zip code.

Figure 3-30: In this query, you are updating the zip code for all customers that have a code between 33605 to 33606.

5. Run the query. Access will throw up the message, shown in Figure 3-31, telling you that you are about to update six rows of data and warning you that you will not be able to undo this action. This is the number you were expecting to see, as the test you ran earlier returned six records. Since everything checks out, click Yes to confirm and update the records.

Figure 3-31: Click Yes to continue with your update action.

TRICKS OF THE TRADE: USING EXPRESSIONS IN YOUR UPDATE QUERIES

You will come across situations where you will have to execute record-specific updates. That is, you are not updating multiple records with one specific value; instead, you are updating each record based on an expression.

To demonstrate this concept, start a query in Design view based on the SalesHistory table you created in the "Make-Table Queries" section of this chapter. Build your query like the one shown in Figure 3-32.

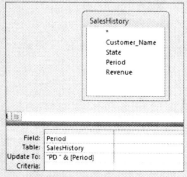

Figure 3-32: This update query uses an expression to make record-specific updates.

This query is telling Access to update the Period to concatenate the text "PD " (note the space after PD) with the value in the Period field.

After you run this query, all the values in the Period field will have a prefix of PD. For example, 200801 will be updated to PD 200801.

Remember, this is just one example of an expression you can use to update your records. You can use almost any expression with an update query, ranging from mathematical functions to string operations.

A Word on Updatable Datasets

Not all datasets are updatable. That is, you may have a dataset that Access cannot update for one reason or another. If your update query fails, you will get one of these messages: "Operation must use an updatable query" or "This Recordset is not updateable."

Your update query will fail if any one of the following applies:

▪ **Your query is using a join to another query:** To work around this issue, create a temporary table that you can use instead of the joined query.

▪ **Your query is based on a crosstab query, an aggregate query, a Union query, or a subquery that contains aggregate functions:** To work around this issue, create a temporary table that you can use instead of the query.

- **Your query is based on three or more tables and there is a many-to-one-to-many relationship:** To work around this issue, create a temporary table that you can use without the relationship.

- **Your query is based on a table where the Unique Values property is set to Yes:** To work around this issue, set the Unique Values property of the table to No.

- **Your query is based on a table on which you do not have Update Data permissions or is locked by another user:** To work around this issue, ensure you have permissions to update the table, and that the table is not in Design view or locked by another user.

- **Your query is based on a table in a database that is open as read-only or is located on a read-only drive:** To work around this issue, obtain write access to the database or drive.

- **Your query is based on a linked ODBC table with no unique index or a Paradox table without a primary key**: To work around this issue, add a primary key or a unique index to the linked table.

- **Your query is based on a SQL pass-through query:** To work around this issue, create a temporary table that you can use instead of the query.

Crosstab Queries

A *crosstab query* is a special kind of aggregate query that summarizes values from a specified field and groups them in a matrix layout by two sets of dimensions: one set down the left side of the matrix and the other set listed across the top of the matrix. Crosstab queries are perfect for analyzing trends over time or providing a method for quickly identifying anomalies in your dataset.

The anatomy of a crosstab query is simple. You need a minimum of three fields to create the matrix structure that will become your crosstab: The first field makes up the row headings, the second field makes up the column headings, and the third field makes up the aggregated data in the center of the matrix. The data in the center can represent a Sum, Count, Average, or any other aggregate function. Figure 3-33 demonstrate the basic structure of a crosstab query.

Region Name	QTR1	QTR2	QTR3	QTR4
Region A	data	data	data	data
Region B	data	data	data	data
Region C	data	data	data	data

Figure 3-33: This is the basic structure of a crosstab query.

There are two methods for creating a crosstab query: using the Crosstab Query Wizard and creating a crosstab query manually using the query design grid.

Using the Crosstab Query Wizard

The Crosstab Query Wizard comes in handy for beginners. Use this wizard when you want a simple guide through the steps of creating a crosstab query.

To activate the Crosstab Query Wizard:

1. In the ribbon, select the Create tab.

2. Select the Query Wizard button. This will bring up the New Query dialog box, shown in Figure 3-34.

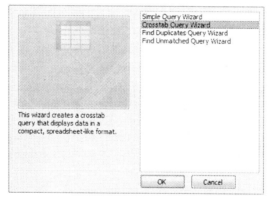

Figure 3-34: Select Crosstab Query Wizard from the New Query dialog box.

3. Select Crosstab Query Wizard from the selection list and then click the OK button.

4. The first step in the Crosstab Query Wizard is to identify the data source you will be using. As you can see in Figure 3-35, you can choose either a query or a table as your data source. In this example, you'll use the Dim_Transactions table as your data source. Select Dim_Transactions and then click the Next button.

5. The next step is to identify the fields you would like to use as the row headings. Select the ProductID field and click the button with the > symbol on it to move it to the Selected Items list. At this point, your dialog box should look like Figure 3-36. Notice that the ProductID field is shown in the sample diagram at the bottom of the dialog box.

NOTE You can select up to three fields to include in your crosstab query as row headings. Remember that Access treats each combination of headings as a unique item. That is, each combination is grouped before the records in each group are aggregated.

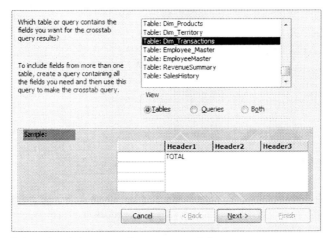

Figure 3-35: Select the data source for your crosstab query.

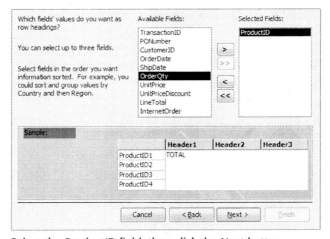

Figure 3-36: Select the ProductID field; then click the Next button.

6. The next step is to identify the field you would like to use as the column heading for your crosstab query. Keep in mind that there can be only one column heading in your crosstab. Select the OrderDate field from the field list. Again, notice in Figure 3-37 that the sample diagram at the bottom of the dialog box updates to show the OrderDate.

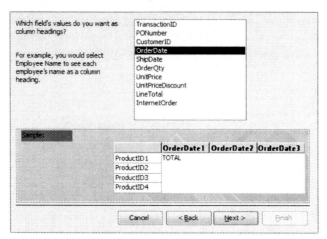

Figure 3-37: Select the OrderDate field; then click the Next button.

NOTE If the field used as a column heading includes data that contains a period (.), an exclamation mark (!), or a bracket ([or]), those characters will be changed to an underscore character (_) in the column heading. This does not happen if the same data is used as a row heading. This behavior is by design, as the naming convention for field names in Access prohibits use of these characters.

7. If your column heading is a date field, as the OrderDate is in this example, you will see the step shown here in Figure 3-38. In this step, you will have the option of specifying an interval to group your dates by. Select Quarter here and notice that the sample diagram at the bottom of the dialog box updates accordingly.

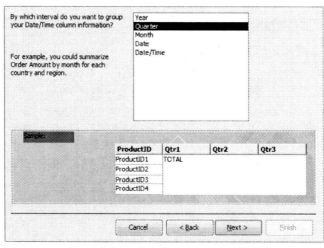

Figure 3-38: Select Quarter and then click the Next button.

8. You're almost done. In the second-to-last step, shown in Figure 3-39, you identify the field you want to aggregate and the function you want to use. Select the LineTotal field from the Fields list and then select Sum from the Functions list.

   If you look at the sample diagram at the bottom of the dialog box, you will get a good sense of what your final crosstab query will do. In this example, your crosstab will calculate the sum of the LineTotal field for each ProductID by Quarter.

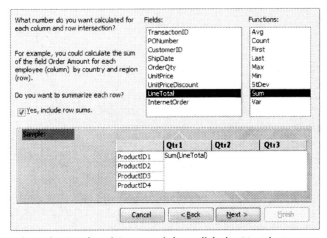

Figure 3-39: Select LineTotal and Sum, and then click the Next button.

> **NOTE** Notice the check box next to "Yes, include row sums." This box is checked by default to ensure that your crosstab query includes a "Total" column that contains the sum total for each row. If you do not want this column, simply remove the check from the checkbox.

9. The final step, shown in Figure 3-40, is to name your crosstab query. In this example, you are naming your crosstab "Product Summary by Quarter." After you name your query, you have the option of viewing your query or modifying the design. In this case, you want to view your query results, so simply click the Finish button.

   In just a few clicks, you have created a powerful look at the revenue performance of each product by quarter (Figure 3-41).

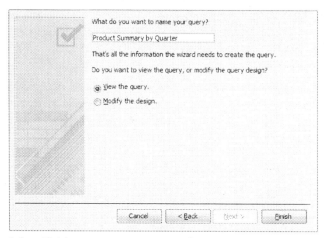

Figure 3-40: Select Finish to see your query results.

ProductID	Total Of LineTotal	Qtr 1	Qtr 2	Qtr 3	Qtr 4
709	$28,663.80	$3,787.20	$8,000.40	$9,485.40	$7,390.80
710	$353,507.05	$69,334.85	$64,463.10	$62,870.60	$156,838.50
718	$732,725.50		$171,432.25	$414,166.75	$147,126.50
719	$5,853,748.80	$1,244,884.20	$1,541,942.70	$1,616,661.00	$1,450,260.90
720	$495,413.50			$495,413.50	
732	$160,733.00	$23,115.00	$49,948.50	$36,247.00	$51,422.50
733	$57,352.00		$22,411.50	$13,065.00	$21,875.50
753	$9,373,695.50	$2,286,041.00	$2,949,132.00	$1,824,659.50	$2,313,863.00
755	$582,601.20	$145,650.30	$166,482.60	$103,370.40	$167,097.90
756	$526,095.55	$133,975.65	$155,210.75	$85,507.75	$151,401.40
757	$250,742.10	$82,378.10	$83,924.30		$84,439.70
759	$517,812.55	$116,694.85	$147,762.65	$124,890.65	$128,464.40
760	$1,580,850.30	$340,331.65	$430,951.80	$480,024.00	$411,552.75

Figure 3-41: A powerful analysis in just a few clicks.

TIP To quickly add all of a table's fields to the query design grid, double click the table's title bar. This will select all of the fields (except the asterisk). Now you can drag all of the selected fields to the grid at once.

TRICKS OF THE TRADE: TURNING YOUR CROSSTAB QUERY INTO HARD DATA

You will undoubtedly encounter scenarios where you will have to convert your crosstab query into hard data in order to use the results on other analysis. A simple trick in doing this is to use your saved crosstab query in a Make-Table query to create a new table with your crosstab results.

Start by creating a new select query in Design view and add your saved crosstab query. In Figure 3-42, you will notice that you are using the "Product

TRICKS OF THE TRADE: TURNING YOUR CROSSTAB QUERY INTO HARD DATA

Summary by Quarter" crosstab you just created. Bring in the fields you want to include in your new table.

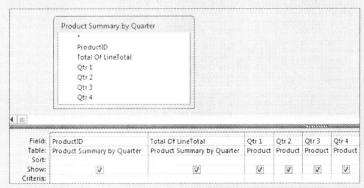

Figure 3-42: Create a select query using the crosstab query as your source data.

At this point, simply convert your query into a Make-Table query and run it. After you run your Make-Table, you will have a hard table that contains the results of your crosstab.

Creating a Crosstab Query Manually

Although the Crosstab Query Wizard makes it easy to create a crosstab in just a few clicks, it does come with its own set of limitations that may inhibit your data analysis efforts. The following list describes the limitations you will encounter when using the Crosstab Query Wizard:

- You can only select one data source on which to base your crosstab. This means that if you need to crosstab data residing across multiple tables, you will need to take extra steps to create a temporary query in order to use as your data source.

- There is no way to filter or limit your crosstab query with criteria.

- You are limited to only three row headings.

- You cannot explicitly define the order of your column headings.

The good news is that you can create a crosstab query manually through the query design grid. As you will learn in the sections to follow, creating your crosstab manually allows you greater flexibility in your analysis.

1. Create the aggregate query shown in Figure 3-43. Notice that you are using multiple tables to get the fields you need. One of the benefits of creating a crosstab query manually is that you don't have to use just one data source. You can use as many sources as you need in order to define the fields in your query.

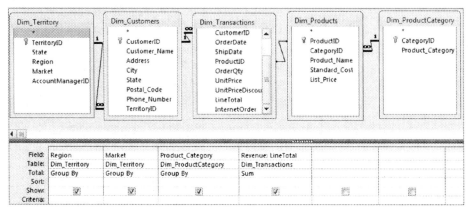

Figure 3-43: Create an aggregate query as shown here.

2. In the ribbon, select the Design tab. From the Design tab, select the Crosstab button. At this point, you will notice a row in your query grid called Crosstab, as shown in Figure 3-44. The idea is to define what role each field will play in your crosstab query. Under each field in the Crosstab row, you will select where the field will be a row heading, a column heading, or a value.

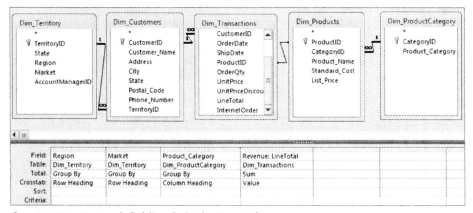

Figure 3-44: Set each field's role in the Crosstab row.

3. Run the query to see your crosstab in action.

When building your crosstab in the query grid, keep the following in mind:

- You must have a minimum of one row heading, one column heading, and one Value field.
- You cannot define more than one column heading.
- You cannot define more than one value heading.
- You are *not* limited to only three row headings.

TRICKS OF THE TRADE: CREATING A CROSSTAB VIEW WITH MULTIPLE VALUE FIELDS

One of the rules of a crosstab query is that you cannot have more than one Value field. However, there is a trick to get work around this limitation and analyze more than one metric with the same data groups. To help demonstrate how this works, follow these steps:

1. Create a crosstab query as shown in Figure 3-45 and save it as **Crosstab-1**. Your column heading is a custom field that has the region name and the word "Revenue" next to it.

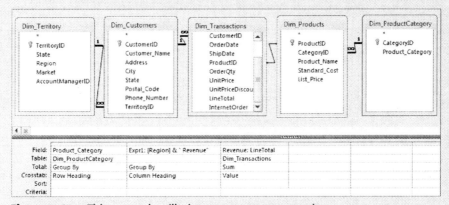

Figure 3-45: This crosstab will give you a revenue metric.

2. Create another crosstab query as shown in Figure 3-46 and save it as **Crosstab-2**. Again, your column heading is a custom field that gives you the region name and the word "Transactions" next to it.

3. Create a select query that will join the two crosstab queries on the row heading. In the example shown in Figure 3-47, the row heading is the Product_Category field. Bring in all the fields in the appropriate order.

(continued)

TRICKS OF THE TRADE: CREATING A CROSSTAB VIEW WITH MULTIPLE VALUE FIELDS (continued)

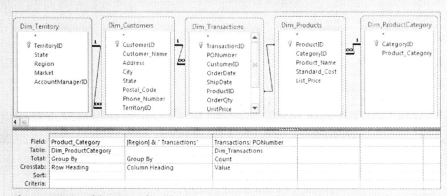

Figure 3-46: This crosstab will give you a transaction count metric.

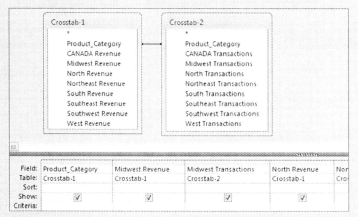

Figure 3-47: This query joins two crosstabs, allowing you to use multiple value fields in a crosstab format.

4. **Run this query. The result will be an analysis that incorporates both crosstab queries, effectively giving you multiple value fields.**

NOTE Keep in mind that if you have more than one row heading, you will have to create a join on each row heading.

Customizing Your Crosstab Queries

As useful as crosstab queries can be, you may find that you need to apply some of your own customizations in order to get the results you need. In this section, you will explore a few of the ways to customize your crosstab queries to meet your needs.

■ **Defining criteria in a crosstab query:** The ability to filter or limit your crosstab query is another benefit of creating a crosstab query manually. To define a filter for your crosstab, simply enter the criteria as you normally would for any other aggregate query. Figure 3-48 demonstrates this concept.

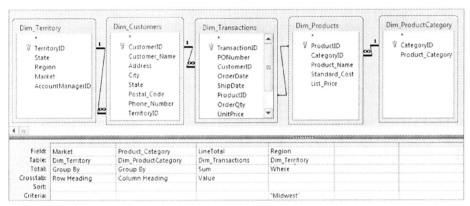

Figure 3-48: You can define a criterion to filter your crosstab queries.

■ **Changing the sort order of your crosstab column headings:** By default, crosstab queries sort their column headings in alphabetical order. For example, the crosstab query in Figure 3-49 will produce a dataset where the column headings read this order: Canada, Midwest, North, Northeast, South, Southeast, Southwest, and West.

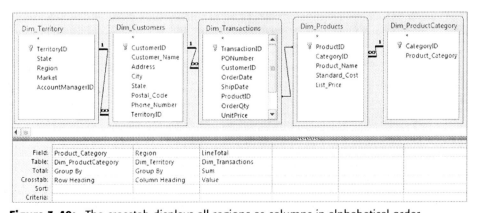

Figure 3-49: The crosstab displays all regions as columns in alphabetical order.

This may be fine in most situations, but if your company headquarters is in California, the executive management may naturally want to see the West region first. You can explicitly specify the column order of a crosstab query by changing the Column Headings attribute in the Query Properties.

To get to the Column Headings attribute:

1. Open the query in Design view.

2. Right click in the grey area above the white query grid and select Properties. This activates the Query Properties dialog box, shown in Figure 3-50.

3. Enter the order you would like to see the column headings by changing the Column Headings attribute.

TIP Adjusting the Column Headings attribute comes in handy when you are struggling with showing months in month order instead of alphabetical order. Simply enter the month columns in the order you would like to see them. For example: Jan, Feb, Mar, Apr, May, Jun, Jul, Aug, Sep, Oct, Nov, Dec.

Property Sheet	▼ ×
Selection type: Query Properties	
General	
Description	
Default View	Datasheet
Column Headings	"West","Canada","Midwest","North","Northeast","South","Southeast","Southwest"
Run Permissions	User's
Source Database	(current)
Source Connect Str	
Record Locks	No Locks
Recordset Type	Dynaset
ODBC Timeout	60
Orientation	Left-to-Right
Subdatasheet Name	
Link Child Fields	
Link Master Fields	
Subdatasheet Height	0"
Subdatasheet Expanded	No

Figure 3-50: The Column Headings attribute is set to have the column read in this order: West, Canada, Midwest, North, Northeast, South, Southeast, and Southwest.

When working with the Column Headings attribute, keep the following in mind:

▪ Each column name should be in quotes and separated by commas. If you omit the quotes, Access will insert them for you.

▪ Accidentally misspelling a column name results in that column being excluded from the crosstab results and a dummy column with the misspelled name being included with no data in it.

- You must enter every column you want to include in your crosstab report. Excluding a column from the Column Headings attribute excludes that column from the crosstab results.

- Clearing the Column Headings attribute ensures that all columns are displayed in alphabetical order.

Summary

Data analysis often goes beyond selecting small extracts of data. The scope of data analysis also includes grouping and comparing data; updating and deleting data; performing calculations on data; and shaping and reporting data. Unfortunately, many Excel users don't realize that Access has built-in tools and functionality designed specifically to handle each of these tasks.

Aggregate queries allow you to quickly group and summarize data, aggregating the returned dataset into totals, averages, counts, and more. Similarly, crosstab queries summarize values and group them in a matrix layout, perfect for analyzing trends over time or providing a method for quickly identifying anomalies in your dataset.

Action queries go beyond just selecting data by actually performing some action on the returned results. The action performed depends on the type of action query you are using. There are four types of action queries: Make-Table queries, delete queries, append queries, and update queries:

- *Make-Table* queries create a new table consisting of the data resulting from the query.

- *Delete* queries delete records from a table based on the definitions and criteria you specify in the query.

- *Append* queries append records to a table based on the definitions and criteria you specify in your query. In other words, with an append query, you can add the results of your query to the end of a table, effectively adding rows to the table.

- *Update* queries allow you to edit large amounts of data at one time.

Utilizing the tools and functionality outlined in this chapter will help you carry out all your analytical processes *within* Access, saving you time, increasing your productivity, and reducing the chance for error.

Basic Analysis Techniques

In This Part

Transforming Your Data with Access

Data transformation generally entails certain actions that are meant to "clean" your data—actions such as establishing a table structure, removing duplicates, cleaning text, removing blanks, and standardizing data fields.

You will often receive data that is unpolished or "raw." That is to say, the data may have duplicates, blank fields, inconsistent text, and so on. Before you can perform any kind of meaningful analysis on data in this state, it's important to go through a process of data transformation, or data cleanup.

While many people store their data in Access, few use it for data transformation purposes, often preferring to export the data to Excel, perform any necessary cleanup there, and then import the data back to Access. The obvious motive for this behavior is familiarity with the flexible Excel environment. However, exporting and importing data simply to perform such easy tasks can be quite inefficient, especially if you are working with large datasets.

This chapter introduces you to some of the tools and techniques in Access that make it easy to clean and massage your data without turning to Excel.

Finding and Removing Duplicate Records

Duplicate records are absolute analysis killers. The effect duplicate records have on your analysis can be far-reaching, corrupting almost every metric, summary, and analytical assessment you produce. For this reason, finding and removing duplicate records should be your first priority when you receive a new dataset.

Defining Duplicate Records

Before you jump into your dataset to find and remove duplicate records, it's important to consider how you define a duplicate record. To demonstrate this point, look at the table shown in Figure 4-1, where you see 11 records. Out of the 11 records, how many are duplicates?

SicCode	PostalCode	CompanyNumber	DollarPotential	City	State	Address
1389	77032	11147805	$9,517.00	houston	tx	6000 n sem heirten pk
1389	77032	11147843	$9,517.00	houston	tx	43410 e herdy rd
1389	77042	11160116	$7,653.00	houston	tx	40642 rachmend ave s
1389	77051	11165400	$9,517.00	houston	tx	5646 helmis rd
1389	77057	11173241	$9,517.00	houston	tx	2514 san filape st ste 6
1389	77060	11178227	$7,653.00	houston	tx	100 n sem heirten pkw
1389	77073	11190514	$9,517.00	houston	tx	4660 rankan rd # 400
1389	77049	11218412	$7,653.00	houston	tx	4541 mallir read 6
1389	77040	13398882	$18,379.00	houston	tx	3643 wandfirn rd
1389	77040	13399102	$18,379.00	houston	tx	3643 wandfirn rd
1389	77077	13535097	$7,653.00	houston	tx	44160 wisthiamir rd st

Figure 4-1: Are there duplicate records in this table? It depends on how you define one.

If you were to define a duplicate record in Figure 4-1 as a duplication of just the SicCode, you would find 10 duplicate records. That is, out of the 11 records shown, one record has a unique SicCode while the other 10 are duplications. Now, if you were to expand your definition of a duplicate record to a duplication of both SicCode and PostalCode, you would find only two duplicates: the duplication of PostalCodes 77032 and 77040. Finally, if you were to define a duplicate record as a duplication of the unique value of SicCode, PostalCode, and CompanyNumber, you would find no duplicates.

This example shows that having two records with the same value in a column does not necessarily mean you have a duplicate record. It's up to you to determine which field or combination of fields best defines a unique record in your dataset.

Once you have a clear idea what field, or fields, best make up a unique record in your table, you can easily test your table for duplicate records by attempting to set them as a primary or combination key. To demonstrate this test, open the LeadList table in Design view; then tag the CompanyNumber field as a primary key. If you try to save this change, you get the error message shown in Figure 4-2. This message means there is some duplication of records in your dataset that needs to be dealt with.

The changes you requested to the table were not successful because they would create duplicate values in the index, primary key, or relationship. Change the data in the field or fields that contain duplicate data, remove the index, or redefine the index to permit duplicate entries and try again.

OK   Help

Figure 4-2: If you get this error message when trying to set a primary key, you have duplicate records in your dataset.

Finding Duplicate Records

If you have determined that your dataset does indeed contain duplicates, it's generally a good idea to find and review the duplicate records before removing them. Giving your records a thorough review ensures that you don't mistake a record as a duplicate and remove it from your analysis. You may find that you are mistakenly identifying valid records as duplications, in which case you need to include another field in your definition of what makes up a unique record.

The easiest way to find the duplicate records in your dataset is to run the Find Duplicates Query Wizard. Follow these steps:

1. To start this wizard, go up to the application Ribbon and select the Create tab.

2. Click the Query Wizard button. This activates the New Query dialog box shown in Figure 4-3.

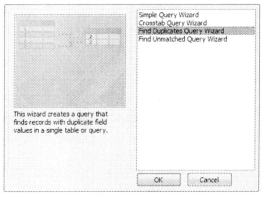

Simple Query Wizard
Crosstab Query Wizard
Find Duplicates Query Wizard
Find Unmatched Query Wizard

This wizard creates a query that finds records with duplicate field values in a single table or query.

OK   Cancel

Figure 4-3: Select the Find Duplicates Query Wizard and then click the OK button.

3. Select Find Duplicates Query Wizard and then click the OK button.

4. Select the particular dataset you will use in your Find Duplicate query. Notice you can use queries as well as tables. Select the LeadList table, as shown in Figure 4-4.

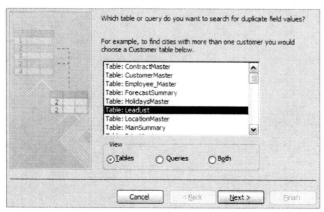

Figure 4-4: Select the dataset in which you want to find duplicates; then click Next.

5. Identify which field, or combination of fields, best defines a unique record in your dataset. In the example shown in Figure 4-5, the CompanyNumber field alone defines a unique record. Click Next.

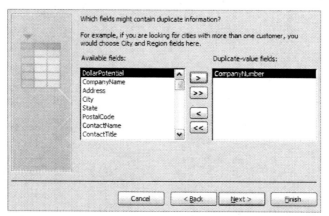

Figure 4-5: Select the field or fields that make up a unique record in your dataset.

6. Shown in Figure 4-6, identify any additional fields you would like to see in your query. Click the Next button.

7. Finish off the wizard by naming your query and clicking the Finish button as shown in Figure 4-7.

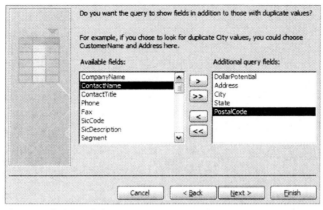

Figure 4-6: Select the field or fields you want to see in your query.

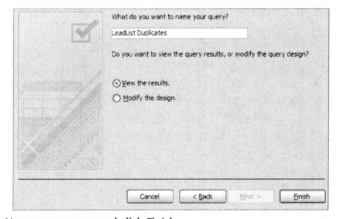

Figure 4-7: Name your query and click Finish.

Once you click Finish, your new Find Duplicates query immediately opens for your review. Figure 4-8 shows the resulting query. Now that Access has found the records that are repeating, you can remove duplicates simply by deleting the duplicate records.

NOTE The records shown in your Find Duplicates query are not only the duplications. They include one unique record plus the duplication. For example, in Figure 4-8, you will notice that there are four records tagged with the CompanyNumber 11145186. Three of the four are duplicates that can be removed, while one should remain as a unique record.

CompanyNumber	DollarPotential	Address	City	State	PostalCode
10625840	$47,039.00	1100 landirs rd	n little rock	ar	72117
10625840	$47,039.00	1100 landirs rd	n little rock	ar	72117
11145186	$60,770.00	5364 lost fwy	houston	tx	77029
11145186	$60,770.00	5364 lost fwy	houston	tx	77029
11145186	$60,770.00	5364 lost fwy	houston	tx	77029
11145186	$60,770.00	5364 lost fwy	houston	tx	77029
11166089	$60,770.00	6632 biffalo spiidway	houston	tx	77054
11166089	$60,770.00	6632 biffalo spiidway	houston	tx	77054
11166089	$60,770.00	6632 biffalo spiidway	houston	tx	77054
11166089	$60,770.00	6632 biffalo spiidway	houston	tx	77054
11220179	$60,770.00	40420 tilge rd	houston	tx	77095
11220179	$60,770.00	40420 tilge rd	houston	tx	77095
11220179	$60,770.00	40420 tilge rd	houston	tx	77095
11220179	$60,770.00	40420 tilge rd	houston	tx	77095

Figure 4-8: Your Find Duplicates query.

Removing Duplicate Records

If you are working with a small dataset, removing the duplicates can be as easy as manually deleting records from your Find Duplicates query. However, if you are working with a large dataset, your Find Duplicates query may result in more records than you care to manually delete. Believe it when someone tells you that manually deleting records from a 5,000 row–Find Duplicates query is an eyeball-burning experience. Fortunately, there is an alternative to burning out your eyeballs.

The idea is to remove duplicates en masse by taking advantage of Access' built-in protections against duplicate primary keys. To demonstrate this technique, follow these steps:

1. Right-click the LeadList table and select Copy.

2. Right-click again and select Paste. At this point, the Paste Table As dialog box, shown in Figure 4-9, activates.

Figure 4-9: Activate the Paste Table As dialog box to copy your table's structure into a new table called "LeadList_NoDups."

3. Name your new table "LeadList_NoDups" and select Structure Only from the Paste Options section. This creates a new empty table that has the same structure as your original.

4. Open your new "LeadList_NoDups" table in Design view and set the appropriate field or combination of fields as primary keys. Again, it's up to you to determine which field or combination of fields best defines a unique record in your dataset. As you can see in Figure 4-10, the CompanyNumber field alone defines a unique record; therefore, only the CompanyNumber field is set as a primary key.

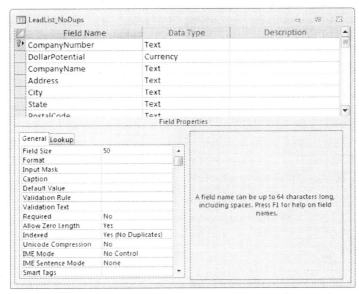

Figure 4-10: Set as a primary key the field or fields that best define a unique record.

5. Pause here a moment and review what you have so far. At this point, you should have a table called LeadList and a table called LeadList_NoDups. The LeadList_NoDups table is empty and has the CompanyNumber field set as a primary key.

6. Create an Append query that appends all records from the LeadList table to the LeadList_NoDups table. When you run the Append query, you get a message similar to the one shown in Figure 4-11.

Figure 4-11: Now you can append all records, excluding the duplicates.

Because the CustomerNumber field in the LeadList_NoDups table is set as the primary key, Access does not allow duplicate customer numbers to be appended. In just a few clicks, you have effectively created a table free from duplicates. You can now use this duplicate-free table as the source for any subsequent analysis!

TRICKS OF THE TRADE: REMOVING DUPLICATES WITH ONE MAKE-TABLE QUERY

Start a Make-Table query in Design view, using as the data source the dataset that contains the duplicates. Right-click on the grey area above the white query grid and select Properties. This activates the Property Sheet dialog box shown in Figure 4-12.

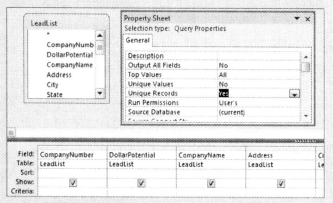

Figure 4-12: Running a Make-Table query with the Unique Values property set to Yes ensures that your resulting table contains no duplicates.

All you have to do here is change the Unique Values property to Yes. Close the Property Sheet dialog box and run the query.

Common Transformation Tasks

Besides duplicate records, you will find that many of the unpolished datasets that come to you requires other types of transformation actions. This section covers some of the more common transformation tasks you will have to perform.

Filling in Blank Fields

Oftentimes, you have fields that contain empty values. These values are considered ''Null''—a value of nothing. Nulls are not necessarily a bad thing. In fact, if used properly, they can be an important part of a well-designed relational database. Note, however, that an excessive number of Null values in your data can lead to an unruly database environment. Too many Nulls in a database makes querying and coding for your data more difficult because you must test for Nulls in almost every action you take.

Your job is to decide whether to leave the Nulls in your dataset or fill them in with an actual value. When deciding this, consider the following general guidelines:

- **Use Nulls Sparingly:** Working with, and coding for, a database is a much less daunting task when you don't have to test for Null values constantly.

- **Use alternatives when possible:** A good practice is to represent missing values with some logical missing value code whenever possible.

- **Never use Null values in number fields:** Use Zeros instead of Nulls in a currency or a number field that feeds into calculations. Any mathematical operation performed using a field containing even one Null value results in a Null answer (the wrong answer).

Filling in the Null fields in your dataset is as simple as running an Update query. In the example shown in Figure 4-13, you are updating the Null values in the DollarPotential field to zero.

Figure 4-13: This query updates the Null values in the DollarPotential field to a value of 0.

It's important to note that there are two kinds of blank values: Null and empty string (""). When filling in the blank values of a text field, include the empty string as a criterion in your Update query to ensure that you don't miss any fields. In the example shown in Figure 4-14, you are updating the blank values in the Segment field to "Other."

Figure 4-14: This query updates blank values in the Segment field to a value of "Other."

Concatenating

It's always amazing to see anyone export data out of Access and into Excel, only to concatenate (join two or more character strings end to end) and then re-import the data back into Access. You can easily concatenate any number of ways in Access with a simple Update query.

Concatenating Fields

Look at the Update query shown in Figure 4-15. In this query, you are updating the MyTest field with the concatenated row values of the Type field and the Code field.

Figure 4-15: This query concatenates the row values of the Type field and the Code field.

TIP It's a good idea to create a test field to test the effects of your data transformation actions before applying changes to the real data.

Take a moment to analyze the following query breakdown:

- [Type]: This tells Access to use the row values of the Type field.
- &: The ampersand is a character operator that joins strings together.
- [Code]: This tells Access to use the row values of the Code field.

Figure 4-16 shows the results of this query.

Code ·	Type ·	MyTest ·
100199	DB	DB100199
200	DB	DB200
100199	DB	DB100199
100199	DB	DB100199
100199	DB	DB100199
100199	DB	DB100199
100199	DB	DB100199
100199	DB	DB100199
100199	DB	DB100199
100199	DB	DB100199
200	DB	DB200
100199	DB	DB100199
200	DB	DB200

Figure 4-16: The MyTest field now contains the concatenated values of the Type field and the Code field.

WARNING When running Update queries that perform concatenations, make sure the field you are updating is large enough to accept the concatenated string. For example, if the length of your concatenated string is 100 characters long, and the Field Size of the field you are updating is 50 characters, your concatenated string will be cut short without warning.

Augmenting Field Values with Your Own Text

You can augment the values in your fields by adding your own text. For example, you may want to concatenate the row values of the Type field and the Code field, but separate them with a colon. The query in Figure 4-17 does just that.

Figure 4-17: This query concatenates the row values of the Type field and the Code field and separates them with a colon.

Take a moment to analyze the following query breakdown:

- [Type]: This tells Access to use the row values of the Type field.
- &: The ampersand is a character operator that joins strings together.

- " : ": This text will add a colon and a space to the concatenated string.
- [Code]: This tells Access to use the row values of the Code field.

Figure 4-18 shows the results of this query.

Code	Type	MyTest
100199	DB	DB: 100199
200	DB	DB: 200
100199	DB	DB: 100199
100199	DB	DB: 100199
100199	DB	DB: 100199
100199	DB	DB: 100199
100199	DB	DB: 100199
100199	DB	DB: 100199
100199	DB	DB: 100199
100199	DB	DB: 100199
200	DB	DB: 200
100199	DB	DB: 100199
200	DB	DB: 200

Figure 4-18: The MyTest field now contains the concatenated values of the Type field and the Code field, separated by a colon.

NOTE When specifying your own text in a query, you must enclose the text in quotes.

Changing Case

Making sure the text in your database has the correct capitalization may sound trivial, but it's important. Imagine you receive a customer table that has an address field where all the addresses are lowercase. How is that going to look on labels, form letters, or invoices? Fortunately, for those who are working with tables containing thousands of records, Access has a few built-in functions that make changing the case of your text a snap.

The LeadList table shown in Figure 4-19 contains an Address field that is in all lowercase letters.

Address	City	State	PostalCode
46 gin criaghten w ebrems dr	agawam	ma	01001
426 bewlis rd	agawam	ma	01001
651 sheimekir ln	agawam	ma	01001
44 almgrin dr	agawam	ma	01001
35 mall ln	brimfield	ma	01010
460 fillir rd	chicopee	ma	01020
320 mimeraal dr ste 4	chicopee	ma	01020
4010 shiradan st	chicopee	ma	01022
5046 wistevir rd	chicopee	ma	01022
40 meple st	east longmeado	ma	01028
242 biich st	holyoke	ma	01040
42 whatang ferms rd	holyoke	ma	01040
100 whatniy ave	holyoke	ma	01040
242 biich st	holyoke	ma	01040
4566 mean st	holyoke	ma	01040

Figure 4-19: The address field is in all lowercase letters.

To fix the values in the Address field, you can use the StrConv function, which converts a string to a specified case.

ABOUT THE STRCONV FUNCTION

To use the StrConv function, you must provide two required arguments: the string to be converted, and the conversion type.

```
StrConv(string to be converted, conversion type)
```

The string to be converted is simply the text you are working with. In a query environment, you can use the name of a field to specify that you are converting all the row values of that field.

The conversion type tells Access whether you want to convert the specified text to all uppercase, all lowercase, or proper case. There are constants that identify the conversion type:

- **Conversion type 1: Converts the specified text to uppercase characters.**

- **Conversion type 2: Converts the specified text to lowercase characters.**

- **Conversion type 3: Converts the specified text to proper case. That is, the first letter of every word is uppercase.**

Examples:

```
StrConv("My Text",1) would be converted to "MY TEXT".
StrConv("MY TEXT",2) would be converted to "my text".
StrConv("my text",3) would be converted to "My Text".
```

The Update query shown in Figure 4-20 will convert the values of the Address field to the proper case.

Figure 4-20: Use StrConv to convert text values to proper case.

NOTE You can also use the Ucase and Lcase functions to convert your text to uppercase and lowercase text. These functions are highlighted in Appendix D of this book.

TRICKS OF THE TRADE: SORTING BY CAPITALIZATION

Ever needed to sort on the capitalization of the values in a field? The query in Figure 4-21 demonstrates a trick that sorts a query where all the values whose first letter is lowercase are shown first.

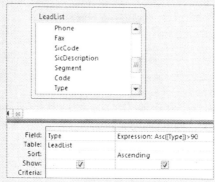

Figure 4-21: This query returns a dataset whose values begin with lowercase letters.

How does this work? The `Asc` function converts a string to its Ascii code. For example, `Asc("A")` returns 65 because 65 is the ASCII code for the uppercase letter A.

If you pass a whole word to the `Asc` function, it only returns the ASCII code for the first letter. Now in ASCII codes, uppercase letters A–Z are respectively represented by codes 65–90, while the lowercase letters a–z are respectively represented by codes 97–122.

The function `Asc([Type])>90` asks the question, "Is the ASCII code returned by the string greater than 90?" The answer is either True or False (-1 or 0). If the answer is true, then the first letter of the string is lowercase; otherwise, the first letter is uppercase.

Figure 4-22 shows the results of the query with the Expression field displayed.

Type ▾	Expression ▾
db	-1
db	-1
db	-1
db	-1
db	-1
DB	0
DB	0
DB	0
DB	0
DB	0
DB	0

Figure 4-22: This query is sorted in ascending order on the Expression field. Sorting this field in descending order displays values starting with uppercase letters first.

Removing Leading and Trailing Spaces from a String

When you receive a dataset from a mainframe system, a data warehouse, or even a text file, it is not uncommon to have field values that contain leading and trailing spaces. These spaces can cause some abnormal results, especially when you are appending values with leading and trailing spaces to other values that are clean. To demonstrate this, look at the dataset in Figure 4-23.

State	SumOfDollarPotential
ca	$26,561,554.00
ny	$7,483,960.00
tx	$13,722,782.00
ca	$12,475,489.00
ny	$827,563.00
tx	$7,669,208.00

Figure 4-23: The leading spaces are preventing an accurate aggregation.

This is intended to be an Aggregate query that displays the sum of the dollar potential for California, New York, and Texas. However, the leading spaces are causing Access to group each state into two sets, preventing you from discerning the accurate totals.

You can easily remove leading and trailing spaces by using the `Trim` function. Figure 4-24 demonstrates how you update a field to remove the leading and trailing spaces by using an Update query.

NOTE Using the `Ltrim` function removes only the leading spaces, while the `Rtrim` function removes only the trailing spaces. These functions are highlighted in Appendix D of this book.

Figure 4-24: Simply pass the field name through the `Trim` function in an Update query to remove the leading and trailing spaces.

Finding and Replacing Specific Text

Imagine that you work in a company called BLVD, Inc. One day, the president of your company informs you that the abbreviation "blvd" on all addresses is now deemed an infringement on your company's trademarked name, and must be changed to "Boulevard" as soon as possible. How would you go about meeting this new requirement? Your first thought may be to use the built-in Find and Replace functionality that exists in all Office applications. However, when your data consists of hundreds of thousands of rows, the Find and Replace function will only be able to process a few thousand records at a time. This clearly would not be very efficient.

The `Replace` function is ideal in a situation like this. As you can see in the following sidebar, the `Replace` function replaces a specified text string with a different string.

ABOUT THE REPLACE FUNCTION

There are three required arguments in a `Replace` function and three optional arguments:

```
Replace(Expression, Find, Replace[, Start[, Count[, Compare]]])
```

- `Expression` **(required): The full string you are evaluating. In a query environment, you can use the name of a field to specify that you are evaluating all the row values of that field.**

- `Find` **(required): The substring you need to find and replace.**

- `Replace` **(required): The substring used as the replacement.**

- `Start` **(optional): The position within expression to begin the search; default is 1.**

- `Count` **(optional): Number of occurrences to replace; default is all occurrences.**

- `Compare` **(optional): The kind of comparison to use; see Appendix D for details**

For example:

```
Replace("Pear", "P", "B") would return "Bear".
Replace("Now Here", " H", "h") would return "Nowhere".
Replace("Microsoft Access", "Microsoft ", "") would return
"Access".
```

Figure 4-25 demonstrates how you would use the Replace function to meet the requirements in the scenario above.

Figure 4-25: This query finds all instances of "blvd" and replaces them with "Boulevard."

Adding Your Own Text in Key Positions Within a String

When transforming your data, you sometimes have to add your own text in key positions with a string. For example, in Figure 4-26, you will see two fields. The Phone field is the raw phone number received from a mainframe report, while the MyTest field is the same phone number transformed into a standard format. As you can see, the two parentheses and the dash were added in the appropriate positions within the string to achieve the correct format.

Phone	MyTest
6455106666	(645)510-6666
6451663624	(645)166-3624
2054224534	(205)422-4534
6456356000	(645)635-6000
2056664330	(205)666-4330
2056545453	(205)654-5453
2055126444	(205)512-6444
2056524200	(205)652-4200
2054315536	(205)431-5536
2055464230	(205)546-4230
2055632504	(205)563-2504
2056334153	(205)633-4153

Figure 4-26: The phone number has been transformed into a standard format by adding the appropriate characters to key positions with the string.

The edits demonstrated in Figure 4-26 were accomplished by using the Right function, the Left function, and the Mid function in conjunction with each other. See the sidebar that follows for more information on these functions.

ABOUT THE RIGHT, LEFT, AND MID FUNCTIONS

The Right, Left, and Mid functions allow you to extract portions of a string starting from different positions:

■ The Left function returns a specified number of characters starting from the leftmost character of the string. The required arguments for the Left function are the text you are evaluating and the number of characters you want returned. For example, Left("70056-3504", 5) would return 5 characters starting from the leftmost character ("70056").

■ The Right function returns a specified number of characters starting from the rightmost character of the string. The required arguments for the Right function are the text you are evaluating and the number of characters you want returned. For example, Right("Microsoft", 4) would return four characters starting from the rightmost character ("soft").

(continued)

ABOUT THE RIGHT, LEFT, AND MID FUNCTIONS *(continued)*

- The `Mid` function returns a specified number of characters starting from a specified character position. The required arguments for the `Mid` function are the text you are evaluating, the starting position, and the number of characters you want returned. For example, `Mid("Lonely", 2, 3)` would return three characters starting from the second character, or character number two in the string ("one").

> **TIP** In a `Mid` function, if there are fewer characters in the text being used than the length argument, the entire text will be returned. For example, `Mid("go",1,10000)` will return "go." As you will see later in this chapter, this behavior comes in handy when you are working with nested functions.

Figure 4-27 demonstrates how the MyTest field was updated to the correctly formatted phone number.

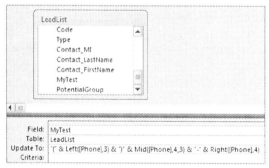

Figure 4-27: This query will update the MyTest field with a properly formatted phone number.

QUERY BREAKDOWN

Take a moment to analyze the query breakdowns that follows.

- `" ("`: This text adds an open parenthesis to the resulting string.
- `&`: The ampersand is a character operator that joins strings together.
- `Left([Phone],3)`: This function extracts the left three characters of the **[Phone]** field.
- `&`: The ampersand is a character operator that joins strings together.
- `") "`: This text adds a close parenthesis to the resulting string.
- `&`: The ampersand is a character operator that joins strings together.

QUERY BREAKDOWN

- `Mid([Phone],4,3)`: **This function extracts the three characters of the [Phone] field starting from character number 4.**
- `&`: **The ampersand is a character operator that joins strings together.**
- `"-"`: **This text adds a dash to the resulting string.**
- `&`: **The ampersand is a character operator that joins strings together.**
- `Right([Phone],4)`: **This function extracts the right four characters of the [Phone] field.**

TRICKS OF THE TRADE: PADDING STRINGS TO A SPECIFIC NUMBER OF CHARACTERS

You may encounter a situation where key fields are required to be a certain number of characters in order for your data to be able to interface with peripheral platforms such as ADP or SAP.

For example, imagine that the CompanyNumber field shown in Figure 4-28 must be 10 characters long. Those that are not 10 characters must be padded with enough leading zeros to create a 10-character string.

CompanyNumber ▾
113
13792992
14230866
630
2298
3082
3128
19641288
3909
4758
13972608
2568
6788
7499
7873

Figure 4-28: You need to pad the values in the CompanyNumber field with enough leading zeros to create a 10-character string.

The secret to this trick is to add 10 zeros to every company number, regardless of the current length, then pass them through a `Right` function that extracts only the right 10 characters. For example, company number 29875764 would first be converted to 000000000029875764, then would

(continued)

TRICKS OF THE TRADE: PADDING STRINGS TO A SPECIFIC NUMBER OF CHARACTERS *(continued)*

go into a `Right` function that extracted out only the right 10 characters; `Right("000000000029875764",10)`. This would leave you with **0029875764**.

Although this is essentially two steps, you can accomplish this with just one Update query. Figure 4-29 demonstrates how this is done. This query first concatenates each company number with "0000000000" and then passes that concatenated string through a `Right` function that extracts only the left 10 characters.

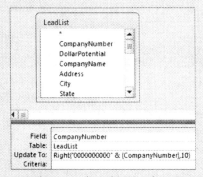

Figure 4-29: This query updates each value in the CompanyNumber field to a 10-character string with leading zeros.

Figure 4-30 shows the results of this query.

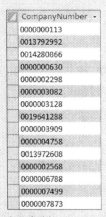

Figure 4-30: The CompanyNumber field now contains 10 character company numbers.

Parsing Strings Using Character Markers

Have you ever gotten a dataset where two or more distinct pieces of data were jammed into one field and separated by commas? For example, a field called Address may have a string that represents "Address, City, State, Zip." In a proper database, this string is parsed into four fields.

In Figure 4-31, you can see that the values in the ContactName field are strings that represent "Last name, First name, Middle initial." You need to parse this string into three separate fields.

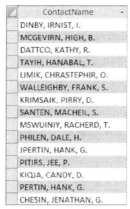

ContactName
DINBY, IRNIST, I.
MCGEVIRN, HIGH, B.
DATTCO, KATHY, R.
TAYIH, HANABAL, T.
LIMIK, CHRASTEPHIR, O.
WALLEIGHBY, FRANK, S.
KRIMSAIK, PIRRY, D.
SANTEN, MACHEIL, S.
MSWUINIY, RACHERD, T.
PHILEN, DALE, H.
JPERTIN, HANK, G.
PITIRS, JEE, P.
KIQJA, CANDY, D.
PERTIN, HANK, G.
CHESIN, JENATHAN, G.

Figure 4-31: You need to split the ContactName field into last name, first name and middle initial.

Although this is not a straightforward undertaking, it can be done fairly easily with the help of the InStrInStr function, which is detailed in the following sidebar.

ABOUT THE INSTRINSTRINSTR FUNCTION

The InStrInStr **function searches for a specified string in another string and returns its position number. There are two required arguments in an** InStrInStr **function and two optional arguments.**

```
InStr([Start], String, Find, [Compare])
```

- Start **(optional): This is the character number to start the search; default is 1.**
- String **(required): This is the string to be searched.**
- Find **(required): This is the string to search for.**
- Compare **(optional): This specifies the type of string comparison.**

(continued)

ABOUT THE INSTRINSTRINSTR FUNCTION *(continued)*

For example:

- `InStr("Alexander, Mike, H",",")` **would return 10 because the first comma of the string is character number 10.**

- `InStr(11,"Alexander, Mike, H",",")` **would return 16 because the first comma from character number 11 is character number 16.**

If the `InStr` **function only returns a number, how can it help you? Well, the idea is to use the** `InStr` **function with the** `Left`, `Right`, **or** `Mid` **functions in order to extract a string. For example, instead of using a hard-coded number in your** `Left` **function to pass it the required length argument, you can use a nested** `InStr` **function to return that number. For example,** `Left("Alexander, Mike",9)` **is the same as** `Left("Alexander, Mike",` `InStr("Alexander, Mike", ",")-1)`.

> **NOTE** **When you are nesting an** `InStr` **function inside of a** `Left`, `Right`, **or** `Mid` **function, you may have to add or subtract a character, depending on what you want to accomplish. For example:**
>
> `Left("Zey, Robert", InStr("Zey, Robert", ",")) would return "Zey,".`
>
> **Why is the comma included in the returned result? The** `InStr` **function returns 4 because the first comma in the string is the fourth character. The** `Left` **function then uses this 4 as a length argument, effectively extracting the left four characters: "Zey,".**
>
> **If you want a clean extract without the comma, you will have to modify your function to read like this:**
>
> `Left("Zey, Robert", InStrInStr("Zey, Robert", ",")-1)`
>
> **Subtracting 1 from the** `InStr` **function would leave you with 3 instead of 4. The** `Left` **function then uses this 3 as the length argument, effectively extracting the left three characters: "Zey".**

The easiest way to parse the contact name field, shown in Figure 4-23, is to use two Update queries.

> **WARNING** **This is a somewhat tricky process, so you will want to create and work in test fields. This ensures that you give yourself a way back from any mistakes you may make.**

Query 1

The first query, shown in Figure 4-32, parses out the last name in the ContactName field and updates the Contact_LastName field. It then updates the Contact_FirstName field with the remaining string.

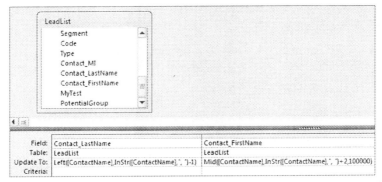

Figure 4-32: This query updates the Contact_LastName and Contact_FirstName fields.

If you open the LeadList table, you can see the impact of your first Update query. Figure 4-33 shows your progress so far.

Contact_LastName	Contact_FirstName
MCGEVIRN	HIGH, B.
DATTCO	KATHY, R.
TAYIH	HANABAL, T.
LIMIK	CHRASTEPHIR, O.
WALLEIGHBY	FRANK, S.
KRIMSAIK	PIRRY, D.
SANTEN	MACHEIL, S.
MSWUINIY	RACHERD, T.
PHILEN	DALE, H.
JPERTIN	HANK, G.
PITIRS	JEE, P.
KIQIA	CANDY, D.
PERTIN	HANK, G.
CHESIN	JENATHAN, G.

Figure 4-33: Check your progress so far.

Query 2

The second query, shown in Figure 4-34, updates the Contact_FirstName field and the Contact_MI.

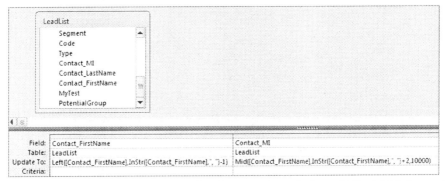

Figure 4-34: This query parses out the first name and the middle initial from the Contact_FirstName field.

After you run your second query, you can open your table and see the results, shown in Figure 4-35.

ContactName	Contact_LastName	Contact_FirstName	Contact_MI
DINBY, IRNIST, I.	DINBY	IRNIST	I.
MCGEVIRN, HIGH, B.	MCGEVIRN	HIGH	B.
DATTCO, KATHY, R.	DATTCO	KATHY	R.
TAYIH, HANABAL, T.	TAYIH	HANABAL	T.
LIMIK, CHRASTEPHIR, O.	LIMIK	CHRASTEPHIR	O.
WALLEIGHBY, FRANK, S.	WALLEIGHBY	FRANK	S.
KRIMSAIK, PIRRY, D.	KRIMSAIK	PIRRY	D.
SANTEN, MACHEIL, S.	SANTEN	MACHEIL	S.
MSWUINIY, RACHERD, T.	MSWUINIY	RACHERD	T.
PHILEN, DALE, H.	PHILEN	DALE	H.
JPERTIN, HANK, G.	JPERTIN	HANK	G.
PITIRS, JEE, P.	PITIRS	JEE	P.
KIQJA, CANDY, D.	KIQJA	CANDY	D.
PERTIN, HANK, G.	PERTIN	HANK	G.
CHESIN, JENATHAN, G.	CHESIN	JENATHAN	G.

Figure 4-35: With two queries, you have successfully parsed the ContactName field into three separate fields.

Summary

Data transformation is the process of cleaning up your data. Before you can perform any kind of meaningful analysis on data in this state, it's important to go through a process of data cleanup. Although Access has several built-in functions and tools that allow you to transform data, most users find themselves exporting data to Excel in order to perform these tasks.

As this chapter shows, there is no need to take the extra effort of moving records to Excel to transform data. Access can easily perform various types of data cleanup to include removing duplicates, concatenating strings of text, filling in blank fields, parsing characters, replacing text, changing case, and augmenting data with your own text.

CHAPTER 5

Working with Calculations and Dates

The truth is that few organizations can analyze their raw data at face value. More often than not, some preliminary analysis with calculations and dates must be carried out before a big-picture analysis can be performed. Again, Excel is the preferred platform for working with calculations and dates. However, as you will learn in this chapter, Access provides a wide array of tools and built-in functions that make working with calculations and dates possible.

Using Calculations in Your Analysis

If you are an Excel user trying to familiarize yourself with Access, one of the questions you undoubtedly have is "Where do the formulas go?" In Excel, you have the flexibility to enter a calculation via a formula directly into the dataset you are analyzing. You do not have this ability in Access. So where do you store calculations in Access?

As you have already learned, things work differently in Access. The natural structure of an Access database forces you to keep your data separate from your analysis. In this light, you will not be able to store a calculation (a formula) in your dataset. Now, it is true that you can store the calculated results as hard data, but using tables to store calculated results is problematic for several reasons:

- Stored calculations take up valuable storage space.

- Stored calculations require constant maintenance as the data in your table changes.

- Stored calculations generally tie your data to one analytical path.

Instead of storing the calculated results as hard data, it is a better practice to perform calculations in "real-time," at the precise moment when they are required. This ensures the most current and accurate results and does not tie your data to one particular analysis.

Common Calculation Scenarios

In Access, calculations are performed using expressions. An *expression* is a combination of values, operators, or functions evaluated to return a separate value to be used in a subsequent process. For example, 2+2 is an expression that returns the integer 4, which can be used in a subsequent analysis. Expressions can be used almost anywhere in Access to accomplish various tasks: in queries, forms, reports, data access pages, and even tables to a certain degree. In this section, you learn how to expand your analysis by building real-time calculations using expressions.

Using Constants in Calculations

Most calculations typically consist of hard-coded numbers or constants. A *constant* is a static value that does not change. For example, in the expression [List_Price]*1.1, 1.1 is a constant; the value of 1.1 will never change. Figure 5-1 demonstrates how a constant can be used in an expression within a query.

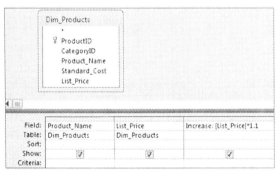

Figure 5-1: In this query, you are using a constant to calculate a 10 percent price increase.

In this example, you are building a query that will analyze how the current price for each product compares to the same price with a 10 percent increase. The expression, entered under the alias "Increase," will multiply the List_Price field of each record with a constant value of 1.1, calculating a price that is 10 percent over the original value in the List_Price field.

Using Fields in Calculations

Not all your calculations require you to specify a constant. In fact, many of the mathematical operations you will carry out are performed on data that already resides in fields within your dataset. You can perform calculations using any fields formatted as numbers or currency.

For instance, in the query shown in Figure 5-2, you are not using any constants. Instead, your calculation is executed using the values in each record of the dataset. This is similar to referencing cell values in an Excel formula.

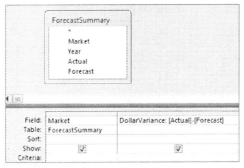

Figure 5-2: In this query, you are using two fields in a Dollar Variance calculation.

Using the Results of Aggregation in Calculations

Using the result of an aggregation as an expression in a calculation allows you to perform multiple analytical steps in one query. In the example in Figure 5-3, you are running an aggregate query. This query executes in the following order.

1. The query firsts group your records by market.

2. The query calculates the count of orders and the sum of revenue for each market.

3. The query assigns the aliases you have defined respectively ("Order-Count" and "Rev").

4. The query then uses the aggregation results for each branch as expressions in your "AvgDollarPerOrder" calculation.

Using the Results of One Calculation as an Expression in Another

Keep in mind that you are not limited to one calculation per query. In fact, you can use the results of one calculation as an expression in another calculation. Figure 5-4 illustrates this concept.

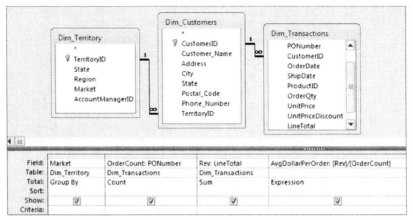

Figure 5-3: In this query, you are using the aggregation results for each market as expressions in your calculation.

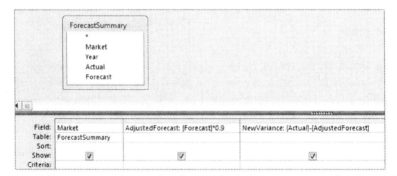

Figure 5-4: This query uses the results of one calculation as an expression in another.

In this query, you are first calculating an adjusted forecast and then using the results of that calculation in another calculation that returns the variance of Actual versus Adjusted Forecast.

Using a Calculation as an Argument in a Function

Look at the query in Figure 5-5. The calculation in this query returns a number with a fractional part. That is, it returns a number that contains a decimal point followed by many trailing digits. You want to return a round number, however, making the resulting dataset easier to read.

To force the results of your calculation into an integer, you can use the Int function. Int is a mathematical function that removes the fractional part of a number and returns the resulting integer. This function takes one argument, a number. However, instead of hard-coding a number into this function, you can use your calculation as the argument. Figure 5-6 demonstrates this concept.

NOTE You can use calculations that result in a number value in any function where a number value is accepted as an argument.

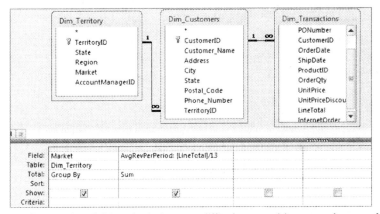

Figure 5-5: The results of this calculation are difficult to read because they are fractional numbers that have many digits trailing a decimal point. Forcing the results into round numbers makes for easier reading.

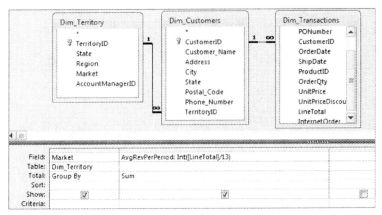

Figure 5-6: You can use your calculation as the argument in the `Int` function, allowing you to remove the fractional part of the resulting data.

Using the Expression Builder to Construct Calculations

If you are not yet comfortable manually creating complex expressions with functions and calculations, Access provides the Expression Builder. The Expression Builder guides you through constructing an expression with a few clicks of the mouse. Avid Excel users may relate the Expression Builder to the Insert Function wizard found in Excel. The idea is that you build your expression by simply selecting the necessary functions and data fields.

To activate the Expression Builder, right-click inside the cell that contains your expression and select Build, as shown in Figure 5-7.

NOTE In fact, you can activate the Expression Builder by right-clicking anywhere you would write expressions, including: control properties in forms, control properties in reports, field properties in tables, as well as in the query design grid.

Figure 5-7: Activate the Expression Builder by right-clicking inside the Field row of the query grid and selecting Build.

As you can see in Figure 5-8, the Expression Builder has four panes to work in. The upper pane is where you enter the expression. The lower panes show the different objects available to you. In the lower-left pane, you can see the five main database objects: tables, queries, forms, reports, and functions.

Double-click any of the five main database objects to drill down to the next level of objects. By double-clicking the Functions object, for example, you can drill into the Built-In Functions folder, where you will see all the functions available to you in Access. Figure 5-9 shows the Expression Builder set to display all the available math functions.

NOTE If you are using Access 2007, your Expression Builder will look slightly different from the one shown in Figure 5-9. However, the basic functionality remains the same. Thus, you can use the concepts illustrated in this section even with Access 2007.

Figure 5-8: The Expression Builder displays all the database objects you can use in your expression.

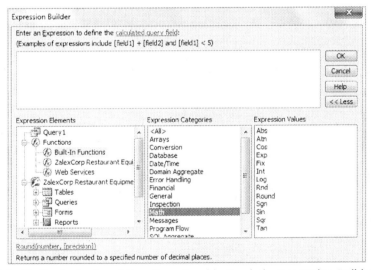

Figure 5-9: Similar to the Insert Function wizard in Excel, the Expression Builder displays all the functions available to you.

The idea is that you double-click the function you need and Access automatically enters the function in the upper pane of the Expression Builder. In the example shown in Figure 5-10, the selected function is Round. As you can see, the function is immediately placed in the upper pane of the Expression Builder, and Access shows you the arguments needed to make the function work. In this case, you need a Number argument and a Precision argument.

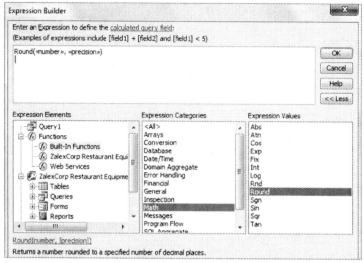

Figure 5-10: Access tells you which arguments you need to make the function work.

If you don't know what an argument means, simply highlight the argument in question and click the Help button. Access will activate a help window that provides an explanation of the function. As shown in Figure 5-11, for example, the Round function requires a number to be rounded and an optional numdecimalplaces argument, which, in this case, indicates the number of decimal places used in the rounding operation.

Figure 5-11: Help files are available to explain each function in detail.

As you can see in Figure 5-12, instead of using a hard-coded number in the `Round` function, an expression returns a dynamic value. This calculation divides the sum of [TransactionMaster]![Line_Total] by 13. Since the `numdecimalplaces` argument is optional, that argument is omitted.

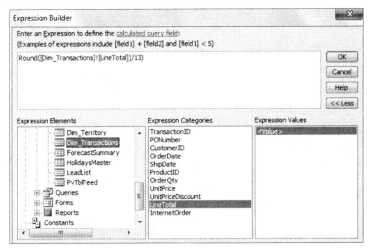

Figure 5-12: The function here rounds the results of the calculation, ([TransactionMaster]![Line _ Total])/13.

When you are satisfied with your newly created expression, click the OK button to insert it in the query grid. Figure 5-13 shows that the new expression has been added as a field. Note that the new field has a default alias of Expr1; you can rename this something more meaningful.

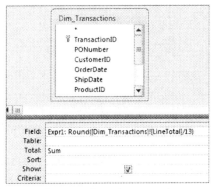

Figure 5-13: Your newly created expression gives you the average revenue by period for all transactions.

Common Calculation Errors

No matter what platform you use to analyze your data, you always run the risk of generating errors when you work with calculations. No magic function in Access can help you prevent errors in your analysis. However, you can take a few fundamental actions to avoid some of the most common calculation errors.

Understanding the Order of Operator Precedence

You might remember from your algebra days that when working with a complex equation executing multiple mathematical operations, the equation does not necessarily evaluate left to right. Some operations have precedence over others and therefore must occur first. The Access environment has similar rules regarding the order of operator precedence. When you are using expressions and calculations that involve several operations, each operation is evaluated and resolved in a predetermined order. It is important to know the order of operator precedence in Access. An incorrectly built expression may cause errors in your analysis.

The order of operations for Access is as follows:

1. Evaluate items in parentheses.

2. Perform exponentiation (^ calculates exponents).

3. Perform negation (- converts to negative).

4. Perform multiplication (* multiplies) and division (/ divides) at equal precedence.

5. Perform addition (+ adds) and subtraction (- Subtract) at equal precedence.

6. Evaluate string concatenation (&).

7. Evaluate comparison and pattern matching operators (>, <, =, <>, >=, <=, Like, Between, Is) at equal precedence.

8. Evaluate logical operators in the following order: Not, And, Or.

NOTE Operations equal in precedence are performed from left to right.

How can understanding the order of operations ensure that you avoid analytical errors? Consider this basic example: The correct answer to the calculation (20+30)*4 is 200. However, if you leave off the parentheses (as in 20+30*4), Access will perform the calculation like this: 30*4 = 120 + 20 = 140. The order of operator precedence mandates that Access perform multiplication before subtraction. Therefore, entering 20+30*4 gives you the wrong answer. Because the order of operator precedence in Access mandates that all operations in parentheses be evaluated first, placing 20+30 inside parentheses ensures the correct answer.

Watching Out for Null Values

A *Null value* represents the absence of any value. When you see a data item in an Access table that is empty or has no information in it, it is considered Null.

The concept of a Null value causing errors in a calculation might initially seem strange to Excel power users. In Excel, if there is a Null value within a column of numbers, the column can still be properly evaluated because Excel simply reads the Null value as zero. This is not the case in Access. If Access encounters a Null value, it does not assume that the Null value represents zero. Instead, it immediately returns a Null value as the answer. To illustrate this behavior, build the query shown in Figure 5-14.

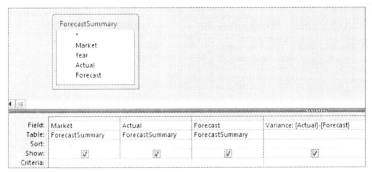

Figure 5-14: To demonstrate how Null values can cause calculation errors, build this query in Design view.

Run the query, and you will see the results shown in Figure 5-15. Notice that the Variance calculation for the first record does not show the expected results; instead, it shows a Null value. This is because the forecast value for that record is a Null value.

Looking at Figure 5-15, you can imagine how a Null calculation error can wreak havoc on your analysis, especially if you have an involved analytical process. Furthermore, Null calculation errors can be difficult to identify and fix. This is a good place to remind you that you should rarely use Null values in your tables. Instead, you should use a logical value that represents "no data" (for example, 0, "NA," or "Undefined").

That being said, you can avoid Null calculation errors by using the Nz function, which enables you to convert any Null value to a value you specify.

Market	Actual	Forecast	Variance
Baltimore	$8,571.00		
Buffalo	$2,103,749.00	$2,163,175.64	($59,426.64)
California	$3,970,922.40	$3,743,168.24	$227,754.16
CANADA	$1,300,568.10	$1,198,797.92	$101,770.18
Charlotte	$8,586,372.20	$7,969,278.04	$617,094.16
Chicago	$159,293.00	$140,286.23	$19,006.77
Dakotas	$149,198.70	$140,938.93	$8,259.77
Dallas	$2,130,941.40	$2,067,835.02	$63,106.38
Denver	$1,302,986.85	$1,221,948.00	$81,038.85
Florida	$36,117,372.05	$37,622,262.55	($1,504,890.50)
Great Lakes	$614,349.10	$573,346.94	$41,002.16
Kansas City	$950,374.15	$904,571.09	$45,803.06
Knoxville	$17,361.00	$16,564.09	$796.91
New England	$772,343.10	$731,248.87	$41,094.23
Omaha	$744,337.50	$687,854.12	$56,483.38

Figure 5-15: As you can see, when any variable in your calculation is Null, the resulting answer is a Null value.

ABOUT THE NZ FUNCTION

The `Nz` function takes two arguments:

`Nz(variant, valueifnull)`

- `variant`: **The data you are working with.**

- `valueifnull`: **The value you want returned if the** `variant` **is Null.**

`NZ([MyNumberField],0)` **converts any Null value in** `MyNumberField` **to zero.**

Armed with this new information, you can adjust the query in Figure 5-14 to utilize the `Nz` function. Since the problem field is Forecast, pass the Forecast field through the `Nz` function. Figure 5-16 shows the adjusted query.

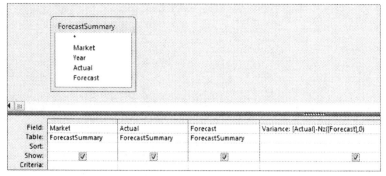

Figure 5-16: Pass the Forecast field through the Nz function to convert Null values to zero.

As you can see in Figure 5-17, the first five records now show a Variance value even though the values in the Forecast field are Null. Note that the NZ function does not physically place a zero in the Null values. The NZ function merely tells access to treat the Nulls as zeros when calculating the Variance field.

Market	Actual	Forecast	Variance
Baltimore	$8,571.00		$8,571.00
Buffalo	$2,103,749.00	$2,163,175.64	($59,426.64)
California	$3,970,922.40	$3,743,168.24	$227,754.16
CANADA	$1,300,568.10	$1,198,797.92	$101,770.18
Charlotte	$8,586,372.20	$7,969,278.04	$617,094.16
Chicago	$159,293.00	$140,286.23	$19,006.77
Dakotas	$149,198.70	$140,938.93	$8,259.77
Dallas	$2,130,941.40	$2,067,835.02	$63,106.38
Denver	$1,302,986.85	$1,221,948.00	$81,038.85
Florida	$36,117,372.05	$37,622,262.55	($1,504,890.50)
Great Lakes	$614,349.10	$573,346.94	$41,002.16
Kansas City	$950,374.15	$904,571.09	$45,803.06
Knoxville	$17,361.00	$16,564.09	$796.91
New England	$772,343.10	$731,248.87	$41,094.23
Omaha	$744,337.50	$687,854.12	$56,483.38

Figure 5-17: The first five records now show a Variance value.

Watching the Syntax in Your Expressions

Basic syntax mistakes in your calculation expressions can also lead to errors. Follow these guidelines to avoid slip-ups:

■ If you are using fields in your calculations, enclose their names in square brackets ([ ]).

■ Make sure you spell the names of the fields correctly.

■ When assigning an alias to your calculated field, be sure you don't use a name that currently exists in the table(s) being calculated.

■ Do not use illegal characters—period (.), exclamation mark (!), square brackets ([ ]) or an ampersand (&)—in your aliases.

Using Dates in Your Analysis

In Access, every possible date starting from December 31, 1899 is stored as a serial number. For example, December 31, 1899 is stored as 1; January 1, 1900 is stored as 2; and so on. This system of storing dates as serial numbers, commonly called the *1900 system*, is the default date system for all Microsoft Office applications. You can take advantage of this system to perform calculations with dates.

Simple Date Calculations

Figure 5-18 shows one of the simplest calculations you can perform on a date. In this query, you are adding 30 to each ship date. This effectively returns the order date plus 30 days, giving you a new date.

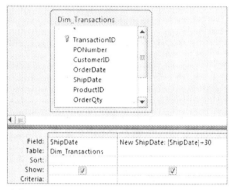

Figure 5-18: You are adding 30 to each ship date, effectively creating a date equal to the ship date plus 30 days.

WARNING To be calculated correctly, dates must reside in a field formatted as a Date/Time field. If you enter a date into a Text field, the date will continue to look like a date, but Access will treat it like a string. The result is that any calculation performed on dates in this Text formatted field will fail. Ensure that all dates are stored in fields formatted as Date/Time.

You can also calculate the number of days between two dates. The calculation in Figure 5-19, for example, subtracts the serial number of one date from the serial number of another date, leaving you the number of days between the two dates.

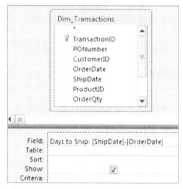

Figure 5-19: In this query, you are calculating the number of days between two dates.

Advanced Analysis Using Functions

As of Access 2010, 25 built-in Date/Time functions are available. Some of these are functions you will very rarely encounter, whereas you'll use others routinely in your analyses. This section discusses a few of the basic Date/Time functions that come in handy in your day-to-day analysis.

The Date Function

Date is a built-in Access function that returns the current system date—in other words, today's date. With this versatile function, you never have to hard-code today's date in your calculations. That is to say, you can create dynamic calculations that use the current system date as a variable, giving you a different result every day. In this section, you look at some of the ways you can leverage the Date function to enhance your analysis.

Finding the Number of Days Between Today and a Past Date

Imagine that you have to calculate aged receivables. You need to know the current date to determine how overdue the receivables are. Of course, you can type the current date by hand, but that can be cumbersome and prone to error.

To demonstrate how to use the Date function, create the query shown in Figure 5-20.

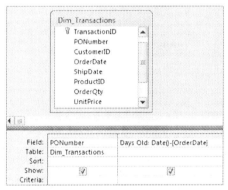

Figure 5-20: This query returns the number of days between today's date and each order date.

Using the Date Function in a Criteria Expression

You can use the Date function to filter out records by including the function in a criteria expression. For example, the query shown in Figure 5-21 returns all records with an order date older than 90 days.

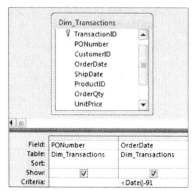

Figure 5-21: No matter what day it is today, this query will return all orders older than 90 days.

Calculating an Age in Years Using the Date Function

Imagine that you have been asked to provide a list of account managers, along with the number of years they have been employed by the company. To accomplish this task, you must calculate the difference between today's date and each manager's hire date.

The first step is to build the query shown in Figure 5-22.

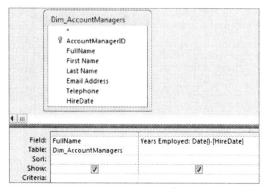

Figure 5-22: You are calculating the difference between today's date and each manager's hire date.

When you look at the query results, shown in Figure 5-23, you realize that the calculation results in the number of days between the two dates, not the number of years.

To fix this, switch back to Design view and divide your calculation by 365.25. Why 365.25? That is the average number of days in a year when you account for leap years. Figure 5-24 demonstrates this change. Note that your original calculation is now wrapped in parentheses to avoid errors due to order of operator precedence.

FullName	Years Employed
Ian Harrell	1364
Kirstie Paulson	1330
Megan Winston	1294
Austen Cope	1222
Maleah Menard	1114
Annabel Locklear	1030
Norman Stackhouse	904
Pauline Mccollum	848
Martin Stamps	831
Rosetta Kimbrough	785
Truman Dubois	750
Carma Gough	686
Tory Hanlon	546
Ashleigh Friedman	489

Figure 5-23: This dataset shows the number of days, not the number of years.

```
Dim_AccountManagers
    *
  ⃗ AccountManagerID
    FullName
    First Name
    Last Name
    Email Address
    Telephone
    HireDate
```

Field:	FullName	Years Employed: (Date()-[HireDate])/365.25
Table:	Dim_AccountManagers	
Sort:		
Show:	✓	✓
Criteria:		

Figure 5-24: Divide your original calculation by 365.25 to convert the answer to years.

A look at the results, shown in Figure 5-25, proves that you are now returning the number of years. All that is left to do is to strip away the fractional portion of the date using the Int function. Why the Int function? The Int function does not round the year up or down; it merely converts the number to a readable integer.

TIP Want to actually round the number of years? You can simply wrap your date calculation in the Round function. The Round function is highlighted in Appendix A of this book.

Wrapping your calculation in the Int function ensures that your answer is a clean year without fractions (see Figure 5-26).

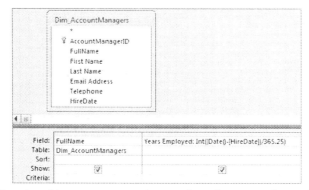

FullName	Years Employed
Ian Harrell	3.73442847364819
Kirstie Paulson	3.64134154688569
Megan Winston	3.54277891354894
Austen Cope	3.34565366187543
Maleah Menard	3.04996577686516
Annabel Locklear	2.81998631074606
Norman Stackhouse	2.47501711156742
Pauline Mccollum	2.32169746748802
Martin Stamps	2.27515400410678
Rosetta Kimbrough	2.1492128678987
Truman Dubois	2.05338809034908
Carma Gough	1.87816563997262
Tory Hanlon	1.49486652977413
Ashleigh Friedman	1.3388090349076

Figure 5-25: Your query now returns years, but you must strip away the fractional portion of your answer.

Figure 5-26: Running this query returns the number of years each employee has been with the company.

You can calculate a person's age by using the same method. Simply replace the hire date with the date of birth.

The Year, Month, Day, and Weekday Functions

The Year, Month, Day, and Weekday functions are used to return an integer that represents their respective parts of a date. These functions require a valid date as an argument. For example:

- Year(#12/31/1997#) returns 1997.
- Month(#12/31/1997#) returns 12.
- Day(#12/31/1997#) returns 31.
- Weekday(#12/31/1997#) returns 4.

NOTE The Weekday function returns the day of the week from a date. In Access, weekdays are numbered from 1 to 7, starting with Sunday. Therefore, if the Weekday function returns 4, the day of the week represented is Wednesday.

Figure 5-27 demonstrates how you use these functions in a query environment.

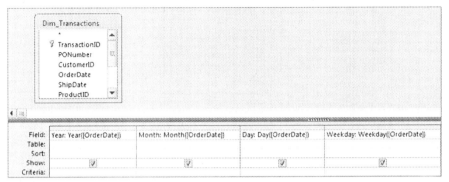

Figure 5-27: The Year, Month, Day, and Weekday functions enable you parse out a part of a date.

TRICKS OF THE TRADE: AN EASY WAY TO QUERY ONLY WORKDAYS

Suppose that you have been asked to provide the total amount of revenue generated by product but only revenue generated during workdays in calendar year 2008. Workdays are defined as days that are not weekends or holidays.

The first thing you need to accomplish this task is a table that lists all the company holidays in 2008. Figure 5-28 shows that a Holidays table can be nothing more than one field listing all the dates that constitute a holiday.

CY_2008_Holidays
Holidays ⋅
1/1/2008
1/19/2008
5/31/2008
7/5/2008
9/6/2008
11/25/2008
11/26/2008
12/23/2008
12/24/2008
12/31/2008

Figure 5-28: In this database, the CY_2008_Holidays table contains a column called Holidays that lists all the dates that counted as company holidays.

(continued)

TRICKS OF THE TRADE: AN EASY WAY TO QUERY ONLY WORKDAYS
(continued)

Once you have established a table that contains all the company holidays, it's time to build the query. Figure 5-29 demonstrates how to build a query that filters out non-workdays.

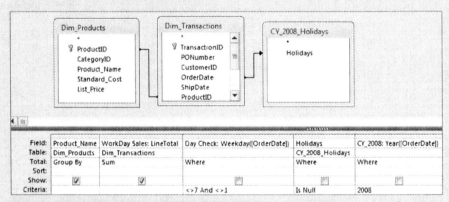

Figure 5-29: Using the CY_2008_Holidays table and a simple Weekday function, you can filter out non-workdays.

Take a moment to analyze what is going on in Figure 5-29.

1. **You create a left join from** TransactionMaster **to** CY_2008_Holidays **to tell Access that you want all the records from TransactionMaster.**

2. **You then use the** Is Null **criteria under Holidays. This limits the** TransactionMaster **to only those dates that do not match any of the holidays listed in the** CY_2008_Holidays table.

3. **You then create a field called Day Check where you are returning the weekday of every service date in the** TransactionMaster.

4. **You filter the newly created Day Check field to filter out those weekdays that represent Saturdays and Sundays (1 and 7).**

5. **Finally, you filter for only those records whose order date falls in the year 2008.**

The DateAdd Function

A common analysis for many organizations is to determine on which date a certain benchmark is reached. For example, most businesses want to know on what date an order becomes 30 days past due. Furthermore, on what date should the customer receive a warning letter? An easy way to perform these types of analyses is to use the DateAdd function. The DateAdd function returns a date to which a specified interval has been added.

ABOUT THE DATEADD FUNCTION

The DateAdd function returns a date to which a specified interval has been added. There are three required arguments in the DateAdd function.

DateAdd(*interval, number, date*)

- interval (required): The interval of time want to use. The intervals available are as follows:

  - "yyyy": Year

  - "q": Quarter

  - "m": Month

  - "y": Day of year

  - "d": Day

  - "w" : Weekday

  - "ww": Week

  - "h": Hour

  - "n": Minute

  - "s": Second

- number (required): The number of intervals to add. A positive number returns a date in the future, whereas a negative number returns a date in the past.

- date (required): The date value with which you are working.

For example:

- DateAdd("ww",1,#11/30/2008#) **returns 12/7/2008.**

- DateAdd("m",2,#11/30/2008#) **returns 1/30/2009.**

- DateAdd("yyyy",-1,#11/30/2008#) **returns 11/30/2007.**

The query shown in Figure 5-30 illustrates how the DateAdd function determines the exact date a specific benchmark is reached. You are creating two new fields with this query: Warning and Overdue. The DateAdd function in the Warning field returns the date that is three weeks from the original order date. The DateAdd function in the Overdue field returns the date that is one month from the original order date.

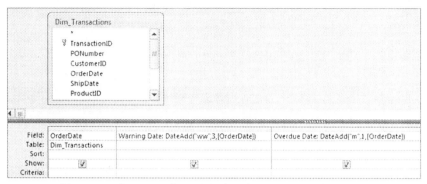

Figure 5-30: This query gives you the original order date, the date you should send a warning letter, and the date that the order is 30 days overdue.

Grouping Dates into Quarters

Why would you need to group your dates into quarters? Most databases store dates rather than quarter designations. Therefore, if you want to analyze data on a quarter-over-quarter basis, you have to convert dates into quarters. Surprisingly, there is no Date/Time function that allows you to group dates into quarters. There is, however, the Format function.

The Format function belongs to the Text category of functions and allows you to convert a variant into a string based on formatting instructions. From the perspective of analyzing dates, you can pass several valid instructions to a Format function.

- Format(#01/31/2004#, "yyyy") returns 2004.
- Format(#01/31/2004#, "yy") returns 04.
- Format(#01/31/2004#, "q") returns 1.
- Format(#01/31/2004#, "mmm") returns Jan.
- Format(#01/31/2004#, "mm") returns 01.
- Format(#01/31/2004#, "d") returns 31.
- Format(#01/31/2004#, "w") returns 7.
- Format(#01/31/2004#, "ww") returns 5.

NOTE Keep in mind that the value returned when passing a date through a Format function is a string that cannot be used in subsequent calculations.

The query in Figure 5-31 shows how you group all the order dates into quarters and then group the quarters to get a sum of revenue for each quarter.

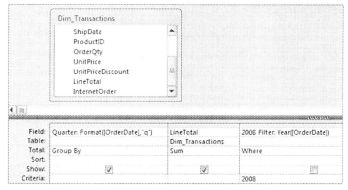

Figure 5-31: You can group dates into quarters by using the `Format` function.

If you want to get fancy, you can insert the `Format` function in a crosstab query, using Quarter as the column (see Figure 5-32).

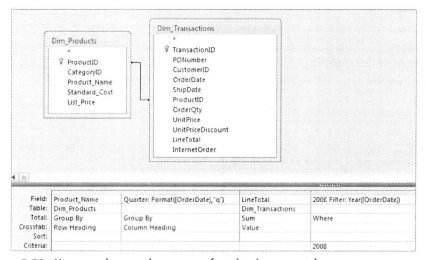

Figure 5-32: You can also use the `Format` function in a crosstab query.

As you can see in Figure 5-33, the resulting dataset is a clean look at revenue by product, by quarter.

Product_Name	1	2	3	4
Filter Sheets 13 1/2" X 24"	$11,970.00	$22,548.75	$55,258.00	$29,307.25
Filter Sheets 14" X 22"	$28,284.60	$57,696.10	$190,679.15	$129,965.20
Filter Sheets 16 1/2" X 25 1/2"	$3,018.35	$3,402.60	$58,183.40	$63,390.65
Filter Sheets 16 3/8" X 24 3/8"	$49,286.10	$101,954.70	$106,431.90	$111,335.50
Food Warmer Pickup Stations 24"W		$7,901.60	$15,529.50	$9,389.10

Figure 5-33: You have successfully grouped your dates into quarters.

The DateSerial Function

The `DateSerial` function allows you to construct a date value by combining given year, month, and day components. This function is perfect for converting disparate strings (that together represent a date) into an actual date.

ABOUT THE DATESERIAL FUNCTION

The `DateSerial` **function has three arguments:**

`DateSerial(Year, Month, Day)`

- `Year` **(required): Any number or numeric expression from 100 to 9999.**

- `Month` **(required): Any number or numeric expression.**

- `Day` **(required): Any number or numeric expression.**

For example, `DateSerial(2004, 4, 3)` **returns April 3, 2004.**

The wonderful thing about the `DateSerial` function is that you can pass other date expressions as arguments. For example, pretend that the system date on your PC is August 1, 2005. For those of you who have been paying attention, this means that the `Date` function would return August 1, 2005. That being the case, the following expression would return August 1, 2005:

```
DateSerial ( Year(Date()) , Month(Date()) , Day(Date()) )
```

NOTE `Year(Date())` **returns the current year,** `Month(Date())` **returns the current month, and** `Day(Date())` **returns the current day.**

So how is this helpful? Well, now you can put a few twists on this by performing calculations on the expressions within the `DateSerial` function. Consider some of the possibilities:

- Get the first day of last month by subtracting `1` from the current month and using `1` as the `Day` argument.

```
DateSerial(Year(Date()), Month(Date()) - 1, 1)
```

- Get the first day of next month by adding `1` to the current month and using `1` as the `Day` argument.

```
DateSerial(Year(Date()), Month(Date()) + 1, 1)
```

- Get the last day of the previous month by using `0` as the `Day` argument.

```
DateSerial(Year(Date()), Month(Date()), 0)
```

- Get the last day of the current month by adding 1 to the current month and using 0 as the Day argument.

```
DateSerial(Year(Date()), Month(Date()) +1, 0)
```

TIP Passing a 0 to the **Day** argument automatically gets you the last day of the month specified in the **DateSerial** function. This is because Access will interpret the 0 as bleeding into the previous month. That is to say from an Access point of view, if 1 is the first day of the month, then 0 means you want to go into the previous month.

The New Calculated Data Type

With Access 2010, Microsoft introduced a new data type called *Calculated*. This new data type allows you to embed calculations directly inside your tables. That is to say, you can create a field that holds no real data, only a predefined calculation—similar to using a formula in a cell in Excel.

Database purists are sure to shun this new functionality because it goes against the rule that calculations should never be stored. Stored calculations require constant maintenance as the data in your table changes. Not to mention that stored calculations generally tie your data to one analytical path.

So why would Microsoft tweak such a long-standing database rule? The reason has to do with the Internet. In the near future, Access databases will have the ability to work on the Web. That is to say, users can interact with Access databases, forms, and reports online. Calculated data types are the first step in giving Access developers a way to employ calculations online without resorting to background queries and code (which may not be available to a user while connected through the Internet).

That being said, offline scenarios that have a calculated data type can save you time because they perform relatively simple operations that won't unduly lock down or hinder your table architecture.

Take a moment to go through a simple scenario where you can use the Calculated data type. Follow these steps:

1. In your sample database, you'll find a table called 2009_Projections. Right-click 2009_Projections and select Design view. Notice that one of the fields in the table is Percent Increase (see Figure 5-34). You could calculate a 2009 Target field that shows a real-time calculation of the projection for each market.

2. Add the new field and select the Calculated data type, as shown here in Figure 5-35. The Expression Builder will immediately activate.

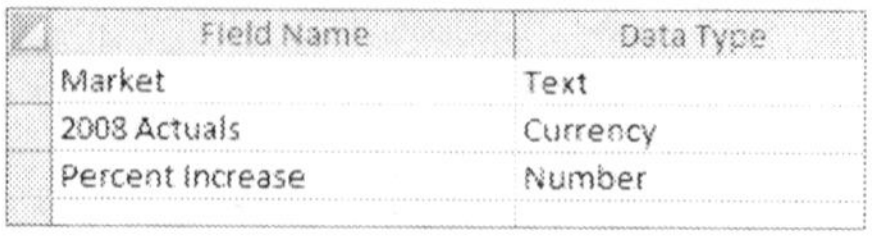

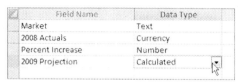

Figure 5-34: Your table contains Percent Increase. You would like to add a 2009 Projection field.

Field Name	Data Type
Market	Text
2008 Actuals	Currency
Percent Increase	Number
2009 Projection	Calculated

Figure 5-35: Add your new field and set the data type to Calculated.

3. The idea is to enter your calculation in the upper pane, as demonstrated in Figure 5-36. In this example, you are performing a simple operation that adds the Percent Increase to the 2008 Actual.

4. Once your expression is set, you can format the calculated field as needed. In Figure 5-37, the 2009 Projection field is formatted to show as a currency.

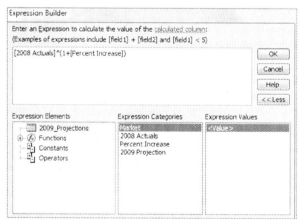

Figure 5-36: Enter your expression.

If all went well, you'll have a new calculated field. As you can see in Figure 5-38, the new 2009 Projection field looks and feels like a standard field. However, this field will recalculate on-the-fly if any of the linked variables are changed. To test this, change any of the values under Percent Increase. Once you change a value, the associated 2009 projection will change.

Field Name	Data Type	
Market	Text	
2008 Actuals	Currency	
Percent Increase	Number	
2009 Projection	Calculated	▾

General	Lookup	
Expression	[2008 Actuals]*(1+[Percent Increase])
Result Type	Currency
Format	Currency
Decimal Places	Auto

Figure 5-37: Apply the needed formatting to the new Calculated field.

Market ▾	2008 Actuals ▾	Percent Increase ▾	2009 Projection ▾
Baltimore	$8,571.00	10%	$9,428.10
Buffalo	$2,103,749.00	11%	$2,335,161.39
California	$3,970,922.40	13%	$4,487,142.31
CANADA	$1,300,568.10	11%	$1,443,630.59
Charlotte	$8,586,372.20	5%	$9,015,690.81
Chicago	$159,293.00	7%	$170,443.51
Dakotas	$149,198.70	9%	$162,626.58
Dallas	$2,130,941.40	12%	$2,386,654.37
Denver	$1,302,986.85	13%	$1,472,375.14
Florida	$36,117,372.05	8%	$39,006,761.81
Great Lakes	$614,349.10	12%	$688,070.99
Kansas City	$950,374.15	5%	$997,892.86
Knoxville	$17,361.00	6%	$18,402.66

Figure 5-38: Although your newly created calculated field looks and feels like a standard field, it will recalculate on-the-fly.

WARNING Be aware the Calculated data types will only work in Access 2010 databases. They are not backward compatible. That means that Access 2007 or prior versions cannot use any field designated as a Calculate data type.

Summary

Not many Excel analysts know that Access has the ability to perform calculations. In fact, the most common question asked about Access is "Where do the formulas go?" The reality is that Access provides a wide array of tools and built-in functions that make performing calculations possible.

The first thing to remember is that calculations are typically not stored in Access tables as formulas are stored in Excel. There are several reasons for this:

■ Stored calculations take up valuable storage space.

■ Stored calculations require constant maintenance as the data in your table changes.

■ Stored calculations generally tie your data to one analytical path.

Instead of storing the calculated results as hard data, calculations in Access are typically performed in "real-time" with the use of various types of queries.

Microsoft has introduced a change to this long-standing rule with the Calculated data type. This new data type allows you to embed calculations directly inside your tables. Although this is generally shunned, you can use the Calculated data type to perform simple operations that won't unduly lock down or hinder your table architecture.

In addition to performing mathematical calculations, Access can perform calculations with dates. This is because Access stores all dates as serial numbers with December 31, 1899 being day 1. You can take advantage of this system to perform queries using date calculations. For example, you can find all orders over 90 days old, you can calculate the seniority of each employee, you can calculate the due date of an order, and the list goes on.

Performing Conditional Analysis

Up until now, your analyses have been straightforward. You build a query, you add some criteria, you add a calculation, you save the query, then you run the query whenever you need to. What happens however, if the criteria that governs you analysis changes frequently, or if your analytical processes depend on meeting certain conditions? In these situations, you would use a *conditional analysis*; an analysis whose outcome depends on a pre-defined set of conditions. Barring VBA code, several tools and functions enable you to build conditional analyses, some of which are parameter queries, the IIf function, and the Switch function. In this chapter, you learn how these tools and functions can help you save time, organize your analytical processes, and enhance your analysis.

Using Parameter Queries

You will find that when building your analytical processes, it's often difficult to anticipate every single combination of criteria that may be needed. This is where parameter queries can help.

A *parameter query* is an interactive query that prompts you for criteria before the query runs. A parameter query is useful when you need to ask a query different questions using different criteria each time it runs. To get a firm understanding of how a parameter query can help you, build the query in Figure 6-1. With this query, you want to see the all purchase orders logged during the 200705-system period.

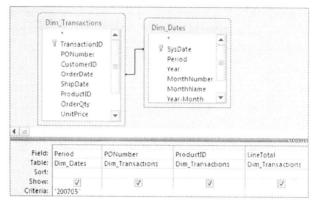

Figure 6-1: This query has a hard-coded criterion for system period.

Although this query gives you what you need, the problem is that the criterion for system period is hard-coded as 200705. That means if you want to analyze revenue for a different period, you essentially have to rebuild the query. Using a parameter query allows you to create a conditional analysis; that is, an analysis based on variables you specify each time you run the query. To create a parameter query, simply replace the hard-coded criteria with text that you have enclosed in square brackets ([ ]), as shown in Figure 6-2.

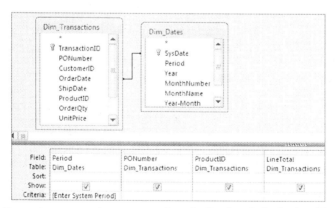

Figure 6-2: To create a parameter query, replace the hard-coded criteria with text enclosed in square brackets [ ].

Running a parameter query forces the Enter Parameter Value dialog box to open and ask for a variable. Note that the text you typed inside the brackets of your parameter appears in the dialog box. At this point, you would simply enter your parameter, as shown in Figure 6-3.

Figure 6-3: Enter your criteria in the Enter Parameter Value dialog box and click OK.

How Parameter Queries Work

When you run a parameter query, Access attempts to convert any text to a literal string by wrapping the text in quotes. However, if you place square brackets ([ ]) around the text, Access thinks that it is a variable and tries to bind some value to the variable using the following series of tests:

1. Access checks to see if the variable is a field name. If Access identifies the variable as a field name, that field is used in the expression.

2. If the variable is not a field name, Access checks to see if the variable is a calculated field. If Access determines the expression is indeed a calculated field, it simply carries out the mathematical operation.

3. If the variable is not a calculated field, Access checks to see if the variable is referencing an object such as a control on an open form or open report.

4. If all else fails, the only remaining option is to ask the user what the variable is, so Access displays the Enter Parameter Value dialog box, showing the text you entered in the Criteria row.

Ground Rules of Parameter Queries

As with other functionality in Access, parameter queries come with their own set of ground rules that you should follow in order to use them properly.

- You must place square brackets ([ ]) around your parameter. If you do not, Access automatically converts your text into a literal string.

- You cannot use the name of a field as a parameter. If you do, Access simply replaces your parameter with the current value of the field.

- You cannot use a period (.), an exclamation mark (!), or square brackets ([]) in your parameter's prompt text.

- You must limit the number of characters in your parameter's prompt text. Entering parameter prompt text that is too long may result in your prompt being cut off in the Enter Parameter Value dialog box. Moreover, you should make your prompts as clear and concise as possible.

TIP If you really want to use a field name in your parameter's prompt, you can follow the field name with other characters. For example, instead of using [Period], you could use [Period: ?]. As you read this, keep in mind that there is nothing magic about the colon (:) or the question mark (?). Any character will do. The idea is to allow Access to differentiate between your parameter and the field name while matching the original field name as closely as possible.

Working with Parameter Queries

The example shown in Figure 6-2 uses a parameter to define a single criterion. Although this is the most common way to use a parameter in a query, there are many ways to exploit this functionality. In fact, it is safe to say that the more innovative you get with your parameter queries, the more elegant and advanced your impromptu analysis will be. This section covers some of the different ways you can use parameters in your queries.

Working with Multiple Parameter Conditions

You are not in any way limited in the number of parameters you can use in your query. Figure 6-4, on the other hand, demonstrates how you can utilize more than one parameter in a query. When you run this query, it prompts you for both a system period and a product ID, allowing you to dynamically filter on two data points without ever having to rewrite your query.

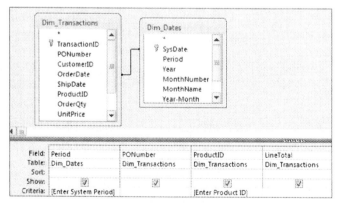

Figure 6-4: You can employ more than one parameter in a query.

Combining Parameters with Operators

You can combine parameter prompts with any operator you would normally use in a query. Using parameters in conjunction with standard operators allows you to dynamically expand or contract the filters in your analysis without rebuilding your query. To demonstrate how this works, build the query shown here in Figure 6-5.

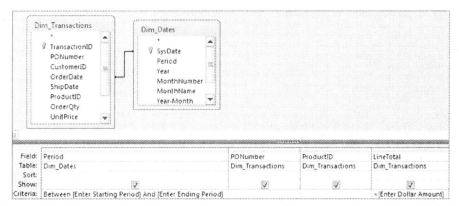

Figure 6-5: This query combines standard operators with parameters in order to limit the results.

This query uses the BETWEEN . . . AND operator and the > (greater than) operator to limit the results of the query based on the user-defined parameters. Because three parameter prompts are built into this query, it prompts you for inputs three times: once for a starting period, once for an ending period, and once for a dollar amount. The number of returned records depends on the parameters you input. For instance, if you input 200701 as the starting period, 200703 as the ending period, and 5000 as the dollar amount, you get 1700 records.

Combining Parameters with Wildcards

One of the problems with a parameter query is that if the parameter is ignored when the query runs, the query returns no records. One way to get around this problem is to combine your parameter with a wildcard so that if the parameter is ignored, all records are returned. To demonstrate how you can use a wildcard with a parameter, build the query shown here in Figure 6-6. When you run this query, it will prompt you for a period. Because you are using the wildcard, you have the option of filtering out a single period by entering a period designator into the parameter, or you can ignore the parameter to return all records.

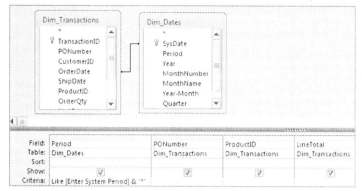

Figure 6-6: If the parameter in this query is ignored, the query returns all records, thanks to the wildcard (*).

TIP Using the wildcard with a parameter also allows users to enter in a partial parameter and still get results. Suppose, for example, that the criteria in your parameter query is:

```
Like [Enter Lastname] & "*"
```

Entering A as the parameter would return all last names that start with the letter A.

Or, suppose the criteria in your parameter query is:

```
Like "*" & [Enter Lastname] & "*"
```

Entering A would return all last names that contain the letter A.

Using Parameters as Calculation Variables

You are not limited to using parameters as criteria for a query; you can use parameters anywhere you use a variable. In fact, a particularly useful way to use parameters is in calculations. For example, the query in Figure 6-7 enables you to analyze how a price increase will affect current prices based on the percent increase you enter. When you run this query, you are asked to enter a percentage by which you want to increase your prices. Once you pass your percentage, the parameter query uses it as a variable in the calculation.

Using Parameters as Function Arguments

You can also use parameters as arguments within functions. Figure 6-8 demonstrates the use of the DateDiff function employing parameters instead of hard-coded dates. When this query runs, it prompts you for a start date and an end date. The `DateDiff` function then uses these dates as arguments. Again, this allows you to specify new dates each time you run the query without ever having to rebuild the query.

NOTE You will notice that when you run the query in Figure 6-8, you will only have to enter the Start date and the End date one time although they are both used in two places in the query. Once you assign a variable to a parameter, that assignment persists to every future instance of that parameter.

This is also a good time to note that the values you enter into your parameters must fit into the data type required for the function's argument. For example, if you are using a parameter in a date-oriented function (like `DateDiff`), the variable you enter into that parameter must be a date or the function won't work.

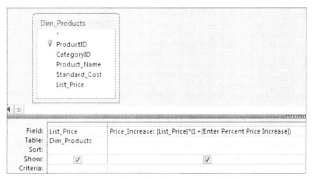

Figure 6-7: You can use parameters in calculations, enabling you to change the calculations variables each time you run the query.

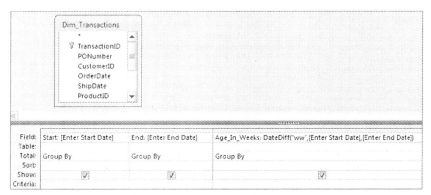

Figure 6-8: You can use parameters as arguments in functions instead of hard-coded values.

TRICKS OF THE TRADE: CREATING A PARAMETER PROMPT THAT ACCEPTS MULTIPLE ENTRIES

The parameter query in Figure 6-9 enables you to dynamically filter results by a variable period that you specify within the parameter. However, this query does not allow you to see results for more than one period at a time.

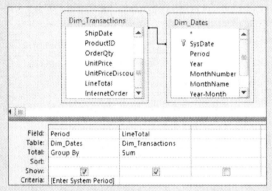

Figure 6-9: This query enables you to filter only one period at a time.

You could use more than one parameter, as shown in the following figure. Unlike the query in Figure 6-9, this query allows you to include more than one period in your query results. However, you are still limited to the number of parameters built into the query (in this case, three) as shown in Figure 6-10.

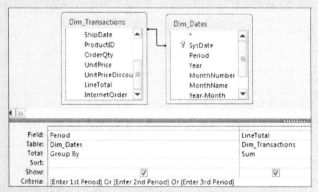

Figure 6-10: This query enables you to filter by three periods at a time instead of one. But what if you need to filter more than three periods?

So how do you allow for any number of parameter entries? The answer is relatively easy. You create a parameter that is passed through an `InStr` function to test for a position number (feel free to revisit Chapter 4 to get a refresher on the `InStr` function).

TRICKS OF THE TRADE: CREATING A PARAMETER PROMPT THAT ACCEPTS MULTIPLE ENTRIES

The query shown in Figure 6-11 demonstrates how to do this.

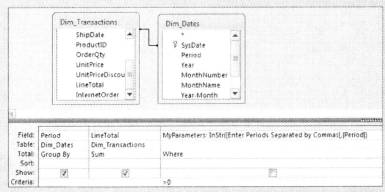

Figure 6-11: This parameter query allows for multiple entries in a parameter.

Notice that the parameter is not being used as criteria for the Period field. Instead, it is being used in an `Instr` function to test for the position number of the variable you enter into the parameter prompt, as follows:

```
InStr([Enter Periods separated by commas],[Period])
```

If the `Instr` function finds your variable, it returns a position number; if not, it returns 0. Therefore, you only want records that returned a position number greater than zero (hence, the criteria for the parameter).

When you run this query, Access displays the standard Enter Parameter Value dialog box (see Figure 6-12). You can then type in as many variables as you want.

Figure 6-12: Simply type as many parameters you want.

Using Conditional Functions

Parameter queries are not the only tools in Access that allow for conditional analysis. Access also has built-in functions that facilitate value comparisons, data validation, and conditional evaluation. Two of these functions are the

IIf function and the Switch function. These conditional functions (also called program flow functions) are designed to test for conditions and provide different outcomes based on the results of those tests. In this section, you learn how to control the flow of your analysis by utilizing the IIf and Switch functions.

The IIf Function

The IIf (immediate if) function replicates the functionality of an IF statement for a single operation. The IIf function evaluates a specific condition and returns a result based on a True or False determination.

ABOUT THE IIf FUNCTION

To use the IIf function, you must provide three required arguments: the expression to be evaluated, a value to be returned if the expression is True, and a value to be returned if the expression is False.

```
IIf(Expression, TrueAnswer, FalseAnswer)
```

- Expression **(required): The expression you want to evaluate.**

- TrueAnswer **(required): The value to return if the expression is True.**

- FalseAnswer **(optional): The value to return if the expression is False. If this argument is omitted, a Null value is returned if the expression evaluates to False.**

TIP Think of the commas in an IIf function as THEN and ELSE statements. Consider the following IIf function, for instance:

```
IIf(Babies = 2 , "Twins", "Not Twins")
```

This function literally translates to: If Babies equals 2, then Twins, else Not Twins.

Using IIf to Avoid Mathematical Errors

To demonstrate a simple problem where the IIf function comes in handy, build the query shown in Figure 6-13.

When you run the query, you'll notice that not all the results are clean. As you can see in Figure 6-14, you are getting some errors due to division by zero. That is to say, you are dividing actual revenues by forecasts that are zero.

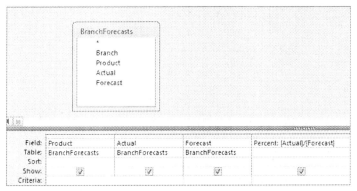

Figure 6-13: This query performs a calculation on the Actual and the Forecast fields to calculate a percent to forecast.

Product ▾	Actual ▾	Forecast ▾	Percent ▾
90830	171	0	#Div/0!
90830	520	658	79.0%
90830	706	727	97.1%
90830	1,025	1,206	85.0%
90830	1,064	1,400	76.0%
90830	1,195	0	#Div/0!
90830	1,370	0	#Div/0!
90830	1,463	0	#Div/0!
90830	1,483	1,786	83.0%
90830	1,522	1,951	78.0%
90830	1,525	0	#Div/0!

Figure 6-14: The errors shown in the results are due to the fact that some revenues are being divided by zeros.

Although this seems like a benign issue, in a more complex, multilayered analytical process, these errors could compromise the integrity of your data analysis. To avoid these errors, you can perform a conditional analysis on your dataset using the IIf function, evaluating the Forecast field for each record before performing the calculation. If the forecast is zero, you bypass the calculation and simply return a value of zero. If the forecast is not zero, you perform the calculation to get the correct value. The IIf function would look like this:

```
IIf([Forecast]=0,0,[Actual]/[Forecast])
```

Figure 6-15 demonstrates how this IIf function is put into action.
As you can see in Figure 6-16, the errors have been avoided.

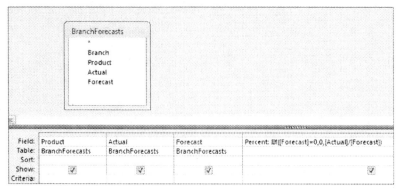

Figure 6-15: This IIf function enables you to test for forecasts with a value of 0 and bypass them when performing your calculation.

Product ▾	Actual ▾	Forecast ▾	Percent ▾
90830	171	0	0.0%
90830	520	658	79.0%
90830	706	727	97.1%
90830	1,025	1,206	85.0%
90830	1,064	1,400	76.0%
90830	1,195	0	0.0%
90830	1,370	0	0.0%
90830	1,463	0	0.0%
90830	1,483	1,786	83.0%
90830	1,522	1,951	78.0%
90830	1,525	0	0.0%

Figure 6-16: The IIf function helped you avoid the division by zero errors.

Using IIf to Save Time

You can also use the IIf function to save steps in your analytical processes and, ultimately, save time. For example, imagine that you need to tag customers in a lead list as either large-sized customers or a small-sized customers, based on their dollar potential and you decide that you will update the MyTest field in your dataset with "LARGE" or "SMALL" based on the revenue potential of the customer. Without the IIf function, you would have to run the two Update queries shown in Figures 6-17 and 6-18 to accomplish this task.

Will the queries in Figures 6-17 and 6-18 do the job? Yes. However, you could accomplish the same task with one query using the IIf function.

The update query shown in Figure 6-19 illustrates how you can use an IIf function as the update expression.

Take a moment and look at the IIf function used as the update expression.

```
IIf([DollarPotential]>=10000,"LARGE","SMALL")
```

Figure 6-17: This query will update the MyTest field to tag all customers that have a revenue potential at or above 10,000 dollars with the word "LARGE."

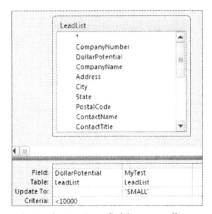

Figure 6-18: This query updates the MyTest field to tag all customers that have a revenue potential less than 10,000 dollars with the word "SMALL."

This function tells Access to evaluate the DollarPotential field of each record. If the DollarPotential field is greater than or equal to 10,000, use the word "LARGE" as the update value. If not, use the word "SMALL."

TIP You can use conditional operators (AND, OR, BETWEEN) within your IIf functions to add a layers to your condition expression. For example, the following function tests for a dollar potential and segment to get a True or a False value.

```
IIf([DollarPotential]>10000 And [Segment]="Metal
    Fabrication","True","False")
```

Figure 6-19: You can accomplish the same task in one query using the IIf function.

Nesting IIf Functions for Multiple Conditions

Sometimes, the condition you need to test for is too complex to be handled by a basic `IF...THEN...ELSE` structure. In such cases, you can use nested `IIf` functions—that is, `IIf` functions embedded in other `IIf` functions. Consider the following example:

```
IIf([VALUE]>100,"A",IIf([VALUE]<100,"C","B"))
```

This function will check to see if VALUE is greater than 100. If it is, *then A* is returned; if not (*else*), a second `IIf` function is triggered. The second `IIf` function checks to see if VALUE is less than 100. If yes, *then C* is returned; if not (*else*), B is returned.

The idea here is that because an `IIf` function results in a True or False answer, you can expand your condition by setting the "False" expression to another `IIf` function instead of to a hard-coded value. This triggers another evaluation. There is no limit to the number of nested `IIf` functions you can use.

Using IIf Functions to Create Crosstab Analyses

Many seasoned analysts use the `IIf` function to create custom crosstab analyses in lieu of using a crosstab query. Among the many advantages of creating crosstab analyses without a crosstab query is the ability to categorize and group otherwise unrelated data items.

In the example shown in Figure 6-20, you are returning the number of account managers hired before and after 2009. Categorizations this specific are not possible with a crosstab query.

The result, shown in Figure 6-21, is every bit as clean and user-friendly as the results would be from a crosstab query.

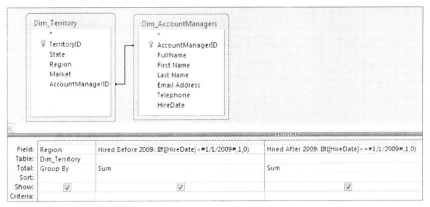

Figure 6-20: This query demonstrates how to create a crosstab analysis without using a crosstab query.

Region ▾	Hired Before 2009 ▾	Hired After 2009 ▾
CANADA	0	5
Midwest	8	0
North	6	0
Northeast	14	0
South	6	0
Southeast	5	0
Southwest	6	0
West	1	5

Figure 6-21: The resulting dataset gives you a clean crosstab-style view of your data.

Another advantage of creating crosstab analyses without a crosstab query is the ability to include more than one calculation in your crosstab report. For example, Figure 6-22 illustrates a query where the sum of units and revenue are returned in crosstab format.

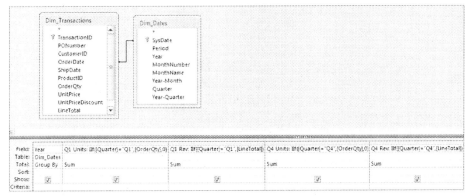

Figure 6-22: Creating crosstab-style reports using the `IIf` function allows you to calculate more than one value.

As you can see in Figure 6-23, the resulting dataset provides a great deal of information in an easy-to-read format. Because a standard crosstab query does not allow more than one value calculations (in this case units and revenue are values), this particular view is not possible with a standard crosstab query.

Year ▾	Q1 Units ▾	Q1 Rev ▾	Q4 Units ▾	Q4 Rev ▾
2006	0		5851	$9,777,639.50
2007	4517	$8,749,969.10	18697	$11,020,743.05
2008	12352	$9,262,135.00	42233	$20,412,540.90
2009	31540	$18,071,842.70	0	

Figure 6-23: This analysis would be impossible to create in a standard crosstab query, where multiple calculations are not allowed.

The Switch Function

The `Switch` function enables you to evaluate a list of expressions and return the value associated with the expression determined to be True. To use the `Switch` function, you must provide a minimum of one expression and one value.

ABOUT THE SWITCH FUNCTION

The power of the `Switch` function comes in evaluating multiple expressions at one time and determining which one is True. The basic syntax for the Switch function is:

```
Switch(Expression, Value)
```

- `Expression` **(required): The expression you want to evaluate.**
- `Value` **(required): The value to return if the expression is True.**

To evaluate multiple expressions, simply add another `Expression` and `Value` to the function, as follows:

```
Switch(Expression1, Value1, Expression2, Value2, Expression3,
Value3)
```

When executed, this `Switch` function evaluates each expression in turn. If an expression evaluates to True, the value that follows that expression is returned. If more than one expression is True, the value for the first True expression is returned (the others are ignored).

If none of the expressions in your `Switch` function evaluate as True, the function returns a Null value. For example, the following function evaluates `Count` and returns a value based on it.

```
Switch([Count] < 10, "Low", [Count] > 15, "High")
```

ABOUT THE SWITCH FUNCTION

If `Count` **comes in between 10 and 15, you get a Null value because none of the expressions include those numbers.**

You can ensure your Switch function returns a value other than Null when none of your expressions evaluate to TRUE. You do this by adding a catch-all expression and provide a value to return if none of your expressions are determined to be True.

```
Switch([Count] < 10, "Low", [Count] > 15, "High", True, "Middle")
```

In this example, adding `True` **as the last expression forces the value** `"Middle"` **to be returned instead of a Null value if none of the other expressions evaluate as True.**

Comparing the IIf and Switch Functions

Although the `IIf` function is a versatile tool that can handle most conditional analysis, the fact is that the `IIf` function has a fixed number of arguments that limits it to a basic `IF...THEN...ELSE` structure. This limitation makes it difficult to evaluate complex conditions without using nested `IIf` functions. While there is nothing wrong with nesting IIF functions, they have the potential to be difficult to read and maintain.

To illustrate this point, consider this scenario: It is common practice to classify customers into groups based on annual revenue, or how much they spend with your company. Imagine that your organization has a policy of classifying customers into four groups: A, B, C, and D (see Table 6-1).

You have been asked to classify the customers in the TransactionMaster table, based on each customer's sales transactions. You can actually do this using either the `IIf` function or the `Switch` function.

Table 6-1: Customer Classifications

ANNUAL REVENUE	CUSTOMER CLASSIFICATION
>= $10,000	A
>=5,000 but < $10,000	B
>=$1,000 but < $5,000	C
<$1,000	D

The problem with using the `IIf` function is that this situation calls for some hefty nesting. That is, you have to use `IIf` expressions within other `IIf` expressions to handle the easy layer of possible conditions. Here is how the expression would look if you opted to use the IIf function:

```
IIf([REV]>=10000,"A",IIf([REV]>=5000,"B",IIf([REV]>=1000,"C","D")))"
```

As you can see, this can get a bit convoluted. So much so, that the chances of making a syntax or logic error are high.

In contrast to the preceding nested IIf function, the following Switch function is rather straightforward:

```
Switch([REV]<1000,"D",[REV]<5000,"C",[REV]<10000,"B",True,"A")
```

This function tells Access that if REV is less than 1000, then return a value of "D". If REV is less than 5000, then return a value of "C". If REV is less than 10000, then return "B". If all else fails, use "A". Figure 6-24 demonstrates how you would use this function in a query.

NOTE You may shrewdly notice that those records that are less than 1000 will also be less than 10,000. So why don't all the records get tagged with a value of "B"? Remember that the Switch function evaluates your expressions from left to right and only returns the value of the first expression that evaluates to True.

In this light, you want to sort the expressions in your Switch function accordingly, using an order that is conducive to the logic of your analysis.

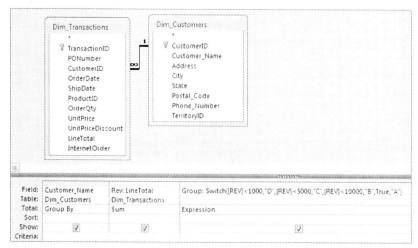

Figure 6-24: Using the Switch function is sometimes more practical than using nested IIf functions. This query will classify customers by how much they spend.

When you run the query, you see the resulting dataset shown in Figure 6-25.

Customer_Name ▾	Rev ▾	Group ▾
ACASCO Corp.	$253.00	D
ACECUL Corp.	$14,771.00	A
ACEHUA Corp.	$9,095.00	B
ACOPUL Corp.	$10,190.00	A
ACORAR Corp.	$4,750.00	C
ACSBUR Corp.	$33.00	D
ADACEC Corp.	$395.00	D
ADADUL Corp.	$5,637.00	B
ADANAS Corp.	$8,573.00	B
ADCOMP Corp.	$4,206.00	C
ADDATI Corp.	$1,020.00	C
ADDOUS Corp.	$921.00	D

Figure 6-25: Each customer is conditionally tagged with a group designation based on annual revenue.

Summary

You will often need to perform analyses where specifications and circumstances for the analysis are variable. That is, the parameters and conditions for the analysis change each time you run it. In such cases, you need to perform a *conditional analysis*—an analysis whose outcome depends on a pre-defined set of conditions. Access has several built-in tools that enable conditional analyses; some of these are parameter queries, the IIf function, and the Switch function.

A *parameter query* is an interactive query that prompts you for criteria before the query runs. You often use this type of query when you need to pass different criteria each time the query runs. Running a parameter query forces the Enter Parameter Value dialog box to open and ask for a variable or criteria. You would simply enter your parameter, as shown in Figure 6-3.

Parameter queries are not the only tools in Access that allow for conditional analysis. Access also has built-in functions that facilitate value comparisons, data validation, and conditional evaluation. These conditional functions (also called program flow functions) are designed to test for conditions and provide different outcomes based on the results of those tests. Two of these functions are the IIf function and the Switch function.

The IIf (immediate if) function replicates the functionality of Excel's IF function, evaluating a specific condition as True or False. The IIf function saves steps in your analytical processes and, ultimately, saves time. The Switch function enables you to evaluate a list of expressions and return the value associated with the expression determined to be True. The power of the Switch function comes in evaluating multiple expressions at one time and determining which one is True.

Leveraging and employing conditional analysis is not only easy but helps save you time, organizes your analytical processes, and ultimately enhances your analysis.

Part

III

Advanced Analysis Techniques

In This Part

Adding Dimension with Subqueries and Domain Aggregate Functions

Often, you will carry out your analyses in layers, each layer of analysis using or building on the previous layer. Building layers into analytical processes is actually very common. For instance, when you build a query using another query as the data source, you are layering your analysis. When you build a query based on a temporary table created by a make-table query, you are also layering your analysis.

All these conventional methods of layering analyses have two things in common.

- They all add a step to your analytical processes. Every query that has to be run in order to feed another query, or every temporary table that has to be created in order to advance your analysis, adds yet another task that must be completed before you get your final results.

- They all require the creation of temporary tables or transitory queries, inundating your database with table and query objects that lead to a confusing analytical process as well as a database that bloats easily.

This is where subqueries and domain aggregate functions can help. *Subqueries* and *domain aggregate* functions allow you to build layers into your analysis within one query, eliminating the need for temporary tables or transitory queries.

NOTE The topic of subqueries and domain aggregate functions requires an understanding of *SQL (Structured Query Language)*. Most beginning Access users don't have the foundation in SQL. If you fall into this category, press the pause button here and review Appendix B of this book. There, you'll receive enough of a primer on SQL to continue this chapter.

Enhancing Your Analysis with Subqueries

Subqueries (sometimes referred to as *subselect queries*) are select queries nested in other queries. The primary purpose of a subquery is to enable you to use the results of one query within the execution of another. With subqueries, you can answer a multiple-part question, specify criteria for further selection, or define new fields for use in your analysis.

The query shown in Figure 7-1 demonstrates how to use a subquery in the design grid. As you look at this, remember that this is just one example of how a subquery can be used. Subqueries are not limited to use as criteria.

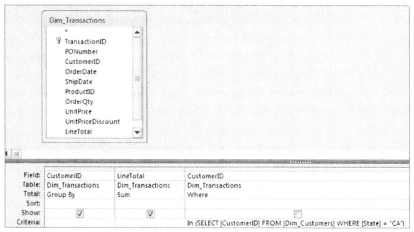

Figure 7-1: To use a subquery in Query Design view, simply enter the SQL statement.

If you were to build the query in Figure 7-1 and switch to SQL view, you would see a SQL statement similar to this one. Can you pick out the subquery? Look for the second SELECT statement.

```
SELECT CustomerID, Sum(LineTotal) AS SumOfLineTotal
FROM Dim_Transactions
WHERE CustomerID IN
(SELECT [CustomerID] FROM [Dim_Customers] WHERE [State] = "CA")
GROUP BY CustomerID
```

NOTE Subqueries must always be enclosed in parentheses.

The idea behind a subquery is that the subquery is executed first, and the results are used in the outer query (the query in which the subquery is embedded) as a criterion, an expression, a parameter, and so on. In the example shown in Figure 7-1, the subquery first returns a list of CustomerIDs for customers in California. Then the outer query uses that list as criteria to filter out any CustomerIDs not in California.

Why Use Subqueries?

You should know that subqueries often run more slowly than standard queries using joins. This is because subqueries either are executed against an entire dataset or are evaluated multiple times—one time per each row processed by the outer query. This makes them slow to execute, especially if you have a large dataset. So why use them?

Many analyses require multiple step processes that use temporary tables or transitory queries. Although there is nothing inherently wrong with temporary tables and queries, an excess number of them in your analytical processes could lead to a confusing analytical process as well as a database that bloats easily.

Even though using subqueries comes with a performance hit, it may be an acceptable trade for streamlined procedures and optimized analytical processes. You will even find that as you become more comfortable with writing your own SQL statements, you will use subqueries in on-the-fly queries to *save* time.

Subquery Ground Rules

There are a few rules and restrictions that you must be aware of when using subqueries.

- Your subquery must have, at a minimum, a SELECT statement and a FROM clause in its SQL string.

- You must enclose your subquery in parentheses.

- Theoretically, you can nest up to 31 subqueries within a query. This number, however, is based on your system's available memory and the complexity of your subqueries.

- You can use a subquery in an expression as long as it returns a single value.

- You cannot use the DISTINCT keyword in a subquery that includes the GROUP BY clause.

Creating Subqueries Without Typing SQL Statements

You may have a tendency to shy away from subqueries because you may feel uncomfortable with writing your own SQL statements. Indeed, many of the SQL statements necessary to perform the smallest analysis can seem daunting.

Imagine, for example, that you have been asked to provide the number of account managers that have a time in service greater than the average time in service for all account managers. Sounds like a relatively simple analysis, and it *is* simple when you use a subquery. But where do you start? Well, you could just write an SQL statement into the SQL view of a query and run it. But the truth is that not many Access users create SQL statements from scratch. The smart ones utilize the built-in functionalities of Access to save time and avoid headaches. The trick is to split the analysis into manageable pieces, as shown in the following steps:

1. Find the average time in service for all account managers. To do this, create the query shown in Figure 7-2.

Figure 7-2: Create a query to find the average time in service for all account managers.

2. Switch to SQL view, shown in Figure 7-3, and copy the SQL statement.

Figure 7-3: Switch to SQL view and copy the SQL statement.

3. Create a query that will count the number of account managers by time in service. Figure 7-4 does just that.

4. Right-click in the Criteria row under the TIS_in_Months field and select Zoom. This opens the Zoom dialog shown in Figure 7-5. The Zoom dialog does nothing more than help you more comfortably work with text that is too long to be easily seen at one time in the query grid.

5. With the Zoom dialog box open, paste the SQL statement you copied previously into to the white input area.

NOTE Remember that subqueries must be enclosed in parentheses, so you want to enter parentheses around the SQL statement you just pasted. You also need to make sure you delete all carriage returns that were put in automatically by Access.

6. Finish off the query by entering a greater than (>) sign in from of your subquery and change the aggregate function of the TIS_in_Months row to a WHERE clause. At this point, your query should look like the one shown in Figure 7-6.

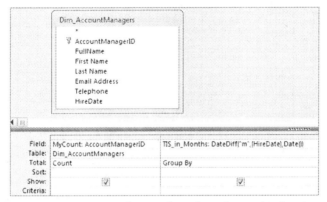

Figure 7-4: Create a query to count the number of employees by time in service.

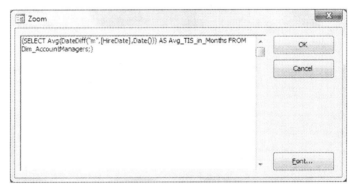

Figure 7-5: Paste the first SQL statement you copied into the Criteria row of the TIS_IN _MONTHS field.

Now if you go to the SQL view of the query shown in Figure 7-6, you will see the following SQL statement:

```
SELECT Count(AccountManagerID) AS MyCount
FROM Dim_AccountManagers
WHERE (((DateDiff("m",[HireDate],Date())))
>(SELECT Avg(DateDiff("m",[HireDate],Date())) AS Avg_TIS_in_Months
FROM Dim_AccountManagers;)));
```

The beauty is that you do not have to type all this syntax. You simply use your knowledge of Access to piece together the necessary actions that needed to be taken in order to get to the answer. As you become more familiar with SQL, you will find that you can create subqueries manually with no problems.

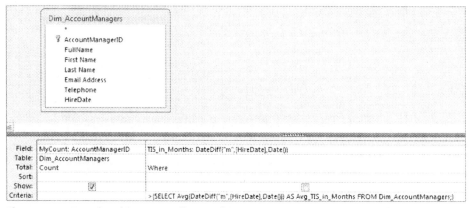

Figure 7-6: Running this query tells you there are 12 account managers that have a time in service greater than the company average.

Using IN and NOT IN with Subqueries

The IN and NOT IN operators enable you to run two queries in one. The idea is that the subquery executes first, and then the outer query uses the resulting dataset to filter the final output.

The example demonstrated in Figure 7-7 first runs a subquery that selects all customers based in CA (California). The outer query then uses the resulting dataset as a criteria to return the sum of LineTotal for only those customers that match the customer numbers returned in the subquery.

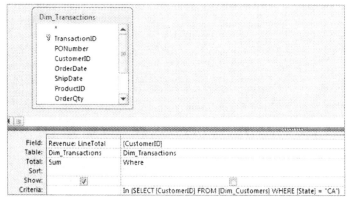

Figure 7-7: This query uses the IN operator with a subquery, allowing you to run two queries in one.

You would use NOT IN to go the opposite way and return the sum of LineTotal for customers that do not match the customer numbers returned in the subquery.

TIP You can find the query examples in this section in the sample database for this book, located at www.wiley.com.

Using Subqueries with Comparison Operators

As its name implies, a comparison operator (=, <, >, <=, >=, <>, and so on) compares two items and returns True or False. When you use a subquery with a comparison operator, you are asking Access to compare the resulting dataset of your outer query to that of the subquery.

For example, to return all customers who have purchases greater than the average purchase for all customers, you can use the following query (Figure 7-8):

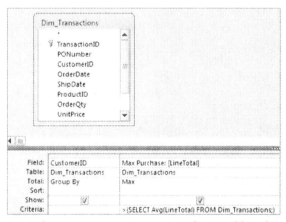

Figure 7-8: Use comparison operators to compare the resulting dataset of your outer query to the results of the subquery.

The subquery runs first, giving you the average purchase for all customers. This is a single value that Access then uses to compare the outer query's resulting dataset. In other words, the max purchase for each customer is compared to the company average. If a customer's maximum purchase is greater than the company average, it is included in the final output; otherwise, it is excluded.

NOTE A subquery used with a comparison operator must return a single value.

Using Subqueries as Expressions

In every example so far, you have used subqueries in conjunction with the WHERE clause, effectively using the results of a subquery as criteria for your outer query. However, you can also use a subquery as an expression, as long as the subquery returns a single value. The query shown in Figure 7-9 demonstrates how you can use a subquery as an expression in a calculation.

Figure 7-9: You are using a subquery as an expression in a calculation.

This example uses a subquery to get the average units sold by the entire company; that subquery returns a single value. You are then using that value in a calculation to determine the variance between each market's average units sold and the average for the company. The output of this query is shown in Figure 7-10.

Market	Market Avg	Variance from Company Avg
Asia	1,142	-612
Australia	1,119	-635
Northern Europe	2,647	893
South America	1,165	-589
Southern Europe	1,800	46
United Kingdom	2,591	837
United States	1,814	60

Figure 7-10: Your query result.

Using Correlated Subqueries

A *correlated query* is essentially a subquery that refers back to a column that is in the outer query. What makes correlated subqueries unique is that while standard subqueries are evaluated one time to get a result, a correlated subquery has to be evaluated multiple times: once for each row processed by the outer query. To illustrate this point, consider the following two SQL statements.

Uncorrelated Subqueries

This SQL statement uses an uncorrelated subquery. How can you tell? The subquery does not reference any column in the outer query. This subquery is evaluated one time to give you the average revenue for the entire dataset.

```
SELECT MainSummary.Branch_Number,
    (SELECT Avg(Revenue)FROM MainSummary)
    FROM MainSummary
```

Correlated Subqueries

This SQL statement uses a correlated subquery. The subquery reaches back into the outer query and references the Branch_Number column, effectively forcing the subquery to be evaluated for every row that is processed by the outer query. The result of this query is a dataset that shows the average revenue for every branch in the company. Figure 7-11 demonstrates how this SQL statement looks in Design View.

```
SELECT MainSummary.Branch_Number,
    (SELECT Avg(Revenue)FROM MainSummary AS M2
    WHERE M2.Branch_Number = MainSummary.Branch_Number) AS AvgByBranch
FROM MainSummary
GROUP BY MainSummary.Branch_Number
```

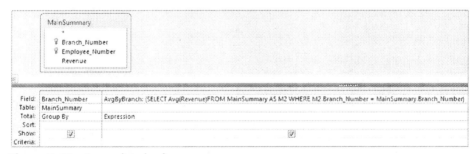

Figure 7-11: A correlated subquery

USING ALIASES WITH CORRELATED SUBQUERIES

Notice that in the correlated subquery, you are using the `AS` clause to establish a table alias of "M2." The reason for this is that the subquery and the outer query are both utilizing the same table. By giving one of the tables an alias, you allow Access to distinguish exactly which table you are referring to in your SQL statement. Although the alias in this SQL statement is assigned to the subquery, you can just as easily assign an alias to the table in the outer query.

Note that the character "M2" holds no significance. In fact, you can use any text string you like, as long as the alias and the table name combined do not exceed 255 characters.

To assign an alias to a table in Design view, simply right-click the field list and select Properties, as shown in Figure 7-12.

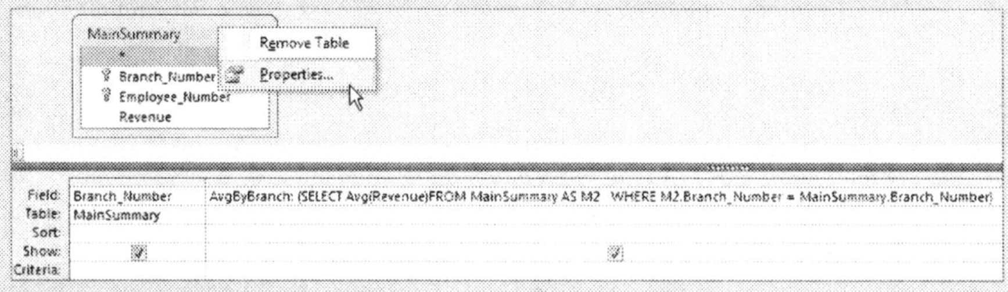

Figure 7-12: Right-click the field list and select Properties.

Next, edit the Alias property to the one you want to use (see Figure 7-13). You know that it takes effect when the name on the Field List changes to your new alias.

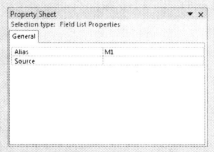

Figure 7-13: Enter the table alias into the Alias property.

TIP Try to give your tables alias names that make sense. For example, if both your outer query and subquery are using the MainSummary table, you can give the table an alias of M1 in your outer query, while naming the same table M2 in your subquery. This gives you an easy visual indication of which table you're referring to.

Using a Correlated Subquery as an Expression

The example shown in Figure 7-9 uses an uncorrelated subquery to determine the variance between each market's average units sold and the average units for the company.

You can apply the same type of technique to correlated subqueries. In the query demonstrated in Figure 7-14, a correlation for each branch number allows you to determine the variance between each employee's annual revenue and the average revenue for that employee's branch.

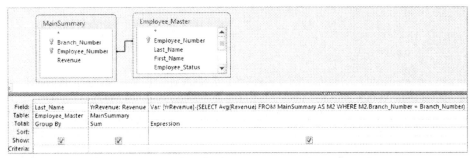

Figure 7-14: You can use a correlated subquery as part of an expression.

Using Subqueries Within Action Queries

Action queries can be fitted with subqueries just as easily as select queries can. Here are a few examples of how you would use a subquery in an action query.

A Subquery in a Make-Table Query

This example illustrates how to use a subquery within a make-table query.

```
SELECT E1.Employee_Number, E1.Last_Name, E1.First_Name
INTO OldSchoolEmployees
FROM Employee_Master as E1
WHERE E1.Employee_Number IN
    (SELECT E2.Employee_Number
    FROM Employee_Master AS E2
    WHERE E2.Hire_Date <#1/1/1995#)
```

A Subquery in an Append Query

This example uses a subquery within an append query.

```
INSERT INTO CustomerMaster (Customer_Number, Customer_Name, State )
SELECT CompanyNumber,CompanyName,State
FROM LeadList
WHERE CompanyNumber Not In
    (SELECT Customer_Number FROM CustomerMaster)
```

A Subquery in an Update Query

This example uses a subquery in an update query.

```
UPDATE PriceMaster SET Price = [Price]*1.1
WHERE Branch_Number In
     (SELECT Branch_Number FROM LocationMaster WHERE Region = "South")
```

A Subquery in a Delete Query

This example uses a subquery in a delete query.

```
DELETE CompanyNumber
FROM LeadList
WHERE CompanyNumber In
     (SELECT Customer_Number FROM CustomerMaster)
```

TRICKS OF THE TRADE: GETTING THE SECOND QUARTILE OF A DATASET WITH ONE QUERY

You can easily pull out the second quartile of a dataset by using a top values subquery.

1. The first step is to create a top values query that returns the top 25 percent of your dataset. Again, you can specify that a query is a top values query by right-clicking the grey area above the white query grid and selecting Properties. Once in the Property Sheet dialog, adjust the Top Values property to return the top Nth value you need as demonstrated in Figure 7-15. For this example, use 25 percent.

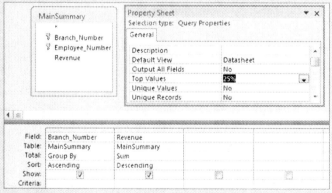

Figure 7-15: Create a query that returns the top 25 percent of your dataset.

2. Next, switch to SQL view, shown in Figure 7-16, and copy the SQL string.

TRICKS OF THE TRADE: GETTING THE SECOND QUARTILE OF A DATASET WITH ONE QUERY

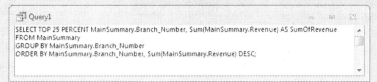

Figure 7-16: Copy the SQL statement that makes up the query.

3. **Switch back to Design view. The idea is to paste the SQL statement you just copied into the Criteria row of the Branch_Number field. To do this, right-click inside the Criteria row of the Branch_Number field and select Zoom. Then paste the SQL statement inside the Zoom dialog box, as shown in Figure 7-17.**

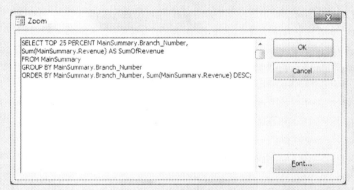

Figure 7-17: Paste the SQL statement into the Criteria row of Branch_Number.

4. **This next part is a little tricky. You need to perform the following edits on the SQL statement in order to make it work for this situation:**

   a. **Because this subquery is a criterion for the Branch_Number field, you only need to select Branch_Number in the SQL statement; therefore, you can remove the line** Sum(MainSummary.Revenue) AS SumOfRevenue.

   b. **Remove the comma at the end of the first line.**

   c. **Delete all carriage returns.**

   d. **Place parentheses around the subquery and put the NOT IN operator in front of it all.**

(continued)

TRICKS OF THE TRADE: GETTING THE SECOND QUARTILE OF A DATASET WITH ONE QUERY *(continued)*

At this point, your Zoom dialog box should look like the one shown in Figure 7-18.

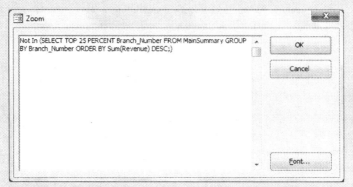

Figure 7-18: Apply a few edits so that the subquery works as criteria.

At this point, you can switch to Design View. If all went well, you query should look similar to Figure 7-19.

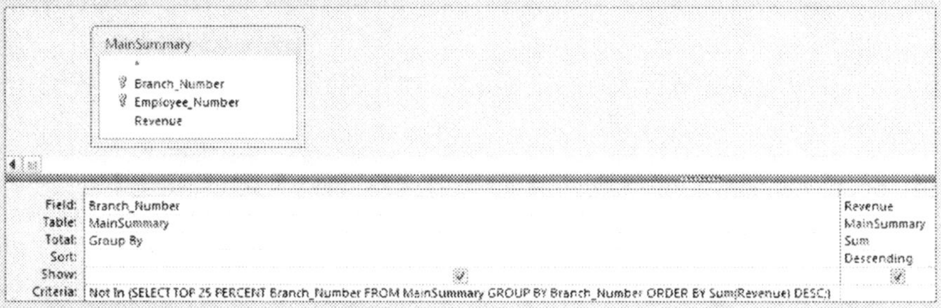

Figure 7-19: Your query is ready to run.

There you have it. Running this query returns the second quartile in the dataset. To get the third quartile, simply replace TOP 25 PERCENT in the subquery with TOP 50 PERCENT; to get the fourth quartile, use TOP 75 PERCENT.

NOTE Be sure to check this book's sample file to get a few more examples that highlight how subqueries can help you find solutions to common analytical needs.

Domain Aggregate Functions

Domain aggregate functions enable you to extract and aggregate statistical information from an entire dataset (a domain). These functions differ from aggregate queries in that aggregate queries group data before evaluating the values, whereas domain aggregate functions evaluate the values for entire datasets; thus, a domain aggregate function never returns more than one value. To get a clear understanding of the difference between an aggregate query and a domain aggregate function, build the query shown in Figure 7-20.

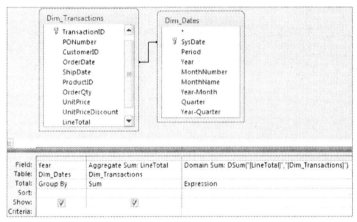

Figure 7-20: This query shows you the difference between an aggregate query and a domain aggregate function.

Run the query to get the results you see in Figure 7-21. You will notice that the Aggregate Sum column contains a different total for each year, whereas the Domain Sum column (the domain aggregate function) contains only one total (for the entire dataset).

Year	Aggregate Sum	Domain Sum
2006	$16,402,702.80	164564683.25
2007	$45,317,067.40	164564683.25
2008	$61,776,867.10	164564683.25
2009	$41,068,045.95	164564683.25

Figure 7-21: You can clearly see the difference between an aggregate query and a domain aggregate function.

NOTE Although the examples in this chapter show the use of domain aggregate functions in query expressions, keep in mind that you can use these functions in macros, modules, or the calculated controls of forms and reports.

THE ANATOMY OF DOMAIN AGGREGATE FUNCTIONS

There are 12 different domain aggregate functions, but they all have the same anatomy:

`FunctionName("[Field Name]","[Dataset Name]", "[Criteria]")`

- `FunctionName`: **This is the name of the domain aggregate function you are using.**

- `Field Name` **(required): This expression identifies the field containing the data with which you are working.**

- `Dataset Name` **(required): This expression identifies the table or query you are working with; also known as the domain.**

- `Criteria` **(optional): This expression restricts the range of data on which the domain aggregate function is performed. If no criterion is specified, the domain aggregate function is performed against the entire dataset.**

NOTE You cannot use a parameter query with a domain aggregate function.

Understanding the Different Domain Aggregate Functions

There are 12 different domain aggregate functions in Access, each one performing a different operation. The Table 7-1 lists each function with its purpose and utility.

Table 7-1: Domain Aggregate Functions

FUNCTION	PURPOSE
DSum	The DSum function returns the sum value of a specified field in the domain. For example, DSum("[LineTotal]", "[Dim_Transactions]") returns the total sum of LineTotal in the Dim_Transactions table.
DAvgf	The DAvg function returns the average value of a specified field in the domain. For example, DAvg("[LineTotal]", "[Dim_Transactions]") returns the average LineTotal in the Dim_Transactions table.
DCount	The DCount function returns the total number of records in the domain. DCount("*", "[Dim_Transactions]"), for example, returns the total number of records in the Dim_Transactions table.

FUNCTION	PURPOSE
DLookup	The DLookup function returns the first value of a specified field that matches the criteria you define within the DLookup function. If you don't supply criteria, the DLookup function returns a random value in the domain. For example, DLookUp("[Last_Name]","[Employee_Master]"," [Employee_Number]='42620' ") returns the value in the Last_Name field of the record where the Employee_Number is 42620.
DMin and DMax	The DMin and DMax functions return the minimum and maximum values in the domain, respectively. DMin("[LineTotal]","[Dim_Transactions]") returns the lowest LineTotal in the Dim_Transactions table, whereas DMax("[LineTotal]","[Dim_Transactions]") returns the highest LineTotal.
DFirst and DLast	The DFirst and DLast functions return the first and last values in the domain, respectively. DFirst("[LineTotal]", "[Dim_Transactions]") returns the first LineTotal in the Dim_Transactions table, whereas DLast("[LineTotal]", "[Dim_Transactions]") returns the last.
DStDev, DStDevP, DVar, and DvarP	You can use the DStDev and DStDevP functions to return the standard deviation across a population sample and a population, respectively. Similarly, the DVar and the DVarP functions return the variance across a population sample and a population, respectively. DStDev("[List_Price]", "[Dim_Products]") returns the standard deviation of all prices in the Dim_Products table. DVar ("[List_Price]", "[Dim_Products]") returns the variance of all prices in the Dim_Products table.

NOTE DLookup functions are particularly useful when you need to retrieve a value from an outside dataset.

Examining the Syntax of Domain Aggregate Functions

Domain aggregate functions are unique in that the syntax required to make them work varies depending on the scenario. This has produced some very frustrated users who have given up on domain aggregate functions altogether. This section describes some general guidelines that help you in building your domain aggregate functions.

Using No Criteria

In this example, you are summing the values in the LineTotal field from the Dim_Transactions table (domain). Your field names and dataset names must always be wrapped in quotes.

```
DSum("[LineTotal]","[Dim_Transactions]")
```

Also, note the use of brackets. Although not always required, it is generally a good practice to use brackets when identifying a field, a table, or a query.

Using Text Criteria

In this example, you are summing the values in the Revenue field from the PvTblFeed table (domain) where the value in the Branch_Number field is 301316. Note that the Branch_Number field is formatted as text. When specifying a criterion that is textual or a string, your criterion must be wrapped in single quotes. In addition, your entire criteria expression must be wrapped in double quotes.

```
DSum("[Revenue]", "[PvTblFeed]", "[Branch_Number] = '301316' ")
```

TIP You can use any valid WHERE clause in the criteria expression of your domain aggregate functions. This adds a level of functionality to domain aggregate functions, as they can support the use of multiple columns and logical operators such as AND, OR, NOT, and so on. An example is:

```
DSum("[Field1]", "[Table]", "[Field2] = 'A' OR [Field2] = 'B'
AND [Field3] = 2")
```

If you are referencing a control inside of a form or report, the syntax will change a bit.

```
DSum("[Revenue]", "[PvTblFeed]", "[Branch_Number] = ↵
' " & [MyTextControl] & " ' " )
```

Notice that you are using single quotes to convert the control's value to a string. In other words, if the value of the form control is 301316, then "[Branch_Number] = ' " & [MyTextControl] & " ' " is essentially translated to read "[Branch_Number] = '301316' ".

Using Number Criteria

In this example, you are summing the values in the LineTotal field from the Dim_Transactions table (domain) where the value in the LineTotal field is greater than 500. Notice that you are not using single quotes, as the LineTotal field is an actual number field.

```
DSum("[LineTotal]", "[Dim_Transactions]", "[LineTotal] > 500 ")
```

If you are referencing a control inside of a form or report, the syntax changes a bit.

```
DSum("[LineTotal]", "[Dim_Transactions]", "[LineTotal] >" ↵
[MyNumericControl])
```

Using Date Criteria

In this example, you are summing the values in the LineTotal field from the Dim_Transactions table (domain) where the value in the OrderDate field is 07/05/2008.

```
DSum("[LineTotal]", "[Dim_Transactions]", "[OrderDate] = #07/05/08# ")
```

If you are referencing a control inside of a form or report, the syntax changes a bit.

```
DSum("[LineTotal]", "[Dim_Transactions]", "[OrderDate] = ↵
#" & [MydateControl] & "#")
```

Notice that you are using number signs to convert the control's value to a date. In other words, if the value of the form control is 07/05/2008, then "[OrderDate] = #" & [MydateControl] & "#" is essentially translated to read "[OrderDate] = #07/05/2008# ".

Using Domain Aggregate Functions

Like subqueries, domain aggregate functions are not very efficient when it comes to performing large-scale analyses and crunching very large datasets. These functions are better suited for use in specialty analyses with smaller subsets of data. Indeed, you most often find domain aggregate functions in environments where the dataset being evaluated is predictable and con-trolled (form example, functions, forms, and reports). This is not to say, however, that domain aggregate functions don't have their place in your day-to-day data analysis. This section walks through some examples of how you can use domain aggregate functions to accomplish some common tasks.

Calculating the Percent of Total

The query shown in Figure 7-22 returns products by group and the sum of LineTotal for each product category. This is a worthwhile analysis, but you can easily enhance it by adding a column that gives you the percent of total revenue for each product.

Product_Category	Revenue
Bar Equipment	$1,806,137.90
Commercial Appliances	$8,634,337.05
Concession Equipment	$10,083,748.40
Fryers	$3,971,959.10
Ovens and Ranges	$58,399,471.75
Refrigerators and Coolers	$43,786,517.10
Warmers	$37,882,511.95

Figure 7-22: You want to add a column that shows the percent of total revenue for each product category.

To get the percent of the total dollar value that each product makes up, you naturally have to know the total dollar value of the entire dataset. This is where a DSum function can come in handy. The following DSum function returns the total value of the dataset:

```
DSum("[LineTotal]","[Dim_Transactions]")
```

Now you can use this function as an expression in the calculation that returns the "percent of total" for each product group. Figure 7-23 demonstrates how.

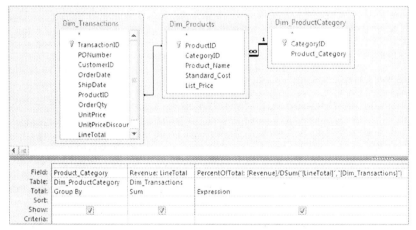

Figure 7-23: Use a DSum function as an expression in a calculation to get "percent of total."

The result, shown in Figure 7-24, proves that this is a quick and easy way to get both total by group and percent of total with one query.

Product_Category ▾	Revenue ▾	PercentOfTotal ▾
Bar Equipment	$1,806,137.90	1.10%
Commercial Appliances	$8,634,337.05	5.25%
Concession Equipment	$10,083,748.40	6.13%
Fryers	$3,971,959.10	2.41%
Ovens and Ranges	$58,399,471.75	35.49%
Refrigerators and Coolers	$43,786,517.10	26.61%
Warmers	$37,882,511.95	23.02%

Figure 7-24: You retrieved both total by group and percent of total with one query.

Creating a Running Count

The query in Figure 7-25 uses a DCount function as an expression to return the number of invoices processed on each specific invoice day.

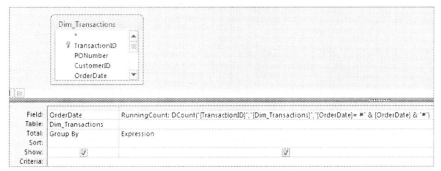

Figure 7-25: This query returns all invoice dates and the number of invoices processed on each date.

Take a moment to analyze what the DCount function is doing.

```
DCount("[TransactionID]","[Dim_Transactions]","[OrderDate]= ↵
#" & [OrderDate] & "#")
```

This DCount function retrieves the count of invoices where the invoice date equals (=) each invoice date returned by the query. In the context of the query shown in Figure 7-25, the resulting dataset shows each invoice date and its own count of invoices.

What would happen if you were to alter the DCount function to tell it to return the count of invoices where the invoice date equals or is earlier than (<=) each invoice date returned by the query, as follows?

```
DCount("[TransactionID]","[Dim_Transactions]","[OrderDate]<= ↵
#" & [OrderDate] & "#")
```

The DCount function would return the count of invoices for each date *and* the count of invoices for any earlier date, thereby giving you a running count.

To put this into action, simply replace the = operator in the DCount function with the <= operator, as shown in Figure 7-26.

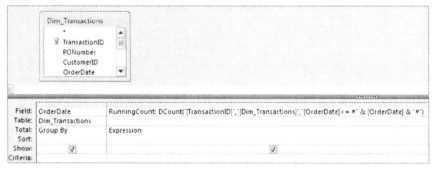

Figure 7-26: Use the <= operator in your DCount function to return the count of invoice dates that equals or is less than the date returned by the query.

Figure 7-27 shows the resulting running count.

OrderDate	RunningCount
7/1/2006	279
7/2/2006	283
7/3/2006	288
7/4/2006	290
7/5/2006	295
7/6/2006	299
7/7/2006	302
7/8/2006	305
7/9/2006	311
7/10/2006	314
7/11/2006	318
7/12/2006	322
7/13/2006	324
7/14/2006	331

Figure 7-27: You now have a running count in your analysis.

TIP You can achieve a running sum instead of a running count by using the DSum function.

Using a Value from the Previous Record

The query in Figure 7-28 uses a DLookup function to return the revenue value from the previous record. This value is placed into a new column called "Yesterday."

This method is similar to the one used when creating a running sum in that it revolves around manipulating a comparison operator in order to change the meaning of the domain aggregate function. In this case, DLookup searches for the revenue value where the invoice date is equal to each invoice date returned by the query minus one (-1). If you subtract one from a date, you get yesterday's date!

```
DLookUp("[Revenue]","[TimeSummary]","[OrderDate] = ↵
#" & [OrderDate]-1 & "#")
```

TIP If you add 1, you get the next record in the sequence. However, this trick does not work with textual fields. This only works with date and numeric fields. If you are working with a table that does not contain any numeric or date fields, create an autonumber field. This gives you a unique numeric identifier that you can use.

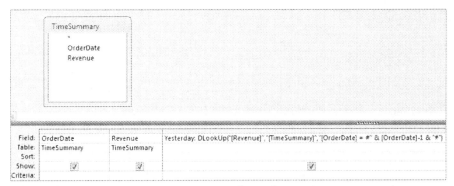

Figure 7-28: This query uses a `DLookup` to refer to the previous revenue value.

Running the query in Figure 7-28 yields the results shown in Figure 7-29.

OrderDate	Revenue	Yesterday
7/1/2006	$716,716.85	
7/2/2006	$18,548.00	716716.85
7/3/2006	$19,515.00	18548
7/4/2006	$9,274.00	19515
7/5/2006	$19,377.00	9274
7/6/2006	$18,548.00	19377
7/7/2006	$10,118.00	18548
7/8/2006	$10,118.00	10118
7/9/2006	$27,822.00	10118
7/10/2006	$13,911.00	27822
7/11/2006	$18,548.00	13911
7/12/2006	$18,548.00	18548
7/13/2006	$9,274.00	18548
7/14/2006	$32,459.00	9274

Figure 7-29: You can take this functionality a step further and perform a calculation on the Yesterday field.

You can enhance this analysis by adding a calculated field that gives you the dollar variance between today and yesterday. Create a new column and enter **[Revenue]-NZ([Yesterday],0)**, as shown in Figure 7-30. Note that the

Yesterday field is wrapped in an NZ function in order to avoid errors caused by null fields.

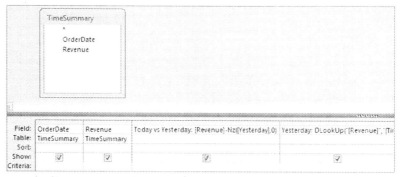

Figure 7-30: Enhance your analysis by adding a variance between today and yesterday.

Figure 7-31 shows the result.

OrderDate	Revenue	Today vs Yesterday	Yesterday
7/1/2006	$716,716.85	$716,716.85	
7/2/2006	$18,548.00	($698,168.85)	716716.85
7/3/2006	$19,515.00	$967.00	18548
7/4/2006	$9,274.00	($10,241.00)	19515
7/5/2006	$19,377.00	$10,103.00	9274
7/6/2006	$18,548.00	($829.00)	19377
7/7/2006	$10,118.00	($8,430.00)	18548
7/8/2006	$10,118.00	$0.00	10118
7/9/2006	$27,822.00	$17,704.00	10118
7/10/2006	$13,911.00	($13,911.00)	27822
7/11/2006	$18,548.00	$4,637.00	13911
7/12/2006	$18,548.00	$0.00	18548
7/13/2006	$9,274.00	($9,274.00)	18548
7/14/2006	$32,459.00	$23,185.00	9274

Figure 7-31: Another task made possible by domain aggregate functions

Summary

Subqueries and domain aggregate functions allow you to build layers into your analysis within one query, eliminating the need for temporary tables or transitory queries. You can leverage both subqueries and domain aggregate functions to streamline your analytical processes, as well as expand and enhance your analysis.

Subqueries are select queries nested within other queries, allowing you to use the results of one query within the execution of another. The idea behind a subquery is that the subquery is executed first, and the results are used in the outer query (the query in which the subquery is embedded) as a criterion, an expression, a parameter, and so on. Although subqueries often run more slowly than standard queries using joins, there are situations where the performance hit may be an acceptable trade for streamlined procedures and optimized analytical processes.

Domain aggregate functions enable you to extract and aggregate statistical information from an entire dataset (a domain). Unlike aggregate queries where the data is grouped before evaluation, domain aggregate functions evaluate the values for the entire dataset. There are 12 different domain aggregate functions: `DSum`, `DAvg`, `DCount`, `DLookup`, `DMin`, `DMax`, `DFirst`, `DLast` `DStDev`, `DStDevP`, `DVar`, and `DVarP`. Domain aggregate functions are ideal for specialty analyses such as calculating the percent of total, creating a running count, creating a running sum, or using values from previous records.

Running Descriptive Statistics in Access

Descriptive statistics allow you to present large amounts of data in quantitative summaries that are simple to understand. When you sum data, count data, and average data, you are producing descriptive statistics. It is important to note that descriptive statistics are used only to profile a dataset and enable comparisons that can be used in other analyses. This is different from *inferential statistics*, where you infer conclusions that extend beyond the scope of the data. To help solidify the difference between descriptive and inferential statistics, consider a customer survey. Descriptive statistics summarize the survey results for all customers and describe the data in understandable metrics, while inferential statistics infer conclusions such as customer loyalty based on the observed differences between groups of customers.

When it comes to inferential statistics, Excel is better suited to handle these types of analyses than Access. Why? First, Excel comes with a plethora of built-in functions and tools that make it easy to perform inferential statistics; tools that Access simply does not have. Secondarily, inferential statistics are usually performed on small subsets of data that can flexibly be analyzed and presented by Excel. Running *descriptive statistics*, on the other hand, is quite practical in Access. In fact, running descriptive statistics in Access versus Excel is often the smartest option due to the structure and volume of the dataset.

TIP The examples shown in this chapter can be found in the sample database for this book. The sample database for this book can be found on `Wrox.com`.

Basic Descriptive Statistics

This section discusses some of the basic tasks you can perform by using descriptive statistics, including:

- Running descriptive statistics with aggregate queries
- Ranking records in a dataset
- Determining the mode and median of a dataset
- Creating random samplings from a dataset

Running Descriptive Statistics with Aggregate Queries

At this point in the book, you have run many Access queries, some of which have been aggregate queries. Little did you know that when you ran those aggregate queries, you were actually creating descriptive statistics. It's true. The simplest descriptive statistics can be generated using an aggregate query. To demonstrate this point, build the query shown in Figure 8-1.

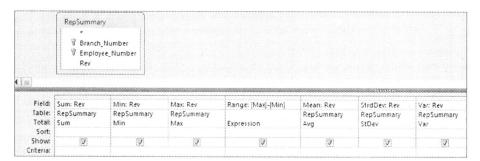

Figure 8-1: Running this aggregate query provides a useful set of descriptive statistics.

Similar to the descriptive statistics functionality found in Excel, the result of this query, shown in Figure 8-2, provides key statistical metrics for the entire dataset.

Sum	Min	Max	Range	Mean	StrdDev	Var
$10,774,159	$86	$137,707	$137,621	$16,009	$21,059	$443,484,375

Figure 8-2: Key statistical metrics for the entire dataset.

You can easily add layers to your descriptive statistics. In Figure 8-3, you are adding the Branch_Number field to your query. This gives you key statistical metrics for each branch.

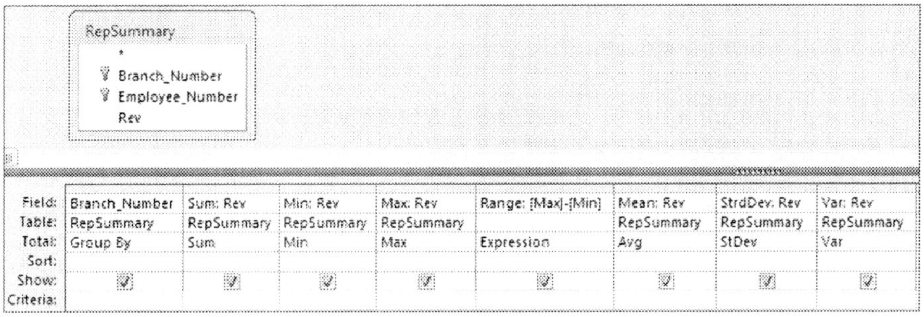

Figure 8-3: Add the Branch_Number field to your query to add another dimension to your analysis.

As you can see in Figure 8-4, you can now compare the descriptive statistics across branches to measure how they perform against each other.

Branch_Number ▾	Sum ▾	Min ▾	Max ▾	Range ▾	Mean ▾	StrdDev ▾	Var ▾
101313	$444,631	$124	$78,824	$78,700	$22,232	$29,111	$847,454,523
101419	$124,597	$99	$46,645	$46,546	$20,766	$19,027	$362,039,701
102516	$63,228	$678	$36,387	$35,709	$21,076	$18,390	$338,192,979
103516	$101,664	$151	$31,428	$31,277	$6,778	$9,338	$87,200,338
173901	$107,216	$402	$33,136	$32,734	$13,402	$13,371	$178,773,758
201605	$69,818	$624	$27,657	$27,033	$8,727	$9,496	$90,165,337
201709	$96,853	$184	$42,778	$42,593	$6,918	$12,375	$153,131,218
201714	$288,714	$145	$57,803	$57,658	$12,553	$15,901	$252,833,070
201717	$450,524	$169	$61,521	$61,352	$34,656	$25,160	$633,007,891
202600	$151,338	$277	$58,473	$58,196	$18,917	$25,557	$653,147,704
202605	$342,537	$147	$62,042	$61,895	$16,311	$17,878	$319,637,725
202714	$113,075	$546	$48,963	$48,417	$16,154	$17,503	$306,365,820
208605	$64,357	$439	$45,740	$45,301	$16,089	$20,721	$429,353,387

Figure 8-4: You have a one shot view of the descriptive statistics for each branch.

Determining Rank, Mode, and Median

Ranking the records in your dataset, getting the mode of a dataset, and getting the median of a dataset are all tasks that data analysts need to perform from time to time. Unfortunately, Access does not provide built-in functionality to perform these tasks easily. This means you have to come up with a way to carry out these descriptive statistics. In this section, you learn some of the techniques you can use to determine rank, mode, and median.

Ranking the Records in Your Dataset

You will undoubtedly encounter scenarios where you have to rank the records in your dataset based on a specific metric such as revenue. A record's rank is not only useful in presenting data; it is also a key variable when calculating advanced descriptive statistics such as median, percentile, and quartile.

The easiest way to determine a record's ranking within a dataset is by using a correlated subquery. The query shown in Figure 8-5 demonstrates how a rank is created using a subquery.

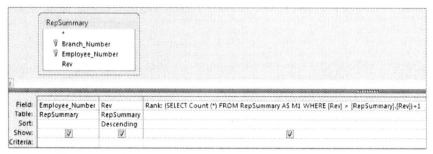

Figure 8-5: This query ranks employees by revenue.

Take a moment to examine the subquery that generates the rank.

```
(SELECT Count(*)FROM RepSummary AS M1 WHERE [Rev]>[RepSummary].[Rev])+1
```

This correlated subquery returns the total count of records from the M1 table (this is the RepSummary table with an alias of M1), where the Rev field in the M1 table is greater than the Rev field in the RepSummary table. The value returned by the subquery is then increased by one. Why increase the value by one? If you don't, the record with the highest value will return 0 because zero records are greater than the record with the highest value. The result would be that your ranking starts with 0 instead of 1. Adding one effectively ensures that your ranking starts with 1.

NOTE Because this is a correlated subquery, this subquery is evaluated for every record in your dataset, giving you a different rank value for each record. Correlated subqueries are covered in detail in Chapter 8. In Appendix B, you'll find a primer on using SQL syntax.

Figure 8-6 shows the result.

TIP This technique is also useful when you want to create an autonumber field within a query.

Getting the Mode of a Dataset

The *mode* of a dataset is the number that appears the most often in a set of numbers. For instance, the mode for 4, 5, 5, 6, 7, 5, 3, 4 is 5.

Employee_Number	Rank	Rev
64621	1	$137,707.14
4136	2	$111,681.81
5060	3	$106,299.32
56422	4	$102,239.87
56405	5	$83,525.72
160034	6	$78,823.82
60425	7	$77,452.50
3466	8	$76,789.52
52635	9	$76,684.54
52404	10	$76,532.26
3660	11	$75,690.33
1336	12	$75,489.77
56416	13	$75,358.76
55144	14	$74,653.99

Figure 8-6: You have created a Rank column for your dataset.

Unlike Excel, Access does not have a built-in Mode function, so you must create your own method of determining the mode of a dataset. Although there are various ways to get the mode of a dataset, one of the easiest is to use a query to count the occurrences of a certain data item, and then filter for the highest count. To demonstrate this method, build the query shown in Figure 8-7.

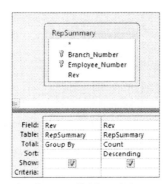

Figure 8-7: This query groups by the Rev field and then counts the occurrences of each number in Rev field. The query is sorted in descending order by Rev.

The results, shown in Figure 8-8, do not seem very helpful, but if you turn this into a top values query, returning only the top one record, you will effectively get the mode.

Change the Top Values property to 1, as shown in Figure 8-9, and you will get one record with the highest count.

As you can see in Figure 8-10, you now have only one Rev figure: the one that occurs most often. This is your mode.

NOTE Keep in mind that in the event of a tie, a top values query shows all records. This effectively gives you more than one mode. You must make a manual determination which mode to use.

Rev	CountOfRev
$158.60	4
$145.02	3
$154.55	3
$185.27	3
$245.78	3
$151.03	3
$122.89	3
$309.11	3
$254.34	2
$650.24	2
$168.82	2
$525.00	2

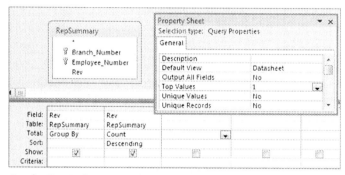

Figure 8-8: Almost there. Turn this into a top values query and you'll have your Mode.

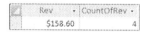

Figure 8-9: Set the Top Values property to 1.

Rev	CountOfRev
$158.60	4

Figure 8-10: This is your mode.

Getting the Median of a Dataset

The *median* of a dataset is the middle number in the dataset. In other words, half of the numbers have values greater than the median, and half have values less than the median. For instance, the median number in 3, 4, 5, 6, 7, 8, 9 is 6 because 6 is the middle number of the dataset.

TIP **Why can't you just calculate an average and be done with it? Sometimes, calculating an average on a dataset that contains outliers can dramatically skew your analysis. For example, if you were to calculate an average on the numbers, 32, 34, 35, 37, and 89, you would get an answer of 45.4. The problem is that 45.4 does not accurately represent the central tendency of this sampling of numbers.**

Using median on this sample makes more sense. The median in this case would be 35, which is more representative of what's going on in this data.

Access does not have a built-in Median function, so you have to create your own method of determining the median of a dataset. An easy way to get the median is to build a query in two steps. The first step is to create a query that sorts and ranks your records. The query shown in Figure 8-11 sorts and ranks the records in the RepSummary table.

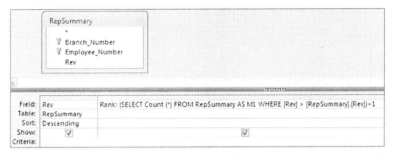

Figure 8-11: The first step in finding the median of a dataset is to assign a rank to each record.

The next step is to identify the middle-most record in your dataset by counting the total number of records in the dataset and then dividing that number by two. This gives you a middle value. The idea is that because the records are now sorted and ranked, the record that has the same rank as the middle value is the median. Figure 8-12 shows the subquery that returns a middle value for the dataset. Note that the value is wrapped in an Int function to strip out the fractional portion of the number.

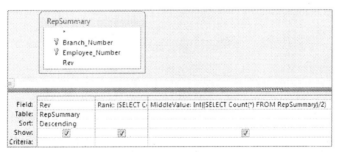

Figure 8-12: The Middle Value subquery counts all the records in the dataset and then divides that number by 2.

As you can see in Figure 8-13, the middle value is 336. You can go down to record 336 to see the median.

Rev ▾	Rank ▾	MiddleValue ▾
$137,707.14	1	336
$111,681.81	2	336
$106,299.32	3	336
$102,239.87	4	336
$83,525.72	5	336
$78,823.82	6	336
$77,452.50	7	336
$76,789.52	8	336
$76,684.54	9	336
$76,532.26	10	336
$75,690.33	11	336
$75,489.77	12	336
$75,358.76	13	336
$74,653.99	14	336

Figure 8-13: Go down to record 336 to get the median value of the dataset.

If you want to return only the median value, simply use the subquery as a criterion for the Rank field, as shown in Figure 8-14.

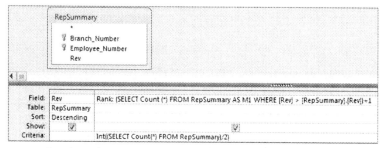

Figure 8-14: Using the subquery as a criterion for the Rank field will ensure that only the median value is returned.

Pulling a Random Sampling from Your Dataset

Although the creation of a random sample of data does not necessarily fall into the category of descriptive statistics, a random sampling is often the basis for statistical analysis.

There are many ways to create a random sampling of data in Access, but one of the easiest is to use the Rnd function within a top values query. The Rnd function returns a random number based on an initial value. The idea is to build an expression that applies the Rnd function to a field that contains numbers, and then limit the records returned by setting the Top Values property of the query.

To demonstrate this method, follow these steps:

1. Start a query in Design view on the TransactionMaster table.

2. Create a Random ID field, as shown in Figure 8-15, and then sort the field (either ascending or descending will work).

NOTE The Rnd function does not work with fields that contain text or Null values. Strangely enough, though, the Rnd function works with fields that contain all numerical values even if the field is formatted as a Text type field.

If your table is made up of fields that only contain text, you can add an Autonumber field to use with the Rnd function. Another option is to pass the field containing text through the Len function, and then use that expression in your Rnd function. For example: Rnd(Len([Mytext])).

Figure 8-15: Start by creating a Random ID field using the Rnd function with the Customer_Number field.

3. Change the Top Values property of the query to the number of random records you want returned. The scenario shown in Figure 8-16 limits this dataset to 1,000 records.

4. Set the Show row for the Random ID field to false and add the fields you want to see in your dataset.

5. Run the query and you will have a completely random sampling of data.

WARNING Re-running the query, switching the view state, or sorting the dataset, results in a different set of random records. If you want to perform extensive analysis on an established set of random records that does not change, you must run this query as a Make-Table query in order to create a hard table.

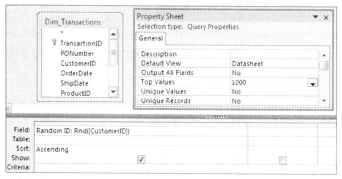

Figure 8-16: Limit the number of records returned by setting the Top Values property of the query.

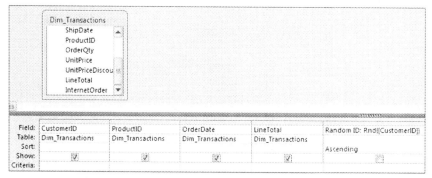

Figure 8-17: Running this query produces a sample 1,000 random records.

Advanced Descriptive Statistics

When working with descriptive statistics, a little knowledge goes a long way. Indeed, basic statistical analyses often lead to more advanced statistical analyses. In this section, you build on the fundamentals you have just learned to create advanced descriptive statistics.

Calculating Percentile Ranking

A *percentile rank* indicates the standing of a particular score relative to the normal group standard. Percentiles are most notably used in determining performance on standardized tests. If a child scores in the 90th percentile on a standardized test, this means that his score is higher than 90 percent of the other children taking the test. Another way to look at it is to say that his score is in the top 10 percent of all the children taking the test. Percentiles are often used in data analysis as a method of measuring a subject's performance in relation to the group as a whole—for instance, determining the percentile ranking for each employee based on annual revenue.

Calculating a percentile ranking for a dataset is simply a mathematical operation. The formula for a percentile rank is `(Record Count-Rank)/Record Count`. The trick is to getting all the variables needed for this mathematical operation.

To start, follow these steps:

1. Build the query you see in Figure 8-18. This query will start by ranking each employee by annual revenue. Be sure to give you new field an alias of "Rank."

2. Add a field that counts all the records in your dataset. As you can see in Figure 8-19, you are using a subquery to do this. Be sure to give your new field an alias of "RCount."

3. Create a calculated field with the expression `(RCount-Rank)/RCount`. At this point, your query should look like the one shown in Figure 8-20.

4. Running the query give you the results shown in Figure 8-21.

Again, the resulting dataset enables you to measure each employee's performance in relation to the group as a whole. For example, the employee ranked sixth in the dataset is in the 99th percentile, meaning this employee earned more revenue than 99 percent of other employees.

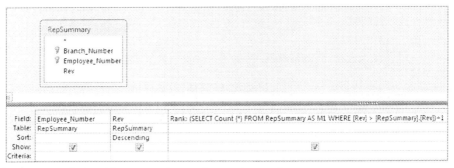

Figure 8-18: Start with a query that ranks employees by revenue.

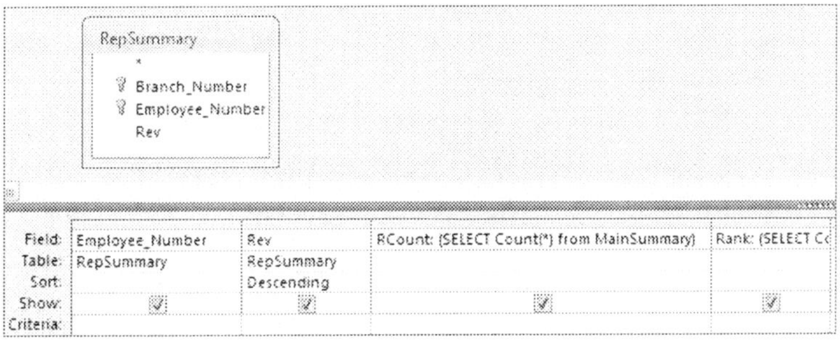

Figure 8-19: Add a field that returns a total dataset count.

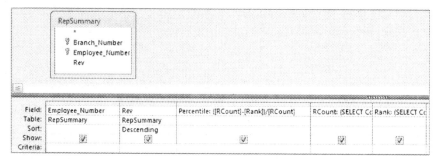

Figure 8-20: The final step is to create a calculated field that gives you the percentile rank for each record.

Rank ▾	Percentile ▾	Employee_Number ▾	Rev ▾	RCount ▾
1	99.85%	64621	$137,707.14	673
2	99.70%	4136	$111,681.81	673
3	99.55%	5060	$106,299.32	673
4	99.41%	56422	$102,239.87	673
5	99.26%	56405	$83,525.72	673
6	99.11%	160034	$78,823.82	673
7	98.96%	60425	$77,452.50	673
8	98.81%	3466	$76,789.52	673
9	98.66%	52635	$76,684.54	673
10	98.51%	52404	$76,532.26	673
11	98.37%	3660	$75,690.33	673
12	98.22%	1336	$75,489.77	673
13	98.07%	56416	$75,358.76	673
14	97.92%	55144	$74,653.99	673

Figure 8-21: You've successfully calculated the percentile rank for each employee.

Determining the Quartile Standing of a Record

A *quartile* is a statistical division of a dataset into four equal groups, with each group making up 25 percent of the dataset. The top 25 percent of a collection is considered to be the first quartile, whereas the bottom 25 percent is considered the fourth quartile. Quartile standings typically are used for the purposes of separating data into logical groupings that can be compared and analyzed individually. For example, if you want to establish a minimum performance standard around monthly revenue, you could set the minimum to equal the average revenue for employees in the second quartile. This ensures you have a minimum performance standard that at least 50 percent of your employees have historically achieved or exceeded.

Establishing the quartile for each record in a dataset does not involve a mathematical operation; rather, it is a question of comparison. The idea is to compare each record's rank value to the quartile benchmarks for the dataset. What are quartile benchmarks? Imagine that your dataset contains 100 records. Dividing 100 by 4 would give you the first quartile benchmark (25). This means that any record with a rank of 25 or less is in the first quartile. To get the second quartile benchmark, you would calculate 100/4*2. To get the third, you would calculate 100/4*3 and so on.

Given that information, you know right away that you need to rank the records in your dataset and count the records in your dataset. Follow these steps:

1. Start by building the query shown in Figure 8-22. Build the Rank field the same way you did in Figure 8-18.

2. Build the RCount field the same way you did in Figure 8-19.

3. Once you create the Rank and RCount fields in your query, you can use these fields in a `Switch` function that tag each record with the appropriate quartile standing. Take a moment and look at the `Switch` function you will be using.

```
Switch([Rank]<=[RCount]/4*1,"1st",[Rank]<=[RCount]/4*2,"2nd",
[Rank]<= [RCount]/4*3,"3rd",True,"4th")
```

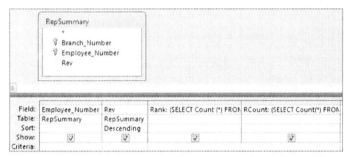

Figure 8-22: Start by creating a field named Rank that ranks each employee by revenue and a field named RCount that counts the total records in the dataset.

This `Switch` function is going through four conditions, comparing each record's rank value to the quartile benchmarks for the dataset.

NOTE For more information on the `Switch` function, see Chapter 6.

Figure 8-23 demonstrates how this `Switch` function fits into the query. Note that you are using an alias of Quartile here.

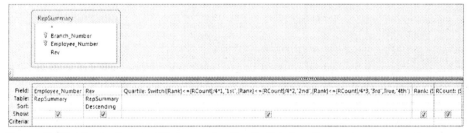

Figure 8-23: Create the quartile tags using the Switch function.

As you can see in Figure 8-24, you can sort the resulting dataset on any field without compromising your quartile standing tags.

Employee_Number	Rev	Rank	Quartile	RCount
104	$9,023.50	294	2nd	673
1044	$447.33	520	4th	673
1050	$179.74	614	4th	673
1054	$54,147.73	55	1st	673
106	$38,013.36	105	1st	673
113	$963.06	458	3rd	673
1130	$67,961.15	18	1st	673
1135	$1,477.21	429	3rd	673
1156	$192.07	602	4th	673
1245	$38,189.81	103	1st	673
1338	$75,489.77	12	1st	673
1344	$12,242.75	268	2nd	673
1416	$1,120.57	445	3rd	673
142	$1,622.30	421	3rd	673

Figure 8-24: Your final dataset can be sorted any way without the danger of losing your quartile tags.

Creating a Frequency Distribution

A *frequency distribution* is a special kind of analysis that categorizes data based on the count of occurrences where a variable assumes a specified value attribute. Figure 8-25 illustrates a frequency distribution created by using the Partition function.

With this frequency distribution, you are clustering employees by the range of revenue dollars they fall in. For instance, 183 employees fall into the 500: 5999 grouping, meaning that 183 employees earn between 500 and 5,999 revenue dollars per employee. Although there are several ways to get the results you see here, the easiest way to build a frequency distribution is to use the Partition function.

Employees	Dollars
158	: 499
183	500: 5499
49	5500: 10499
43	10500: 15499
31	15500: 20499
34	20500: 25499
36	25500: 30499
22	30500: 35499
23	35500: 40499
13	40500: 45499
19	45500: 50499
15	50500: 55499
17	55500: 60499
10	60500: 65499
5	65500: 70499
4	70500: 75499
6	75500: 80499

Figure 8-25: This frequency distribution was created by using the Partition function.

ABOUT THE PARTITION FUNCTION

The `Partition` **function identifies the range that a specific number falls into, indicating where the number occurs in a calculated series of ranges. The** `Partition` **function requires the following four arguments:**

`Partition(Number, Range Start, Range Stop, Interval)`

- `Number` **(required): The number you are evaluating. In a query environment, you typically use the name of a field to specify that you are evaluating all the row values of that field.**

- `Range Start` **(required): A whole number that is to be the start of the overall range of numbers. Note that this number cannot be less than zero.**

- `Range Stop` **(required): A whole number that is to be the end of the overall range of numbers. Note that this number cannot be equal to or less than the** `Range Start`.

- `Interval` **(required): A whole number that is to be the span of each range in the series from** `Range Start` **to** `Range Stop`**. Note that this number cannot be less than one.**

To create the frequency distribution you saw in Figure 8-25, build the query shown in Figure 8-26. As you can see in this query, you are using a `Partition` function to specify that you want to evaluate the Revenue field, start the series range at 500, end the series range at 100,000, and set the range intervals to 5,000.

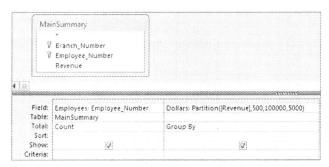

Figure 8-26: This simple query creates the frequency distribution you see in Figure 8-25.

You can also create a frequency distribution by group by adding a Group By field to your query. Figure 8-27 demonstrates this by adding the Branch_Number field.

The result is a dataset (see Figure 8-28) that contains a separate frequency distribution for each branch, detailing the count of employees in each revenue distribution range.

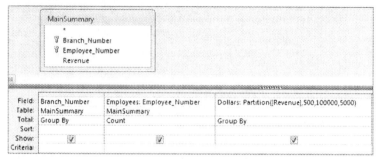

Figure 8-27: This query creates a separate frequency distribution for each branch number in your dataset.

Branch_Number ▾	Employees ▾	Dollars ▾
101313	3	: 499
101313	7	500: 5499
101313	2	5500: 10499
101313	1	15500: 20499
101313	1	20500: 25499
101313	1	25500: 30499
101313	1	45500: 50499
101313	1	60500: 65499
101313	1	70500: 75499
101313	2	75500: 80499
101419	2	: 499
101419	1	10500: 15499
101419	1	25500: 30499
101419	1	30500: 35499
101419	1	45500: 50499
102516	1	500: 5499
102516	1	25500: 30499
102516	1	35500: 40499
103516	4	: 499
103516	6	500: 5499

Figure 8-28: You have successfully created multiple frequency distributions with one query.

TRICKS OF THE TRADE: CREATING A HISTOGRAM CHART IN ACCESS

A *histogram chart* is a graphic representation of a frequency distribution. You can use these types of charts to easily pick out anomalies in a data collection, by following these steps:

1. Start your histogram chart by building the query shown in Figure 8-29.

2. Run the query to display the results of the frequency distribution operation (be sure to run the query). After you run the query, select View▷PivotChart View as shown in Figure 8-30.

   Within a few seconds, Access runs your query and returns the results to a pivot chart object.

TRICKS OF THE TRADE: CREATING A HISTOGRAM CHART IN ACCESS

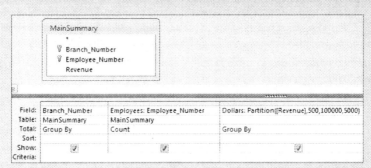

Figure 8-29: Build a query using the Partition function to create a frequency distribution.

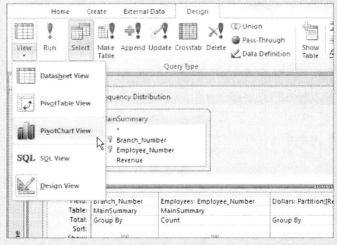

Figure 8-30: Switch to PivotChart View.

3. **Drag thze Branch Number field to the section of the pivot chart that reads Drop Filter Fields Here.**

4. **Drag the Dollars field to the section of the pivot chart that reads Drop Category Fields Here.**

5. **Drag the Employees field to gray plot area in center of the chart.**

   The result is a histogram similar to the one illustrated here in Figure 8-31.

6. **As if that isn't impressive enough, remember you have given yourself the ability to filter by branch number. To filter out one branch,**

(continued)

TRICKS OF THE TRADE: CREATING A HISTOGRAM CHART IN ACCESS *(continued)*

click the drop-down arrow next to the Branch_Number field, shown in Figure 8-32, and remove the check from the All checkbox.

7. **Place a check in the checkbox for the branch you want to show, and then click OK.**

The PivotChart in the Figure 8-33 presents the histogram chart for branch 301316.

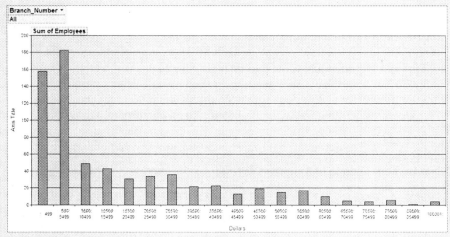

Figure 8-31: Your histogram chart is complete!

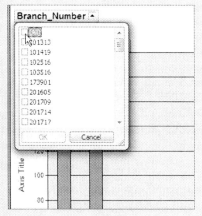

Figure 8-32: To filter by branch, click the drop-down arrow next to the Branch_ Number field.

TRICKS OF THE TRADE: CREATING A HISTOGRAM CHART IN ACCESS

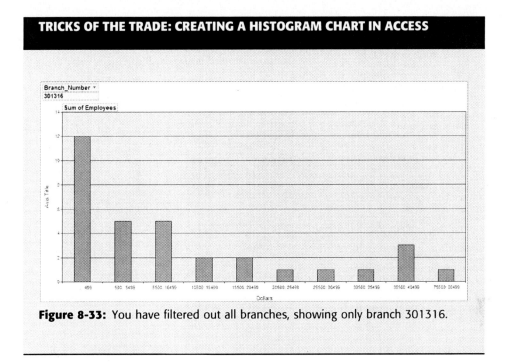

Figure 8-33: You have filtered out all branches, showing only branch 301316.

Summary

Descriptive statistics allow you to profile a dataset and enable comparisons that you can use in other analyses. With descriptive statistics, you can present large amounts of data in quantitative summaries that are meaningful, yet simple to understand. Although many users turn to Excel to perform statistical operations, running descriptive statistics in Access is often the smartest option due to the structure and volume of the data that is to be analyzed.

The simplest descriptive statistics can be generated using aggregate queries (sum, average, min, max, etc.), while more advanced descriptive analyses can be performed by leveraging the power of subqueries and domain aggregate functions. Indeed, using the tools and techniques you have learned thus far, you can create a wide array of descriptive analyses; from determining rank, mode, and median, to creating a frequency distribution.

Scheduling and Running Batch Analysis

In the realm of Microsoft Access, the term "automation" has two meanings. First, it's used to describe the computerization of a process where Access self-regulates a procedure based on predetermined requirements you supply. It's also used to define the means of manipulating another application's objects with the use of Access Visual Basic for Applications (VBA). In the context of this book, the term automation involves the former.

Access provides you with two key methods of automating your analytical processes: macros and VBA. This chapter focuses on using macros to automate your processes and run batch analysis on your data. Why should you care? Well, leveraging macro functionality is not just a cool way to use Access, it offers the following advantages:

- **Higher productivity:** Just because you have the skills to analyze data in Access doesn't mean you have the time. With automation, you can have Access carry out redundant analyses and recurring analytical processes, leaving you free to work on other tasks.

- **Quality control:** Human beings make mistakes. The more you touch a set of analyses, the greater the chance there is for errors. Automation takes humans (you) out of the equation.

- **Reproducibility:** There's an old quip among data analysts: "It's okay to produce the wrong answer, as long as you produce the same wrong answer consistently." Although you obviously don't want to produce a wrong answer, the point is you want to be able to reproduce the analysis you have established. If your answer changes from one analysis to the next, you'll find yourself wondering whether you've done something differently. Automating your analytical processes ensures that Access executes your analyses in the same way every time.

Introduction to Access Macros

Access macros are very different from Excel macros. In Excel, macros are used as a way to record actions that can be played back when needed. Excel macros are analogous to programming a phone to dial a specific telephone number when you hit a special key. In Access, however, macros are used to execute a set of pre-programmed functions, much like a list of menu options on your TV that can be fired when selected. These pre-programmed functions are called *actions*. The idea behind building a macro in Access is to choose a set of actions you want the macro to carry out when it is executed. Figure 9-1 illustrates an Access macro that carries out three actions when run.

Figure 9-1: This macro runs a SQL statement that makes a new table, opens the new table, and throws up a message box.

Again, none of the actions shown in Figure 9-1 were recorded by the user. They are all actions that came pre-packaged for use in a macro.

NOTE With the release of Access 2010, Microsoft decided to move away from the grid format traditionally found in previous versions of Access. To keep the content of this book substantive, the screenshots in this chapter have been limited to those taken from Access 2010.

This means that if you are using Access 2007 to go through the exercises in this chapter, you will notice some of the screenshots will not match what you see on your screen. That's OK. Although the interfaces are different, the basic mechanics and functionality of creating and using macros are the same between Access 2007 and 2010.

In short, you should still be able to follow along with the exercises in this chapter even if you are using Access 2007.

Dealing with Access Macro Security

Before jumping into your first macro, it's important to understand the macro security features in Access.

Access 2010 comes with over 80 macro actions that you can use in your processes. However, the new security features in Access 2007 prevents 20 of those macro actions from running unless the Access database you are working with is trusted. The term *trusted* means that you have explicitly told Access that the macros within the database are of no threat and can be run freely.

For example, when you open the sample database for this book, you should see a security message (Figure 9-2) directly below the Ribbon. This message indicates that because this database is not "trusted," certain actions have been disabled.

Figure 9-2: Databases that are not trusted will have certain features automatically disabled.

This means that certain macro actions will not run at all. For instance, the macro illustrated here in Figure 9-3 contains two SetWarnings macro actions. These macro actions require that the database be trusted before running properly.

NOTE In Figure 9-3, the two SetWarnings macro actions have a triangle icon next to them. These icons provide a convenient visual indicator, letting you know that the action will require a trusted database to run properly.

Figure 9-3: The two SetWarnings macro actions will not run in an un-trusted database.

Attempting to run this macro in a database that is not trusted will result in a message similar to the one shown in Figure 9-4.

Figure 9-4: Running certain actions in an un-trusted databases will cause an error.

TIP The following Access 2010 macro actions require a trusted database to run: CopyObject, DeleteObject, Echo, ImportExportData, ImportExportSpreadsheet, ImportExportText, ImportSharePointList, OpenSharePointList, OpenSharePoint-RecycleBin, OpenVisualBasicModule, PrintOut, QuitAccess, RenameObject, RunApplication, RunSavedImportExport, RunSQL, SaveObject, SendKeys, SetValue, SetWarnings, and ShowToolbar.

If you are running Access 2007, these macro actions require a trusted database to run: CopyDatabaseFile , CopyObject, DeleteObject, Echo, OpenDataAccessPage, OpenDiagram, OpenFunction, OpenModule, OpenStoredProcedure, OpenView, PrintOut, Quit, Rename, RunApp, RunCommand, RunSavedImportExport, RunSQL, Save, SendKeys, SetValue, SetWarnings, ShowToolbar, TransferDatabase, TransferSharePointList, TransferSpreadsheet, TransferSQLDatabase, and TransferText.

Note that although the RunCommand macro action does not, in and of itself, require a trusted database to run, many of its arguments do.

The Quick Fix

The easy fix for a disabled database is to manually enable the content. In Access 2010, you can do this by clicking the Enable button on the security message shown in Figure 9-2.

If you are using Access 2007, you can click the button on the warning messages shown in Figure 9-2. This activates the Microsoft Office Security Options dialog box. From here, simply select the option next to "Enable this content" as demonstrated in Figure 9-5.

Figure 9-5: Once you enable the content in a database, all macros will run fine.

Keep in mind that the Access 2007 quick fix needs to be repeated each time you open the database.

The Long-Term Fix

The best way to work around the security issues in Access 2007 on a long-term basis is to use the database in a *trusted location*, a directory deemed a safe zone where only trusted workbooks are placed. A trusted location allows you to work with a database with no security restrictions, as long as the database is in that location.

To set up a trusted location, follow these steps:

1. In Access 2010, select the File button. For Access 2007, select the Office icon in the upper left-hand corner of the application window.

2. Select the Options button.

3. Click the Trust Center button and select Trust Center Settings.

4. Select the Trusted Locations button.

5. Select Add New Location

6. Click Browse to specify the directory that will be considered a trusted location (such as your MyDocuments directory; or the Documents directory if you're using Windows Vista)

Once a trusted location is specified, all databases opened from that location are, by default, opened with macros enabled.

NOTE In Access 2010, Microsoft has enhanced the security model to remember files that you've deemed trustworthy. That is to say, when you open an Access database and click the Enable button, Access remembers that you trusted the database. Each time you open the database after that, Access will automatically trust it.

Creating Your First Macro

Start by initializing a new macro. To do this, select the Create tab on the Ribbon and then click the Macro button. This will activate the Macro window shown in Figure 9-6.

The idea is to select an action in the Action drop-down box.

TIP As mentioned previously in this chapter, Access, by default, hides any macro action that requires a trusted database to run properly. That is to say, these macro actions will not appear in the Action column drop-down boxes. Therefore, before you get started, click the Show All Actions button on the Design tab of the Ribbon. This ensures that all macro actions are displayed in the Action column drop-down boxes, even those that require a trusted database.

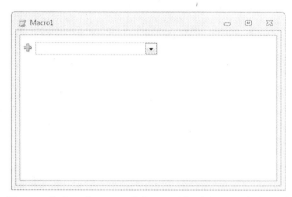

Figure 9-6: The Macro window is essentially a grid where each row defines a specified action to carry out.

The first action you want to run is RunSQL, so select RunSQL from the Action dropdown box. Once you select your action, you will see some new input boxes. These new input boxes are called *action arguments*. Every action comes with a unique set of arguments that you can tailor to fit your needs. As you can see in Figure 9-7, the RunSQL action requires two arguments: SQL Statement and Use Transaction.

Click inside the SQL Statement input field and enter **SELECT Customer_Number INTO MyTable FROM CustomerMaster**. This action will run a make-table query in order to make a new table called MyTable.

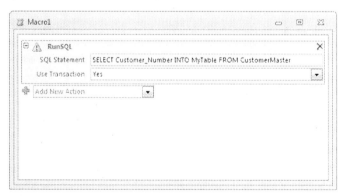

Figure 9-7: Add the RunSQL action and specify its arguments.

Add another action by selecting the OpenTable action from the Action dropdown box. Once the new OpenTable action has been added, enter **MyTable** in the Table Name input field, as shown in Figure 9-8. This action will open the MyTable table.

NOTE Although there is no table called MyTable currently in the database, there will be once the `RunSQL` action runs. In the meantime, the macro doesn't care that there is no table called MyTable and will save with no problem. This illustrates the fact that, unlike VBA modules, macros don't compile to identify unrecognized objects or other errors.

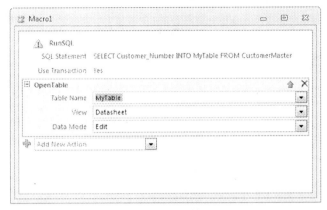

Figure 9-8: Add the `OpenTable` action and specify its arguments.

Add another action by selecting the `MessageBox` action from the Action dropdown box. Once the new `MessageBox` action has been added, enter **Table has been created** in the Message input field, as shown in Figure 9-9. This action will activate a message box.

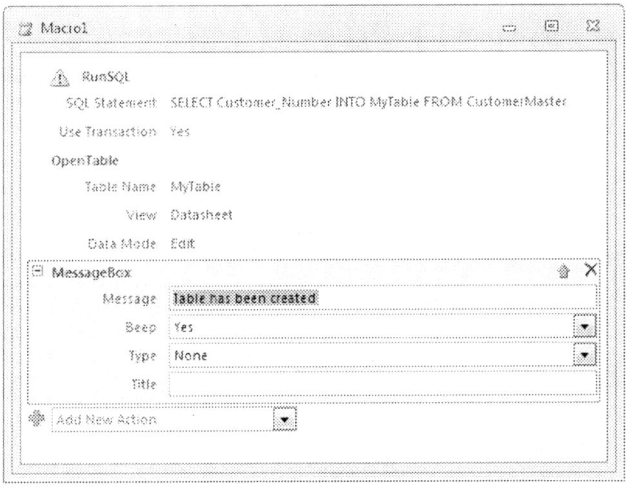

Figure 9-9: Add the `MessageBox` action and specify its arguments.

At this point, save and close your newly created macro. Access will prompt you to give your new macro a name. Once you name your macro, it will be saved in the Macros collection in your Database window. To run it, simply double-click it. If you built your macro correctly, it should paste 9,253 records into a new table called MyTable, and then open the table and throw up a message box that reads, "Table has been created."

NOTE To edit any macro, you can simply right-click the macro and select Design View.

Essential Macro Actions

Trying to determine which macro actions benefit the automation of your data analysis can be overwhelming. A set of 18 macro actions, however, are ideal for automating your analytical processes. When trying to familiarize yourself with the macro actions that are available to you, the actions in this section should be first on your list.

Manipulating Forms, Queries, Reports, and Tables

The following macro actions manipulate forms, queries, reports, and tables:

- `CloseWindow`: Closes a specified form, query, report, or table. This is useful when you want to ensure that a particular object is closed before running a process. In Access 2007, this action is called `Close`.

- `DeleteObject`: Deletes a specified form, query, report, or table. This action comes in handy when you need to delete temporary tables that you created during an analytical process. Note that this macro action requires a trusted database to run properly.

- `OpenQuery`: Runs a specified query or, if indicated, opens the query in Design view. You typically use the action to string multiple `OpenQuery` actions together in order to run a series of queries, effectively running a batch analysis.

- `OpenForm`: Opens a specified form. You can use this action to open a form that supplies the values needed for your analytical process.

- `OpenReport` and `OpenTable`: These actions allow you to open a specified report and table, respectively. These are useful for presenting a final result after your batch analysis.

The Access Environment

The following macro actions affect the Access environment:

- `QuitAccess`: Closes the entire Access application. This action comes in handy when you are running a scheduled process and you want to close the application once the macro has finished executing. Note that in Access 2007, this action is called `Quit`.

- **SetWarnings:** Forces an OK or Yes response to all system messages, effectively suppressing message pop-ups while a macro runs. Without the `SetWarnings` action, you would have to be there to click Yes or OK on every confirmation message that popped up while your macro was running. Note that this macro action requires a trusted database to run properly.

Executing Processes

The following macro actions control the execution of processes:

- **RunCode:** Executes an existing VBA function. This action is ideal when you need to initialize a procedure that can only be accomplished with VBA, such as automating Excel.

- **RunMacro:** Executes another macro. You can use this action in a conditional macro where the resulting decision requires that another macro be executed.

- **RunSQL:** Executes a valid SQL string. Bear in mind that only `Insert`, `Delete`, `Select...Into`, or `Update` statements are valid in the macro environment. This action comes in handy when you need to run action queries, but you don't want to inundate your database with superfluous query objects. Note that this macro action requires a trusted database to run properly.

- **StopMacro:** Stops the current macro. You can use this action in a conditional macro where the resulting decision indicates no further processing is needed.

Outputting Data

The following macro actions export or output data:

- **PrintOut:** Prints the active datasheet, form, or report. This action is ideal for ensuring that a hardcopy of analytical results are produced. Note that this macro action requires a trusted database to run properly.

- **ExportWithFormatting:** Outputs a table, query, form, or report to an external document. Output options include outputting to Excel, Word, HTML, or text. Note that this action is memory intensive and does not work well with very large datasets. In Access 2007, this action is called `OutputTo`.

- **ImportExportData:** Exports and imports data to and from an external database. This action is ideal for backing up your database to an external location. You can even schedule nightly backups of your data using this macro action. Note that this macro action requires a trusted database to run properly. In previous versions of Access, this macro action was called `TransferDatabase`.

- **ImportExportSpreadsheet:** Exports and imports data to and from external spreadsheets. This action comes in handy when you need to push large datasets to and from Excel files. Note that this macro actions require a trusted database to run properly. In Previous versions of Access, this macro action is called `TransferSpreadsheet`.

- **ImportExportText:** Exports and imports data to and from external text files. This action is ideal for automating data pulls from text files. Note that this macro actions require a trusted database to run properly. In Previous versions of Access, this macro action is called `TransferText`.

- **EMailDatabaseObject:** Outputs an object to an Excel, text, PDF, or HTML file, then attaches that file to an email message that can be sent to specified address with additional text. This action works with any 32 bit email program that conforms to Mail Application Programming Interface (MAPI) standards. In Access 2007, this action is called `SendObject`.

Setting Up and Managing Batch Analysis

An analytical process involves a series of queries that run in a logical order, giving you the needed set of analyses. A batch analysis is nothing more than automating the execution of one or more of your analytical processes. In this section, you learn how to set up and manage you own automated batch analysis.

Getting Organized

Creating a batch analysis is as simple as defining which queries and actions you need run. This involves pointing your macro to specific objects. However, if your database is inundated with temporary queries and tables or queries that have no logical name or order, it becomes difficult to determine which object does what, let alone point a macro to the right set of objects. That being said, there are a few things you can do to ensure that you keep your database organized.

Using a Logical Naming Convention

The long-standing guideline on using naming conventions in Access is that you preface each type of object in your database with a prefix describing that object. For example, an appropriate name for a query would be *qryMonthlyRevenue*, a table could be called *tblCustomers*, and a form could be named *frmMain*.

What you are about to read will be considered blasphemy in many Access circles, but the fact is that this is not always the best naming convention you can use.

The database in Figure 9-10 is a good example. This database contains 15 queries that make up two separate analytical processes. As you can see, it's difficult to determine which query belongs to which process.

Figure 9-10: It's difficult to determine which query belongs to which analytical process.

Adding "qry" to each query, as shown in Figure 9-11, doesn't help much in this situation.

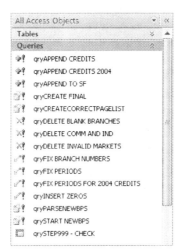

Figure 9-11: Prefixing each query with "qry" does not clear things up at all.

So, what do you do? In a database used primarily for data analysis, the best way to organize your queries is to take advantage of the fact that the default sort order is alphabetical. Preface your query names with text describing the analysis followed by a logical numbering system. For example, instead of AppendCredits, you could use PSmry_2A_AppendCredits. Figure 9-12 demonstrates this naming convention. Keep in mind that there is nothing special about the prefix "PSmry"; it is simply a description that allows for easy recognition of the analyses that have to do with creating the period summary.

NOTE Note the use of the underscore in place of spaces. It's generally a good practice not to use spaces in your object names in order to avoid complications when writing SQL strings or using VBA code.

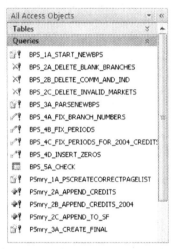

Figure 9-12: With this naming convention, you cannot only distinguish between the two analyses but can also see the correct order each query should be run.

You should also make your object names *upper camel case*, meaning that the first letter of each word is capitalized. This makes your object names easier to read. Figure 9-13 demonstrates this naming convention.

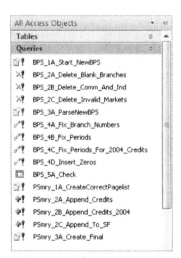

Figure 9-13: Using camel case makes your object names easier to read.

Using the Description Property

Each object has a Description property that you use to describe the object in detail. To adjust an object's description, right-click the object and select Object Properties. This activates a properties dialog box for that object, as shown in Figure 9-14. You can use up to 250 characters to describe the object.

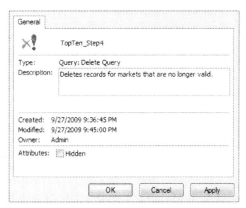

Figure 9-14: Use the Description property to describe the object in detail.

Now you can change your database view to show descriptions along with the names and other details of your Access objects. To do so, right click on the title bar of the navigation pane and select View By ➪ Details as demonstrated in Figure 9-15.

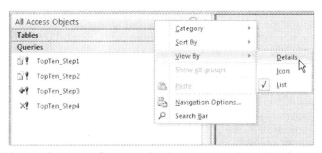

Figure 9-15: Change the view of your navigation pane to show details.

This will show you a series of details to include the description you entered. Figure 9-16 shows a database in Details view.

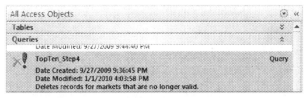

Figure 9-16: You can now see the description you added.

Setting Up a Basic Batch Analysis

Setting up a basic batch analysis involves little more than creating a macro that executes a set of analytical processes in a logical order conducive to your analysis. For example, the database in Figure 9-17 is used to run three queries that work together to accomplish a set of analytics.

Figure 9-17: These three queries make up a simple analytical process.

The macro being built in Figure 9-18 starts with a SetWarnings action to ensure that no system messages interrupt the process. From here, it's simply a question of adding the queries that need to be executed in order.

Figure 9-18: Building a macro to automate the execution of the three queries.

After all queries are added, a second SetWarnings action is called to reinstate system messages. The completed macro is shown in Figure 9-19.

Once this macro is saved, it can be run at any time to execute what can be called a "batch analysis."

NOTE You may notice in Figure 9-19 that the arguments seem to be hidden. This is because the macro is in a collapsed state. This makes the macro easier to read. To collapse your macros, simply right-click any of the actions in the macro and select Collapse All.

Figure 9-19: When completed and saved, the macro can be run anytime as a batch analysis.

TIP If you need to create a macro with a large amount of queries, you can save time by simply dragging each query to the macro design interface (see Figure 9-20). This will automatically create an `OpenQuery` action for you, complete with all the needed arguments.

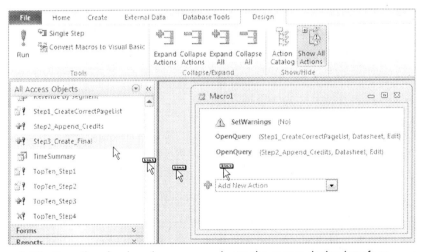

Figure 9-20: Save time by dragging your queries to the macro design interface.

Building Smarter Macros

You can simulate decision-making functionality by building conditions into your macros. A *condition* is a logical expression evaluated in order to return a True or False answer. With conditions, you simulate an `If...Then` scenario or even an `If...Then...Else` scenario.

If ... Then in Access 2010 Macros

To demonstrate how to build a basic If ... Then scenario, start a new macro and add the If macro action. Enter the following as the expression argument: **InputBox("Enter any number")>10**.

This expression activates an input box and asks you to enter a number. The number you enter is then evaluated to determine if it is greater than 10. If the number you enter is greater than 10, the expression will return a True answer, otherwise, it will return a False answer.

At this point, your macro should look similar to Figure 9-21.

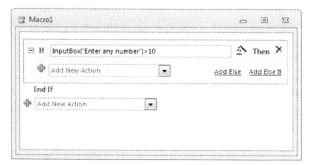

Figure 9-21: Start a new macro with one If action.

In Figure 9-21, you will notice an area between the If and End If where you can assign actions. Any action placed between the If and End If is executed when the conditional expression evaluates to true. Here, select the MessageBox action and enter a message similar to that shown in Figure 9-22.

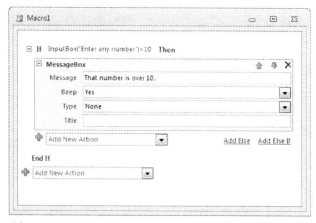

Figure 9-22: Add a messagebox between If and End If.

Close the macro and save it as **IfMacro**. When you run the macro, you'll see the input box shown in Figure 9-23. If you enter a number less than or equal to 10, nothing happens. If you enter a number greater than 10, a message pops up telling you your number is greater than 10.

Figure 9-23: Running the macro activates an input box where you enter your chosen number.

If . . . Then in Access 2007 Macros

If you are using Access 2007, you will not have the If macro action available to you. In order to apply conditions to your macros in Access 2007, you need to activate the Condition column in your macro design interface.

Go up to the Design tab on the application ribbon and click the Conditions button. At this point, your macro design interface will contain a new column called Condition. The idea is to enter your Condition next to the action you want fired if that condition evaluates to True. In Access 2007, the macro for this first exercise would look like Figure 9-24.

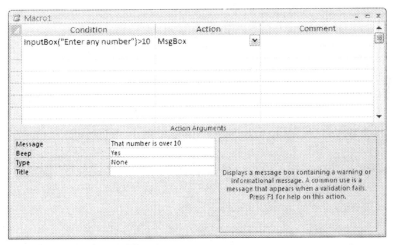

Figure 9-24: Evaluating a condition in Access 2007.

If . . . Then . . . Else in Access 2010 Macros

You can expand the scope of your conditions by adding If...Then...Else functionality. To demonstrate this, create a new macro and enter the following condition in a new If action: **InputBox("Guess How Many Locations There are")=DCount("[Branch_Number]","[LocationMaster]")**. With this condition, you are comparing the user's input to the number of records in the LocationMaster table. If the two are equal, the expression evaluates as True.

In the area between If and End If, Select the MessageBox action, and then select the StopMacro action. At this point, your Macro window should look similar to the one shown in Figure 9-25.

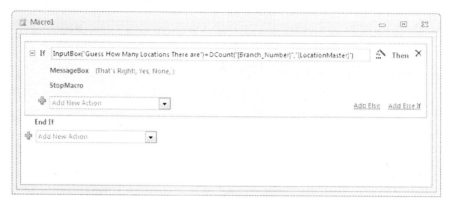

Figure 9-25: If the expression evaluates to true, this macro will fire a congratulatory message box, then stop.

Once you have your basic condition built, click the "Add Else" hyperlink shown in Figure 9-25. This activates a new section where you can specify what action to take if your condition evaluates to false.

In this case, select the MessageBox action, and enter "The Answer is 59" in the Message argument. On the line below that, select the RunMacro Action and enter **ConditionalMacro** as the Macro Name argument.

At this point, your Macro window should look similar to the one shown in Figure 9-26.

Make sure to save the macro and name it ConditionalMacro. Now take a moment to consider what will happen when you run this macro.

1. It will give you an input box where you will guess how many locations there are. It will then compare your answer to the real record count from the LocationMaster table. *If* your answer matches the actual record count, *then* the macro performs actions 2 and 3; *else* the macro skips to action 4. As you can see, this essentially gives you the IF...THEN...ELSE effect.

2. If your macro goes to action 2, it means you got the answer right. A message box is thrown to tell you so.

3. The macro stops.

4. If your macro goes directly to step 4, it means it got the answer wrong. A message box is thrown to tell you the correct answer.

5. The macro is run again to give you another chance.

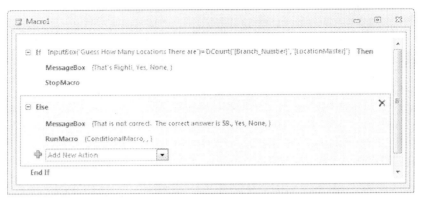

Figure 9-26: : Any action in the Else section will only be run if your condition did not evaluate to true.

If . . . Then . . . Else in Access 2007 Macros

As explained earlier in this chapter (If . . . Then in Access 2007 Macros) conditional macros work differently in Access 2007. In Access 2007, conditional expressions are entered in the Conditions column. This allows you to build simple If . . . Then functionality into your macros.

You can expand simple decision-making functionality into a more complex If . . . Then . . . Else model by entering three periods (also called an "ellipsis") as a condition. Using an ellipsis in the Condition inputs tells the macro to execute the action on that line only if the condition in the preceding line is true.

The previous exercise can be completed in Access 2007 by building the macro shown in Figure 9-27.

Figure 9-27: In Access 2007, you use ellipses in the Condition inputs to invoke the If . . . Then . . . Else functionality.

Taking a closer look at Figure 9-27, you can see the second action in the macro is a message box with an ellipsis condition. This means that the second action will run only if the preceding condition evaluates to true. Since the third action in the macro also has the ellipsis condition, it too will be skipped if the preceding conditions are true.

In short, if the first condition evaluates to true, then the macro will run its course, else the macro will skip to action 4. This, in effect achieves the If . . . Then . . . Else functionality.

Looping with Macros

First, your trustworthy author has to confess that the phrase "looping with macros" is admittedly a tad misleading. *Looping* implies that the macro's actions are continuously being run in the same instance of execution. What is really happening is that the macro is being started repeatedly until a condition is met. However, the fact that you can simulate looping behavior through macros does open up some interesting possibilities for those of you who are not yet comfortable with VBA.

To demonstrate the concept of a looping macro, imagine that you have been asked to provide a list of the top ten customers for each market in the US. Because this will be a monthly exercise, you decide to use macros to automate the process. For this particular scenario, you will need four queries and two macros.

TIP You can find a working version of the example illustrated here in the sample database for this book at www.wiley.com/go/excelanalystguide. Refer to the sample database if you run into problems.

1. Create the make-table query shown in Figure 9-28. Name the table being created **TopTenList**. Running this query will create an empty table that will eventually contain the final results. Be sure to save this query as **TopTen_Step1**.

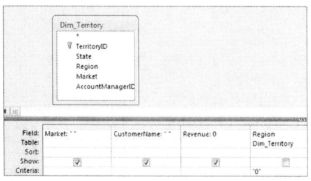

Figure 9-28: Save this make-table query as TopTen_Step1.

> **NOTE** Run the query you created in step 1 at least one time. You will need the table it creates for step 3.

2. Create the make-table query shown in Figure 9-29. Name the table being created **LoopList.** Running this query will create a list of unique market names that will be used to loop through. Be sure to save this query as **TopTen_Step2.**

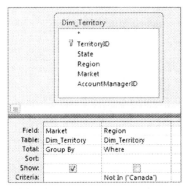

Figure 9-29: Save this take-table query as TopTen_Step2.

> **NOTE** Run the query you created in step 2 at least one time. You will need the table it creates for step 4.

3. Create the append query shown in Figure 9-30. You will append it to the TopTenList table you created in step 1. Note that the Top Values property has been set to 10 in order to return only the top ten values. Also note the criteria under Market. This criteria ensures that only one market is included in the query: the one whose first letter is closest to the letter A. Be sure to save this query as **TopTen_Step3.**

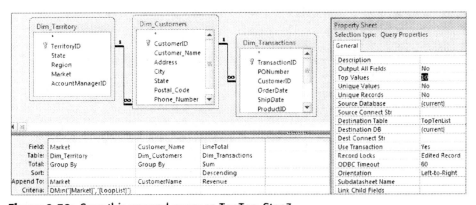

Figure 9-30: Save this append query as TopTen_Step3.

4. Create the delete query shown in Figure 9-31. Running this query deletes the market whose first letter is closest to the letter A from the LoopList. This ensures that the market can never again be used in the TopTen_Step3 query. If you ran this query 14 times, you would eventually run out of markets. Be sure to save this query as **TopTen_Step4**.

Figure 9-31: Save this delete query as TopTen_Step4.

5. Start a new macro and add the following actions:
    ▪ **SetWarnings.** Set the Warnings No argument to No.
    ▪ **OpenQuery.** Set the Query Name argument to TopTen_Step1.
    ▪ **OpenQuery.** Set the Query Name argument to TopTen_Step2.
    ▪ **RunMacro.** Set the Macro Name argument to TopTenB_Child.
    ▪ **SetWarnings.** Set the Warnings No argument to Yes.

    This macro will do the setup work, creating the tables necessary for the looping action. Once the tables are created, it calls the child macro, TopTenB_Child.

    Be sure to save this query as TopTenA_Parent. At this point, your Macro window should look similar to the one shown in Figure 9-32.

Figure 9-32: Save this macro as TopTenA_Parent.

6. Start a new macro and add an If action:
    ▪ **If:** Set the Condition to DCount("[Market]","[LoopList]")>0. This condition specifies that the record count of the Looplist table must be

greater than zero in order to continue with the actions that have the ellipsis condition.

7. Inside the If section, add the following actions:

   ■ **SetWarnings:** Give this action an ellipsis condition. Set the Warnings No argument to No.

   ■ **OpenQuery:** Give this action an ellipsis condition. Set the Query Name argument to TopTen_Step3.

   ■ **OpenQuery:** Give this action an ellipsis condition. Set the Query Name argument to TopTen_Step4.

   ■ **RunMacro:** Give this action an ellipsis condition. Set the Macro Name argument to TopTenB_Child. This action starts the macro over. The idea is that this macro will repeatedly start over until the condition in the first line of the macro is false.

8. Click the "Add Else" hyperlink to add an Else section. Inside the Else section, add the following actions:

   ■ **DeleteObject:** This is the first action that runs when the condition in the first line of the macro is false. Set the ObjectType argument to Table and the Object Name argument to LoopList. This action deletes the LoopList table as it is no longer needed.

   ■ **SetWarnings:** Set the Warnings No argument to Yes.

   ■ **MessageBox:** Set the Message argument to "Top Ten Customers by Market can now be found in the TopTenList table."

   ■ **StopMacro:** This action is used as a clean sweep to ensure no rogue macro actions are still executing.

   When you are done, your Macro window should look similar to the one shown in Figure 9-33. Be sure to save this query as **TopTenB_Child**.

9. There is nothing left to do but run the macro. Double-click the Top TenA_Parent macro to start the loop. After the macro is done, you will get a message telling you that you can find your results in the TopTenList table. Open the table to see the results.

You may be thinking that this is a lot of work. However, remember that you are not only performing some hefty analytics on 17 markets with a click of the mouse, but now that this process is built, you can run it whenever you need to.

TIP Instead of using the OpenQuery action in your macro, which requires that you create a query object, you can use a SQL statement in a RunSQL action. This can help you cut back on the number of superfluous queries in your database.

Keep in mind that the SQL statements used in RunSQL actions cannot be more than 256 characters in length.

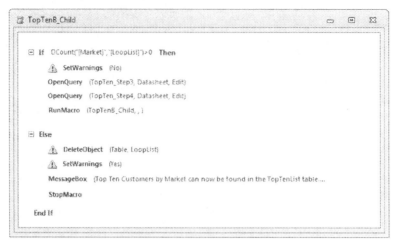

Figure 9-33: Save this macro as TopTenB_Child.

Scheduling Macros to Run Nightly

Although automating a process to run with a click of the mouse is impressive, the ultimate in automation is not even being there. How many times have you heard someone say, "Yeah, I just run a nightly routine" while you nod your head and pretend to know what that means. Meanwhile, you're trudging into work at 5:00 am to make sure you have the reports ready by eight. The good news is that there is an easy way to schedule your macros to run every night, every Monday, on the 15th of every month, or whenever you like.

Unfortunately, as of Office 2010, Access does not yet have an internal macro scheduler. Until the time it does, you can use the Windows Task Scheduler to schedule a macro to run at specific times. The question is, how do you tell Access which macro to run through a completely unrelated program (Windows Task Scheduler)? You have two options: use an AutoExec macro or use a command-line switch.

Using an AutoExec Macro to Schedule Tasks

If you name a macro AutoExec, that macro will be run automatically when your database is opened. How does that help you? The idea is to create a macro that contains your batch analysis and save it as AutoExec. When the Windows Task Scheduler opens your database at 3:00 am, the AutoExec automatically executes your batch analysis.

To demonstrate this, create the macro shown in Figure 9-34. The `MessageBox` action with the Message argument set to read "A bunch of actions are executed" will represent a batch analysis. Using the QuitAccess action makes certain that the database closes once the macro completes execution. Save your newly created macro as **AutoExec**.

Figure 9-34: Create this macro and save it as AutoExec.

TIP If you need to run multiple batch analyses, you can create a "master" macro that runs other macros, and then save it as AutoExec.

Once you save your macro as **AutoExec**, close the database to test it. When you open your database again, you should see the message box you entered into the AutoExec; then the database closes. Now you are ready to schedule your newly created macro with the Windows Task Scheduler.

TIP How do you get back into your database? Simply hold down the Shift key while you open the database. This prevents the AutoExec macro from running.

You may be tempted to remove the QuitAccess action from your macro, but keep in mind that during a nightly routine, you want the database to close automatically. Removing the QuitAccess action will cause the database to stay open.

Remember that the QuitAccess action will only run if the database is trusted as per the new security features highlighted earlier in this chapter.

Using the Windows Task Scheduler

Every version of Windows comes with a built-in Task Scheduler. Although the steps for creating a scheduled task varies from version to version, the basic mechanics are the same. In this walkthrough, the Windows XP task scheduler is being used.

In the Windows Control Panel, find and double-click the icon for the Task Scheduler (Figure 9-35).

TIP If you are having trouble finding the Task Scheduler in your version of Windows, you can use a Run command to find it. To do so, click Start in your

Windows taskbar, and then click Run. This will open the Run dialog box. In the input box provided, enter "control schedtasks" (without the quotes) then press OK.

Another way to get to the Task Scheduler is to right-click My Computer and select the Manage option. This activates the Computer Mangement window where you will find the Task Scheduler.

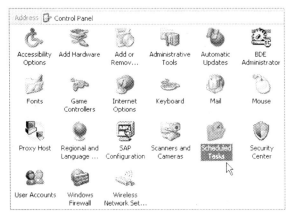

Figure 9-35: Double-click Scheduled Tasks.

Once you are in the Scheduled Tasks folder, double-click the Add Scheduled Task icon to activate the Scheduled Task Wizard shown in Figure 9-36, and then click Next.

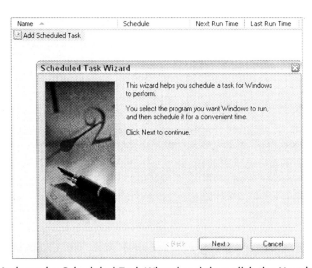

Figure 9-36: Activate the Scheduled Task Wizard and then click the Next button.

The next window, shown in Figure 9-37, asks you to select the program you would like to run. Select Microsoft Office Access 2010 from the program list, and then click the Next button.

Figure 9-37: Select Microsoft Access from the program list, and click Next.

At this point, you will see the window shown in Figure 9-38, where you will name your scheduled task and specify when you want the task to be performed. In this example, the task will be performed daily.

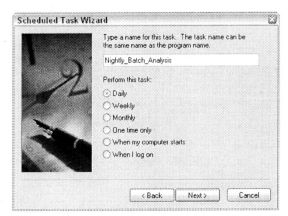

Figure 9-38: Specify when you want the task to be performed, and then click the Next button.

In the next window, you will set up the time and interval for the task. In the example illustrated in Figure 9-39, the task will be performed at 3:00 am every day, starting on March 1, 2010.

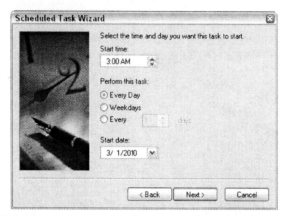

Figure 9-39: Indicate the time and interval you want the task to be performed, and then click Next.

In the next window, shown in Figure 9-40, you will have to enter the user ID and password you use to log in. This is important, as the scheduled task will not run without it.

WARNING If you are using Windows XP, the Task Scheduler will not work without a password. Also, keep in mind that the Windows Task Scheduler does not keep track of expired or changed passwords. You will have to reconfigure your task if you change your password.

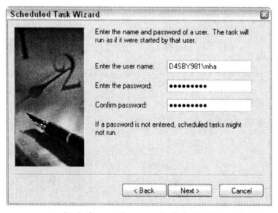

Figure 9-40: Enter your security information, and click the Next button.

Once you get to Figure 9-41, you're almost done. Select the check box next to "Open advanced properties for this task when I click Finish."

The last step is to click on the Browse button, shown in Figure 9-42, and point the Scheduler to the database that contains the AutoExec macro.

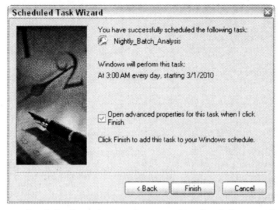

Figure 9-41: Place a check in the advanced properties check box, and click Finish.

Figure 9-42: Click the Browse button and point the Scheduler to your database.

Now you can test the task to make sure it runs properly by right-clicking its name and selecting Run, as demonstrated in Figure 9-43.

Your task is now scheduled! One thing to keep in mind is that the PC on which the task is scheduled obviously must stay on. Also, based on your PC's configuration, you must be logged-in in order for the task to run. That is to say that if you log out, the task may not run. A workaround to this problem is to lock the workstation, which effectively keeps your user ID logged in without compromising security.

Figure 9-43: Be sure to test your task to make sure it runs properly.

Using Command Lines to Schedule Tasks

Command lines are nothing more than commands you can pass to your Access database to modify its startup process. In other words, you can tell Access to do something on startup. For example, the following command line tells the DB1 database to open exclusively and fire the STATS macro.

```
"C:\Program Files\Microsoft Office\Office\msaccess.exe" ↵
"C:\Data\DB1.mdb"/Excl/X STATS
```

A command line is made up of three basic parts:

- The path to the msaccess.exe:

```
"C:\Program Files\Microsoft Office\Office\msaccess.exe" ↵
"C:\Data\DB1.mdb"/Excl/X STATS
```

- The path of the affected database:

```
"C:\Program Files\Microsoft Office\Office\msaccess.exe" ↵
"C:\Data\DB1.mdb"/Excl/X STATS
```

- The command-line switch(es) being used:

```
"C:\Program Files\Microsoft Office\Office\msaccess.exe" ↵
"C:\Data\DB1.mdb"/Excl/X STATS
```

In this example, the /Excl switch tells the database to open exclusively. The /X STATS switch tells the database to run the STATS macro upon opening.

> **TIP** Here's a quick list of the more useful command-line switches:
>
> - /excl opens the specified database exclusively.
> - /ro opens the specified database as read-only.
> - /user starts Access by using the specified user name.
> - /pwd starts Access by using the specified password.

- **/profile** starts Access by using the options in the specified user profile.
- **/compact** compacts and repairs the specified database.
- **/X** *MacroName* starts the specified database and runs the specified macro.
- **/wrkgrp** starts Access by using the specified workgroup information.

When to Use Command Lines to Schedule Tasks Instead of AutoExec

Microsoft recommends that you use an AutoExec macro in lieu of command-line switches. However, there are situations where a command line makes more sense. Consider the following when deciding which method to use to schedule your batch analysis:

- **AutoExec affects the startup of your database every time you open it.** You already know that holding the Shift key while you open the database bypasses the AutoExec macro. However, working with a database where you constantly have to remember to hold down the Shift key can be quite annoying. In contrast, a command-line switch does not become part of the database. This means you can fire it whenever you like. If you regularly work in the same database used to run scheduled tasks, consider using command lines.

- **Each macro can have its own schedule.** The problem with combining all your analytical processes into one AutoExec macro is that you run them *all* when you run AutoExec. If you want to schedule some your analyses to run on Monday while others run on Wednesday, you'll have to create another database with a separate AutoExec macro. Command-lines, on the other hand, allow you to have multiple macros run on different schedules without creating new databases. If you have multiple tasks that need to be scheduled at different time, consider using command lines.

Scheduling a Macro to Run Using a Command Line

To schedule a task using a command line, you would follow the steps you performed in the section "Using the Windows Task Scheduler" (shown in Figures 9-35 through 9-42). In the advanced properties dialog box shown in Figure 9-42, enter the following in the Run input box:

1. The path to msaccess.exe in quotes. In most cases, it will be "C:\Program Files\Microsoft Office\OFFICExx\msaccess.exe," where xx is the version of Office.

2. A space.

3. The path to the database that contains the macro you want to run in quotes.

4. The command-line switch for running a macro (/X MacroName).

The following is an example of a valid command-line switch:

```
"C:\Program Files\Microsoft Office\OFFICE14\msaccess.exe" ↵
"C:\Data\MyDatabase.mdb"/X MyMacro
```

As you can see in Figure 9-44, to use this command line, you would simply enter it into the Run input box.

Your task is now scheduled!

Figure 9-44: Simply enter the command line into the Run input box.

TIP You can create a new shortcut on your desktop and use a command line as the target. This enables you to run a macro from a shortcut, compact and repair your database from a shortcut, and so forth.

Summary

Access macros are used to execute a set of pre-programmed functions called actions. The idea behind building a macro in Access is to choose a set of actions you want the macro to carry out when it is executed. There are over 80 macro actions in Access, each one performing a certain function. These functions range from manipulating Access objects to executing and outputting data analysis. Once you build a macro that automates your analytical processes, you can schedule it to run automatically by using the Windows Task Scheduler. Leveraging macro functionality allows you to automate many of your analytical processes, leading to higher productivity and a reduced chance of human error.

CHAPTER 10

Leveraging VBA to Enhance Data Analysis

Many Access users are not programmers, and it would be fair to say that most do not aspire to be programmers. In fact, most of you are just trying to survive the projects you are juggling now; who has the time to learn VBA?

If you are tempted to take a polite look at this chapter and then move on, you should definitely fight that urge. Why? Because leveraging VBA (Visual Basic for Applications) in your analytical processes can make your life easier in the long run. VBA can help you do things faster and more efficiently. In fact, just a few lines of code can save you hours of work, freeing you up to do other things, and increasing your productivity. Consider some of the advantages that VBA offers:

- VBA can help you automate redundant analyses and recurring analytical processes, leaving you free to work on other tasks.

- VBA allows you to process data without the need to create and maintain queries and macros.

- With VBA, you can automate external programs such as Excel to expand the reporting capabilities.

- With VBA, you can perform complex, multi-layered procedures that involve looping, record-level testing, and `If...Then...ElseIf` statements.

- You can tailor your own error-handling procedures using VBA, allowing you to anticipate and plan for process flow changes in the event of an error.

This chapter covers some fundamental concepts and techniques that will lay the groundwork for your own ideas about how to enhance your analytical processes with VBA.

TIP True to its purpose, all the techniques in this chapter involve writing some basic code. In order to keep things focused on the data analysis aspect of these techniques, this chapter will not be spending much time explaining the VBA behind them. If you are new to VBA, you may want to refer to Appendix A, "Access VBA Fundamentals," which will give you a firm understanding of the basic concepts used in this chapter.

NOTE Keep in mind that the new security features in Access may prevent you from running the procedures found in the sample file. You will need to enable the content in the database in order to use the VBA. Feel free to revisit Chapter 9 to find out how the new security features in Access work and how to enable the content of your database.

Creating and Using Custom Functions

The developers at Microsoft have put in thousands of man-hours developing functions that are expansive enough to fit the needs of most users. In most cases, the functions available in Access more than satisfy user requirements. In fact, many users will never use a majority of the functions available, and will typically gravitate towards only those that fit their current needs.

On the other end of the spectrum, there are those users whose daily operations involve tasks not covered by the functions in Access. These tasks can involve a business-specific calculation or a complex expression that achieves a particular result. In most cases, these tasks are accomplished by building expressions. For example, suppose that your analysis routinely calls for the last day of the current week. Because no built-in function exists to help you determine the last day of the current week, you would use the following expression wherever you need this data:

```
Date() - WeekDay(Date()) + 7
```

The alternative to using such an expression is to build a custom function (sometimes referred to as a user-defined function). *Custom functions* are VBA procedures that expose your expressions to other objects in your database as a function, much like Access's built-in functions. This essentially means that instead of creating and using expressions in a query or form, you build your expressions into a VBA procedure, and then call it whenever you need it. Why bother with custom functions? Well, consider the following inherent advantages to converting your expressions into custom functions.

- Expressions, in and of themselves, generally perform operations that are simple and linear in nature. They don't allow for complex operations that involve looping or If...Then...Else logic. Building a custom function will give you the flexibility to perform complex, multi-layered procedures that involve looping, record-level testing, and If...Then...Else logic.

- Expressions don't allow you to define explicitly what happens in the event of an error. Building a custom function in a VBA environment allows you to include error-handling procedures with your expressions, empowering you to anticipate and plan for process flow changes in the event of an error.

- When you change the definition of an expression, you have to find and modify that expression in every place it is used. A custom function resides in one module; therefore, when there is a change in your expression or procedure, you have to update it in only one location.

- There is an increased risk of error when you are forced to manually type expressions repeatedly. For example, the expression, Date() - WeekDay(Date()) + 7 contains syntax that could easily be keyed incorrectly or omitted. By using a custom function, you ensure that your expression is performed the same way every time, without the risk of a typing mistake.

Creating Your First Custom Function

For your first custom function, you will build a function that will return the last day of the current week.

1. Start a new module by clicking the Create tab on the ribbon and selecting Module as demonstrated in Figure 10-1.

Figure 10-1: Start a new module.

2. Create a new function by entering the following code:

```
Function LastDayThisWeek()
```

NOTE There is nothing special about the name **LastDayThisWeek**. It's simply a descriptive name that coincides with the purpose of the function. When creating your own custom function, it's good practice to give your functions simple names that are descriptive and easy to remember.

3. On the next line, assign the needed expression to the function, giving your custom function its utility.

```
LastDayThisWeek = Date - Weekday(Date) + 7
```

At this point, your module should look similar to the one shown in Figure 10-2.

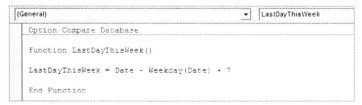

Figure 10-2: You have created your first custom function.

4. Save the module and close it.

To test your newly created custom function, create the query you see in Figure 10-3 and run it. In this query, you first determine the last day of the current week by using your newly created function, and then you use that value to calculate how many days are left in the current week.

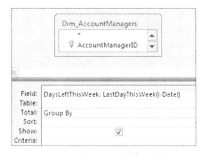

Figure 10-3: This query uses your newly created function to determine how many days are left in the current week.

TRICKS OF THE TRADE: CREATING A CENTRAL REPOSITORY OF CUSTOM FUNCTIONS

You don't have to create a separate module for each custom function in your database; you can create one module to hold them all. In the sample database that comes with this book, you will see a module called "My_Custom_Functions." If you open it, you will see the seven separate custom functions shown in Figure 10-4. These functions can be used separately in various analyses.

This method of storing your custom functions makes finding and editing your functions easy. Figure 10-5 illustrates another advantage of this method. When you activate the Expression Builder, you can drill into all the modules you have created in your database. Having one module that contains all your custom functions provides you a complete list of your functions.

TRICKS OF THE TRADE: CREATING A CENTRAL REPOSITORY OF CUSTOM FUNCTIONS

```
(General)

Option Compare Database
Option Explicit

Function FirstDayThisWeek()
FirstDayThisWeek = Date - Weekday(Date) + 1
End Function

Function LastDayThisWeek()
LastDayThisWeek = Date - Weekday(Date) + 7
End Function

Function FirstDayThisQtr()
FirstDayThisQtr = DateSerial(Year(Date), Int((Month(Date) - 1) / 3) * 3 + 1, 1)
End Function

Function LastDayThisQtr()
LastDayThisQtr = DateSerial(Year(Date), Int((Month(Date) - 1) / 3) * 3 + 4, 0)
End Function

Function LastDayThisMonth()
LastDayThisMonth = DateSerial(Year(Date), Month(Date), 0)
End Function

Function LastDayNextMonth()
LastDayNextMonth = DateSerial(Year(Date), Month(Date) + 1, 0)
End Function

Function FirstDayLastMonth()
FirstDayLastMonth = DateSerial(Year(Date), Month(Date) - 1, 1)
End Function
```

Figure 10-4: Creating one module that holds all your custom functions allows you to quickly find and edit any of your user-defined functions.

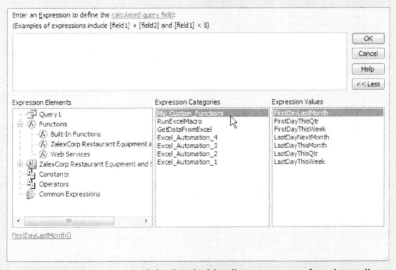

Figure 10-5: Creating one module that holds all your custom functions allows you to quickly find and edit any of your user-defined functions.

Creating a Custom Function that Accepts Arguments

Sometimes the operation performed by your custom function requires arguments that cannot be supplied internally by Access. In these situations, you will need to create a custom function that accepts arguments. To illustrate this concept, look at the query in Figure 10-6.

In this query, the Revenue field is being annualized (that is, the revenue value of each row is being translated to an annual rate for comparative purposes). The nature of this operation requires three arguments: the value being annualized, the number of periods already completed, and the number periods that make up an entire year. As you can see in this query, the value being annualized is revenue, the number of periods completed is 8, and the number periods that make up a year is 12.

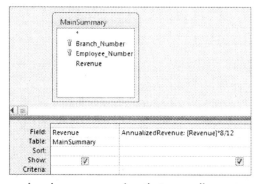

Figure 10-6: This query is using an expression that annualizes a revenue value.

In order to convert this expression to a custom function, you have to allow the user to pass the required arguments. Walk through the following steps:

1. Go into the Visual Basic Editor by pressing Ctrl+Alt on the keyboard. From there, start a new module by selecting Insert ➪ Module.

2. Create and name your new function by entering the following code:

```
Function Annualized()
```

3. Inside the parentheses, declare a variable and type for each argument that will be passed to the function.

```
Function Annualized(MyValue As Long, _
PeriodsCompleted As Integer, PeriodsinYear As Integer)
```

4. On the next line, assign the needed expression to the function, giving your custom function its utility. Instead of using hard-coded values, you will use the values passed to the declared variables.

```
Annualized = MyValue / PeriodsCompleted * PeriodsinYear
```

At this point, your module should look similar to the one shown in Figure 10-7.

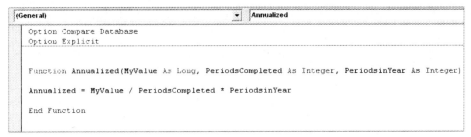

```
(General)                                              ▼  Annualized

    Option Compare Database
    Option Explicit


    Function Annualized(MyValue As Long, PeriodsCompleted As Integer, PeriodsinYear As Integer)

    Annualized = MyValue / PeriodsCompleted * PeriodsinYear

    End Function
```

Figure 10-7: This custom function accepts three variables and uses them in an expression.

To test your newly created Annualized function, create the query you see in Figure 10-8, and then run it. Note that you are using your newly created function in an Alias called "AnlzdRev."

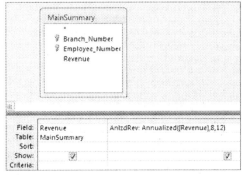

Figure 10-8: This query uses your newly created function to get the annualized revenue for each record.

> **TIP** You can hard-code selected arguments in your custom function to limit the number of arguments that need to be passed. For instance, the following code demonstrates how you can change the procedure for the Annualized function to hard-code the number of periods in a year:

```
Function Annualized(MyValue As Long, PeriodsCompleted As Integer)
Annualized = MyValue / PeriodsCompleted * 12
End Function
```

> As you can see, the number of periods in a year has been hard-coded to 12, so when using this function, you have to pass only two arguments. For example:

```
Annualized([Revenue], 8)
```

A WORD ABOUT USING CUSTOM FUNCTIONS

Up to this point, you have tested your custom functions using queries. Although you will most commonly use your custom functions in queries, it is

(continued)

A WORD ABOUT USING CUSTOM FUNCTIONS *(continued)*

important to note that you can use them anywhere you would use any one of Access's built-in functions. Here are a few examples of how you can utilize your custom functions.

In a query environment, you can use your custom functions in the same ways you would use built-in Access functions. Figure 10-9 demonstrates some of the ways you can use a custom function in a query.

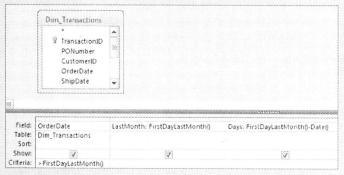

Figure 10-9: Using custom functions in a query

Figure 10-10 illustrates how in a form, you can tie the Control Source for a text box to one of your custom functions. This same method works in Access reports. In this example, this form will automatically execute the `FirstDayLastMonth` function each time it is opened to provide a value to the assigned text box.

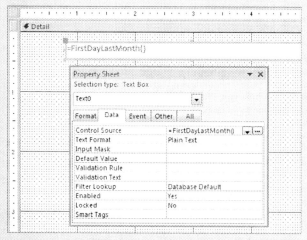

Figure 10-10: Using a custom function in a form

A WORD ABOUT USING CUSTOM FUNCTIONS

Figure 10-11 illustrates how your custom functions can be used in other VBA procedures. This procedure uses the `FirstDayLastMonth` function to find the first day of last month and then puts that date into a message box.

```
(General)

Option Compare Database

Function Mytest()
MsgBox ("The first day last month was " & FirstDayLastMonth() & ".")
End Function
```

Figure 10-11: Using a custom function in another VBA procedure

---

Controlling Analytical Processes with Forms

An Access form is nothing more than a database object that can accept user input and display data using a collection of controls. Access forms are often thought of as part of the presentation layer of a database, primarily being used as the front-end of an application. While it is true that the primary purpose of forms is to act as an interface between Access and a user, this does not mean the user cannot be you (the designer of the database). In this section, you learn how Access forms can be leveraged on the back-end of a database as a data analysis tool that interacts with your analyses and further automates your analytical processes.

The Basics of Passing Data from a Form to a Query

The idea behind passing data from a form to a query is that instead of using parameters in a query to collect the data for your analysis, you collect the data through a form. To get a firm understanding of the basics of passing parameters from a form to a query, perform the following steps:

1. Start by creating a new form. Go to the Create tab on the ribbon and click the Form Design button as demonstrated in Figure 10-12.

2. Go up to the Design tab and select the Text Box control as demonstrated in Figure 10-13; then click anywhere on your form. At this point, you should have a form with one text box control.

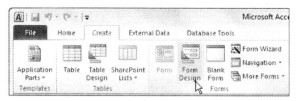

Figure 10-12: Start a new form in Design view.

Figure 10-13: Add a text box control to your form.

3. Right-click the text box and select Properties. Click the All tab, and then give the newly created text box a distinctive name by entering **txtParam** as the Name property, as shown in Figure 10-14.

Figure 10-14: Give your text box control a distinctive name.

NOTE   Each control on your form must have a valid name in the Name property. The Name property is a unique identifier that allows Access to reference a control in other parts of your database. Access automatically assigns generic names to newly created controls. However, you should always make it a point to give each of your controls you own descriptive name. This makes referencing and recognizing your controls much easier.

4. Go back to the Design tab and select the Command Button control, as shown in Figure 10-15, and click anywhere on your form. This will place a command button on your form.

NOTE   If the Command Button Wizard activates, click Cancel to close it. You will not need that wizard for this exercise.

Figure 10-15: Add a command button control to your form.

5. Right-click the newly created command button and select Properties. Click the All tab, and adjust the Name property of your command button to read **btnRunQuery.** Then adjust the Caption property to read **Run Query**.

6. Next, while still in the command button's properties, click the Event tab and then select [Event Procedure] from the On Click event, as shown in Figure 10-16. Next, click the ellipsis button (the button next to the dropdown).

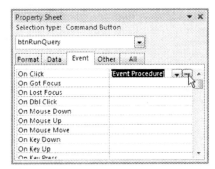

Figure 10-16: Set the On Click event to run an [Event Procedure], and then click the ellipsis button.

7. At this point, you should be inside the VBA editor, where you will enter a DoCmd action that will run the query called "Chapter10_ExampleA." Enter the following code, just as you see in Figure 10-17.

```
DoCmd.OpenQuery "Chapter10_ExampleA", acViewNormal
```

The DoCmd.OpenQuery method enables you to execute any saved query from code. This method is perfect for simple automation processes such as this.

8. Once you are done, save your form as "frmMain" and close it.

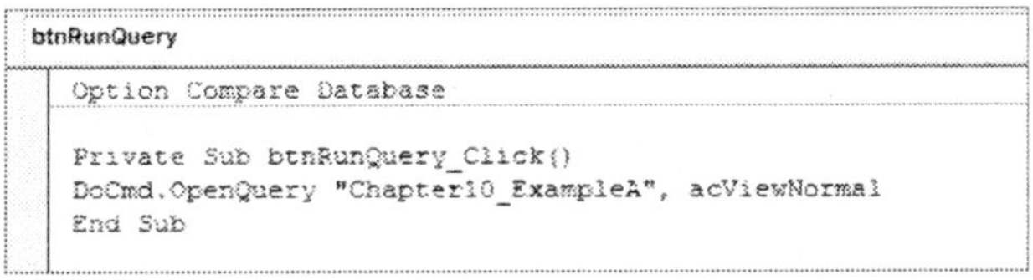

```
btnRunQuery

    Option Compare Database

    Private Sub btnRunQuery_Click()
    DoCmd.OpenQuery "Chapter10_ExampleA", acViewNormal
    End Sub
```

Figure 10-17: Use the Docmd.OpenQuery method to execute the "Chapter10_ExampleA" query.

9. It's time to test. Open the newly created frmMain form and click the Run Query button. If the query runs successfully, you have set up your form correctly. Now you can prepare your query to accept parameters from this form!

10. Open the "Chapter12_Example_A" query in Design view. Enter **[Forms]! [frmMain].[txtParam]** as the criteria for the Period field, as shown in Figure 10-18.

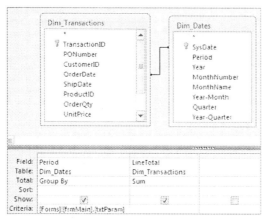

Figure 10-18: This query filters on the Period field based on the value of the txtParam text box in the frmMain form.

11. Save and close the query.

Now you can open the frmMain form and enter a parameter for your query through a form! Enter **200704** in the text box, as shown in Figure 10-19, and then run the query. This returns all revenues earned in the 200704system period.

NOTE You will notice that if you leave the text box blank, your query will not return any results. This is the same issue you encounter using parameter queries. One way to get around this problem is to combine your expression with a wildcard so that if the text box is blank, all records will be returned. In this scenario, for instance, you would change your expression to read:

```
Like [Forms]![frmMain].[txtParam] & "*"
```

Figure 10-19: Now you can pass your parameters to your query through a form.

TIP You can reference any form control that has a value property, including combo boxes, list boxes, text boxes, and option groups.

UNDERSTANDING THE SYNTAX FOR REFERENCING A FORM

Let's take a moment to analyze the syntax used for referencing a form.

■ *Brackets ([ ])*: Brackets are used to identify the name of an object. For instance, if you were referring to the CustomerMaster table, you would refer to it as [CustomerMaster]. If you were referring to a query called TopTen_Step1, you would refer to it as [TopTen_Step1]. This not only helps Access identify objects, but it will also make your code easier to read.

■ *The collection operator (!)*: The collection operator (sometimes referred to as the bang operator) is used to tell Access that the object with which you are working belongs to a particular collection of objects. For example, if you are working with a form called "Main," you would refer to it as [Forms]![Main] because the form [Main] belongs to the Forms collection.

■ *The dot operator (.)*: The dot operator points to a property belonging to an object. For example, while [CustomerMaster] refers to the CustomerMaster table, [CustomerMaster].[City] refers to the City field in the CustomerMaster table. Here is another example. [Forms]![Main] refers to the form "Main", while [Forms]![Main].[Fname] refers to a control called Fname located in "Main."

Enhancing Automation with Forms

Access forms can help you enhance your automated processes using little more than a few controls and some light VBA coding. The idea is to turn your forms into something more than just a tool to pass parameters; you can create a robust central control point for your analysis.

To help illustrate the power of incorporating Access forms into your analysis, open the frmMktRpts form in the sample database, shown in Figure 10-20. The purpose of this form is to control the execution of an analysis that involves creating market reports. The idea is to select a market, run the process that executes a query, and then sends the results to an Excel file in the C:\OffTheGrid directory.

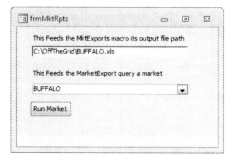

Figure 10-20: This form enables you to control the execution of an analytical process.

Open the form in Design view to see how this works. As you can see, there are three controls on this form.

- **The txtPath text box.** The txtPath text box uses the market value from the combo box to construct a file path. This allows you to dynamically create a separate path for each market. This path is constructed by concatenating two strings and a control reference.

    - **C:\OffTheGrid\.** This is the first part of the file path, pointing to the OffTheGrid directory in the C drive.

    - **[cboLocations].** This is the name of the combo box where you select your market. This becomes the file name.

    - **.xls.** This string finishes the path by assigning the file extension that identifies the file as an Excel file.

If you open the MktExports macro, shown in Figure 10-21, you will notice that the Output File path is referencing this text box. This allows the macro to avoid using a hard-coded file path.

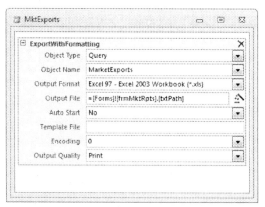

Figure 10-21: You will use the txtPath text box to dynamically feed your macro the Output File path for each market.

■ **The cboLocations combo box**. This combo box helps do two things. First, this combo box feeds the txtPath text box a market to use in the construction of a file path. Second, it feeds the MarketExports query its parameter. If you open the MarketExports query, shown in Figure 10-22, you will notice that filter criteria for the Market field is referencing this combo box. This allows the query to avoid using a hard-coded market.

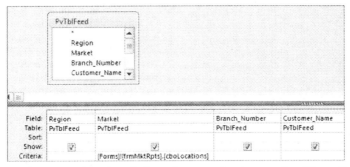

Figure 10-22: You are using the cboLocations combo box as the filter criteria for the Market field.

■ **The btnRunMarket command button.** Right-click this command button and then click Build Event. This will take you to the VBA editor shown in Figure 10-23. As you can see, this button simply runs the MktExports macro, and then throws up a message box announcing the location of your new file.

Figure 10-23: When you click the command button, a DoCmd action will run the macro and then call a message box.

Now that you have a firm grasp of how this form works, you can enhance it even further. Instead of running one market at a time, wouldn't it be useful to run all markets at once? You can do this by using VBA to enumerate through all the markets in the combo box, running the MktExports as you go.

Enumerating Through a Combo Box

Open the frmMktRpts form and take a look at the combo box on the form. The entries, or rows, you see within the combo box are indexed—that is, each row has an index number starting from 0 and continuing to however many rows there are. For example, the first row is index number 0, the second row is index number 1, the third row is index number 2, and so on. The idea behind enumerating through a combo box is to capture one index at a time, and then change the value of the combo box to match the row value assigned to that index number.

1. Start by opening the frmMktRpts form in Design view and adding a second command button.

2. Adjust the Name property of your newly created command button to read **btnRunAll,** and then adjust the Caption property to read **Run All**.

   At this point, your form should look similar to Figure 10-24.

Figure 10-24: Add a second command button called Run All to the form.

3. Right-click the button and select Build Event. Select Code Builder from the Choose Builder dialog box, and then click OK. This opens the VBA Editor. As you can see in Figure 10-25, this creates a separate subprocedure.

```
btnRunAll                                                      ▼   Click

    Option Compare Database


    Private Sub btnRunAll_Click()

    End Sub

    Private Sub btnRunMarket_Click()

        DoCmd.RunMacro "MktExports"
        MsgBox "Your file can be found here:" & Me.txtPath

    End Sub
```

Figure 10-25: Build an On Click event for the newly created btnRunAll command button.

4. Start the code by declaring an integer variable called `IndexNum`. This traps the index number of each entry of the combo box.

```
Dim IndexNum As Integer
```

5. Initiate a `For...Next` loop with the `IndexNum` variable. This line of code ensures that the procedure runs for each index number in the combo box.

```
For IndexNum = 0 To Me.cboLocations.ListCount - 1
```

NOTE Why subtract 1 from the combo box's list count? You must do this to adjust for the fact that index numbers of a combo box start at 0. If there are 10 rows in a combo box, the ListCount property starts counting at 1, returning a count of 10 rows. However, the index numbers in the same combo box range from 0 to 9. Subtracting 1 from the list count removes the extra number and corrects the discrepancy.

6. Set the value of the combo box equal to the value of the row assigned to the current index number. After the new value has been set, run the predefined macro.

```
Me.cboLocations.Value = Me.cboLocations.ItemData(IndexNum)
DoCmd.RunMacro "MktExports"
```

7. Repeat the process for the next index number. The message will alert you when the procedure has completed its execution.

```
Next IndexNum
MsgBox "Your files can be found in the C:\OffTheGrid directory."
```

If you have done everything correctly, your procedure should look similar to Figure 10-26.

8. Save your form and test the newly created functionality by clicking the Run All button.

Figure 10-26: This procedure enumerates through a combo box, running a macro for each entry.

Once the procedure has completed running, look under the C:\OffTheGrid directory to see all the Excel files that where created (see Figure 10-27).

Figure 10-27: All of these Excel files were created with automation.

Needless to say, this example is just one of the hundreds of ways you can enhance your analytical processes using forms. The flexibility and functionality you gain by using a few controls and a handful of code is simply incredible. Even simple techniques such as passing parameters from a form to a query can open the doors to a completely new set of analytical functionality.

Processing Data Behind the Scenes

One of the benefits of using VBA is that you can perform much of your data processing in the background without the use of queries and macros. This can be beneficial in several ways, including that it can:

▪ **Reduce the number of query objects in your database:** Every analytical process has intermediate steps that serve as a means to an end. These steps typically involve action queries that massage and transform the data for the bigger analysis. Too many of these peripheral queries can inundate your database with query objects, making your analytical processes difficult to manage and change. Processing your data in the background using VBA can help you streamline your processes by reducing the number query objects in your database, making both the management and the maintenance of your analyses more practical.

- **Better organize your analytical processes:** Have you ever seen a process that involves queries that link to forms that, in turn, link to macros that reference tables created by other queries, and so on? You will undoubtedly run into analyses that involve complicated processes, and there is nothing wrong with utilizing the tools Access provides. However, engineering overly elaborate systems that involve macros, queries, and forms can make your processes difficult to manage and maintain. Processing your data in the background using VBA can help you centralize your analysis into one procedure, organizing your tasks in a clearly defined set of instructions that are easy to locate, update, and manage.

- **Protect your processes in shared environments:** Processing your data in the background using VBA can help you protect your analytical processes working in a shared database. Building your processes in VBA can reduce the risk of someone changing your queries or accidentally deleting objects.

- **Enhance your processes with VBA:** The more you integrate your analytical processes into VBA, the more you can take advantage of its many benefits such as looping, record-level testing, and error handling.

Anyone who routinely works with Access knows that there are several different ways to accomplish any given task. Processing data using VBA is no different. Indeed, the beauty of VBA is that its flexibility allows you to perform literally any action in countless ways. That being said, it should be obvious that it's impossible to cover every possible way to process data using VBA. Therefore, you will focus on using RunSQL statements. This technique gives you some fundamental controls over your processes through VBA and allows you to move more of your analyses behind the scenes.

Processing Data with RunSQL Statements

By this point, you already know that the query objects you are accustomed to using are simply visual representations of SQL statements. What you may not know is that you don't necessarily need to create a query object in order to process data. You can process data directly through a RunSQL statement. One of the ways to do this is to use the RunSQL method.

The Basics of the RunSQL Method

If you were designing a macro, you would find RunSQL in the list of macro actions. In technical terms, RunSQL is a method belonging to the DoCmd object. Those of you who have been paying attention probably noticed that up until now, you've used OpenQuery when working with a query in a macro environment, and Docmd.OpenQuery when working with a query through code.

In this light, it's important to note the differences between the RunSQL method and OpenQuery method.

- The OpenQuery method executes a saved query, whereas the RunSQL method processes a SQL statement without the need for a saved query.

- The RunSQL method only allows you to execute action queries (make-table, append, delete, and update), whereas the OpenQuery method enables the execution of any type of saved query; including select queries.

- The OpenQuery method is ideal for use in a macro environment. The RunSQL method, on the other hand, is better suited for dynamic back-end processes performed in VBA.

> **NOTE** Among other reasons, RunSQL is better suited for VBA because in a macro environment, the RunSQL action limits you to SQL statements that do not exceed 256 characters. This obviously restricts the functionality of RunSQL in the macro environment. However, there is no such limitation in the VBA environment.

THE ANATOMY OF RUNSQL STATEMENTS

`DoCmd.RunSQL(SQLStatement, UseTransaction)`

RunSQL is a method of the DoCmd object that executes action queries such as append, delete, update, and make-table. This method has the following two arguments:

- *SQLStatement* (required): This is the SQL statement that is to be executed.

- *UseTransaction* (optional): This is a true or false indicator that specifies how Access safeguards your data during the execution of your SQL statement. The default state for this argument is True, which ensures that your SQL statement is tested in a temporary log before final execution. You should rarely set this argument to False.

`DoCmd.RunSQL "Delete * from [MyTable]"` deletes all records from MyTable.

Using RunSQL Statements

Using RunSQL statements in your code is easy. You would simply place each RunSQL statement in your VBA procedure as needed. For instance, the following procedure runs four actions, demonstrating that you can process data without creating one query:

- Makes a table called tblJobCodes
- Inserts a new record into the tblJobCodes table
- Updates the job code "PPL" to "PPL1"
- Deletes the "PPL1" job code

```
Function Look_Ma_No_Queries()

DoCmd.RunSQL "SELECT [Job_Code]INTO [tblJobCodes]FROM ↵
[Employee_Master] GROUP BY [Job_Code]"

DoCmd.RunSQL "INSERT INTO [tblJobCodes] ( [Job_Code] ) SELECT ↵
'PPL' AS NewCode FROM [Employee_Master] GROUP BY 'PPL'"

DoCmd.RunSQL "UPDATE [tblJobCodes] SET [Job_Code] = 'PPL1' ↵
WHERE [Job_Code]='PPL'"

DoCmd.RunSQL "DELETE * FROM [tblJobCodes] WHERE [Job_Code]='PPL1'"

End Function
```

NOTE You will find this procedure in the sample database in the module called Using_RunSQL. Note that each `RunSQL` statement should be one line of code. You see the lines broken up here due to layout specifications.

TIP Having trouble creating SQL statements? Here's a handy trick. Create a query in Design view, and then switch to SQL view. Although you have to adjust the SQL statement a bit, Access does most of the work for you.

Advanced Techniques Using RunSQL Statements

Now that you have a firm understanding of what `RunSQL` statements can do, take a look at some of the advanced techniques that will help enhance your behind-the-scenes processing.

Suppressing Warning Messages

As you execute your `RunSQL` statements, you will notice that Access throws up the same warning messages you would get if you were to run the same actions with stored queries. You can use the `SetWarnings` method to suppress these messages just as you would in a macro. For example, the following code sets warnings to false, runs the `RunSQL` statement, and then sets warnings back to true.

```
DoCmd.SetWarnings False
DoCmd.RunSQL "DELETE * FROM [tblJobCodes] WHERE [Job_Code]='PPL1'"
DoCmd.SetWarnings True
```

Passing a SQL Statement as a Variable

One of the biggest challenges in working with the RunSQL method is managing and making sense of giant SQL statements. It's difficult to determine what is going on in your code when your RunSQL statement runs off the page with over 100 characters in its SQL string. One of the ways to make for easier reading is to pass your SQL statement as a variable. This section demonstrates how passing your SQL statement through a string variable enables you to break up your statement into pieces that are easier to read.

1. Start a procedure and declare a string variable called MySQL.

   ```
   Function Passing_SQL_With_Strings()
   Dim MySQL As String
   ```

2. Start assigning the SQL statement to the MySQL variable. What you're looking for here is structure, a format that makes the SQL statement easy to read and manage within the VBA editor. The first line starts the string. Each subsequent line is concatenated to the previous line. By the last line, the MySQL variable contains the entire SQL string.

   ```
   MySQL = "SELECT TOP 10 Market, Sum(Revenue) AS Rev INTO TopTenList "
   MySQL = MySQL & "FROM PvTblFeed "
   MySQL = MySQL & "GROUP BY PvTblFeed.Market, PvTblFeed.Customer_Name "
   MySQL = MySQL & "ORDER BY Sum(PvTblFeed.Revenue) DESC"
   ```

3. All that is left to do now is pass the MySQL variable to your RunSQL statement, as follows:

   ```
   DoCmd.RunSQL MySQL
   End Function
   ```

NOTE Although there are other ways to concatenate this SQL string without the redundancy of typing *"MySQL = MySQL & ... "*, this method creates a visual block of code that unmistakably lets the person reviewing the code know that all this goes together.

Passing User-Defined Parameters from a Form to Your SQL Statement

Even when you are processing data behind the scenes, you can pass user-defined parameters from a form to create dynamic SQL statements. Here are some examples of how you would pass data from a form to your SQL statements:

Passing Textual Parameters from a Form

In this example, you are passing textual criterion from a form. Note that the expression that points to the user-defined parameter on the form must be wrapped in quotes. In addition, because the data type you are passing is textual, the entire expression is wrapped in single quotes.

```
MySQL = "SELECT Market, Customer_Name, EffDate, TransCount "
MySQL = MySQL & "INTO MyResults "
MySQL = MySQL & "FROM MyTable "
MySQL = MySQL & "WHERE Market='" & [Forms]![frmMain].[cboMarket] & "'"
DoCmd.RunSQL MySQL
```

Passing Numeric Parameters from a Form

In this example, you are passing a numeric criterion from a form. Note that the expression that points to the user-defined parameter on the form must be wrapped in quotes.

```
MySQL = "SELECT Market, Customer_Name, EffDate, TransCount "
MySQL = MySQL & "INTO MyResults "
MySQL = MySQL & "FROM MyTable "
MySQL = MySQL & "WHERE TransCount =" & [Forms]![frmMain].[cboCount] & ""
DoCmd.RunSQL MySQL
```

Passing Date Parameters from a Form

In this example, you are passing date criterion from a form. Note that the expression that points to the user-defined parameter on the form must be wrapped in quotes. In addition, because the data type you are passing is a date, the entire expression is wrapped in a pound sign (#).

```
MySQL = "SELECT Market, Customer_Name, EffDate, TransCount "
MySQL = MySQL & "INTO MyResults "
MySQL = MySQL & "FROM MyTable "
MySQL = MySQL & "WHERE EffDate =#" & [Forms]![frmMain].[cboMarket] & "#"
DoCmd.RunSQL MySQL
```

Summary

Leveraging VBA (Visual Basic for Applications) in your analytical processes can help you automate redundant and recurring analyses, as well as process data without the need to create and maintain queries and macros. Although there are countless ways you can leverage VBA to improve your analytical process, in this chapter you covered three techniques: building custom functions, incorporating Access Forms in your analysis, and using Run SQL commands to run queries behind the scenes.

Custom functions are VBA procedures that expose your expressions to other objects in your database as a function, much like Access's built-in functions. This essentially means that instead of creating and using expressions in a query or form, you build your expressions into a VBA procedure, and then call it whenever you need it. The major advantages to building your own custom functions using VBA is that you have the flexibility to perform complex multi-layered procedures that involve looping, record-level testing, and If...Then...Else logical evaluations while ensuring that your expression is performed the same way every time, without the risk of a typing mistake.

Another way to use VBA to enhance analysis is to incorporate Access forms into your analytical processes. An Access form is nothing more than a database object that can accept user input and display data using a collection of controls. Access forms are often thought of as part of the presentation layer of a database, primarily being used as the front-end of an application. While it is true that the primary purpose of forms is to act as an interface between Access and a user, this does not mean the user cannot be you. Access forms can be leveraged on the back-end of a database as a data analysis tool that interacts with your analyses and further automates your analytical processes.

Finally, you can create and run RunSQL commands using VBA to process data behind the scenes, without the need for query objects or temporary tables. The advantages of using RunSQL commands are:

- You can reduce the number of query objects in your database.

- You can centralize your analysis into one procedure, organizing your tasks in a clearly defined set of instructions that are easy managed.

- You can protect your processes in shared environments, reducing the risk of someone changing your queries or accidentally deleting objects.

Reports, Dashboards, and Visualization in Access

In This Part

Presenting Data with Access Reports

As an Excel analyst, you have no doubt created your fair share of Excel reports; complete with sorting, layout and formatting. But how often have you thought about creating your reports in Access? The truth is that most Excel analysts think of Access solely as a data store. Few analysts consider using Access' reporting layer (the Access Report object).

The *Access Report* is an incredibly powerful component of the Microsoft Access toolset. Acting as the presentation layer for your database, the Access Report allows you to easily integrate your database analysis with polished PDF-style reporting functionality, complete with grouping, sorting, and conditional formatting.

In this chapter, you explore Access Reports and discover how they can add a powerful new dimension to your reporting capabilities.

Access Report Basics

In this section, you create your first Access report and explore the different ways to view that report. After walking through this section, you'll have enough grounding to start building your own Access Reports.

Creating Your First Report

The first step in creating a report in Access is to define the data source for the report. The data used in any Access reports can come from either a Table or a Query. One of the easiest ways to define a data source for a report is to build a query specifically designed to feed your report.

For your first report, you'll use the Query_Products query. Select the query and click Report command found in the Create tab (Figure 11-1).

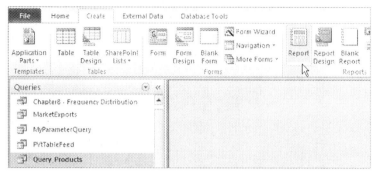

Figure 11-1: Select your query and click the Report command button.

In a few seconds, Access produces a report that looks similar to the one illustrated here in Figure 11-2. As easy as that, you have created your first Access Report.

Query_Products		
Product_Category	Product_Name	List_Price
Bar Equipment	Spindle Drink Mixer Triple Spindle $ 595.00	$595.00
Bar Equipment	One Gallon Blender	$1,099.00
Bar Equipment	Bar Cover	$162.94
Bar Equipment	High Power Blender Easy-To-Clean Electronic Membrane	$375.00
Bar Equipment	High Power Blender With Paddle Switches	$375.00
Bar Equipment	Glass Rimmers Twin Brushes	$17.95
Bar Equipment	Speed Rail 10 Quart/Liter Bottle Capacity	$34.95
Bar Equipment	Glass Rimmers Triple Brushes	$20.43

Figure 11-2: You have created your first Access Report!

Close the report and you will a message asking if you want to save your changes. Clicking the No button leaves you with no report. Clicking the Yes button activates the dialog box you see in Figure 11-3. Here, you name your new report. As you can see, Access defaults the name of the report to the same name as its source. In this case, the name Query_Products is fine.

Figure 11-3: Be sure to save your report.

Viewing Your Report

At this point, you will see your newly created report in the Navigation Pane (Figure 11-4). Simply double click on the report name to open it.

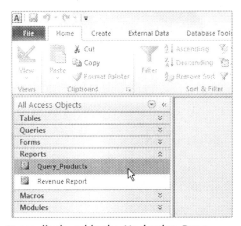

Figure 11-4: All reports are displayed in the Navigation Pane.

Report View

By default, your reports will open in Report view. The Report view simply lets you view and interact with your report as the report user would. You can't edit the data, labels or layout in Report view. However, Access does allow you to apply filters to your reports in real-time.

For instance, imagine you need to quickly find all the Refrigerator products in your newly created report. While in Report View, right-click any product name and select Text Filters ➪ Contains (as demonstrated in Figure 11-5).

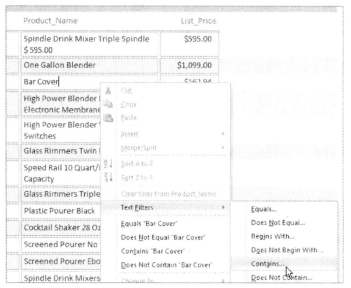

Figure 11-5: Right-click any field while in Report View to see a set of filter options.

This activates the Custom Filter dialog box shown in Figure 11-6. Simply enter your search criteria. In this case, you would enter Refrigerator.

Figure 11-6: Enter your search criteria.

As you can see in Figure 11-7, Access responds by filtering out any product with the word Refrigerator in the product name.

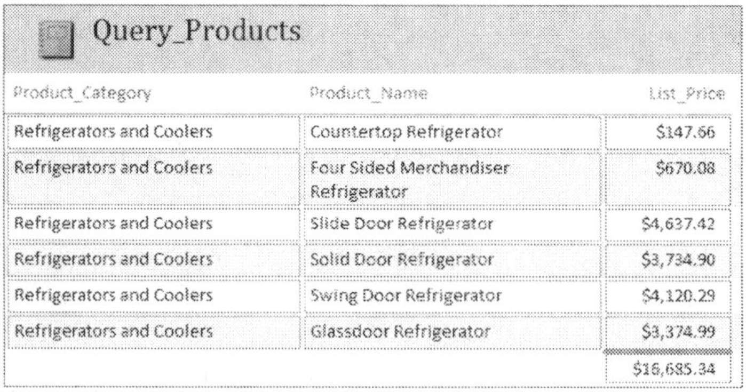

Product_Category	Product_Name	List_Price
Refrigerators and Coolers	Countertop Refrigerator	$147.66
Refrigerators and Coolers	Four Sided Merchandiser Refrigerator	$670.08
Refrigerators and Coolers	Slide Door Refrigerator	$4,637.42
Refrigerators and Coolers	Solid Door Refrigerator	$3,734.90
Refrigerators and Coolers	Swing Door Refrigerator	$4,120.29
Refrigerators and Coolers	Glassdoor Refrigerator	$3,374.99
		$16,685.34

Query_Products

Figure 11-7: You can now review all Refrigerator products.

Layout View

The Layout view, introduced in Access 2007, allows you to edit the look and feel of your report while seeing how it will be displayed to the end user. To get to Layout view, open your Access report and select View ➪ Layout View in the Home tab.

Once your report is in Layout view, you can do things like change the report title, change the data labels, resize columns, remove individual fields, or add new fields. For example, with your report open in Layout view, you can choose a theme for your report (See Figure 11-8). You will immediately notice that your changes take effect in real-time. You don't have to switch back to Report view to see the effect of your change; it shows up right there live on your screen.

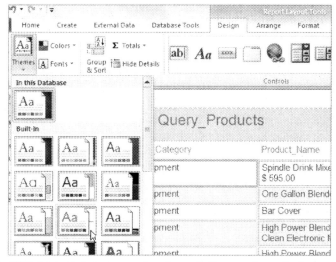

Figure 11-8: With Layout view, you get a dynamic live preview of what your report will look like as you change themes.

Design View

The Design view allows you design your report in the traditional grid interface. For the Access novice, deciphering a report in Design view can be a little intimidating. However, once you understand the basics, creating reports will become much more intuitive and simple. To get to Design view, open your Access report and select View ➪ Design View in the Home tab.

Opening the Query_Products report in Design view brings up the screen shown in Figure 11-9.

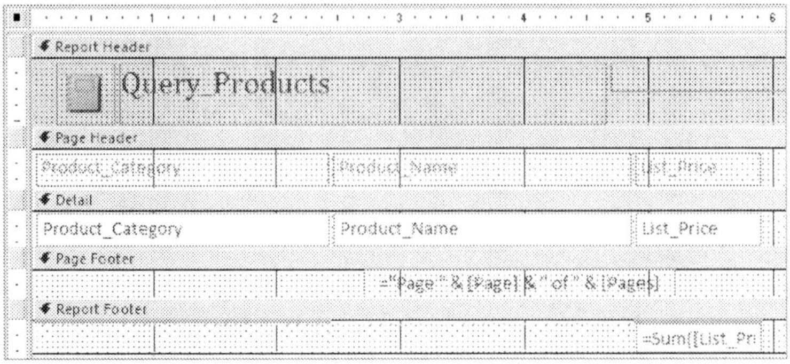

Figure 11-9: The Query_Products report in Design view.

Notice that this report has five distinct sections: Report Header, Page Header, Detail, Page Footer, and Report Footer. These sections are typically what you see when you initially create your reports in Access. Take a moment to explore what each section is designed to do:

- **Report Header:** This typically contains a label that serves as the main title for your report. Just like a header in Word, anything placed in the header section of the Access Design view shows up at the top of your report. As you can see, Access was nice enough to include an auto logo along with a report title; therefore that logo also shows up at the top of your report. It's important to note that items in the Report Header section need not be simple labels. They can be data driven as well, such as page number, current date, or virtually any other data element.

- **Page Header:** This typically contains labels that serve as the heading for each page in your report. Again, items in the Page Header section need not be simple labels. They can be data fields, page count, a date indicator, or virtually any other data element. While it's not evident in this view, you can have different sub-header types. In each instance the header section gives you a place for data that will repeat only once at the top of each logical section, be it report, page, or grouping. You will explore sub-headers and grouping later in this chapter.

TIP You can hover the cursor over the bottom boundary of any section and the cursor will change to a resizing arrow. Simply drag the bottom boundary up or down and you will resize that section of your report. Resizing the sections effectively changes the distance between the sections, allowing you to reduce the white space in your report, expand a section to make room for additional fields, or simply create bit more space to move around easier while working in a particular section.

- **Detail:** This section houses the actual data of your report. As you can see, each data field in your report is represented by a single text box. You can manipulate the content and formatting of any given field by right-clicking a field and selecting Properties. This activates the Property Sheet pane, shown in Figure 11-10. This pane allows you to easily edit and format the chosen field simply by adjusting the properties found here.

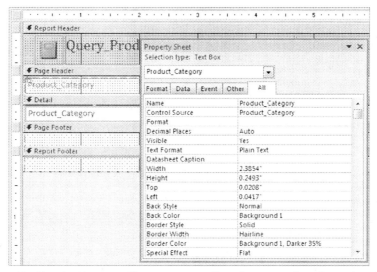

Figure 11-10: Use the Property Sheet pane to adjust the properties of any given field.

Page Footer

The Page Footer section is virtually identical to the Page Header section. The only difference is that labels and data in the footer section come at the end of each page view in the report. Common data elements in the footer include page number, date, and labels. As you can see in Figure 11-9, your report has a data driven page number field inserted in the footer section.

ADDING REPORT ELEMENTS TO YOUR HEADERS AND FOOTERS

It's always handy to have your report headers and footers display information about your report; specifically page numbering and report dates. Although Access does apply these report elements by default, you may want to create these elements manually or change their format and content.

You can apply these elements using the Page Numbers and Date and Time buttons found in the Header/Footer group of the Design tab (Figure 11-11).

(continued)

ADDING REPORT ELEMENTS TO YOUR HEADERS AND FOOTERS *(continued)*

Each of these command buttons opens a dialog box that allows you to configure the report element to suit your needs. For example, Figure 11-12 illustrates the Page Numbers dialog box that configures the format of the report's page numbering.

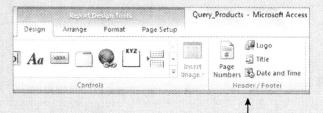

Figure 11-11: You can apply report elements using the Page Numbers and Date and Time buttons.

Figure 11-12: The Insert Page Numbers dialog box

Report Footer

The Report Footer section is virtually identical to the Report Header section. The only difference is that labels and data in the footer come at the end of the report. Common data elements in the footer include page number, date, and labels.

Creating and Modifying Grouped Reports

In this section, you begin to explore the true power of Access reports by illustrating grouping, sorting, and totaling techniques. You'll explore a set of specific example reports, using both the Design and Layout views to complete them.

Grouping

Grouping your report is one of the easiest and most powerful ways to enhance your reports by adding layers of analyses. To explore grouping, open your Query_Products report in Layout View.

Once your report is opened, select the Group and Sort menu item found in the Design tab. This activates the Group, Sort, and Total pane, shown at the bottom of Figure 11-13.

Figure 11-13: The Group, Sort, and Total pane in Layout view

Notice that there are two menu items in the Group, Sort, and Total pane—Add a group and Add a sort. Select the Add a group menu item. Doing so brings up a drop down menu asking on which field we wish to group by (see Figure 11-14).

Figure 11-15 illustrates the applied grouping. Notice how Access moves your grouping field (Product_Category) to the far left of the report. In addition, product categories are now listed only once instead of repeatedly for each of the branch's service reps.

Figure 11-16 demonstrates how a bit of formatting work can make your groupings stand out. In this example, the font for the Product_Category field has been increased and made bold. Also, a little color has been added to the background to make it look more like a heading.

Figure 11-14: You want to group by the Product_Catetgory field.

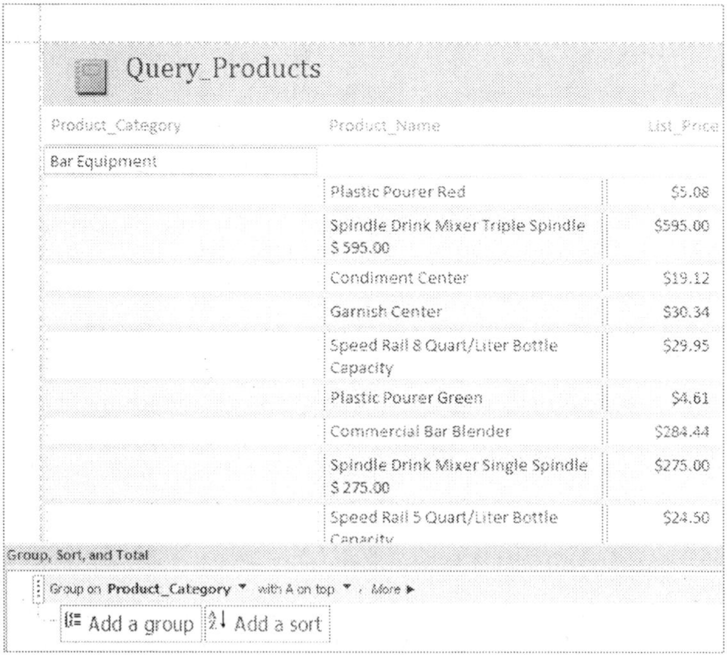

Figure 11-15: Your grouping has been applied.

Figure 11-16: Apply some formatting to make your grouping stand out.

Sorting and Totaling

Fortunately, Access's Layout view makes sorting and totaling very easy and intuitive. Switch back to Layout view and take a closer look at the Group, Sort, and Total pane. As you can see in Figure 11-17, this pane now shows you the existing groupings.

Figure 11-17: The Group, Sort and Total pane shows you the groupings that have been applied to your reports.

The first line of the Group, Sort, and Total pane tells you that Access is grouping the report first by Product_Category, and sorting Product_Category in ascending order (with A on top). The second line is indented slightly. This is Access's way of sorting and grouping hierarchy within the report.

If you wish to manipulate anything related to the top group and sort, Product_Category, then you need to work with the menu items on the top line. For additional grouping or sorting underneath Product_Category, you would work with the menu items. In this example, you want to add a sorting by the ListPrice column. That is to say, you want to sort the product by its list price.

1. Start clicking the Add a sort menu item. As you can see in Figure 11-18, this activates a drop down menu asking you to select the field by which you want to sort. Choose the ListPrice field.

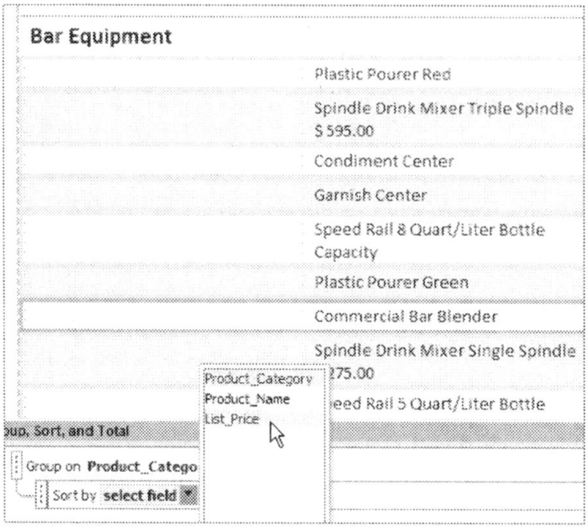

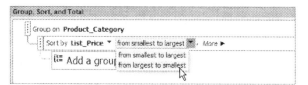

Figure 11-18: Choose the field you want to sort by.

2. You'll notice that a new line appears in the Group, Sort, and Total pane. This line represents the sorting you just applied. Since the sales amount must be sorted in descending order, change the sort direction as demonstrated in Figure 11-19.

Figure 11-19: Change the sort direction by using the dropdown selectors.

At this point, the products under each category should be sorted in descending order by list price.

This looks great, but this report could really use a total product count for each category. That is to say, you want to display a number which represents the count of products in that category.

In Layout view, go to the Group, Sort, and Total pane and select the More drill down button for the Product_Category grouping. Figure 11-20 demonstrates how.

Figure 11-20: Select the More drill down button.

As promised, you will see more options for your grouping. One of these is the totals option, which is set to "with no totals" by default. Click the dropdown selector for the totals option to reveal the Totals dialog box illustrated in Figure 11-21.

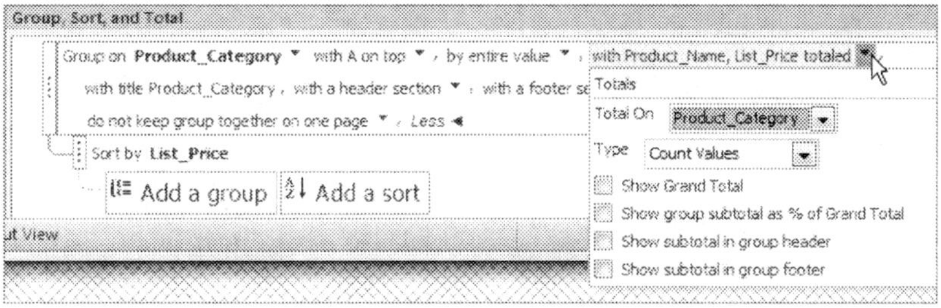

Figure 11-21: Activate the Totals menu.

The Totals dialog box can be a bit tricky. The top menu item is a dropdown box where you choose a field to total. Notice that the default selection is the first field in your report. Again, you want to count the number of products. To do so, follow these steps:

1. Select the Product_Name field from the Total On dropdown menu.

2. Select Count of Records from the Type dropdown menu.

3. Click the Show in group footer box at the bottom of our menu. This tells Access to display the total in the footer section of your category groupings.

At this point, your Totals dialog box should look similar to the one shown in Figure 11-22.

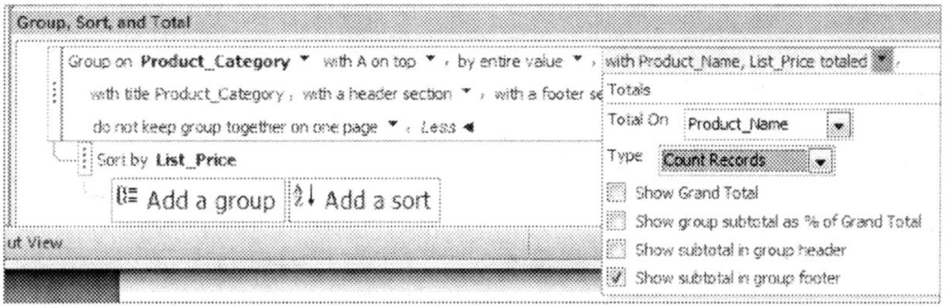

Figure 11-22: Your completed Totals dialog box

Take a moment to save your report; then switch to Report view. Figure 11-23 illustrates what the grouping, sorts, and totals look like for Fryers category. With just few clicks of the mouse, you've added layering to your report, making it much easier to comprehend.

Fryers	
Fry Basket Black Handle	$12.43
Fryer Brush	$13.37
Fry Basket Blue Handle	$16.22
Cheesecloth Filter 15 10" Filters	$16.28
Fry Basket Coated Handle	$19.52
Fry Basket Yellow Handle	$22.84
Taco Basket 6 Shells	$23.75
Filter Sheets 121/2" X 173/4"	$28.93
Filter Sheets 131/2" X 24"	$35.44
Filter Sheets 163/8" X 243/8"	$40.52
Filter Sheets 161/2" X 251/2"	$53.30
Filter Sheets 14" X 22"	$59.11
Taco Basket 8 Shells	$80.58
13	

Figure 11-23: Your product list is much easier to read.

TRICKS OF THE TRADE: SOLVING PAGE BREAK ISSUES

A common problem in grouped, multi-page reports occurs when users go to print. Very often, a page break occurs during the middle of a grouping or even right after a group heading, making it difficult for the user to read. Fortunately, there is an easy fix in Access's Layout view.

Open your report in Layout view and expand the submenu for your grouping under the Group, Sort, and Total menu. Once the menu is expanded, you will see an option titled "do not keep group together on one page." Using the dropdown selector, change that option to "keep whole group together on one page" as demonstrated in Figure 11-24.

Figure 11-24: Avoid page break issues by choosing to keep your groups together.

Creating a Report from Scratch

In the previous exercise, you let Access generate your report automatically. Although this option is convenient, you may want to have a more involved hand in what your report looks and feels like. In this section, you'll discover how to create an Access report from scratch, starting from a blank slate.

For this endeavor, you'll walk through the creation of a specific type of report called an Alpha Roster. An *Alpha Roster* is a fancy name for an alphabetically grouped and sorted report, usually showing addresses, contact information, or something similar. This particular report will show customer information grouped by the first letter of the customer's name and sorted alphabetically.

Creating Your Source Data

The first thing you need is some source data. Instead of creating a separate external query for this, you'll build your data source directly into the Report object.

1. Go to the Create tab of the Access Ribbon and select Report Design.

2. Once in Design view, ensure the Property Sheet pane is activated by right clicking inside the white area of the report and selecting Properties (you can also select F4 on your keyboard).

3. Make sure the Selection Type dropdown menu in the Property Sheet pane is set to Report.

4. Now select the Data tab and click the ellipsis button (the button with the three dots) next to the Record Source property (Figure 11-25).

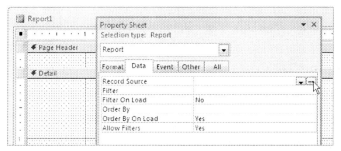

Figure 11-25: Choose to build the data source using the Query Builder.

Selecting these three dots invokes the Query Builder, which you can use just as you would if you were building a standard query.

5. At this point, you can create the query you see here in Figure 11-26. As you want to make an alphabetical listing of customers, you will choose the most relevant pieces of data.

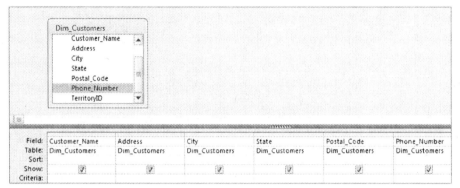

Figure 11-26: Query design for your customer roster.

6. Now you must save your query to ensure it remains as the report record source. Click the close button from the Design menu and select the Yes button when presented with the message box shown in Figure 11-27.

Figure 11-27: Be sure to save your changes by clicking the Yes button when asked to save your query.

As a quick check, go to the Property Sheet pane and examine the Record-Source property of your report to make sure it contains your newly created query. If the query saved properly, you should see SQL syntax similar to that shown in Figure 11-28. If you don't see anything, repeat steps 4 through 6.

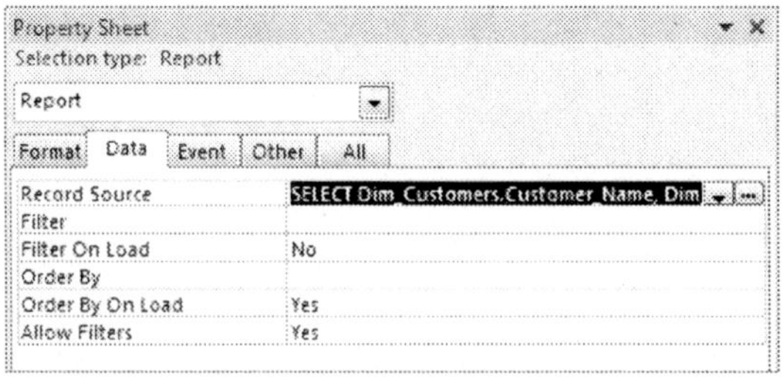

Figure 11-28: Check the RecordSource property to ensure your query was saved.

Building the Report in Design View

Once you have a data source defined, you can start designing your report. Because you are building your report from scratch, you'll have to add and arrange your report's content yourself. Follow these steps to build your report:

1. From the Design tab of the ribbon, select the Add Existing Fields button. This opens the Field List pane.

2. The idea is to drag the fields you want on your report. Drag the fields you need over to the detail section of your report as demonstrated in Figure 11-29.

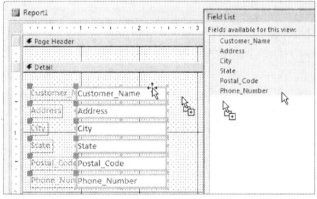

Figure 11-29: Drag the appropriate fields to the Detail area.

Now you have the basic data elements for your Customer roster. Before you go on, take some time to position your data fields and clean up your labels until it they look like Figure 11-30.

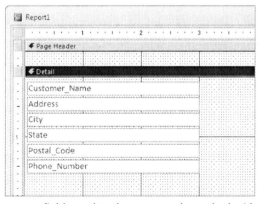

Figure 11-30: Format your fields so that they are neatly stacked without their labels.

TIP For quick and easy positioning of data and labels, highlight your fields and labels and then go to the Arrange tab on the ribbon and select Stacked. Access automatically aligns and distributes your labels and data into a neat block.

Remember that you want your report grouped and sorted alphabetically. So naturally, the next step is to add a grouping.

3. From the Design tab on the ribbon, click the Group and Sort icon.

4. You will see the same Group, Sort, and Total menu you saw earlier. From this menu, group the Customer_Name field by clicking the Add Group button and selecting Customer_Name.

5. Expand the menu by clicking More and select the third dropdown menu (to the right of the text "with A on top").

As you can see in Figure 11-31, this menu gives different options for how to group by the Name field. Select to group by first character of the Customer_Name field.

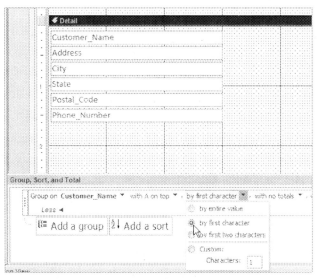

Figure 11-31: Group the customer names by first character.

Now you have a grouping that bundles all companies with the same first letter of their name. Things are starting to come together now, but you still aren't quite done. You need a field that explicitly shows users what grouping (what letter of the alphabet) they are viewing. For this, you must add a field to the group header section.

6. In the Design tab, click the Text Box control as demonstrated in Figure 11-32.

Figure 11-32: Click the Text Box control to add a new Text Box.

7. Place the new Text Box in the group header section of the Name field. Be sure to delete the label that came with the Text Box; then align the Text Box to the left (Figure 11-33).

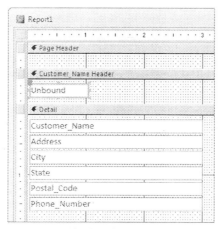

Figure 11-33: Place the Text Box in the header section for the Name field.

8. Type the following in your new Text Box:

```
=LEFT([Customer_Name],1)
```

The LEFT function parses out the leftmost characters of a text string. It requires two arguments: the string to be parsed and the number of characters to parse. The preceding code returns the single leftmost character in the Customer_Name text string.

9. Take a moment to format your new text box so that the font is 24-pitch and bold. While you're at it, go ahead and make the Customer_Name field bold as well.

At this point, you can switch to Report view and admire your newly created report. Figure 11-34 illustrates what your report should look like.

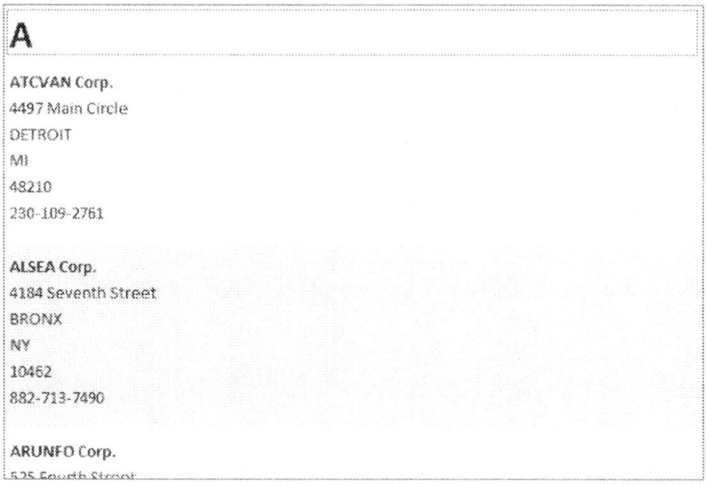

A

ATCVAN Corp.
4497 Main Circle
DETROIT
MI
48210
230-109-2761

ALSEA Corp.
4184 Seventh Street
BRONX
NY
10462
882-713-7490

ARUNFO Corp.
525 Fourth Street

Figure 11-34: Your alphabetically sorted customer roster

TRICKS OF THE TRADE: MULTI-COLUMN REPORT LAYOUT

To make better use of report space, you can change the column layout to two columns. In Design view, select the Columns icon from the Page Setup tab on the Ribbon. This activates the dialog box in Figure 11-35:

■ The Grid Settings section tells Access that you want two columns per sheet instead of the default, which is one column.

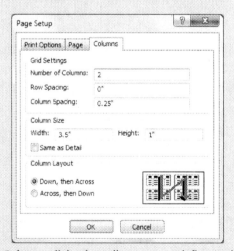

Figure 11-35: The Columns dialog box allows you to define multi-column layouts.

TRICKS OF THE TRADE: MULTI-COLUMN REPORT LAYOUT

■ **The Column Size section allows you to define the column widths so that your multiple columns will actually fit on the page.**

■ **The Column Layout section defines how your columns should flow. For example, the "Down, then Across" setting tells Access that the data should be organized first by going down the page and then starting another column when the end of the page is reached.**

Summary

Access Reports act as the presentation layer for your database and allows you to easily integrate your database analysis with polished PDF-style reporting.

Access Reports allow you to build data-driven reports right from the tables and queries in your database. You can either use the convenient Report Wizard to generate an Access Report or can create your Reports from scratch. Access Reports offer a full array of customization options, including: grouping, sorting, and formatting. The convenience and productivity improvements you can gain from Access reports are only limited by your creativity and initiative!

CHAPTER 12

Using Pivot Tables and Pivot Charts in Access

A pivot table is one of the most robust analytical tools found in Excel. With a pivot table, you can group, summarize and perform a wide variety of calculations in a fraction of the time it takes to do so by hand. The most impressive functionality of a pivot table is the ability to interactively change its content, shape data, and alter its overall utility. You can drag and drop fields, dynamically change your perspective, recalculate totals to fit the current view, and interactively drill down to the detail records.

If pivot tables are your passion and the reason you use Excel, then you had better lean in close as I tell you a secret: You have the power of pivot tables at your fingertips right there in your Access database. That's right. Access comes with its own version of the pivot table, allowing you to customize your analysis on the fly without re-writing your queries or turning to code.

In this chapter, you will discover that you can apply your knowledge of Excel pivot tables to Access, creating both pivot table and pivot chart analyses. You will learn how leveraging these powerful tools to change the way you analyze your Access data and the way you create your Excel exports.

> **TIP** This chapter focuses on using the power of pivot tables and pivot charts in Access. We assume that you are familiar with both the mechanics and the benefits of using pivot tables and pivot charts in Excel. If you are new to pivot tables altogether, consider picking up *Excel 2007 Pivot Table Data Crunching*, ISBN: 0789736012.

Pivot Tables in Access?

For years, pivot tables could only be found in Excel. The closest equivalent to this functionality in pre-2000 versions of Access was the traditional Crosstab query, which didn't come close to the analytical power of pivot tables. The first attempts at an "Access pivot table" came with Access 2000 where users had the ability to embed an Excel pivot table report inside of a Form. Unfortunately, this feature was a bit clunky and left users with an interface that felt clumsy at best. However, Access 2000 also introduced a promising new technology in the form of Office Web Components. Office Web Components allowed users to create interactive web pages with functionality normally found only in Excel. One of these components was the PivotTable Component. Although this component did expose pivot table functionality to Access, the fact that it was limited for use only on Data Access Pages (asp and html-based Web pages), made it an impractical tool for day-to-day data analysis.

With the release of Office XP, Microsoft gave Access users the ability to use the PivotTable and PivotChart components in both the Query and Form environments. This finally allowed for practical data analysis using pivot tables in Access. Alas, this functionality remained relatively untouched by many users, as it was relatively difficult to find in previous versions.

In later versions of Access, the PivotTable and PivotChart components still exist and have been brought to the forefront. So the only question for you is, why should you get excited about using pivot tables in Access?

From a data analysis point of view, pivot tables and pivot charts are some of the most powerful data-crunching tools found in Access today. Consider these capabilities:

- You can create multi-dimensional analysis that far surpasses the limitations of traditional Crosstab Queries.
- You can interactively change your analysis without re-writing your query.
- You can dynamically sort, filter, group, and add custom calculations with a few clicks of the mouse.
- You have drill-down capabilities that allow you to collapse and expand analytical details without writing code.
- You can perform more of your analysis in Access instead of spending time exporting raw data back and forth to Excel.

The Anatomy of a Pivot Table

Figure 12-1 shows an empty pivot table. As you can see a pivot table is comprised of four areas. Because how you choose to utilize these areas defines both the utility and the appearance of your pivot table, it's important to understand the functionality of each area.

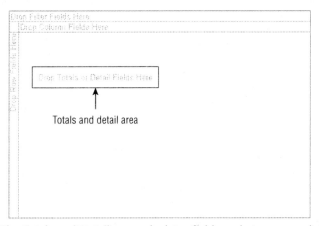

Figure 12-1: An empty pivot table in Access.

The Totals and Detail Area

The Totals and Detail area, highlighted in Figure 12-2, is the area that calculates and supplies the details for your report. You can recognize this area by the words *Drop Totals or Detail Fields Here*. This area tends to be confusing for first time users because it has a dual role. First, it displays aggregate totals such as Sum of Revenue, Count of Units, and Average of Price. Secondarily, it stores detailed row data that is exposed upon expansion of Row and Column fields.

Figure 12-2: The Totals and Detail area calculates fields and stores record details.

The Row Area

The Row area, highlighted in Figure 12-3, is the area that creates the headings down the left side of the pivot table. You can recognize this area by the words *Drop Row Fields Here.* Dropping a field into the Row Area will display each unique value in that field down the left side of the pivot table. The types of data fields that you would drop here are things you would want to group and categorize; for example, locations, customer names, and products.

Row area

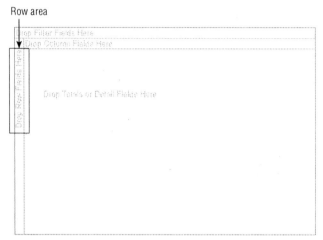

Figure 12-3: The Row area displays values down the left side of the pivot table.

The Column Area

The Column area, highlighted in Figure 12-4, makes up the headings that span across the top of the pivot table. You can recognize this area by the words *Drop Column Fields Here.* Dropping a field into the Column area will display each unique value in the field in a column-oriented perspective. The Column area is ideal for showing trending over time. Some examples of fields you would drop here would be Months, Periods, and Years.

The Filter Area

The Filter area, highlighted in Figure 12-5, allows for dynamic filtering of your pivot table based on a value in a field. You can recognize this area by the words *Drop Filter Fields Here.* The fields dropped here would be things you would want to isolate and focus on, such as locations, employee names, and products.

Column area

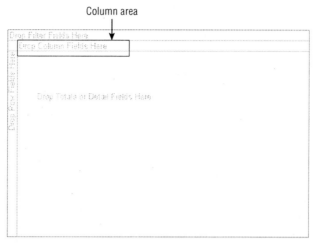

Figure 12-4: The Column area displays values across the top of the pivot table.

Filter area

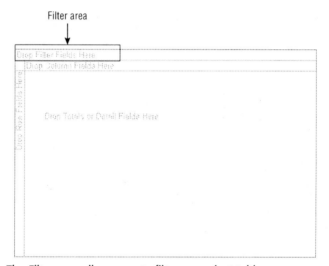

Figure 12-5: The Filter area allows you to filter your pivot table.

Creating a Basic Pivot Table

Start by building the query you see here in Figure 12-6, and then do the following:

1. Click the Design tab and click View ➪ PivotTable View.

   At this point, you will see an empty pivot table, shown here in Figure 12-7 and a list of fields that are in your dataset.

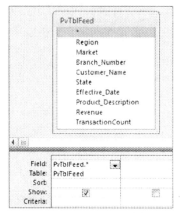

Figure 12-6: Build your query then switch to PivotTable view.

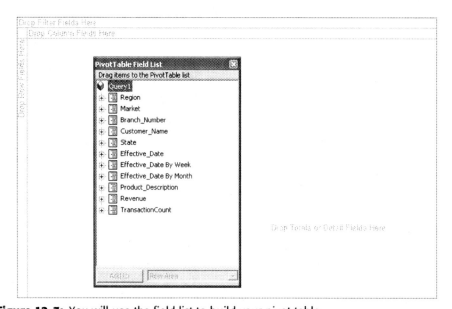

Figure 12-7: You will use the field list to build your pivot table.

2. Drag the fields you need into the pivot table's drop areas. How do you know which field goes where? To answer this question, consider two things: what are you measuring, and how do you want it presented? The answer to the first question tells you which fields in your data source you need to work with, and the answer to the second tells you where to place the fields. For example, to measure the amount of revenue by region, you automatically know that you need to work with the Revenue field and

the Region field. In addition, you want regions to go down the left side of the report and revenues to be calculated for each region. Therefore, you know that the Region field will go into the Row area while the revenue field will go into the Detail area.

3. Start by selecting the Region field from your field list and drag it to the Row area as shown here in Figure 12-8.

   TIP If you accidently close out your PivotTable Field List, simply right-click inside the pivot table and select Field List to reactivate it. You can also find this command on the PivotTable Tools Design Tab in the Show/Hide group.

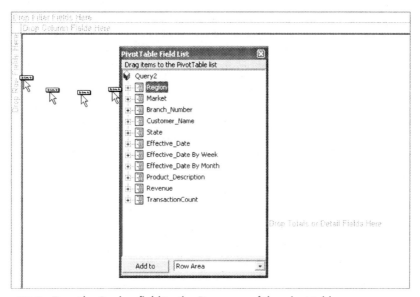

Figure 12-8: Drag the Region field to the Row area of the pivot table

4. Select the Revenue field, then select Data area from the drop-down box at the bottom of the PivotTable field list as shown in Figure 12-9. Click the Add To button.

   NOTE Why not just drag the Revenue field to the Detail area? The reason is that the Pivot Table Web Component requires that you view detail data before you add totals. So, if you simply drag the Revenue field to the Data area, the pivot table does not display the sum of revenue. Instead it displays the detailed revenue for each record in your dataset.

   NOTE Keep in mind that in order to use the method shown in Figure 12-9, the field you are adding must be a numeric or currency field.

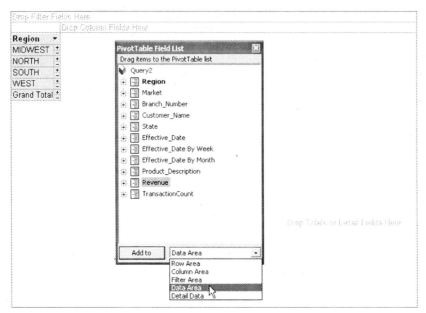

Figure 12-9: Add the Revenue field using the field list drop-down.

At this point, your pivot table should look like the one shown in Figure 12-10.

Region	▼	Sum of Revenue
MIDWEST		$1,848,890.66
NORTH		$2,779,015.40
SOUTH		$3,141,451.17
WEST		$3,004,832.22
Grand Total		$10,774,189.46

Figure 12-10: You have created your first pivot table report!

5. You can add some dimension to this report by the dragging the Product-Description field to the Column area. As you can see in Figure 12-11, doing this you now have a cross tabular view of revenue by region and product.

6. Add the Market field to the Row area and drag the Region field to the Filter area (the area that reads *Drop Filter Fields Here*). Your pivot table should look like the one shown in Figure 12-12. With just a few mouse clicks, you not only have a totally new perspective on the same data, but you can now filter by region.

	Product_Description ▼		
	Cleaning & Housekeeping Services	Facility Maintenance and Repair	Fleet Maintenance
	+ −	+ −	+ −
Region ▼	Sum of Revenue	Sum of Revenue	Sum of Revenue
MIDWEST ±	$174,518.08	$463,078.85	$448,800.61
NORTH ±	$534,284.19	$606,748.65	$610,791.49
SOUTH ±	$283,170.17	$846,508.06	$1,046,229.86
WEST ±	$146,623.34	$444,825.85	$521,976.06
Grand Total ±	$1,138,595.78	$2,361,161.41	$2,627,798.02

Figure 12-11: Drag the ProductDescription field to the Column area of the pivot table.

Region ▼			
All			
	Product_Description ▼		
	Cleaning & Housekeeping Services	Facility Maintenance and Repair	Fleet Maintenance
	+ −	+ −	+ −
Market ▼	Sum of Revenue	Sum of Revenue	Sum of Revenue
BUFFALO ±	$66,844.23	$69,568.80	$86,461.34
CALIFORNIA ±	$37,401.55	$281,203.86	$337,224.62
CANADA ±		$294,258.33	$273,175.05
CHARLOTTE ±	$170,341.83	$223,346.86	$245,119.74
DALLAS ±	$18,807.34	$136,844.19	$156,152.05
DENVER ±	$12,563.96	$160,325.12	$170,188.42
FLORIDA ±	$20,448.86	$410,039.45	$556,003.84
KANSASCITY ±	$65,439.45	$132,119.42	$133,170.10
MICHIGAN ±	$243,451.28	$65,079.56	$66,408.19
NEWORLEANS ±	$73,572.13	$76,277.55	$88,954.24
NEWYORK ±	$223,988.68	$177,841.95	$184,746.91
PHOENIX ±	$96,685.78	$125,522.50	$150,788.58
SEATTLE ±	$12,536.02	$38,099.49	$33,962.86
TULSA ±	$96,514.67	$170,634.31	$145,442.10
Grand Total ±	$1,138,595.78	$2,361,161.41	$2,627,798.02

Figure 12-12: Adding the Market field and dragging the Region field to the Filter area allows you to analyze market revenue for a specific region.

A WORD ABOUT DRAGGING FIELDS FROM ONE AREA TO ANOTHER

When you are dragging your fields from one area of a pivot table to another, your cursor will turn into a mini pivot table. That is to say, your cursor turns into an icon that represents your pivot table. As you move your cursor from one area of your actual pivot table to the next, you will notice that different parts of the icon will be shaded. The shaded area corresponds to the area over which you are currently hovering. This allows you to easily discern the area in which you are about to drop your field. The key to telling which area you are hovering over is to watch the shaded area of the cursor as shown in Figure 12-13.

TIP If you need to remove a field from your pivot table, an alternative to dragging it off is right-clicking the field name and select Remove.

(continued)

A WORD ABOUT DRAGGING FIELDS FROM ONE AREA TO ANOTHER *(continued)*

Row Field

Column Field

Detail Field

Filter Field

Remove Field

Figure 12-13: Watch the shaded area of the cursor to determine where you are about to drop your field.

Creating an Advanced Pivot Table with Details

This section, demonstrates how you can incorporate record details into your pivot table, effectively building an analysis that can drill down to the record level. First, create the pivot table shown in Figure 12-14 by following these steps:

1. Start by building the query you see in Figure 12-6, then in the Design tab and click View ⇨ PivotTable View.

2. Drag the Market and Product_Description fields to the Row area of the pivot table.

3. Select the Revenue field, then select Data area from the drop-down box at the bottom of the PivotTable Field List and click the Add To button.

   Take a moment and look at what you have so far. You've created a basic analysis that reveals the amount of revenue by product for each market. Now you can enhance this analysis by adding customer details to the pivot table. This will allow you to drill into a product segment and view all the customers that make up that product's revenue.

4. Select the Customer_Name field; then select Detail Data from the drop-down box at the bottom of the PivotTable field and click the Add To button.

5. Select the Effective_Date field; then select Detail Data from the drop-down box at the bottom of the PivotTable field and click the Add To button.

Market	Product_Description		Sum of Revenue
⊟ BUFFALO	Cleaning & Housekeeping Services		$66,844.23
	Facility Maintenance and Repair		$69,568.80
	Fleet Maintenance		$86,461.34
	Green Plants and Foliage Care		$34,830.18
	Landscaping/Grounds Care		$65,464.84
	Predictive Maintenance/Preventative Maintenance		$127,309.32
	Total		$450,478.72
⊟ CALIFORNIA	Cleaning & Housekeeping Services		$37,401.55
	Facility Maintenance and Repair		$281,203.86
	Fleet Maintenance		$337,224.62
	Green Plants and Foliage Care		$830,422.28
	Landscaping/Grounds Care		$248,343.46
	Predictive Maintenance/Preventative Maintenance		$520,155.87
	Total		$2,254,751.64
⊟ CANADA	Facility Maintenance and Repair		$294,258.33
	Fleet Maintenance		$273,175.05
	Green Plants and Foliage Care		$15,965.46
	Landscaping/Grounds Care		$76,751.57
	Predictive Maintenance/Preventative Maintenance		$116,097.37
	Total		$776,247.78

Figure 12-14: Build the pivot table shown here.

6. Select the Revenue field, then select Detail area from the drop-down box at the bottom of the PivotTable field and click the Add To button.

At this point, it looks as though your pivot table hasn't changed. However, if you click the plus sign next to any one of the products segments, you now see the customer details for every customer that contributed to that segment's total revenue. Figure 12-15 illustrates this.

Market	Product_Description		Customer_Name ▾	Effective_Date ▾	Revenue ▾
⊟ BUFFALO	Cleaning & Housekeeping Services		BAUDUS Corp.	1/13/2004	$5,417.95
			CUNUME Corp.	1/19/2004	$3,750.89
			FSULLA Corp.	6/9/2004	$1,250.30
			GOSBOR Corp.	1/7/2004	$3,750.89
			KUYSTU Corp.	1/20/2004	$3,750.89
			LATREB Corp.	1/5/2004	$6,668.24
			LATRUN Corp.	2/2/2004	$2,083.83
			PPGAND Corp.	1/29/2004	$3,750.89
			SPUCAA Corp.	1/8/2004	$10,835.90
			VARGAN Corp.	1/8/2004	$3,750.89
			VUUDUS Corp.	1/12/2004	$5,417.95
			LUXANG Corp.	1/19/2004	$6,668.85
			PRUUUC Corp.	9/27/2004	$1,025.98
			SUNUCA Corp.	1/14/2004	$2,564.94
			THEHAL Corp.	1/21/2004	$3,077.93
			Sum of Revenue		$66,844.23
	Facility Maintenance and Repair		Sum of Revenue		$69,568.80
	Fleet Maintenance		Sum of Revenue		$86,461.34
	Green Plants and Foliage Care		Sum of Revenue		$34,830.18
	Landscaping/Grounds Care		Sum of Revenue		$65,464.84
	Predictive Maintenance/Preventative Maintenance		Sum of Revenue		$127,309.32
	Total		Sum of Revenue		$450,478.72

Figure 12-15: Your now have the ability to drill down into the details that make up your revenue totals.

TIP You can drill into all details at one time by right-clicking the column field names and selecting Show Details. Conversely, you can hide the details by right-clicking the column field names and selecting Hide Details.

WARNING Incorporating record details into your pivot tables is a technique that should be limited to smaller datasets. Because the PivotTable component opens a separate ADO recordset for each cell it contains, accessing a large amount of details through your pivot table can lead to performance issues. If you absolutely need to view all row and column details for a large dataset, you should consider using a Query or a Form.

Saving Your Pivot Table

It's important to remember that when you are building your analysis with a pivot table, you are actually working with a query in a *PivotTable View*. Therefore, when you save your analysis it will save as a query. You will notice that the next time you open the query it will open in Datasheet View. This doesn't mean your pivot table is lost. Just switch back to PivotTable View to see your pivot table.

If you want your query to run in PivotTable View by default, just change the Default View property of the query. To do this:.

1. Open your query in Design View. You will see the Property Sheet button in the Design tab under the Show/Hide group.

2. Select the Property Sheet button. This activates the Property Sheet dialog box shown in Figure 12-16. Change the Default View property to PivotTable. The next time you open your query, it will open in PivotTable view.

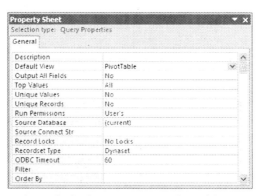

Figure 12-16: Change the Default View property to PivotTable.

Sending Your Access Pivot Table to Excel

Once you are happy with your Access pivot table analysis, you may want to share your pivot table with the world. You can distribute your Access-made pivot table via Excel. To do so, open your query in PivotTable view. Then in the Design tab, click the Export to Excel button. This will send your pivot table to Excel where you can format it and mail it out as a professionally made analysis.

The nifty thing about this technique is that only the pivot cache is sent to Excel. That is to say, the raw data behind the pivot table is not sent to the workbook to be placed in a separate sheet. This means a smaller file size and a cleaner looking workbook.

> **TIP** What if you also want your users have access to the raw data? Because Access only transfers the pivot table and not the raw data, are you out of luck? No. To get the raw data, simply double-click the bottom-right-most Grand Total value of your pivot table. This drills into the pivot cache and outputs the raw data that makes up your pivot table. The output goes to a separate worksheet in the same workbook.

Pivot Table Options

You will often find that the pivot tables you create often need to be tweaked in order to get the result you're looking for. This section covers some of the pivot table options you can adjust in order to enhance your analysis. To prepare for the examples in this section, create the pivot table shown in Figure 12-17 by following these steps:

1. Build the query you see in Figure 12-6, then in the Design tab, select View ⇨ PivotTable View.

2. Drag the Region, Market and Customer_Name fields to the Row area of the pivot table.

3. Select the Revenue field, then select Data area from the drop-down box at the bottom of the PivotTable Field List and click the Add To button.

4. Select the TransactionCount field; then select Data area from the drop-down box at the bottom of the PivotTable field and click the Add To button.

Region	▾ Market	▾ Customer_Name ▾	Sum of Revenue	Sum of TransactionCount
⊟ MIDWEST	⊟ DENVER	ADOMSC Corp.	$1,190.30	6
		ADVANC Corp.	$1,709.64	12
		ALLAAN Corp.	$625.25	4
		ALLFAN Corp.	$448.02	4
		ALPANE Corp.	$4,578.26	25
		ALUXAN Corp.	$1,139.76	8
		AMPRUT Corp.	$448.02	4
		AMPUST Corp.	$5,592.04	30
		AMUSYS Corp.	$937.88	6
		ANAQAE Corp.	$1,172.20	8
		ANATUD Corp.	$4,644.84	24
		ANCLEM Corp.	$716.28	6
		ANDALU Corp.	$997.29	7
		ANDART Corp.	$2,421.99	17
		ANDUQU Corp.	$1,318.73	9
		ANDUSS Corp.	$448.02	4
		ANFANA Corp.	$434.06	4
		ANGUSS Corp.	$1,318.73	9

Figure 12-17: Build the pivot table shown here.

Expanding and Collapsing Fields

It's always difficult to perform an effect analysis on a large volume of data. So when you are analyzing a large amount of data in a pivot table such as the one shown in Figure 12-17, it's helpful to see small chunks of data at a time.

To facilitate this need, Access allows you to expand or collapse detail easily when you click the plus and minus signs shown in the pivot tables. You can also expand or collapse all values in a field at once. For example, when you right-click the Market field and select Collapse, as seen in Figure 12-18, all the customer details for each market are hidden, which makes this pivot table easier to read. Now you can analyze the customer detail for one market at a time when you click the plus sign for that market.

Changing Field Captions

As you know by now, Access often attempts to name aggregated fields with its own name such as *Sum of TransactionCount*. You can imagine how titles like this can be confusing to the consumer. You can customize your field captions by changing the Caption property of the field.

To demonstrate this, follow these steps:

1. Right-click Sum of TransactionCount field heading and select Properties. This activates the Properties dialog box shown here in Figure 12-19.

2. Click the Captions tab and enter **Count of Transactions** in the Caption input box.

3. Close the dialog box and your changes will immediately take effect.

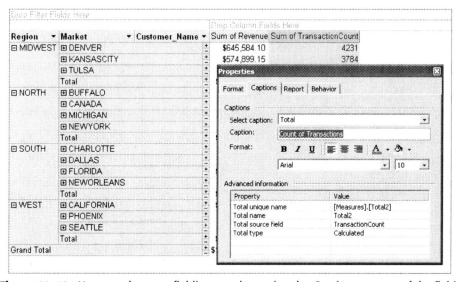

Region	▾	Market	▾	Customer_Name	▾	Sum of Revenue	Sum of TransactionCount
⊟ MIDWEST		⊞ DENVER				$645,584.10	4231
		⊞ KANSASCITY				$574,899.15	3784
		⊞ TULSA				$628,407.41	4417
		Total				$1,848,890.66	12432
⊟ NORTH		⊞ BUFFALO				$450,478.72	2625
		⊞ CANADA				$776,247.78	4981
		⊞ MICHIGAN				$678,708.11	3689
		⊞ NEWYORK				$873,580.79	4808
		Total				$2,779,015.40	16103
⊟ SOUTH		⊞ CHARLOTTE				$890,514.49	5389
		⊞ DALLAS				$467,086.11	3392
		⊞ FLORIDA				$1,450,397.76	11486
		⊞ NEWORLEANS				$333,452.80	1920
		Total				$3,141,451.17	22187
⊟ WEST		⊞ CALIFORNIA				$2,254,751.64	13617
		⊞ PHOENIX				$570,254.17	3222
		⊞ SEATTLE				$179,826.42	1053
		Total				$3,004,832.22	17892
Grand Total						$10,774,189.46	68614

Figure 12-18: Collapsing fields makes your pivot tables easier to read.

Figure 12-19: You can change a field's name by setting the Caption property of the field.

Sorting Data

By default, pivot tables are initially sorted in ascending order. However, you may prefer to present your data in an order that makes more sense in your situation. To change the sort order of a particular field or aggregation, simply right-click the chosen field or aggregation and select Sort and then Sort Ascending or Sort Descending.

Grouping Data

A particularly useful feature in pivot tables is the ability to create a new layer of analysis by grouping and summarizing unrelated data items. Imagine that you need to group the products shown in Figure 12-20 into two segments: outside services (Green Plants and Foliage Care and Landscaping/Grounds Care) and inside services (the rest of the items on the list).

Product_Description	▾ Sum of Revenue
Cleaning & Housekeeping Services	$1,138,595.78
Facility Maintenance and Repair	$2,361,161.41
Fleet Maintenance	$2,627,798.02
Green Plants and Foliage Care	$1,276,790.55
Landscaping/Grounds Care	$1,190,911.60
Predictive Maintenance/Preventative Maintenance	$2,178,932.11
Grand Total	$10,774,189.46

Figure 12-20: You need to group these products into two groups.

To accomplish this task, follow these steps:

1. Hold down the Ctrl key on your keyboard and select both Green Plants and Foliage Care and Landscaping/Grounds Care.

2. Right-click and select Group Items as shown here in Figure 12-21.

   At this point, your pivot table should look similar to the one shown in Figure 12-22. As you can see, you have essentially created a new field with two data items: Group1 and Other.

3. All that's left do is to change the captions on these newly created objects to reflect their true meaning. You do this simply by right-clicking the field name and select Properties. This activates the Properties dialog box where you can click the Captions tab and edit the Caption input box.

Figure 12-23 illustrates what the final report with a new Product Segment field should look like.

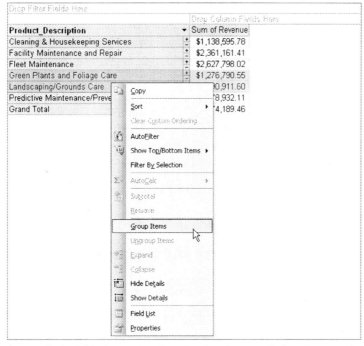

Figure 12-21: Include fields in a group by selecting them and choosing Group Items from the right-click menu.

Product_Description1 ▾	Product_Description	Sum of Revenue
⊟ Group1	Green Plants and Foliage Care	$1,276,790.55
	Landscaping/Grounds Care	$1,190,911.60
	Total	$2,467,702.15
⊟ Other	Cleaning & Housekeeping Services	$1,138,595.78
	Facility Maintenance and Repair	$2,361,161.41
	Fleet Maintenance	$2,627,798.02
	Predictive Maintenance/Preventative Maintenance	$2,178,932.11
	Total	$8,306,487.31
Grand Total		$10,774,189.46

Figure 12-22: You have successfully grouped your items into a single data item!

Product Segment ▾	Product_Description	Sum of Revenue
⊟ Outside Services	Green Plants and Foliage Care	$1,276,790.55
	Landscaping/Grounds Care	$1,190,911.60
	Total	$2,467,702.15
⊟ Inside Services	Cleaning & Housekeeping Services	$1,138,595.78
	Facility Maintenance and Repair	$2,361,161.41
	Fleet Maintenance	$2,627,798.02
	Predictive Maintenance/Preventative Maintenance	$2,178,932.11
	Total	$8,306,487.31
Grand Total		$10,774,189.46

Figure 12-23: In just a few clicks, you have added another layer to your analysis.

NOTE The Properties dialog is non-modal. That means you can select different objects without closing it. This is especially helpful when you're changing the caption on multiple objects. For example, you can change the Product_Description1 caption, and then select the Group1 object and change *its* caption —all without closing the Properties dialog.

One last note about grouping data. If you activate your field list and drill into the Product_Description field, as shown in Figure 12-24, you will notice that you newly created grouping is listed there as a sub field. This means you can treat this field as any other in your field list. To delete your grouping, right-click its entry in the field list and select Delete.

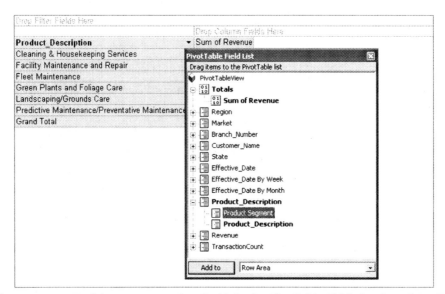

Figure 12-24: To delete your grouping, find it in the PivotTable Field List; then right-click it, and then click Delete.

Using Date Groupings

Notice that in Figure 12-25, you have a field called Effective _Date and directly underneath that field you see Effective_Date by Week and Effective_Date by Month. Unlike Excel where you would have to explicitly create date groupings, Access automatically creates these groupings for any field that is formatted as a date field.

Figure 12-26 illustrates how you can simply drag these date grouping onto your pivot table just as you would any other field.

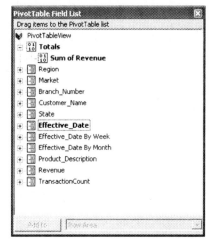

Figure 12-25: Access automatically creates date groupings for any field formatted as a date field.

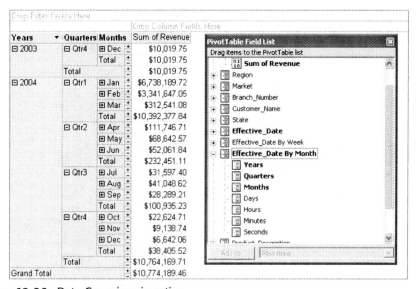

Figure 12-26: Date Groupings in action.

NOTE If your dates aren't expanded as shown in Figure 12-26, you can expand a field by right-clicking on the field header and choosing Expand.

One drawback to using the Access-provided date groupings is that you can't separate them. For instance, you cannot drag the Year grouping into the Column area then drag the Month grouping into the Row area.

Filter for Top and Bottom Records

Filtering your pivot table to show the top or bottom Nth records can be done with just a few clicks of the mouse. In the example illustrated in Figure 12-27, you have a list of customers and want to limit the list to the top ten customers by sum of revenue. Right-clicking the Customer_Name field heading will expose a shortcut menu where you can select Show Top/Bottom Items ⇨ Show only the Top ⇨ 10.

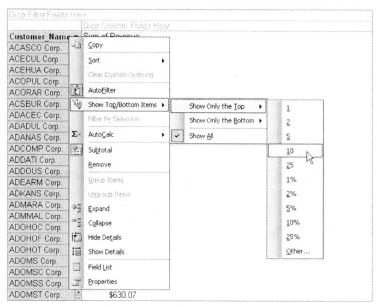

Figure 12-27: An example of how easy it is to filer top 10 customers.

As you can see in Figure 12-27, the filtering options also include the ability to filter by percent of records. You can remove the applied filter by right-clicking the field heading and selecting AutoFilter.

TIP There are actually two methods you can use to remove an applied filter from a field.

▪ **Method 1: Right-click the field heading and select AutoFilter.**
▪ **Method 2: Right-click the field heading and clicking Show Top/Bottom Items ⇨ Show All.**

Method 1 has an added advantage in that it allows you to reapply the last known filter to the field at any time by right-clicking the field heading and selecting AutoFilter. Method 2, however, clears the filter settings altogether.

Adding a Calculated Total

Once you create a pivot table, you may find it useful to expand your analysis by performing calculations on summary totals. To demonstrate this, follow these steps:

1. Create the pivot table shown here in Figure 12-28. This analysis calculates total revenue and total count of transactions. Upon reviewing these results, you determine that you need to get an average dollar per transaction.

Market		Sum of Revenue	Sum of TransactionCount
BUFFALO		$450,478.72	2625
CALIFORNIA		$2,254,751.64	13617
CANADA		$776,247.78	4981
CHARLOTTE		$890,514.49	5389
DALLAS		$467,086.11	3392
DENVER		$645,584.10	4231
FLORIDA		$1,450,397.76	11486
KANSASCITY		$574,899.15	3784
MICHIGAN		$678,708.11	3689
NEWORLEANS		$333,452.80	1920
NEWYORK		$873,580.79	4808
PHOENIX		$570,254.17	3222
SEATTLE		$179,826.42	1053
TULSA		$628,407.41	4417
Grand Total		$10,774,189.46	68614

Figure 12-28: You need to calculate the average dollar per transaction for each market.

2. In the Design tab, click Formulas ⇨ Create Calculated Total. This will set off two events. First, a new field called New Total will appear in your pivot table as shown in Figure 12-29 (see the column right next to the Market column). Second, the Properties dialog box for this field will activate.

   The idea here is to enter the calculation you need into the dialog box.

3. Enter **Dollars per Transaction** into the Name input box.

4. Delete the 0 from the large input box below Name.

5. Select Sum of Revenue (Total) from the drop-down then click the Insert Reference To button.

6. Type a forward slash (/) to indicate division.

7. Select Sum of TransactionCount (Total) from the drop-down, then click the Insert Reference To button.

   At this point, your dialog box should look similar to Figure 12-30.

8. Click the Change button.

9. In the Format tab, click Currency from the Number input box.

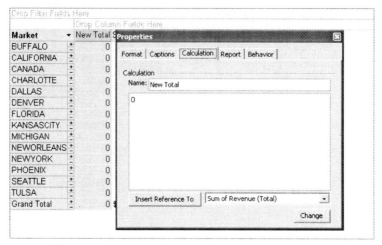

Figure 12-29: Adding a new calculated total will create a new field in your pivot table.

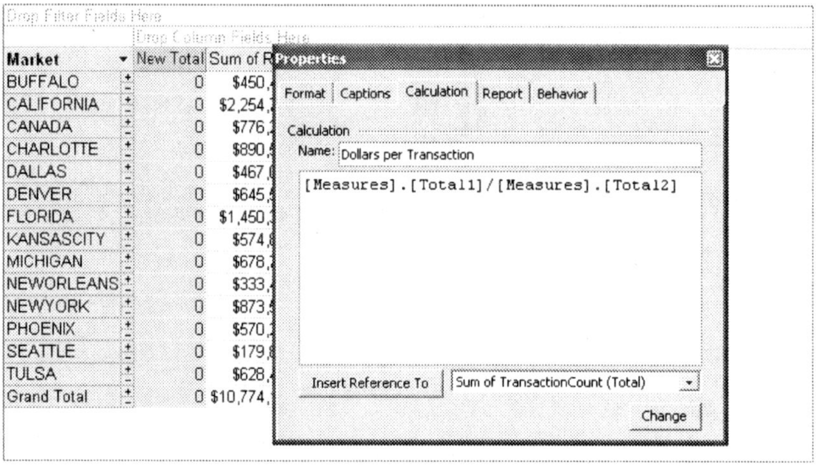

Figure 12-30: Your dialog box should look like this.

As you can see in Figure 12-31, your new calculation looks and acts like any other Totals field in your pivot table.

To adjust the calculation behind your calculated total, right-click on the field heading and select Properties. This will open the Properties dialog box where you can change the calculation in the Calculation tab.

To delete your calculated total, right-click on its entry in the field list, shown here in Figure 12-32, and select Delete.

NOTE You can also create Calculated Detail Field using the same steps illustrated above. However, it's generally a better idea to perform calculations on details in the actual query as opposed to a pivot table. This way, Microsoft ACE (ACE is the Access replacement for Microsoft Jet) performs the calculation instead of the PivotTable component, making your PivotTable view perform better.

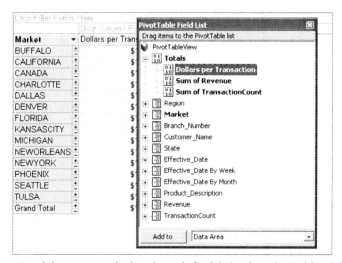

Market		Dollars per Transaction	Sum of Revenue	Sum of TransactionCount
BUFFALO		$171.61	$450,478.72	2625
CALIFORNIA		$165.58	$2,254,751.64	13617
CANADA		$155.84	$776,247.78	4981
CHARLOTTE		$165.25	$890,514.49	5389
DALLAS		$137.70	$467,086.11	3392
DENVER		$152.58	$645,584.10	4231
FLORIDA		$126.28	$1,450,397.76	11486
KANSASCITY		$151.93	$574,899.15	3784
MICHIGAN		$183.98	$678,708.11	3689
NEWORLEANS		$173.67	$333,452.80	1920
NEWYORK		$181.69	$873,580.79	4808
PHOENIX		$176.99	$570,254.17	3222
SEATTLE		$170.78	$179,826.42	1053
TULSA		$142.27	$628,407.41	4417
Grand Total		$157.03	$10,774,189.46	68614

Figure 12-31: You have enhanced your analysis with a calculated total.

Figure 12-32: To delete your calculated total, find it in the PivotTable Field List; then right-click it, and then click Delete.

Working with Pivot Charts in Access

A pivot chart is essentially a pivot table in chart form. Once you learn the basics of using a pivot table, a pivot chart will feel quite intuitive.

Pivot Chart Fundamentals

There are slight differences in the anatomy of a pivot chart. Figure 12-33 shows an empty pivot chart where you can see four distinct areas. Just as in pivot tables, how you choose to utilize these areas defines both the utility and the appearance of your pivot chart.

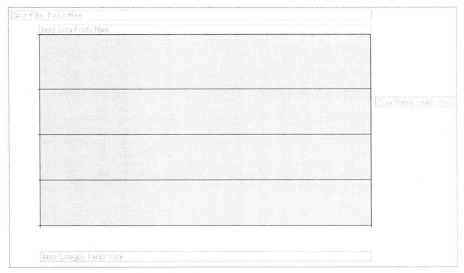

Figure 12-33: An empty pivot chart in Access.

Data Area

The Data area, highlighted in Figure 12-34, is the area that calculates and supplies the data points for your chart. You can recognize this area by the words *Drop Data Fields Here*.

Series Area

The Series area, highlighted in Figure 12-35, is the area that makes up the Y axis of your chart. You can recognize this area by the words *Drop Series Fields Here*. This area corresponds is equivalent to the Column area of a pivot table. In other words, if you create a pivot table and switch to PivotChart view, the fields in the Column area of the pivot table will become the Y axis series.

Category Area

The Category area, highlighted in Figure 12-36, is the area that makes up the X axis of your chart. You can recognize this area by the words *Drop*

Category Fields Here. This area is equivalent to the Row area of a pivot table. In other words, if you create a pivot table and switch to PivotChart view, the fields in the Row area of the pivot table will become categories in the X axis.

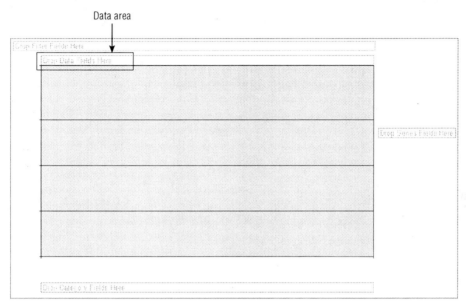

Figure 12-34: The Data area supplies the data points for your chart.

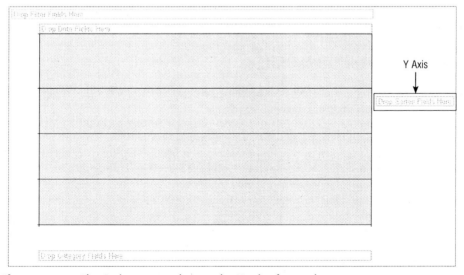

Figure 12-35: The Series area makes up the Y axis of your chart.

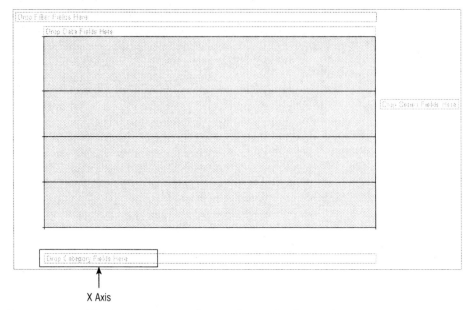

Figure 12-36: The Category area makes up the X axis of your chart.

Filter Area

The Filter area, highlighted in Figure 12-37, allows for dynamic filtering of your pivot chart based on a value in a field. You can recognize this area by the words *Drop Filter Fields Here.* This area is identical to the Filter area of a pivot table.

Creating a Basic Pivot Chart

To create a pivot chart, start by building a query in design view, as shown here in Figure 12-38. Next, follow these steps:

1. In the Design tab, click View ➪ PivotChart View.

   At this point, you will see an empty pivot chart, shown here in Figure 12-39 and a list of fields that are in your dataset.

2. Just as in a pivot table, the idea is to drag the fields you need into the pivot chart's drop areas. Build a basic chart by dragging the Revenue field to the Data area, then the Market field to the Category area.

3. Drag the Region field to the Filter area. Your completed chart should look like the one illustrated here in Figure 12-40.

NOTE You may notice that the pivot charts produced by Access are not as polished as the ones Excel produces. This is because Access uses the old Office Web Component technology that was primarily designed for reporting on the web. Excel, on the other hand, uses the slick new graphics engine introduced with Office 2007.

Filter area

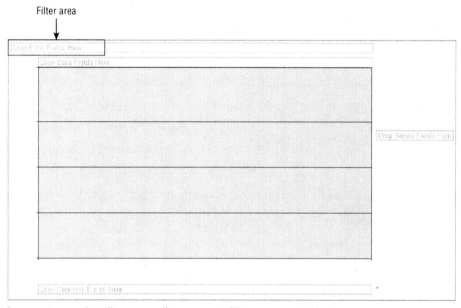

Figure 12-37: The Filter area allows you to filter your pivot chart.

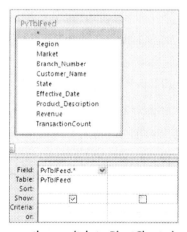

Figure 12-38: Build your query; then switch to PivotChart view.

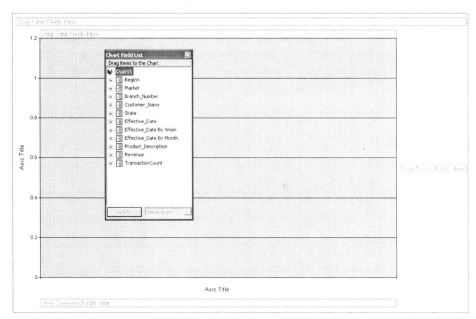

Figure 12-39: You will use the field list to build your pivot table.

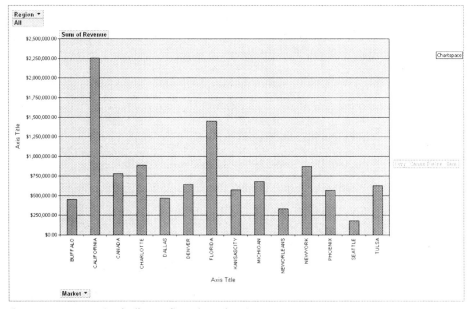

Figure 12-40: You've built you first pivot chart!

Formatting Your Pivot Chart

The key to formatting a pivot chart in Access is to remember that everything revolves around property settings. Each object on the chart has its own properties that you can adjust. To demonstrate this, follow these steps:

1. Right-click your pivot chart and select Properties. This will activate the Properties dialog box shown in Figure 12-41.

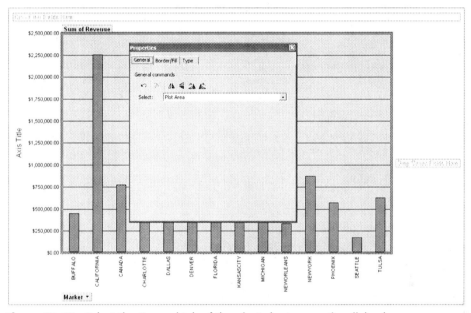

Figure 12-41: Select the General tab of the pivot chart properties dialog box.

2. Go to the General tab. The idea here is to select the object with which you want to work in order to expose the adjustable properties. For example, if you wanted to add labels to your series, you would select Series from the Select drop-down as demonstrated here in Figure 12-42.

3. With the Series properties exposed, you can tailor its properties to suit your needs. In Figure 12-43, you are adding data labels to you pivot chart.

4. Of course, data labels have properties that can be modified as well. In the General tab of the Properties dialog box, select the series data labels you just added. As you can see in Figure 12-44, the Select drop-down list has been updated to include "Series Data Labels 1."

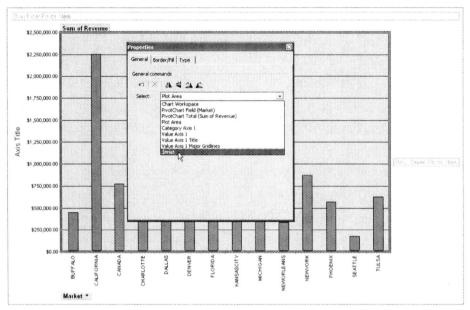

Figure 12-42: Selecting the Series object exposes its modifiable properties.

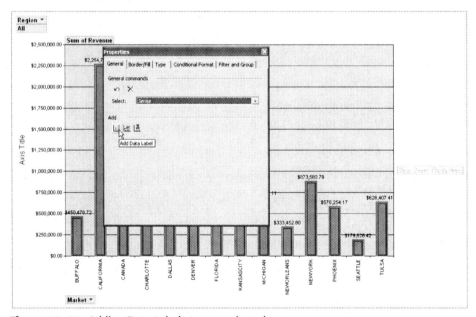

Figure 12-43: Adding Data Labels to your pivot chart.

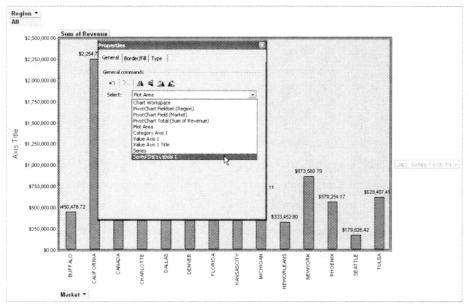

Figure 12-44: The Select dropdown list is updated every time you add a new object to your chart.

Twenty minutes of experimenting with each object's properties will give you a solid level of proficiency at formatting pivot charts in Access.

NOTE As of this writing, you cannot export pivot charts from Access to Excel. Again, this is due to the fact that Access and Excel use entirely different charting engines.

Summary

From a data analysis point of view, pivot tables and pivot charts are some of the most powerful data-crunching tools found in Access. With a pivot table, you can group, summarize, and perform a wide variety of calculations in a fraction of the time it takes by hand. In addition, you can interactively change the content and shape of your analysis by dragging data fields to one area of the pivot table to another. This allows you to dynamically change your perspective, recalculate totals to fit the current view, and interactively drill down to the detail records. Pivot charts enhance your analytical tools by allowing you to display your pivot tables graphically—in chart form. By applying your knowledge of Excel pivot tables to Access, you can completely change the way you analyze your Access data.

Enhancing Queries and Reports with Visualizations

Access isn't typically a tool you would think of when considering a dashboard style reporting tool. The reporting tools in Access, as slick as they are, don't readily lend themselves to data visualizations. That is to say, Access doesn't offer a whole lot in the way of dashboarding graphics. What's so great about visualization?

When you present your data through a visual interface, you can highlight key trends, point out comparisons, and focus in on outliers. Think of how much time it takes your end-users to process the table-driven reports you produce. Now imagine giving your users a visual interface that they can absorb at-a-glance. Adding visual components to your reporting arsenal not only makes you more effective at reporting data, but it helps your end-users become more effective at consuming data.

In this chapter, you explore some of the techniques that will help you go beyond tables filled with numbers. At the end of this chapter, you'll be turning your bland queries and reports into innovative visual interfaces.

Basic Visualization Techniques

Data visualizations don't always refer to fancy graphics. In fact, something as basic as specially formatted font or colored fields can be considered visualizations. In this section, you start with some simple techniques that will help spruce up your reporting.

Using Number Formatting Tricks to Enhance Reporting

As a general rule, you should always make your reporting easy to read and absorb. To that end, you should consider formatting the numbers in your reports to help your audience consume the needed information they need without confusion or hindrance. Why? Because it's never fun to count the zeros in a large number, especially when you're staring at 10 pitch font.

Here are some general best practices when it comes to formatting numbers for reporting:

- Always use commas to make numbers easier to read (for example, instead of 2345, show 2,345).

- Only use decimal places if that level of precision is required. For instance, there is rarely benefit for showing the decimal places in a dollar amount such as $123.45. Likewise in percentages, use only the minimum number of decimals required to represent the data effectively. For example instead of 43.21 percent, you may be able to get away with 43 percent.

- Only use the dollar symbol when you need to clarify that you are referring to monetary values. If you have a chart or table that contains all revenue values, and there is a label clearly stating this, you can save room and pixels by leaving out the dollar symbol.

- Format very large numbers to thousands or millions place. For instance, instead of displaying 16,906,714, you can format the number to read 16.9 M.

You can easily format numbers in Access by adjusting the Format property of your value fields. To test this, go to the sample database you downloaded with this book, and open the Access Report called "Revenue By 2007 vs 2008."

As you can see in Figure 13-1, there are a ton of numbers here. Instead of inundating your users with unnecessary digits, you can truncate the dollar values to thousands.

Follow these steps to format the numbers:

1. Switch to Design View by going up to the Ribbon and clicking View ⇨ Design View.

2. Click the 2007 field to set focus on it.

3. You will see a Design tab in the Ribbon. Go to the Design tab and click the Property Sheet button.

4. This activates the Property Sheet pane. Here, click the Format tab and enter **$#,##0," k"** into the Format property (see Figure 13-2).

5. Click the 2008 field and apply the same number formatting.

Northeast

	2007	2008
Baltimore	$4,120	$8,571
Buffalo	$1,367,770	$2,103,749
New England	$582,930	$772,343

South

	2007	2008
Dallas	$2,190,698	$2,130,941
Florida	$26,844,140	$36,117,372

Southeast

	2007	2008
Charlotte	$6,404,954	$8,586,372
Knoxville	$0	$17,361

Figure 13-1: To make this report easier to read, dollar values can be shown in thousands.

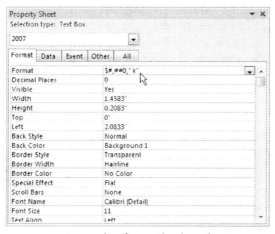

Figure 13-2: Enter your custom number formatting into the Format property.

Let's take a moment to analyze the syntax you just used: (**$#,##0," k"**).

- The dollar symbol ($) obviously tells Access that this is a currency value.

- The pound signs along with the first comma (#,##0) defines a basic structure for any number that uses this format. In this case, #,##0 tells Access that commas should be used in any number larger than 999.

- The comma after the 0 tells Access to truncate the number to the thousands place.

- The letter k wrapped in quotes (" k ") adds a visual indicator that these numbers are in thousands.

Switch back to report view to see the result of your change. If all went well, your report should now look like one shown here in Figure 13-3.

Northeast		
	2007	2008
Baltimore	$4 k	$9 k
Buffalo	$1,363 k	$2,104 k
New England	$583 k	$772 k
South		
	2007	2008
Dallas	$2,191 k	$2,131 k
Florida	$26,844 k	$36,117 k
Southeast		
	2007	2008
Charlotte	$6,405 k	$3,586 k
Knoxville	$0 k	$17 k

Figure 13-3: You have successfully applied your custom number format.

This is just one example of a custom number format you can apply to reduce the clutter in your reports. You can employ literally hundreds of alternative formats. Table 13-1 lists just a few of the common format syntax and how they can affect your numbers.

Table 13-1: Common Custom Number Syntax

ORMAT SYNTAX	HOW 6,404,954 WOULD BE DISPLAYED
#,##0	6,404,954
#,##0,	6,405
#,##0," k"	6,405 k
#,##0,," M"	6 M
$#,##0,	$6,405
$#,##0," k"	$6,405 k
$#,##0,," M"	$6 M

Using Conditional Formatting in Access

Conditional Formatting is the term given to the functionality where Access dynamically changes the formatting of a value based on a set of conditions you define. Conditional formatting allows your audience to, at a glance, make split-second determinations on which values are "good" and which are "bad," all based on formatting.

Conditional formatting is one of those functionalities in Access that offer countless ways of achieving a result. In this section, you cover a few basic examples of how conditional formatting can visually enhance your Access reporting. If you've worked with conditional formatting in Excel, this will be familiar territory.

Apply Conditional Formatting to a Field Based on its Own Value

The simplest way to apply conditional formatting is to test whether a field's value meets a specific criterion. For your first encounter with conditional formatting in Access, take a moment to walk through an example.

1. Go to the sample database you downloaded with this book, and open the Access Report called Revenue by Segments.

2. Switch to Design View by going up to the Ribbon and clicking View ⇨ Design View.

3. Click the SumofSales_Amount field; then find the Format tab on the Ribbon. There, click the Conditional Formatting button shown in Figure 13-4.

Figure 13-4: Selecting the Conditional Formatting button.

4. The Conditional Formatting dialog box will open (see Figure 13-5). Click the New Rule button.

Figure 13-5: Choose to start a new rule.

The New Formatting Rule dialog box will activate. Take a look at Figure 13-6. Because you are applying a condition to the current field based on its own values, the only adjustments that have to be made are to the operator dropdown and the criteria field.

5. As you can see in Figure 13-6, you are applying a formatting rule to any value less than 50000. Select less than from the operator dropdown, and then enter 50000 in the criteria input.

6. While you are still on this dialog box, assign a format you want applied to any value meeting your criteria.

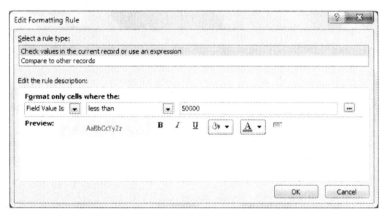

Figure 13-6: Apply a new format for any value under 50,000.

7. Click the OK button to finalize your conditional formatting. Figure 13-7 illustrates what your report will look like when you switch back to Report View.

Midwest

Chicago

Segment	Revenue	% of Revenue
Bar Equipment	$3,188	1%
Commercial Appliances	$9,081	2%
Concession Equipment	$18,218	5%
Fryers	$9,847	2%
Ovens and Ranges	$133,416	33%
Refrigerators and Coolers	$124,565	31%
Warmers	$104,243	26%
Sum	$402,538	

Kansas City

Segment	Revenue	% of Revenue
Bar Equipment	$41,892	2%
Commercial Appliances	$61,404	3%
Concession Equipment	$57,301	3%

Figure 13-7: You've successfully applied your first conditional formatting in Access.

With your newly applied conditional formatting, you can easily pick out the entry under 50,000. Although this is a relatively benign example, conditional formatting can prove useful in guiding your end-users toward key metrics on your report.

Apply Conditional Formatting Based on another Control's Value

Often times, you may need to set conditional formatting on a particular field based the values of another field. In these cases, you'll have to configure your conditional formatting slightly differently.

1. Open the Revenue By Segment report again in Design View.

2. Click the SumofSales_Amount field, and then click Conditional Formatting on the Format tab in the Ribbon.

3. Because you have already set up a conditional format, you now have the Edit Rule button illustrated in Figure 13-8. From here, you can choose to create a new rule, or to edit the existing rule. Click the Edit Rule button.

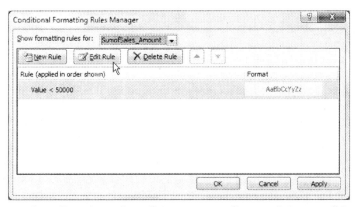

Figure 13-8: The Edit Rule option allows you to edit an existing conditional formatting rule.

At this point, you will be taken to the Edit Formatting Rule dialog box shown in Figure 13-9. In this example, you want to edit the rule to check the PcntSales field. If the PcntSales Field is less than 20 percent, you want to apply your conditional formatting.

4. As you can see in Figure 13-9, the Expression Is qualifier is being used this time. Any time you are evaluating your criteria against another field, you will choose the "Expression is" qualifier. On the same dialog box, enter **[Pcnt Sales]** <**.20**. This expression tells Access to evaluate the PcntSales field. If the value in that field is less than 20 percent, then the SumofSales_Amount field will be formatted.

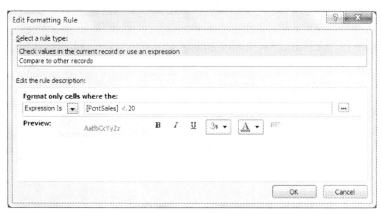

Figure 13-9: Use an expression to point to the field you need to evaluate.

5. Click the OK button to finalize your conditional formatting. If you're following along, your report should look similar to the one shown here in figure 13-10.

Midwest		
Chicago		
Segment	Revenue	% of Revenue
Bar Equipment	$3,168	1%
Commercial Appliances	$9,081	2%
Concession Equipment	$18,218	5%
Fryers	$9,847	2%
Ovens and Ranges	$133,416	33%
Refrigerators and Coolers	$124,565	31%
Warmers	$104,243	26%
Sum	$402,538	
Kansas City		
Segment	Revenue	% of Revenue
Bar Equipment	$41,892	2%
Commercial Appliances	$61,404	3%

Figure 13-10: Your conditional formatting is now based on the values in the percent of Revenue field.

Clearing Conditional Formatting

If you find that you no longer need to conditionally format a particular field, you can follow these steps to clear the conditional formatting rule.

1. Open your report in Design View.

2. Click the control from which you want the conditional formatting removed.

3. Click Conditional Formatting on the Format tab in the Ribbon.

4. In the Conditional Formatting dialog box, select the condition you want removed and then click the Delete Rule button.

5. Click OK to confirm.

Advanced Visualization Techniques

Up until now, you've been working with the visualization tools that are native to Access. Now it's time to move off the reservation a bit.

In this section, you explore a few techniques that go beyond the built-in functionality of Access. As you go through the rest of this chapter, you'll discover how a little outside-the-box thinking can expand your reporting capabilities and improve your ability to communicate through dashboard-style visualizations.

Enhancing Queries and Reports with Data Bars

Figure 13-11 shows a query that contains what seems to be a bar chart. This type of data visualization is typically referred to as in-cell charting (charting directly in a table, providing a visualization of the data shown). The cool thing is that the in-cell charting achieved here is the result of a simple calculation and the STRING function.

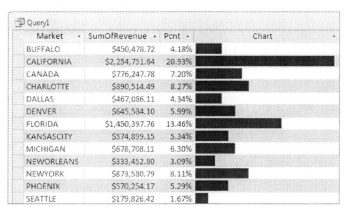

Figure 13-11: The in-cell charting seen here is nothing more than a query trick using the STRING function.

Introducing the STRING Function

The STRING function repeats a given character a specified number of times. For example, if you were to type the expression =STRING(10, 's'), the returned value would be ssssssssss (the "s" character repeated 10 times). To see this in action, build the query you see in Figure 13-12.

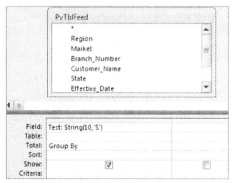

Figure 13-12: Testing the STRING function in a query

When you run this query, as promised, you will see a series of ten S's. Now you can alter this query so that instead of using a letter, you would use a character that, when repeated, looks kind of like a chart.

For this, you can use the ChrW function. The ChrW function returns Unicode characters based on a character number. For instance, ChrW(9608) returns a block that, when repeated several times, looks like a bar chart. Here is how you would use it with the STRING function.

```
String(10, ChrW(9608)
```

Figure 13-13 demonstrates how this is used in a query.

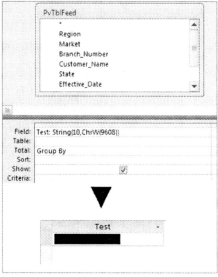

Figure 13-13: Using ChrW(9608) with the STRING function in a query produces a series of block characters reminiscent of a bar chart.

Obviously, it doesn't make sense to hard-code the number of times to repeat the character. You would ideally point the STRING function to some sort of field or mathematical operation that gives you a number of times to repeat. Figure 13-14 illustrates an example where the Revenue field is used in a mathematical operation to arrive at an appropriate number of times to repeat the block character.

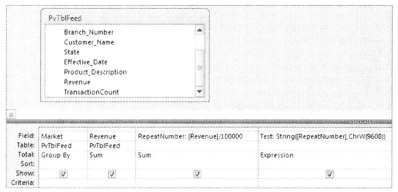

Figure 13-14: In situations where you have large values, you can divide the vales by 10, 100, 1000, etc. in order to calculate an appropriate repeat number.

As you can see in Figure 13-15, you couldn't just use the raw Revenue field to feed the STRING function. There would be too many block characters, and the function would fail. So the RepeatNumber field is calculated to derive a repeat number that works.

Market	SumOfRevenue	RepeatNumber	Test
BUFFALO	$450,478.72	4.50	
CALIFORNIA	$2,254,751.64	22.55	
CANADA	$776,247.78	7.76	
CHARLOTTE	$890,514.49	8.91	
DALLAS	$467,086.11	4.67	
DENVER	$645,584.10	6.46	
FLORIDA	$1,450,397.76	14.50	
KANSASCITY	$574,899.15	5.75	
MICHIGAN	$678,708.11	6.79	
NEWORLEANS	$333,452.80	3.33	
NEWYORK	$873,580.79	8.74	
PHOENIX	$570,254.17	5.70	
SEATTLE	$179,826.42	1.80	

Figure 13-15: The results of your test query

Another way to limit the number of times a character is repeated is to calculate a maximum repeat number. You can do this by getting a bit fancy and using Access' DSUM function. To understand this, take a look at Figure 13-16.

The expression in the RepeatNumber column basically tells Access to take the value being referenced and divide it by the sum for the entire range. This returns a percent weighting, which is then multiplied by 100. Stand back and think about what this means. The maximum number of characters that can possibly be returned by this formula is 100, no matter how big the revenue figures are.

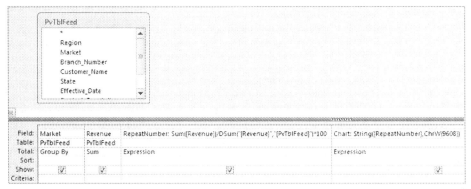

Figure 13-16: Use the DSUM Function to establish a ceiling on your repeat number.

NOTE You may be wondering why you would not just use the data bars conditional formatting feature, or for that matter, a chart? First, data bars are not backwards compatible. Meaning anyone who doesn't have Access 2010 won't be able to use them. Second, their gradient style may not conform to the overall look and feel of your dashboard. As for standard charts, they take up much more space than in-cell charting. Plus they add overhead to your file. In-cell charting gives you an easy to implement alternative that doesn't require a lot of real-estate or setup.

Extending Data Bars to Reports

Because these clever new data bars are expression driven, they can be used practically anywhere you can use an expression. In Figure 13-17, a new TextBox has been added to the Revenue by Segments report, and a STRING expression is used to create a data bar.

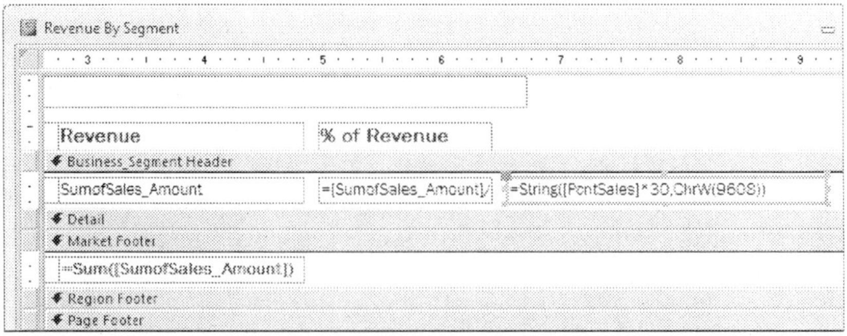

Figure 13-17: You can use your new data bar anywhere you can enter an expression.

Figure 13-18, shows the data bars in Report view. Note that because these data bars are text based, they can be formatted just like any other text.

Revenue by Segment

CANADA

CANADA

Segment	Revenue	% of Revenue	
Bar Equipment	$35,975	1%	
Commercial Appliances	$71,272	2%	
Concession Equipment	$205,875	5%	
Fryers	$129,636	3%	
Ovens and Ranges	$1,183,773	32%	
Refrigerators and Coolers	$1,728,601	46%	
Warmers	$392,969	10%	

Figure 13-18: These data bars can also be formatted to be different colors and sizes.

Sprucing up Queries and Reports with Symbols

With the release of Office 2007, Excel introduced new conditional formatting rules that allow you to show dashboard-esque icons to your cells. With these icons, you can represent performance using different shapes and colors. Unfortunately, no such functionality exists in your cache of Access 2010 tools.

A creative alternative is using the fancy characters and symbols you can get from the ChrW function. You were introduced to the ChrW function earlier in this chapter ("Enhancing Queries and Reports with Data Bars"). If you'll remember, the ChrW function returns Unicode characters based on a character number. For instance, ChrW(9608) returns a block character. These characters allow you to mimic Excel's icon sets, using symbols to provide users a visual representation of performance.

Before walking through an example, look at Table 13-2. Here, you will see some of the Unicode characters often seen on dashboard reports. Again, the idea is to pass the character number through the ChrW function. For example, ChrW(9650) would return an up arrow symbol.

To understand the benefit of using symbols in reporting, go to the sample database you downloaded with this book, and open the Access Report called Revenue By 2007 vs 2008.

As you can see in Figure 13-19, this report compares revenues in 2008 to those in 2007. Obviously, the goal of this report is to convey the movement up or down in revenue from one year to another.

Table 13-2: Unicode Character Codes and Their Associated Symbols

CHARACTER CODE	ASSOCIATED SYMBOL	CHARACTER CODE	ASSOCIATED SYMBOL
8592	←	9668	◀
8593	↑	9670	◆
8594	→	9671	◇
8595	↓	9679	●
8598	↖	9680	◐
8599	↗	9681	◑
8600	↘	9682	◒
8601	↙	9683	◓
8678	⇐	9684	◔
8679	⇑	9685	◕
8680	⇒	9698	◢
8681	⇓	9699	◣
9607	▌	9700	◤
9608	█	9701	◥
9650	▲	10003	✓
9658	►	10007	✗
9660	▼	10025	☆

Midwest		
	2007	2008
Chicago	$72,046	$159,293
Kansas City	$462,950	$950,374
Omaha	$751,101	$744,338
Tulsa	$691,890	$987,687

North		
	2007	2008
Dakotas	$152,431	$149,199
Great Lakes	$536,618	$614,349

Northeast		
	2007	2008
Baltimore	$4,120	$8,571
Buffalo	$1,367,770	$2,103,749
New England	$582,930	$772,343

Figure 13-19: Open the Revenue By 2007 vs 2008 report.

In order to help absorb this data faster, let's add a set of up and down arrows representing the increase or decrease in revenue from 2007 to 2008.

1. Switch to Design View by going up to the Ribbon and clicking View ➪ Design View.

2. Add a new TextBox next to the 2008 field (Figure 13-20).

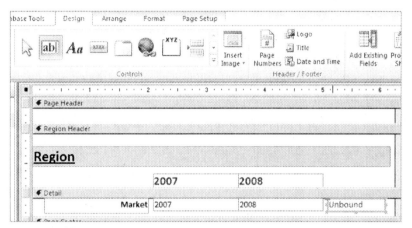

Figure 13-20: Add a TextBox.

3. In the newly added TextBox, enter the following IIf statement: **=IIf([2008]>[2007],ChrW(9650),ChrW(9660))**. This checks if the 2008 revenue is greater than 2007. If so, then an up arrow is return via the ChrW function. If not, a down arrow is returned. Your screen should look similar to that shown in Figure 13-21.

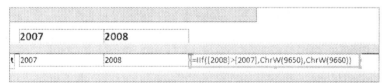

Figure 13-21: Build an IIf statement that evaluates revenue and returns either an up arrow or down arrow.

4. Since you're knee-deep in creating a visualization, you might as well add some conditional formatting. Click your newly created TextBox and select Conditional Formatting from the Format tab. This activates the Conditional Formatting Rules Manager dialog box.

5. Click the New Rule button.

6. Select the "Expression Is" qualifier, then enter **[2008]>[2007]** in the condition input (see Figure 13-22). This formats all arrows where the revenue from 2008 is greater than 2007 (up arrows). Needless to say,

you want to select formatting that corresponds with good performance. Format the Font Color green.

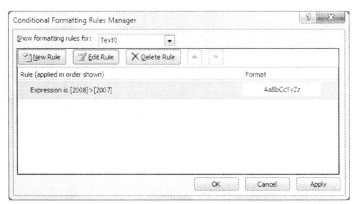

Figure 13-22: Create a conditional formatting for up arrows.

7. Press OK to confirm your changes and to return to the Conditional Formatting Rules Manager.

8. Now you'll need to add conditional formatting to those records where 2007 is greater than 2008. Click the New Rule button.

9. Select the "Expression Is" qualifier, then enter **[2007]>[2008]** in the condition as demonstrated in Figure 13-23. This formats all arrows where the revenue from 2007 is greater than 2008 (down arrows). For the down arrows, format the Font Color Red.

Figure 13-23: Create a conditional formatting for down arrows.

10. Take some time to format your arrows; make them bigger, align them to the other fields, and so on. If all went well, your report should look similar to Figure 13-24.

Midwest

	2007	2008	
Chicago	$72,046	$159,293	▲
Kansas City	$462,950	$950,374	▲
Omaha	$751,101	$744,338	▼
Tulsa	$691,890	$987,687	▲

North

	2007	2008	
Dakotas	$152,431	$149,199	▼
Great Lakes	$536,618	$614,349	▲

Northeast

	2007	2008	
Baltimore	$4,120	$8,571	▲
Buffalo	$1,367,770	$2,103,749	▲
New England	$582,930	$772,343	▲

Figure 13-24: With your new visualizations, you easily pick out the poor performers.

Using Your Own Dashboard Graphics in Access

Figure 13-25 shows a dashboard report (gauges included) that contains data related to internet revenue. Believe it or not, this report was done in Access. If you open the sample database for this book, you will find a Report object called Dashboard Report.

Market	Total Revenue	Internet Revenue	%of Sales Via Internet	
California	$11,363,506.25	$7,986,770.00	70%	
CANADA	$3,748,101.15	$2,465,913.25	66%	
Charlotte	$21,563,040.45	$1,875,035.00	9%	
Chicago	$402,537.75	$274,313.75	68%	

Figure 13-25: Amazingly, this report was created in Access.

Storing External Graphics in an Access Table

The starting point to this technique is obviously graphics. You'll need to decide which graphics to use. For illustrative purposes, Figure 13-26 shows a directory that has several bitmap files (each one containing a representation of a gauge). Note how the title of each file is a number. When creating graphics for dashboarding purposes, the idea is to name each file a number corresponding to a value from 1 to 100. So file 50 represents 50 percent, file 40 represents 40 percent, and so on.

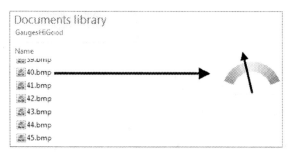

Figure 13-26: Figure 13-26: Start with a set of bitmap files, each representing a value from 1 to 100.

NOTE The sample database for this book already contains a table ('Dashboard-Graphics') which contains a series of images ideal for dashboarding. This section is an illustrative look at how you would go about building your own dashboard graphics table.

Once you have graphics, you'll need to store them someplace. This is where Access tables come in. Figure 13-27 demonstrates a basic structure for a table designed to hold graphics. As you can see, you need only three columns to start.

- A number column that holds numbers 1–100
- A percent column that holds .01–1
- An OLEObject column that holds the Bitmap graphics

GraphicsTable	
Field Name	**Data Type**
ValueNum	Number
ValuePcnt	Number
GaugesHiGood	OLE Object

Figure 13-27: The basic table structure needed to store graphics for dashboarding purposes

TIP OLE (Object Linking and Embedding) is a Microsoft technology that allows an application to store data packages such as text files, sound files, or picture files. The OLE Object field type in Access uses this technology to embed and store external data files directly into an Access database. Embedding files using an OLE Object field ensures that the embedded files travel with the database when distributed or moved.

Once Access has a place to store your graphics, you'll need to get your graphics into the table. Several multiple methods are available to do this. The easiest manual way is to drag them into the OLEObject field. Simply drag each graphic into the record corresponding to its value. For example, the bitmap file titled 40 would go into the record where the ValueNum field is 40 and the ValuePcnt field is .40. Figure 13-28 demonstrates how you would drag graphic files into the OLE Object field.

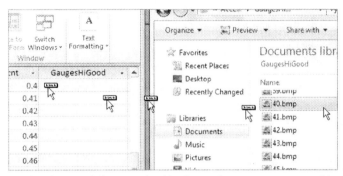

Figure 13-28: The drag and drop method is the easiest way to get graphics into an OLE Object field.

When all is said and done, you would have a "graphics table" where each record represents a number value from 1 to 100. Each number and percent value corresponds to the appropriate bitmap file (see Figure 13-29).

ValueNum	ValuePcnt	GaugesHiGood
40	0.4	Bitmap Image
41	0.41	Bitmap Image
42	0.42	Bitmap Image
43	0.43	Bitmap Image
44	0.44	Bitmap Image
45	0.45	Bitmap Image
46	0.46	Bitmap Image
47	0.47	Bitmap Image
48	0.48	Bitmap Image
49	0.49	Bitmap Image
50	0.5	Bitmap Image
51	0.51	Bitmap Image
52	0.52	Bitmap Image
53	0.53	Bitmap Image
54	0.54	Bitmap Image

Figure 13-29: A completed graphics table

Using the Graphics Table

Using a graphics table is as easy as linking it to any analysis using the ValueNum or ValuePcnt columns. Figure 13-30 demonstrates how you would use a query to tie your graphics table to another dataset. In this case, the Pcnt

Internet Revenue field is joined to the ValuePcnt field I the graphics table. This results in the appropriate image being associated to each value in the Pcnt Internet Revenue field.

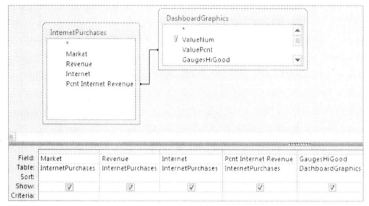

Figure 13-30: The OLEObject column (the column that holds the bitmaps) in this example is called "GaugesHiGood."

After the query is saved, you can use it as the source for various reports and forms. Figure 13-31 shows that you can build reporting views in Access forms as well as Access reports.

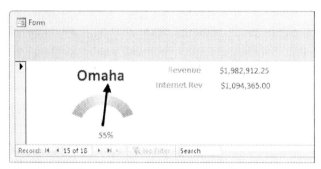

Figure 13-31: You can build your dashboards directly on forms.

Using Multiple Sets of Graphics

Keep in mind that you can have more than one OLEObject field in your graphics table. This allows you to have all kinds of different visual representations of 1–100. If you open the DashboardGraphics table found in the sample database for this book, you will see multiple columns representing different graphics.

Figure 13-32 demonstrates how using multiple graphics fields is as easy as selecting the desired graphic in a query.

InternetPurchases
*
Market
Revenue
Internet
Pcnt Internet Revenue
DashboardGraphics
*
ValueNum
ValuePcnt
GaugesHiGood
GaugesLowGood
ProgressBarHiGood
ProgressBarLowGood
ProgressColumnHiGood
ProgressColumnLowGood
Field: Market | Revenue | Internet | Pcnt Internet Revenue | ProgressBarHiGood
Table: InternetPurchases | InternetPurchases | InternetPurchases | InternetPurchases | DashboardGraphics
Sort:
Show:
Criteria:

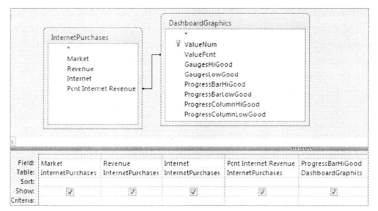

Figure 13-32: This query identifies the progress bar as the graphic used.

Running this query produces the report in Figure 13-33.

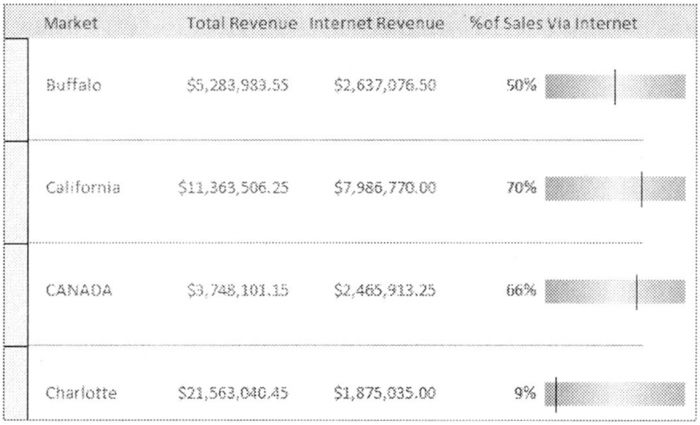

Market
Total Revenue
Internet Revenue
%of Sales Via Internet
Buffalo $5,283,983.55 $2,637,076.50 50%
California $11,363,506.25 $7,986,770.00 70%
CANADA $3,748,101.15 $2,465,913.25 66%
Charlotte $21,563,040.45 $1,875,035.00 9%

Figure 13-33: The progress bar report

Summary

Adding data visualizations to your reporting allows you to highlight key trends, point out comparisons, and focus in on outliers. It not only makes you more effective at reporting data, but it helps your end-users become more effective at consuming data.

Using Access' conditional formatting functionality is an easy way to quickly add visualizations to your reports. Conditional formatting allows your audience to, at-a-glance, make split-second determinations on which values are "good" and which are "bad," all based on formatting.

Outside of rudimentary conditional formatting, Access doesn't offer a whole lot in the way of data visualization and dashboarding graphics. But with a bit of imagination, you can create your own visualizations. Two examples covered in this chapter are data bars using the STRING function and fancy symbols using the ChrW function. Alternatively, thanks to Access' ability to store OLE objects, you can store and use your own graphics in reporting.

Advanced Excel and Access Integration Techniques

In This Part

Getting Access Data into Excel

Throughout this book, you've been exposed to the concept of using Access as the data layer, and Excel as the presentation layer. This obviously suggests that data has to be moved from Access to Excel. In this chapter, you explore a few basic techniques that will help you efficiently move Access data into your Excel workbook.

The Different Methods for Importing Access Data

While it's important to know the numerous ways to get our Access data into Excel, it's equally important to know when a particular method is more efficient than another! In this section, you'll be introduced to several methods for getting data into Excel and examine what circumstances make one method better suited than another.

The Drag and Drop Method

For simplicity and ease, you just can't beat the Drag and Drop method. Try this: Simultaneously open an empty Excel workbook and an Access database from which you want to import. In this case, you can use the ZalexCorp sample database you downloaded with this book. Now resize each application's window such that they are both fully visible on your screen.

Hover on the Access table or query you wish to transfer into Excel. Now press and hold the left mouse button and move the mouse cursor over to the blank worksheet in Excel as demonstrated in Figure 14-1. Release the mouse to see the data move to Excel.

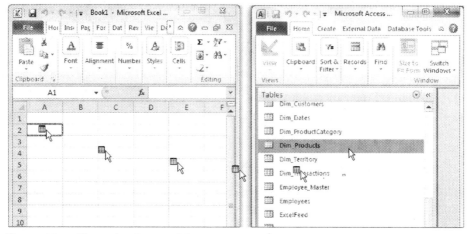

Figure 14-1: Illustrating Drag and Drop

The Drag and Drop method comes in handy when you are doing a quick one-time analysis where you need a specific set of data in Excel. It is not so useful if:

- You expect this step to occur routinely, as a part of a repeated analysis or report.

- You expect the users of your Excel report to get or refresh the report data via this method.

- It's not possible or convenient for you to simply open up Access at the time you need the data.

Under the preceding scenarios, it is much better to use another technique.

Using the Export Wizard from Access

You may remember from Chapter 2 that Access has a built-in Import wizard for importing data from various sources. Well, Access also has an Export wizard. It's relatively simple to use.

1. With the ZalexCorp sample database open, click the Dim_Products table one time to select it.

2. With the table selected, browse to the External Data tab on the Ribbon and select the Excel icon under the Export group. This activates the wizard shown in Figure 14-2.

   As you can see in Figure 14-2, you have a few discretionary options you can specify in the Excel Export wizard. You can specify the file location, the file type and some format preservation options.

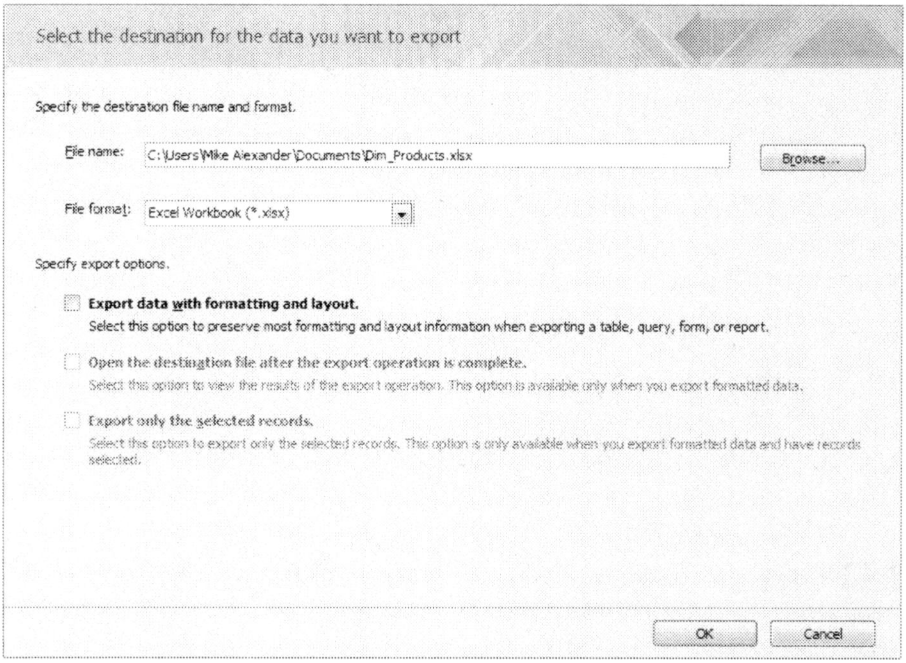

Figure 14-2: Export Data to Excel wizard in Access.

NOTE You may export your Access object to an existing Excel file instead of creating a new file. However, you should be aware of several things. By default, the name of the exported object becomes the name of the table or query in Access. Be cautious if you have an object with the same name in your Excel workbook, as it may be overwritten. For example, if you export the "PriceMaster" table to an Excel worksheet that already has a worksheet named PriceMaster, Excel will overwrite the worksheet. Second, make sure the workbook to which you are exporting is closed. If you try to export to an open workbook, you will likely get an error in Access.

3. Select the Export data with formatting and layout option. Notice that a second menu option becomes available that asks if you wish to open the file for viewing after export. Select that as well and click OK.

   Immediately, Excel opens to show you the exported data.

In Access, the last page in the Export wizard (Figure 14-3) asks if you want to save your export steps. Saving your export steps can be useful if you expect to frequently send that particular query or table to Excel.

The benefit of this method is that, unlike dragging and dropping, the ability to save export steps allows you to automate your exports by using macros.

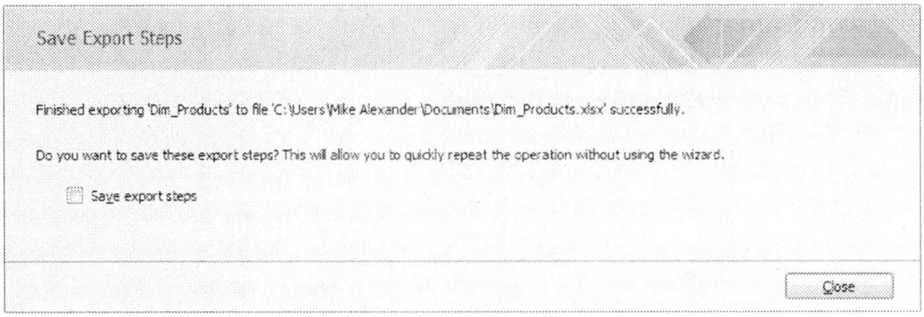

Figure 14-3: Be sure to utilize the Save Export Steps option if you are going to Export your data frequently.

The limitation of this export method is that it is done within Access. If you are making an Excel report where data refresh must be under the Excel user's control, this method is not viable. In this circumstance, importing data from the Excel menu and/or using MS Query in Excel is the more viable option.

TIP Use the RunSavedImportExport macro action to automate the exporting of data using "saved export steps." Feel free to review Chapter 9 for a refresher on how to use macros.

Using Get External Data from Excel

The option to pull data from Access has been available in Excel for many versions; it was just buried several layers deep in somewhat cryptic menu titles. This made getting Access data into Excel seem like a mysterious and tenuous proposition for many Excel analysts. With the introduction of the Ribbon in Excel 2007, Microsoft made importing Access data from Excel a little less nebulous, including the option right on the Ribbon under the Data tab.

Using the Get External Data method in Excel allows you to establishing a refreshable data connection between Excel and Access. To see the power of this method, walk through these steps:

1. Open a new Excel workbook and select the Data tab on the Ribbon.

2. Simply click the From Access icon found in the Get External Data group.

   This activates the Select Database dialog box you see in Figure 14-4. The idea is to browse for your Access database. If the database from which you wish to import is local, simply browse to the file location and open it. If you have an Access database on a network drive at your employer, you may also select that database as well — provided you have the proper authorization and access.

3. Navigate to the sample database found under C:\OffTheGrid (see Figure 14-4): then click the Open button.

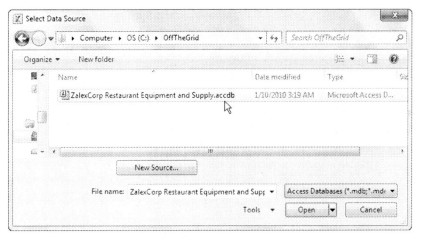

Figure 14-4: Choose your source database.

4. In some environments, a series of Data Link Properties dialog boxes will activate, asking for credentials (username and password). Most Access databases do not require login credentials, but if your database does require a username and password, enter them in the Data Link Properties. Otherwise, press the OK button to go to the next step.

5. Once you reach this step, the Select Table dialog box (Figure 14-5) activates and allows you to choose a table or query from your database. Choose Revenue by Period query and click the OK button.

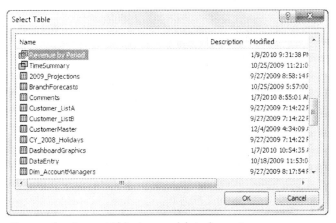

Figure 14-5: Choose the Access Object you wish to import.

At this point, you will see the Import Data dialog box shown in 14-6. This dialog box allows you to define where and how to import the table. As you can see, you have the option of importing the data into a Table, a PivotTable, or a PivotChart/PivotTable combination.

In this scenario, you want the raw data to be written directly onto your spreadsheet, so you'll choose the Table option.

NOTE If you choose PivotTable or PivotChart, the data is saved to a pivot cache without writing the actual data to the spreadsheet. This allows your pivot table to function as normal without having to import potentially hundreds of thousands of data rows twice (once for the pivot cache and once for the spreadsheet).

6. Select Table as the output view and define cell A1 as the output location (see Figure 14-6). Click the OK button to finalize your selections.

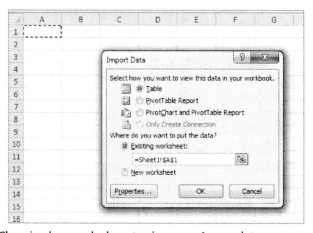

Figure 14-6: Choosing how and where to view your Access data

Your reward for all the work will be a table similar to that shown in Figure 14-7, which contains the imported data from your Access database.

Region	Market	Business Segment	SumofSales Amount
CANADA	CANADA	Bar Equipment	35975.25
CANADA	CANADA	Commercial Appliances	71272.1
CANADA	CANADA	Concession Equipment	205874.6
CANADA	CANADA	Fryers	129636.2
CANADA	CANADA	Ovens and Ranges	1183772.75
CANADA	CANADA	Refrigerators and Coolers	1728600.95
CANADA	CANADA	Warmers	392969.3
Midwest	Chicago	Bar Equipment	3168
Midwest	Chicago	Commercial Appliances	9081
Midwest	Chicago	Concession Equipment	18218
Midwest	Chicago	Fryers	9846.8

Figure 14-7: Your imported Access data!

The incredibly powerful thing about importing data this way is that it's refreshable! That's right. If you import data from Access using this technique,

Excel creates a table that you can refresh by right-clicking and selecting Refresh, as demonstrated in Figure 14-8. When you *Refresh* your imported data, Excel reconnects to your Access database and imports the data again. As long as a connection to your database is available, you can refresh it with a mere click of the mouse.

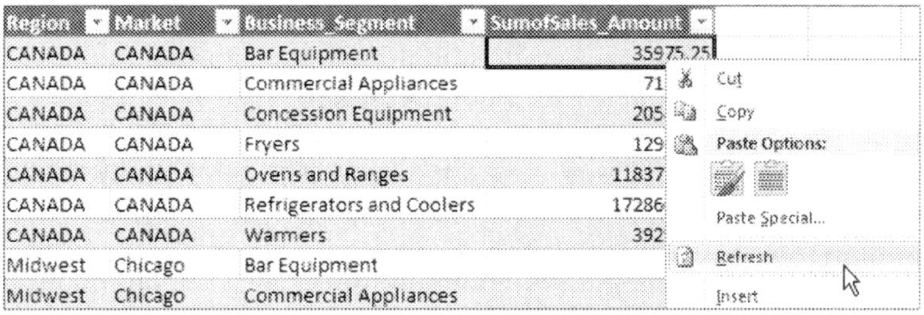

Figure 14-8: As long as a connection to your database is available, you can refresh your table with the latest data.

Again, a major advantage to using the Get External Data method is that it allows you to establish a refreshable data connection between Excel and Access. This means, in most cases, you can set up the connection one time and then just refresh the data connection when needed. You can even record an Excel macro to refresh the data on some trigger or event. This is ideal for automating the transfer of data from Access.

The disadvantage to this method is that you have to take the data as it is in Access. That is to say, you give up the ability to utilize sorts, filters, and table joins to customize the data you bring into Excel.

Using MS Query

Microsoft Query (affectionately known as MS Query) is a stand-alone program, installed with the Office suite, which can connect to external data sources from Excel. MS Query has one distinct advantage over the other methods for importing Access data into Excel: flexibility.

When transferring data using any of the previously mentioned methods, you can only import an existing table or query as is. That is to say, there is no opportunity to parse, filter or sort the data on the fly before importing it.

Not so with MS Query! With MS Query, you don't have to rely on the original tables or queries to be filtered or configured in a particular way. You can apply your own filters and sorts to your data pulls (through MS Query), essentially creating custom views that don't necessarily exist in the source database.

NOTE MS Query may or may not be installed on your system, based on how you performed your Office installation. Keep in mind that if you do not have the MS

Query program installed on your system, you cannot link to external data sources in Excel. To install MS Query you need your Microsoft Office installation disk. Start the Microsoft Office Setup and choose to customize your installation. While you are customizing your installation, look for Office Tools. You will find an entry called Microsoft Query under Office Tools. Make sure you set it to the Run from My Computer option and then complete the installation.

Starting MS Query

Begin by going to the Get External Data menu under the Data tab of the Excel ribbon. To start Microsoft Query, you choose the From Other Sources option and then select From Microsoft Query from the dropdown menu. Figure 14-9 shows what the menu will look like.

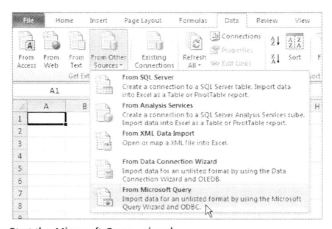

Figure 14-9: Start the Microsoft Query wizard.

After Microsoft Query opens, you will see the Choose Data Source dialog box illustrated in Figure 14-10. This is where you start building your MS Query import.

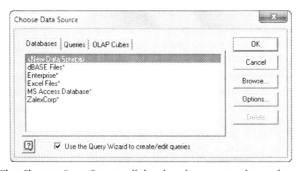

Figure 14-10: The Choose Data Source dialog box is your starting point.

Setting up Your Data Source

For this exercise, you will source data from the ZalexCorp database you downloaded with the sample files for this book. To set this database as an available data source, follow these steps:

1. From the Choose Data Source dialog, choose <New data source> from the Databases tab and click OK. This opens the Create New Data Source dialog box.

2. Type a name for your data source at the top of the dialog box, for example, ZalexCorp (see Figure 14-11).

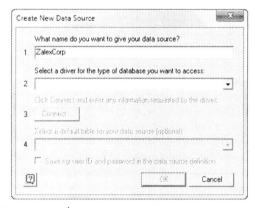

Figure 14-11: Name your new data source.

3. In the dropdown list box below, choose a type of driver for the database to which you want to connect. From this dropdown menu, make sure you select Microsoft Access Driver (*.mdb, *.accdb), as shown in Figure 14-12.

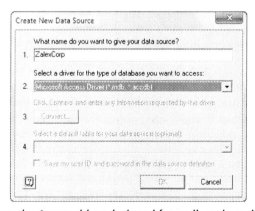

Figure 14-12: Choose the Access driver designed for .mdb and .accdb files.

4. Click Connect. This opens the ODBC Microsoft Access Setup dialog box illustrated in Figure 14-13.

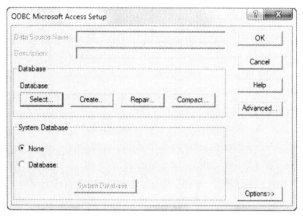

Figure 14-13: The ODBC Microsoft Access Setup dialog box

5. Click the Select button in the Database section to browse for your database in the Select Database dialog box (see Figure 14-14). In this example, you will select the ZalexCorp database found in the C:\OffTheGrid directory.

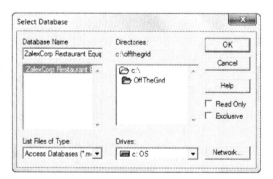

Figure 14-14: Select your target database.

6. After you have selected your database, continue to click OK until you come back to the Choose Data Source dialog box. ZalexCorp now shows up in the list of databases (see Figure 14-15).

Now that your ZalexCorp data source is set up, MS Query remembers its location, allowing you to use it repeatedly without the need to point to it each time you need to use it.

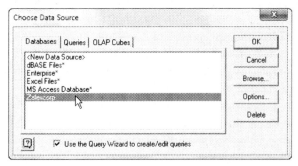

Figure 14-15: ZalexCorp is now in the list of available data sources.

TIP Microsoft Query works equally well for non-local databases (those that reside on a networked drive or even on the Web). In the Select Database dialog box, you'll find a dropdown menu with a list of computer drives available to you.

If your target database is on a network drive that is already mapped to your computer, choosing it is as simple as choosing that drive from the dropdown menu, and browsing the file hierarchy until you find the database you are looking for.

If your database is on a network that isn't mapped to your computer, simply click the Network button (shown in the lower right of the dialog box in Figure 14-14). This fires up a wizard to help you connect to a network drive or folder to which you are not currently mapped.

Building Your Custom Data Pull

Now that you have your ZalexCorp database set as an available data source, you can start building your own custom data pull. If you've closed the MS Query wizard, start it back up by going to the Data tab of the Excel Ribbon, choosing the From Other Sources option and then selecting From Microsoft Query.

1. Select your ZalexCorp datasource, as demonstrated in Figure 14-16, and click OK.

2. As you can see in Figure 14-17, you are presented with a dialog box that shows tables and queries within the ZalexCorp database. Select the Revenue by Period object and click the button with the right-pointing arrow.

3. In the next step, you can change the order of the data fields by clicking the up and down arrows to the right of the Columns in your query list box. Arrange the columns so that Region and Market come before Period as demonstrated in Figure 14-18. Click the Next button.

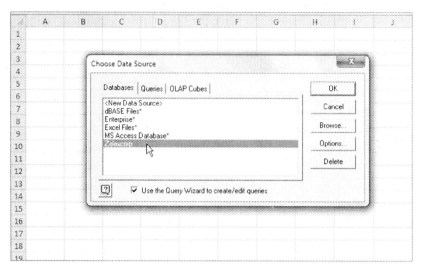

Figure 14-16: Select your ZalexCorp data source.

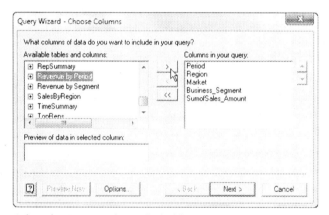

Figure 14-17: Select the Revenue by Period object.

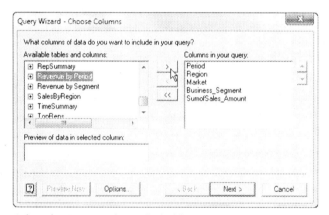

Figure 14-18: Move the Period column after Region and Market.

4. The next pane of the query wizard gives you the option of applying your own criteria to filter your data before importing (see Figure 14-19). Select the Period field to enable the filter options on the right. Once filtering is enabled, select "is greater than" from the condition dropdown. Then select 200812 in the criteria input box. Click the Next button.

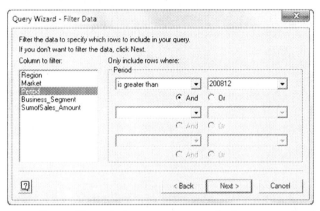

Figure 14-19: Set a filter telling MS Query to return only those records where the Period is greater than 200812.

5. In the next step, you're offered the opportunity to sort your query results. In this scenario, you want to sort by Period in ascending order, then by SumofSalesAmount in descending order. Figure 14-20 illustrates what this step looks like after the needed sorts have been applied. Click the Next button.

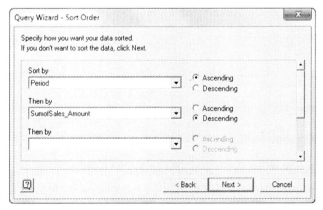

Figure 14-20: You can apply your own sorting to your query results.

6. The last screen of the wizard asks you whether you want to return your data to Excel or further modify the query in Microsoft Query. Choose to view our data in Excel and click the Finish button.

7. At this point, you should see the Import dialog box shown in Figure 14-21. Here, elect to return the data to a Table in cell A1, and then click the OK button.

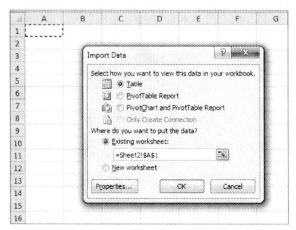

Figure 14-21: Return your results to a Table on your spreadsheet.

If all went well, you should have a table similar to that shown in Figure 14-22. Note that as designed, your query results contain only records where the Period is greater than 200812. Also, the columns have the correct order and sorting.

	A	B	C	D	E
1	Region	Market	Period	Business Segment	SumofSales Amount
2	South	Florida	200901	Warmers	1216003.3
3	South	Florida	200901	Refrigerators and Coolers	724743
4	South	Florida	200901	Ovens and Ranges	526507.5
5	West	California	200901	Refrigerators and Coolers	240063
6	Southeast	Charlotte	200901	Warmers	210336.4
7	South	Florida	200901	Commercial Appliances	173578.4
8	South	Florida	200901	Concession Equipment	139441.25
9	West	California	200901	Ovens and Ranges	100405.6
10	Southwest	Denver	200901	Refrigerators and Coolers	96733
11	West	California	200901	Warmers	85768.5
12	South	Dallas	200901	Refrigerators and Coolers	81530
13	South	Florida	200901	Fryers	79506.95

Figure 14-22: You've successfully created your first MS Query!

You can refresh the data by right-clicking anywhere inside your query table and selecting the Refresh button. You can also click the Refresh button found in the Design tab which activates when you cursor is inside the query table.

Again, while setting up an MS Query seems like a lot of work, the ability to parse, filter and sort data on the fly gives MS Query a distinct advantage over the previously mentioned methods for transferring data.

TRICKS OF THE TRADE: MANAGING EXTERNAL DATA PROPERTIES

Your query tables have a few adjustable properties exposed via the Properties dialog box. You can get to the properties of a particular External data table by clicking on the target table and selecting the Properties icon under the Data Tab (see Figure 14-23).

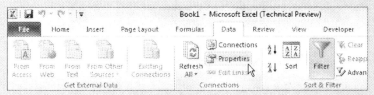

Figure 14-23: Getting to the properties of an external data table dialog box.

Activating the properties of a query table calls up the dialog box shown in Figure 14-24. Adjusting these properties allows you to further customize your query tables to suit your needs. Take a moment to familiarize yourself with some of the useful options on this dialog box.

Figure 14-24: The External Data Properties dialog box.

- **Include row numbers:** This property is unchecked by default. Checking this property will create a dummy column that contains row numbers. The first column of your dataset will be this row number column upon refresh.

- **Adjust column width:** This property is checked by default, telling Excel to adjust the column widths each time the data is refreshed. Removing this check will cause the column widths to remain the same.

- **Preserve column/sort/filter/layout:** If this is checked, the order of the columns and rows of the Excel range remains unchanged.

(continued)

TRICKS OF THE TRADE: MANAGING EXTERNAL DATA PROPERTIES
(continued)

This way, you can rearrange and sort the columns and rows of the external data in your spreadsheet without worrying about blowing away your formatting each time you refresh. Unchecking this property makes the Excel range look like the query.

■ **Preserve cell formatting:** This is checked by default, telling Excel to keep the applied cell formatting when you refresh.

■ **Insert cells for new data, delete unused cells:** This is the default setting for data range changes. When data rows decrease, you may have errors in adjacent cells that reference your external range. The cells these formulas referenced are deleted, so you will get a #VALUE error in your formula cells.

■ **Insert rows for new data, clear unused cells:** When the unused cells are cleared instead of deleted, the formula may no longer return an error. Instead, it continues to reference cells from the original range—even though some of them are blank now. This could still give you erroneous results.

■ **Overwrite cells for new data, clear unused cells:** The third option should be the same as option two when rows decrease as unused cells are cleared.

Summary

There are several basic techniques you can use to move Access data into your Excel workbooks. The most basic of these is the Drag and Drop method, where you literally drag access tables and queries onto a spreadsheet. Although this method comes in handy when you are doing a quick one-time analysis, it's not ideal when your analytical processes require that the data coming from Access be refreshed on a routine basis.

Another method of transferring data is to use Access' own Export wizard. This method is easy and it is ideal for automating exports to Excel using macros. However, if you are making an Excel report where data refresh must be under the Excel user's control, this method is not for you.

Excel's Get External Data functionality is yet another method you can employ to transfer data from Access to Excel. With a simple wizard guiding your way, it's extremely easy to get up and running with this option. The advantage to using the Get External Data method is that it allows you to establish a refreshable data connection between Excel and Access. The disadvantage to this method is that you have to take the data as it is in Access. That is to say, you give up the ability to utilize sorts, filters, and table joins to customize the data you bring into Excel.

The last method covered in this chapter is MS Query. MS Query is a standalone application that works with Excel to pull external data via queries. Like the Get External Data method, MS Query allows you to create refreshable data connections between Excel and Access. But MS Query has a distinct advantage over the Get External Data method in that it allows you to customize your query results. That is to say, MS Query enables you to apply your own filters and sorts to your data pulls, essentially creating custom views that don't necessarily exist in the source database.

With these basic options at your disposal, you should have no problem integrating Excel and Access.

Using VBA to Move Data between Excel and Access

Throughout the first few chapters of this book, you have discovered several ways to move data between Access and Excel. Although many of those techniques will suit your needs just fine, each one retains an aspect of manual involvement. That is to say, each one involves manual setup, management, and maintenance. In this chapter, you explore how to leverage VBA (along with some data connection technologies) to make your life even easier by making your data transfer processes virtually hands free.

Note the phrase, "along with some data connection technologies." The reality is that VBA, in and of itself, does not have the capability to connect and manipulate external data. You need to combine VBA with a helper technology to work with external data sources. Although many technologies allow you to automate your data processes, you will focus on using ADO (ActiveX Data Objects) and SQL (Structured Query Language)—commonly pronounced "sequel."

Why bother using VBA when the manual processes work just fine? First, VBA allows you to process data without the need to create and maintain multiple queries and macros. Also with VBA, you can perform complex, multi-layered procedures that involve looping, record-level testing, and `If...Then...Else` checks without the need to inundate your processes with many queries and temporary tables. Finally, the one-two-three combination of VBA, ADO, and SQL is extremely powerful and relatively easy to understand and implement. In fact, as you go through this chapter, you will immediately start to think about the ways the techniques found here will help you optimize your Excel and Access integration projects.

> **NOTE** True to its purpose, all the techniques in this chapter involve writing some basic code. In order to keep this chapter focused on the data analysis aspect of these techniques, this chapter does not spending much time explaining the VBA behind them. If you are new to VBA, you may want to visit Appendix A, which gives you a basic understanding of the concepts used in this chapter.

Understanding ADO Fundamentals

When trying to grasp the basics of ADO, it helps to think of ADO as a tool that will help you accomplish two tasks: Connecting to a data source and specifying the dataset with which to work. In the following section, you will explore the fundamental syntax you will need to know in order to do just that.

The Connection String

The first thing you must do is connect to a data source. In order to do this, you must give VBA a few pieces of information. This information is passed to VBA in the form of a connection string. A *connection string* is fundamentally nothing more than a text string that holds a series of variables (also called *arguments*), which VBA uses to identify and open a connection to a data source. Although connection strings can get pretty fancy with a myriad of arguments and options, there are a handful of arguments that are commonly used when connecting to either Access or Excel. If you're new to ADO, it helps to focus on these commonly used arguments:

- `Provider`: The `Provider` argument tells VBA what type of data source with which you are working. When using Office 2007 or Office 2010 as the data source, the `Provider` syntax will read:

  `Provider=Microsoft.ACE.OLEDB.12.0`

  If your data process needs to run on a machine that does not have Office 2007 or Office 2010 on it, you need to use the `Provider` for earlier versions of Access and Excel:

  `Provider=Microsoft.Jet.OLEDB.4.0`

- `Data Source`: The `Data Source` argument tells VBA where to find the database or workbook that contains the data needed. With the `Data Source` argument, you pass the full path of the database or workbook. For example:

  `Data Source=C:\Mydirectory\Northwind 2007.accdb`

- `Extended Properties`: The `Extended Properties` argument is typically used when connecting to an Excel workbook. This argument tells VBA that the data source is something other than a database. When working with an Excel 2007 or 2010 workbook, this argument would read:

  `Extended Properties=Excel 12.0`

If your data process needs to run on a machine that does not have Office 2007 or Office 2010 on it, you must use the `Extended Properties` for the earlier versions of Excel:

```
Extended Properties=Excel 8.0
```

- `User ID`: The `User ID` argument is optional and only used if a user ID is required to connect to the data source:

```
User Id=MyUserId
```

- `Password`: The `Password` argument is optional and only used if a password is required to connect to the data source:

```
Password=MyPassword
```

Take a moment now to see a few examples of how these arguments are put together to build a connection string:

- Connecting to an Access database:

```
"Provider=Microsoft.ACE.OLEDB.12.0;" & _
"Data Source= C:\MyDatabase.accdb"
```

TIP **You will notice that each argument is surrounded by quotes and we are using the ampersand (&) along with an underscore (_). This is a simple technique used to break up the text string into readable parts. The code above is the same as writing:**

```
"Provider=Microsoft.ACE.OLEDB.12.0;Data Source= C: MyDatabase.accdb"
```

The purpose of breaking up the text string into parts is to make the code easy to read and manage within the Visual Basic Editor. The first line starts the string, and each subsequent line is concatenated to the previous line with the ampersand (&). The underscore (_), preceded by a space, is used as a continuation marker, indicating that the code on the next line is part of the code on the current line. This is similar to the way a hyphen is used in writing to continue a word broken into two lines.

- Connecting to an Access database with password and user ID:

```
"Provider=Microsoft.ACE.OLEDB.12.0;" & _
"Data Source= C:\MyDatabase.accdb;" & _
"User ID=Administrator;" & _
"Password=AdminPassword"
```

- Connecting to an Excel workbook:

```
"Provider=Microsoft.ACE.OLEDB.12.0;" & _
"Data Source=C:\MyExcelWorkbook.xlsx;" & _
"Extended Properties=Excel 12.0"
```

- Access connection string that will run on systems without Office 2007 installed:

```
"Provider=Microsoft.Jet.OLEDB.4.0;" & _
"Data Source= C:\MyDatabase.mdb"
```

■ Excel connection string that will run on systems without Office 2007 installed:

```
"Provider=Microsoft.Jet.OLEDB.4.0;" & _
"Data Source=C:\MyExcelWorkbook.xls;" & _
"Extended Properties=Excel 8.0"
```

Declaring a Recordset

In addition to building a connection to your data source, you must define the data set with which you need to work. In ADO, this dataset is referred to as the *Recordset*. A `Recordset` object is essentially a container for the records and fields returned from the data source. The most common way to define a `Recordset` is to open an existing table or query using the following arguments (see Table 15-1):

```
Recordset.Open Source, ConnectString, CursorType, LockType
```

Table 15-1: Recordset Arguments

ARGUMENT	DEFINITION
Source	Represents the data to be extracted. This is typically a table, query or SQL statement that retrieves records. Initially, you use tables and queries to select records from a data source. Later in this chapter, you learn how to build SQL statements to fine tune data extracts on the fly.
ConnectString	Represent the connection string used to connect to your chosen data source.
CursorType	Represents how a `Recordset` allows you to move through the data to be extracted. Types are shown in Table 15-2.
LockType	The argument to specify whether the data returned by the `Recordset` can be changed. Commonly used LockTypes are shown in Table 15-3.

The `CursorTypes` commonly used are shown in Table 15-2.

The following sections provide a few examples of how to declare a `Recordset` using the arguments you just covered.

Return Read Only Data from a Table or Query

Any of these `Recordset` declarations would return a `Recordset` that is read only. Note that you can use a table name or a SQL statement in each one of these examples:

```
MyRecordset.Open "MyTable", ConnectString
MyRecordset.Open "SQL", ConnectString, adOpenForwardOnly,adLockReadOnly
```

Table 15-2: Common Cursor Types

adOpenForwardOnly	This is the default setting; if you don't specify a CursorType, the Recordset will automatically be adOpenForwardOnly. This CursorType is the most efficient type because it only allows you to move through the Recordset one way, from beginning to end. This is ideal for reporting processes where data only needs to be retrieved and not traversed. Keep in mind that you cannot make changes to data when using this CursorType.
adOpenDynamic	This CursorType is typically used in processes where there is a need for looping, moving up and down through the dataset, or the ability to dynamically see any edits made to the dataset. This CursorType is typically memory and resource intensive and should be used only when needed.
adOpenStatic	This CursorType is ideal for returning results quickly because it essentially returns a snapshot of your data. However, this is different from the adOpenForwardOnly CursorType as it allows you to navigate the returned records. In addition, when using this CursorType, the data returned can be made updateable by setting its LockType to something other than adLockReadOnly.

Table 15-3: Common Lock Types

adLockReadOnly	This is the default setting; if you don't specify a LockType, the Recordset will automatically be set to adLockReadOnly. This is typically used when there is no need to change the data that is returned.
adLockOptimistic	This LockType allows you to freely edit the data of the records that are returned.

Return Updateable Data from a Table or Query

Any of these Recordset declarations would return updateable data. Note that you can use a table name or a SQL statement in each one of these examples:

```
MyRecordset.Open "SQL", ConnectString, adOpenStatic, adLockOptimistic
MyRecordset.Open "SQL", ConnectString, adOpenDynamic, adLockOptimistic
```

Writing Your First ADO Procedure

Now it's time to put together the ADO fundamentals you have explored thus far to create your first ADO procedure. In this section, you build a procedure that transfers an Access table into an Excel spreadsheet.

Referencing the ADO Object Library

Before you do anything with ADO, you must first set a reference to the ADO Object Library. Just as each Microsoft Office application has its own set of objects, properties and methods, so does ADO. Since Excel does not inherently know the ADO Object Model, you need to point Excel to the ADO reference library, as shown in the following steps:

1. Open a new Excel workbook and the Visual Basic Editor.

TIP Remember that in both Excel and Access you can access the VBE with the shortcut Alt + F11. Alternatively, you can access the VBE in Excel by selecting the Developer tab from the ribbon, and then selecting the Visual Basic icon.

Depending on how Excel is set up, the Developer tab may not show up in your Ribbon by default. If it is not there, simply go to the top-left corner of the Ribbon and click the File tab in Excel 2010 (the Office icon in Excel 2007) and select Excel Options In the Personalize menu, you will see a check box entitled "Show Developer tab in ribbon." Make sure this box is checked.

2. Once you are in the Visual Basic Editor, go up to the application menu and select Tools ⇨ References. This opens the References dialog box illustrated in Figure 15-1.

3. Scroll down until you locate latest version of the Microsoft ActiveX Data Objects Library. Place a checkmark beside this entry and click OK.

NOTE It is normal to have several versions of the same library displayed in the References dialog box. It's generally best to select the latest version available. You will notice that in Figure 15-1, Microsoft ActiveX Data Objects Library 2.8 is used. Don't be too concerned if you only have earlier versions available; the examples in this chapter will run fine with those earlier versions.

4. After you click the OK button, you can open the Reference dialog box again to ensure that your reference is set. You will know that your selection took effect, when the Microsoft ActiveX Data Objects Library is displayed at the top of the Reference dialog box with a check next to it (Figure 15-2).

NOTE You have just walked through setting a reference to the Microsoft ActiveX Data Objects Library using Excel. Keep in mind that these are the steps you take when you perform the same task in Access.

Also keep in mind that the references you set in any given workbook or database are not applied at the application level. This means that you need to repeat these steps with each new workbook or database you create.

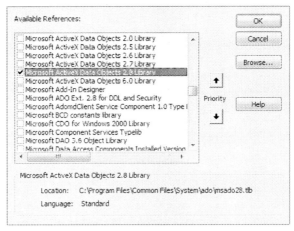

Figure 15-1: Select the latest version of the Microsoft ActiveX Data Objects Library.

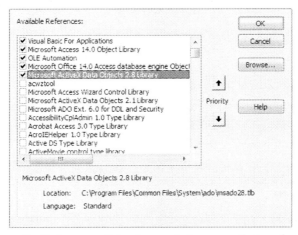

Figure 15-2: Open the References dialog box again to ensure that a reference to Microsoft ActiveX Data Objects Library has indeed been set.

Writing the Code

Once you have a reference set to the ADO Object Library, start a new module in the Visual Basic Editor by selecting Insert ➪ Module. Start a new Sub procedure called GetAccessData. In that procedure, enter the following code:

```
Sub GetAccessData()

'Step 1: Declare your Variables
    Dim MyConnect As String
    Dim MyRecordset As ADODB.Recordset

'Step 2: Declare your Connection String
    MyConnect = "Provider=Microsoft.ACE.OLEDB.12.0;" & _
               "Data Source=
C:\OffTheGrid\ZalexCorp Restaurant Equipment and Supply.accdb"

'Step 3: Instantiate and Specify your Recordset
    Set MyRecordset = New ADODB.Recordset
    MyRecordset.Open "Query_Products", MyConnect, adOpenStatic,
adLockReadOnly

'Step 4: Copy the Recordset to Excel
    Sheets("Your First ADO Procedure").Select
    ActiveSheet.Range("A2").CopyFromRecordset MyRecordset

'Step 5: Add Column Labels
    With ActiveSheet.Range("A1:C1")
        .Value = Array("Product", "Description", "Segment")
        .EntireColumn.AutoFit
    End With

End Sub
```

TIP Installing the sample files for this book ensures that you have the Access database referenced in the previous code. You will also find a workbook called Chapter15_SampleFiles.xls containing this procedure along with the others found in this chapter.

When writing your own procedures, you will alter the connection string to reference the path for your data source.

Take a moment to think about what you are doing in each step:

1. **Declaring the necessary variables:** Declare two variables: a string variable to hold the connection string, and a Recordset object to hold the results of the data pull. In this example, the variable called MyConnect holds the connection string identifying the data source. Meanwhile, the variable called MyRecordset holds the data returned by the procedure.

2. **Declaring the connection string:** Define the connection string for the ADO procedure. In this scenario, you are connecting to the ZalexCorp Restaurant Equipment and Supply.accdb found on the C drive.

3. **Assigning data to your Recordset:** Once you've defined your data source, you can fill your `Recordset` with some data. Specify that your Recordset is read-only and filled with data from the Query_Products query found in the ZalexCorp Restaurant Equipment and Supply Access database. When writing your own procedures, you can replace the Query_Products query name with that of your own tables.

   Also notice that you must set the `MyRecordset` variable to a new `ADODB.Recordset` (Set `MyRecordset` = New `ADODB.Recordset`). VBA requires that you instantiate the `Recordset` object before it can be used.

4. **Copying the Recordset into Excel:** By the time you reach this step, the `MyRecordset` object is filled with data from the Query_Products query. Now, you use Excel's `CopyFromRecordset` method to get it out and into your spreadsheet. This method requires two pieces of information: The location of the data output and the `Recordset` object that holds the data you need. In this example, you are copying the data in the `MyRecordset` object onto the sheet called "Your First ADO Procedure" starting at cell A2.

5. **Adding column labels:** Interestingly enough, the `CopyFromRecordset` method does not return column headers or field names. Step 5 is where you add the column headers yourself. You are telling Excel to fill cells A1 through C1 with the respective values in the array. Then you tell Excel to AutoFit those columns so that all the data can be seen.

Using the Code

Be sure to save your changes, and then close the Visual Basic Editor. At this point, you can run your procedure simply by running the GetAccessData macro.

Better still, you can get fancy and assign the macro to a button. This gives you and other users an easy way to call the ADO procedure whenever you need to refresh the data extract from Access. Follow these steps:

1. Select the Insert icon from the Developer tab on the Excel ribbon.

2. Click the Form button as demonstrated in Figure 15-3; then click anywhere on your spreadsheet to drop the button on the sheet. You will immediately see the Assign Macro dialog box shown here in Figure 15-4.

3. Click the macro name to assign the macro to the button.

4. Click OK.

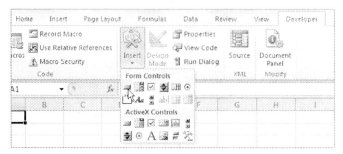

Figure 15-3: Insert a Form button.

Figure 15-4: Assign a macro to the button.

The reward for all your efforts will be a worksheet that pulls data directly from Access at the click of a button! Remember, this is all without the use of third party applications (MS Query) or manual manipulation. With ADO and VBA, you can build all the necessary components at one time in a nicely packaged macro, and then simply forget about it. As long as the defined variables in your code (that is, the data source path, the Recordset, the output path) do not change, then your ADO-based procedures will require virtually zero maintenance.

Writing your First ADO/SQL Data Extract

Writing a data extract procedure with ADO and SQL is very similar to writing an ADO procedure to extract data directly from an Access table. The difference is that instead of specifying a table name as the data source, you pass a SQL statement that defines the data you need. Start a new module and enter the following code.

```
Sub GetAccessData_With_SQL()

'Step 1: Declare your variables
    Dim MyConnect As String
    Dim MyRecordset As ADODB.Recordset
    Dim MySQL As String

'Step 2: Declare your connection string
    MyConnect = "Provider=Microsoft.ACE.OLEDB.12.0;" & _
                "Data Source=  C:\OffTheGrid\ZalexCorp Restaurant
Equipment and Supply.accdb"

'Step 3: Build your SQL statement
 MySQL ="SELECT Region, Market, Product_Description," & _
        " Sum(Revenue) AS Rev, Sum(TransactionCount) AS Units" & _
        " FROM PvTblFeed" & _
        " GROUP BY Region, Market, Product_Description"

'Step 4: Instantiate and specify your recordset
    Set MyRecordset = New ADODB.Recordset
    MyRecordset.Open MySQL, MyConnect, adOpenStatic, adLockReadOnly

'Step 5: Copy the recordset to Excel
    Sheets("ADO and SQL").Select
    ActiveSheet.Range("A2").CopyFromRecordset MyRecordset

'Step 6: Add column labels
    With ActiveSheet.Range("A1:E1")
        .Value = Array("Region", "Market", "Product_Description", _
        "Revenue", "Transactions")
        .EntireColumn.AutoFit
    End With

End Sub
```

TIP Be sure that you have set a reference to the ADO Object Library as outlined in "Referencing the ADO Object Library" earlier in this chapter.

Feel free to check out Appendix B if you need a refresher on SQL syntax fundamentals.

Running this code queries the Access database and aggregates records on the fly to return data to an Excel sheet. Let's take a moment to talk about what you are doing in each step.

1. **Declaring the necessary variables:** Declare three variables: a string variable to hold the connection string, a `Recordset` object to hold the results of the data pull, and a second string variable to hold your SQL statement. In this example, the variable called MyConnect holds the connection string identifying the data source. Meanwhile, the variable called MyRecordset holds the data returned by the procedure and the variable called MySQL holds the SQL statement.

2. **Declaring the connection string:** Define the connection string for the ADO procedure. In this scenario, you are connecting to the ZalexCorp Restaurant Equipment and Supply.accdb database found on the C drive.

3. **Building the SQL statement:** Assign a SQL statement in the form of a text string to the MySQL variable. You'll notice that the SQL statement is broken up into separate strings, each string followed by the ampersand (&) along with an underscore (_). This technique breaks up the complete SQL string into readable parts, making the code easier to read and manage. The first line starts the string, and each subsequent line is concatenated to the previous line with the ampersand (&). The underscore (_), preceded by a space, is used as a continuation marker, indicating that the code on the next line is part of the code on the current line.

4. **Assigning data to your Recordset:** Specify that your `Recordset` is read-only and is filled with data returned from your SQL statement.

5. **Copying the `Recordset` into Excel:** Use Excel's `CopyFromRecordset` method to get the returned dataset into your spreadsheet. In this example, you copy the data in the `MyRecordset` object onto the sheet called "ADO and SQL" starting at cell A2.

6. **Adding column labels:** Add header columns by telling Excel to fill cells A1 through E1 with the respective values in the array. Then you tell Excel to AutoFit those columns so that all the data can be seen.

Using Criteria in your SQL Statements

Passing criteria through your SQL statements allows you to evaluate each record in your dataset and selectively filter only the ones you need. This affords you tremendous flexibility that you can only achieve through SQL. Take a moment to review a few example SQL statements that use criteria to filter records.

TIP To get a sense of the impact of using criteria, try replacing the SQL statement in the example you just walked through with any one of the statements listed in the following sections.

Set Numeric Criteria

Setting numeric criteria is quite simple; just select the operator you want and you're done. In this example, you are selecting only those records that show revenues greater than $2,000.

```
" SELECT * FROM PvTblFeed" & _
" WHERE Revenue > 2000"
```

Set Textual Criteria

When setting criteria that is textual or text type, you need to wrap your text in single quotes. In this example, you are selecting only records that belong to the Denver market.

```
" SELECT * FROM PvTblFeed" & _
" WHERE Market = 'Denver'"
```

Set Date Criteria

When setting criteria for a date type field, you need to wrap your criteria in pound (#) signs. The pound signs tags the criteria string as a date. In this example, you are selecting only those records that have an effective date after June 30, 2004.

```
" SELECT * FROM PvTblFeed" & _
" WHERE Effective_Date > #30/Jun/2004#"
```

Set Multiple Criteria

It's important to mention that you are not limited to one criterion. You can evaluate multiple criteria with your SQL statements by simply using the AND operator. In the example shown here, you are selecting only those records that have an effective date after June 30, 2004 and belong to the Denver market.

```
" SELECT * FROM PvTblFeed" & _
" WHERE (Effective_Date > #6/30/2004#) AND (Market = 'Denver')"
```

You can evaluate multiple criteria using the OR operator as demonstrated in the next example. Here, you are selecting only records that belong to either the Denver market or the Charlotte market.

```
" SELECT * FROM PvTblFeed" & _
" WHERE (Market = 'Denver') OR (Market = 'Charlotte'")
```

> **TIP** You will note that in the multiple criteria examples each criterion is wrapped in parentheses. The parentheses are not actually necessary; the SQL statement is valid without the parentheses. However, the parentheses are useful in visually separating the criteria, allowing for easy reading.

Using the LIKE Operator with ADO

Access users will note that the wildcard character used in the WHERE clause is not the asterisk (*) that is typically used in Access. Instead, the percent sign (%) is used. This is because the SQL statement will be passed through ADO, which only validates the percent sign as a wildcard character.

```
" SELECT * FROM PvTblFeed" & _
" WHERE (Market Like 'C%')"
```

TROUBLESHOOTING ERRORS IN YOUR SQL STATEMENTS

Troubleshooting a SQL statement in VBA can be one of the most frustrating exercises you will undertake, primarily for two reasons:

- You are working in an environment where the SQL statement is broken up into pieces. Although this makes it easier to determine what the SQL statement is doing, it makes debugging problematic since you cannot readily see the statement as a whole.

- The error messages you get when SQL statements fail are often vague, leaving you to guess what the problem may be.

Here's a handy little trick you can implement to make troubleshooting a SQL statement a bit easier. Pass your SQL statement to a message box. The message box will enable you to see your SQL statement as a whole and more easily point out where the discrepancy lies. Take, for example, the following SQL statement:

```
MySQL ="SELECT Region, Market, Product_Description," & _
    " Sum(Revenue) AS Rev, Sum(TransactionCount) AS Units" & _
    "FROM PvTblFeed" & _
    "GROUP BY Region, Market, Product_Description"
```

This particular statement fails and throws the error shown in Figure 15-5. The trick is to pass the MySQL string variable to a message box as demonstrated here:

```
MySQL ="SELECT Region, Market, Product_Description," & _
    " Sum(Revenue) AS Rev, Sum(TransactionCount) AS Units" & _
    "FROM PvTblFeed" & _
    "GROUP BY Region, Market, Product_Description"
MsgBox (MySQL)
```

TROUBLESHOOTING ERRORS IN YOUR SQL STATEMENTS

Microsoft Visual Basic

Run-time error '3141':

The SELECT statement includes a reserved word or an argument name
that is misspelled or missing, or the punctuation is incorrect.

| Continue | End | Debug | Help |

Figure 15-5: This error message is vague and practically useless.

As you can see in Figure 15-6, this activates a message box that contains
your SQL statement in its entirety. Here, you can review the SQL and determine that the culprits for the error are two missing spaces, one before the
FROM clause and one before the GROUP BY clause.

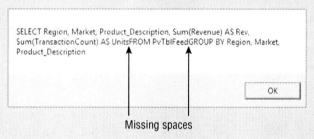

SELECT Region, Market, Product_Description, Sum(Revenue) AS Rev,
Sum(TransactionCount) AS UnitsFROM PvTblFeedGROUP BY Region, Market,
Product_Description

OK

Missing spaces

Figure 15-6: Using a message box allows you to more easily pinpoint errors in
your SQL statements.

That's right; two measly spaces cause the entire SQL statement to fail.
Remember, these lines of code are not separate SQL statements; they are
actually pieces of one SQL statement that have been broken down into parts.
They are pieced back together when the function is executed. In that light, you
have to consider, and include, all syntax that is necessary to create a valid
SQL statement, including spaces. In this example, the fix for the error is simply
to add a space before the FROM and GROUP BY clauses.

```
MySQL ="SELECT Region, Market, Product_Description," & _
    " Sum(Revenue) AS Rev, Sum(TransactionCount) AS Units" & _
    " FROM PvTblFeed" & _
    " GROUP BY Region, Market, Product_Description"
```

Common Scenarios Where VBA Can Help

There are literally countless ways you can use the fundamentals you have learned in this chapter. Of course, it would be impossible to go through each example here. However, there are some common scenarios where VBA can greatly enhance integration between Excel and Access.

Query Data from an Excel Workbook

Up until now, you have used Access as the data source for your data pulls. However, use can also use an Excel workbook as a data source. To do so, you would simply build a SQL statement that references the data within the Excel workbook. The idea is to pinpoint the dataset in Excel to query by passing a sheet name, a range of cells, or a named range to the SQL statement.

- **Query the Entire Worksheet:** To query all of the data on a specific worksheet, you would pass the name of that worksheet followed by the dollar sign ($) as the table name in your SQL statement. Be sure to encapsulate the worksheet name with square brackets. For example:

  `"SELECT * FROM [MySheet$]"`

  NOTE If the worksheet name contains spaces or characters that are not alphanumeric, you will need to wrap the worksheet name in single quotes. For instance: `Select * from ['January; Forecast vs. Budget$']`

- **Query a Range of Cells:** To query a range of cells within a given worksheet, you would first identify the sheet as described above, and then add the target range. For example:

  `"SELECT * FROM [MySheet$A1:G17]"`

- **Query a Named Range:** To query a named range, simply use the name of the range as the table name in your SQL statement. For example:

  `"SELECT * FROM MyNamedRange"`

The code shown here demonstrates how to query data from an Excel worksheet. In this example, the entire used range in the SampleData worksheet is queried to return only those records that belong to the North Region.

```
Sub GetData_From_Excel_Sheet()

'Step 1: Declare your variables
    Dim MyConnect As String
    Dim MyRecordset As ADODB.Recordset
    Dim MySQL As String
```

```
'Step 2: Declare your connection string
    MyConnect ="Provider=Microsoft.ACE.OLEDB.12.0;" & _
              "Data Source=
C:\OffTheGrid\Chapter15_SampleFile.xlsm;" & _
              "Extended Properties=Excel 12.0"

'Step 3: Build your SQL Statement
    MySQL = " SELECT * FROM [SampleData$]" & _
            " WHERE Region ='NORTH'"

'Step 4: Instantiate and specify your recordset
    Set MyRecordset = New ADODB.Recordset
    MyRecordset.Open MySQL, MyConnect, adOpenStatic, adLockReadOnly

'Step 5: Clear previous contents
    Sheets("Excel Data Pull").Select
    ActiveSheet.Cells.Clear

'Step 6: Copy the recordset to Excel
    ActiveSheet.Range("A2").CopyFromRecordset MyRecordset

'Step 7: Add column labels
    With ActiveSheet.Range("A1:F1")
        .Value = Array("Region", "Market", "Product_Description", _
        "Revenue", "Transactions", "Dollar per Transaction")
        .EntireColumn.AutoFit
    End With

End Sub
```

To query an Excel workbook, follow these steps:

1. **Declaring the necessary variables:** Declare three variables: a string variable to hold the connection string, a Recordset object to hold the results of the data pull, and a second string variable to hold your SQL statement. In this example, the variable called MyConnect will hold the connection string identifying the data source. Meanwhile, the variable called MyRecordset holds the data that is returned by the procedure and the variable called MySQL holds the SQL statement.

2. **Declaring the connection string:** Define the connection string for the ADO procedure. In this scenario, you are connecting to an Excel workbook, thus the reason for the Extended Properties argument.

3. **Building the SQL statement:** Assign a SQL statement in the form of a text string to the MySQL variable. Here, you build the SQL statement just as though you were working with a database, only you pass the worksheet name as the table. Note that NORTH is encased in single quotes. In SQL statements, you can use single and double quotes interchangeably.

4. **Assigning data to your RecordSet:** You specify that your `Recordset` is read-only and is filled with data returned from your SQL statement.

5. **Clearing cell contents:** Clear the Excel Data Pull worksheet before copying the `Recordset`. This ensures that all data from the previous pull are removed before bringing in fresh data.

6. **Copying the Recordset into Excel:** Use Excel's `CopyFromRecordset` method to get the returned dataset into your spreadsheet. In this example, you copy the data in the `MyRecordset` object onto the sheet called Excel Data Pull starting at cell A2.

7. **Adding column labels:** Add header columns by telling Excel to fill cells A1 through F1 with the respective values in the array. Then tell Excel to AutoFit those columns so that all the data can be seen.

Append Records to an Existing Excel Table

There are often times when you don't necessarily want to overwrite the data in your Excel worksheet when you bring in fresh data. Instead, you may want to simply add or append data to the existing table.

In a typical scenario, you would hard-code the location or range where you want a given Recordset to be copied. In these situations, this location must dynamically change to reflect the first empty cell in your worksheet. The code that follows demonstrates this technique.

```
Sub Append_Results()

'Step 1: Declare your variables
    Dim MyConnect As String
    Dim MyRecordset As ADODB.Recordset
    Dim MyRange As String

'Step 2: Declare your connection string
    MyConnect = "Provider=Microsoft.ACE.OLEDB.12.0;" & _
                "Data Source= C:\OffTheGrid\ZalexCorp Restaurant
 Equipment and Supply.accdb"

'Step 3: Instantiate and specify your recordset
    Set MyRecordset = New ADODB.Recordset
    MyRecordset.Open "Query_Products", MyConnect, adOpenStatic,
adLockReadOnly

'Step 4: Find first empty row and use that to build a dynamic range
    Sheets("AppendData").Select
    MyRange = "A" & _
    ActiveSheet.Cells.SpecialCells(xlCellTypeLastCell).Row + 1
```

```
'Step 5: Copy the Recordset to First Empty Row
    ActiveSheet.Range(MyRange).CopyFromRecordset MyRecordset

End Sub
```

The following steps show how to append records to an existing Excel table:

1. **Declaring the necessary variables:** In Step 1, you declare three variables: a string variable to hold the connection string, a `Recordset` object to hold the results of the data pull, and a second string variable to hold text that represent a cell reference. In this example, the variable called `MyConnect` holds the connection string identifying the data source. Meanwhile, the variable called `MyRecordset` holds the data that is returned by the procedure and the variable called `MyRange` holds a text string that represent a cell reference.

2. **Declaring the connection string:** Define the connection string for the ADO procedure. In this scenario, you are connecting to the ZalexCorp Restaurant Equipment and Supply.accdb database found on the C drive.

3. **Assigning data to your Recordset:** Specify that your `Recordset` is read-only and is filled with data from the Query_Products query found in the ZalexCorp Restaurant Equipment and Supply Access database.

4. **Finding the first empty cell:** Dynamically determine the first available empty cell that can be used as the output location for the data pull. First, find the first empty row. This is relatively easy to do thanks to Excel's SpecialCells method, which helps you find the last used cell in the worksheet, and then extracts the row number of that cell. This gives you the last used row. To get the row number of the first empty row you simply add 1; the next row down from the last used row will inherently be empty.

   The idea is to concatenate the `SpecialCells` routine with a column letter (in this case `"A"`) to create a string that represents a range. For example, if the first empty row turns out to be 10, then the code shown below would return `"A10"`.

   ```
   "A" & ActiveSheet.Cells.SpecialCells(xlCellTypeLastCell).Row + 1
   ```

   Trapping this answer in the `MyRange` string variable allows you to pass the answer to the `CopyFromRecordset` method in Step 5.

5. **Copying the Recordset into Excel:** Use Excel's `CopyFromRecordset` method to get the returned dataset into your spreadsheet. In this example, you are copying the data in the `MyRecordset` object onto the sheet called "AppendData" starting at the cell that has been dynamically defined by the `MyRange` string.

Append Excel Records to an Existing Access Table

You will undoubtedly find a time when you need to pull data from an Excel file into an Access table. Again, there are several ways to get Excel data in Access, but using the one-two-three combination of VBA, ADO and SQL can provide some flexibility that is not easily attained using other methods.

The code that follows demonstrates how to query data from an Excel worksheet and append the results to an existing Access table. In this example, the SampleData worksheet is queried to return only those records that belong to the North Region.

Note that this code is designed to be run from Access. That is to say, you add this code to your Access database to *pull* data from Excel.

```
Sub GetData_From_Excel_Sheet()

'Step 1: Declare your variables
    Dim MyConnect As String
    Dim MyRecordset As ADODB.Recordset
    Dim MyTable As ADODB.Recordset
    Dim MySQL As String

'Step 2: Declare your connection string
    MyConnect = "Provider=Microsoft.ACE.OLEDB.12.0;" & _
                "Data Source=C:\OffTheGrid\Chapter15_SampleFile.xlsm;"& _
"Extended Properties=Excel 12.0"

'Step 3: Build your SQL statement
    MySQL = " SELECT * FROM [SampleData$]" & _
            " WHERE Region ='NORTH'"

'Step 4: Instantiate and specify your recordset
    Set MyRecordset = New ADODB.Recordset
    MyRecordset.Open MySQL, MyConnect, adOpenStatic, adLockReadOnly

'Step 5: Instantiate and specify your Access table
    Set MyTable = New ADODB.Recordset
    MyTable.Open "ExcelFeed", CurrentProject.Connection, _
adOpenDynamic, adLockOptimistic

'Step 6: Loop through each record and add to the table
    Do Until MyRecordset.EOF
    MyTable.AddNew
        MyTable!ActiveRegion = MyRecordset!Region
        MyTable!ActiveMarket = MyRecordset!Market
        MyTable!Product = MyRecordset!Product_Description
        MyTable!Revenue = MyRecordset!Revenue
        MyTable!Units = MyRecordset!Transactions
        MyTable![Dollar Per Unit] = MyRecordset![Dollar Per Transaction]
    MyTable.Update
```

```
MyRecordset.MoveNext
Loop

End Sub
```

Use the following steps to append Excel records to an existing Access table:

1. **Declaring the necessary variables:** Declare four variables:

    ▪ `MyConnect` is a `String` variable that holds the connection string identifying the data source.

    ▪ `MyRecordset` is a `Recordset` object that holds the results of the data pull.

    ▪ `MyTable` is a `Recordset` object that provides the structure of the existing table.

    ▪ `MySQL` is a `String` variable that holds your SQL statement.

2. **Declaring the connection string:** Define the connection string for the ADO procedure. In this scenario, you are connecting to an Excel workbook, thus the reason for the Extended Properties argument.

3. **Building the SQL statement:** Assign a SQL statement in the form of a text string to the MySQL variable. Here, you build the SQL statement just as though you were working with a database, only you pass the worksheet name as the table.

4. **Assigning data to your Recordset:** Specify that your `Recordset` is read-only and is filled with data returned from your SQL statement.

5. **Open the target Access table into a Recordset:** Open the pre-existing local ExcelFeed table into a `Recordset`. Two things to note about the Recordset declaration in Step 5:

    ▪ Notice that the connection argument is referencing the internal connection `CurrentProject.Connection`. You use this standard connection to assign a local table to a Recordset.

    ▪ The `CursorType` and `LockType` arguments are `adOpenDynamic` and `adLockOptimistic`, respectively. This ensures that the local table can be updated to append the new records.

6. **Loop through the Query Results and add each record to the table:** Use a loop through the records in the results Recordset and add each record to the local ExcelFeed table. Start the loop by declaring what the procedure will do until MyRecordset hits the end of the file. This tells VBA to keep looping through the MyRecordset Recordset until it hits the EOF (end of file). Next, you use the `AddNew` method of the `Recordset` to add a new empty record to the local ExcelFeed table represented by the MyTable Recordset.

From here, you simply fill the fields in the empty record you just created with the values that were returned from your SQL statement.

NOTE Note that each field in the ExcelFeed table (represented by the MyTable Recordset) has its counterpart in the MyRecordset Recordset.

Querying Text Files

For many, text files are not only a source of data but also very much part of daily data operations. Given this fact, it's worth looking into how to pull data from text files using ADO and SQL. The connection string used to source a text file is as follows:

```
MyConnect = "Provider=Microsoft.ACE.OLEDB.12.0;" & _
            "Data Source= C:\Integration\;" & _
            "Extended Properties=Text"
```

A closer look at the `Data Source` argument reveals that only the file's directory is specified as the source for the data; not the actual file itself. The `Extended Properties` argument is set to `Text`.

Outside the difference in the construct of the connection string, querying a text file is very much similar to querying an Excel workbook.

```
Sub GetData_From_Text_File()
'Step 1: Declare your variables
    Dim MyConnect As String
    Dim MyRecordset As ADODB.Recordset
    Dim MySQL As String

'Step 2: Declare your connnection string
    MyConnect = "Provider=Microsoft.ACE.OLEDB.12.0;" & _
                "Data Source=C:\OffTheGrid\;" & _
                "Extended Properties=Text"

'Step 3: Build your SQL statement
    MySQL = " SELECT * FROM SalesData.csv"

'Step 4: Instantiate and specify your recordset
    Set MyRecordset = New ADODB.Recordset
    MyRecordset.Open MySQL, MyConnect, adOpenStatic, adLockReadOnly

'Step 5: Clear previous contents
    Sheets("Query Text").Select
    ActiveSheet.Cells.Clear

'Step 6: Copy the recordset to Excel
```

```
        ActiveSheet.Range("A2").CopyFromRecordset MyRecordset

'Step 7: Add column labels
    With ActiveSheet.Range("A1:F1")
        .Value = Array("Region", "Market", "Product_Description", _
        "Revenue", "Transactions", "Dollar per Transaction")
        .EntireColumn.AutoFit
    End With

End Sub
```

Summary

Although there are many methods for moving data between Access and Excel using the interfaces of those two programs, many of them retains an aspect of manual involvement. VBA can help make your data transfer processes virtually hands free.

VBA, in and of itself, does not have the capability to connect and manipulate external data. You need to combine VBA with helper technologies such as ADO (ActiveX Data Objects) and SQL (Structured Query Language). ADO is a tool that helps you accomplish two tasks: connect to a data source and specify the dataset with which to work. SQL allows you to customize your data processes, giving you the flexibility to filter, group and sort your results.

The one-two-three combination of VBA, ADO and SQL is extremely powerful and relatively easy to understand and implement. Using these three tools together, you can process data without the need to create and maintain multiple queries and macros. You can also perform complex, multi-layered procedures that involve looping, record-level testing, and If...Then...Else checks without the need to inundate your processes with many queries and temporary tables.

Exploring Excel and Access Automation

In the last few chapters, you have learned several ways to automate your analytical processes to achieve higher productivity, controlled analysis, and reproducibility. In this chapter, automation takes on different meaning. *Automation* here will define the means of manipulating or controlling one application with another. Why would you even want to control one application with another? Think about all the times you have crunched data in Access only to bring the results into Excel for presentation and distribution. Think about all the times you have sent Excel data to Access only to open Access and run a set of queries or output a report.

The reality is that each of these applications has its strengths, which you routinely leverage through manual processes. So why not automate these processes? The goal of this chapter is to give you a solid understanding of how to use automation to control Excel from Access and vice versa.

Understanding the Concept of Binding

Each program in the Microsoft Office Suite comes with its own Object Library. As you know, the *Object Library* is a kind of encyclopedia of all the objects, methods, and properties available in each Office application. Excel has its own Object Library, just as Access has its own Object Library, just as all the other Office applications have their own Object Library. In order for Excel to be able to speak to another Office program such as Access, you have to bind it to that program.

Binding is the process of exposing the Object Library for a server application to a client application. There are two types of binding: early binding and late binding.

NOTE In the context of this discussion, a *client application* is the application that is doing the controlling, while the *server application* is the application being controlled.

Early Binding

With *early binding*, you explicitly point a client application to the server application's Object Library in order to expose its object model during design-time, or while programming. Then you use the exposed objects in your code to call a new instance of the application as such:

```
Dim XL As Excel.Application
Set XL = New Excel.Application
```

Early binding has several advantages:

- Because the objects are exposed at design-time, the client application can compile your code before execution. This allows your code to run considerably faster than with late binding.

- Since the Object Library is exposed during design time, you have full access to the server application's object model in the Object Browser.

You have the benefit of using IntelliSense. *IntelliSense* is the functionality you experience when you type a keyword and a dot (.) or an equal sign (=) and you see a popup list of the methods and properties available to you.

- You automatically have access to the server application's built-in constants.

Late Binding

Late binding is different in that you don't point a client application to a specific Object Library. Instead, you purposely keep things ambiguous, only using the CreateObject function to bind to the needed library at run-time, or during program execution.

```
Dim XL As Object
Set XL = CreateObject("Excel.Application")
```

Late binding has one main advantage: Late binding allows your automation procedures to be version-independent. That is, your automation procedure will not fail due to compatibility issues between multiple versions of a component. For example, suppose you decide to use early binding and set a reference to the Excel Object Library on your system. The version of the available library on your system will be equal to your version of Excel. The problem is that if your users have an earlier version of Excel on their machine, your automation procedure will fail. You do not have this problem with late binding.

BINDING CONVENTIONS IN THIS BOOK

For the purposes of this book, early binding is used for a couple of reasons:

■ **The design time benefits of early binding, such as IntelliSense, is ideal for discovering and experimenting with the methods and properties that come with Excel and Access.**

■ **This chapter is written in the context of building procedures that help you increase productivity, not building an application that many users use. In that light, version issues do not come into play, negating the need for late binding.**

Automating Excel from Access

Processes where Access data is moved to Excel lend themselves quite nicely to automation. This is primarily due to the nature of these two programs. Access typically serves as the data layer in most analytical processes, while Excel serves as the presentation. Because of this dynamic, you may find that you often send Access data to Excel to build charts, pivot tables, or some other presentation mechanism displaying the data. Excel Automation can literally take you out of the report building process, creating and saving Excel reports without any human interaction.

Creating your First Excel Automation Procedure

For your first Excel automation trick, you will build a procedure in Access that automatically opens a new Excel workbook and adds a worksheet:

1. Open the ZalexCorp Restaurant Equipment and Supply.accdb sample database on www.wrox.com.

2. Start a new module by clicking the Create tab in the ribbon and selecting Module. If you are using Access 2007, you need to select Macro ➪ Module.

3. Before you do anything, you must set a reference to the Excel Object Library. To do this, go up to the application menu and select Tools ⇨ References. The Reference dialog box shown in Figure 16-1 will activate.

4. Scroll down until you find the entry "Microsoft Excel *XX* Object Library," where the *XX* is your version of Excel. Place a check in the checkbox next to the entry, as shown here in Figure 16-1, and then click the OK button.

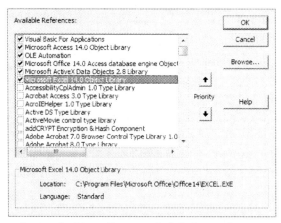

Figure 16-1: Select the Excel Object Library and click the OK button.

NOTE If you don't set a reference to the Excel Object Library, Access gives you a compile error, producing you this message:

```
Compile error: User-defined type not defined.
```

The good news is that once you set a reference to the Excel Object Library in a particular database, it is set for good in that database.

Now that you have referenced the Excel Object Library, you can start writing code. Enter the following code in your newly created module.

```
Function MyFirstAutomationCode()

'Step1:  Declare the variables you will work with.
    Dim xl As Excel.Application
    Dim xlwkbk As Excel.Workbook
    Dim xlsheet As Excel.Worksheet

'Step 2:  Start Excel, then add a workbook and a worksheet.
    Set xl = New Excel.Application
    Set xlwkbk = xl.Workbooks.Add
```

```
    Set xlsheet = xlwkbk.Worksheets.Add

'Step 3:  Make Excel visible
    xl.Visible = True

'Step 4:  Memory Clean up.
    Set xl = Nothing
    Set xlwkbk = Nothing
    Set xlsheet = Nothing


End Function
```

The following outlines what the steps in the code do:

1. **Declaring the necessary variables:** In step 1, declare three variables:
   - xl is an object variable that exposes the Excel Application object
   - xlwkbk is an object variable that exposes the Excel Workbook object
   - xlsheet is an object variable that exposes the Excel Worksheet object

2. **Starting a new instance of Excel with a new Workbook and Worksheet:** In step 2, first create a new instance of Excel and assign that instance to your xl object variable. From here, the xl object variable is your tie into the Excel application, exposing all objects, properties and variables that you would normally have if you were working directly in Excel.

   Next, you open a new workbook by using the Workbooks.Add method of the xl object variable. Note that you are assigning the new workbook to your xlwkbk variable. At this point, your xlwkbk variable actually represents a real workbook, exposing all objects, properties and variables that you would normally have if you were working with a workbook directly in Excel.

   Finally, you add a new worksheet by using the Worksheets.Add method of the xlwkbk object variable. Note that you are assigning the new worksheet to your xlsheet variable. At this point, your xlsheet variable actually represents a real worksheet, exposing all objects, properties and variables that you would normally have if you were working with a worksheet directly in Excel.

3. **Making Excel visible:** By default, an instance of Excel created via automation is not visible. Although not necessary, it's generally a good practice to make the instance of Excel visible for a couple of reasons. First, should anything go wrong during the procedure, debugging becomes easier if you can see the Excel spreadsheet. Secondly, you can easily close the instance of Excel in debug mode by closing out the Excel window. If the instance is not visible, you have to kill it by going into the Windows Task Manager and ending the process there.

4. **Cleaning up memory by closing the open objects:** In step 4, it is generally good practice to release the objects assigned to your variables. This reduces the chance of any problems caused by rogue objects that may remain open in memory. As you can see in the code, you simply set the variable to Nothing.

Congratulations! You have just created your first automation procedure.

Automating Data Export to Excel

Now that you have successfully created your first automation procedure, it's time to try something more meaningful; sending Access data to Excel, the first step in creating an Excel report from your Access analysis.

Sending one Recordset to Excel

The process of sending your Access data to Excel can generally be broken down into three main actions:

1. First, you identify the dataset you want to send to Excel and assign it to a Recordset object.

2. Next, you open Excel and copy the Recordset to a spreadsheet using Excel's CopyFromRecordset method.

3. Finally, since the CopyFromRecordset method does not transfer column headings, you must add your dataset's column headings and add them to the spreadsheet.

Let's go through the following example procedure, where you send the PvTblFeed table to a tab called "Pivot Table Feed."

```
Function SendRecordset()

'Step1: Declare the objects and variables you will work with
    Dim MyRecordset As ADODB.Recordset
    Dim xl As Excel.Application
    Dim xlwkbk As Excel.Workbook
    Dim xlsheet As Excel.Worksheet
    Dim i As Integer

'Step 2: Start Excel, then add a workbook and a worksheet
    Set xl = New Excel.Application
    Set xlwkbk = xl.Workbooks.Add
    Set xlsheet = xlwkbk.Worksheets.Add
    xlsheet.Name = "Pivot Table Feed"

'Step3: Make the instance of Excel visible
    xl.Visible = True
```

```
'Step 4: Assign a dataset to the recordset object
    Set MyRecordset = New ADODB.Recordset
    MyRecordset.Open "PvTblFeed", CurrentProject.Connection

'Step 5: Copy the records to the active Excel sheet
    With xlsheet
    xl.Range("A2").CopyFromRecordset MyRecordset
    End With

'Step 6: Add column heading names to the spreadsheet
    For i = 1 To MyRecordset.Fields.Count
    xl.ActiveSheet.Cells(1, i).Value = MyRecordset.Fields(i - 1).Name
    Next i

'Step 7: Memory Clean up
    Set MyRecordset = Nothing
    Set xl = Nothing
    Set xlwkbk = Nothing
    Set xlsheet = Nothing

End Function
```

The following outlines what the steps in the code do:

1. **Declaring the necessary objects and variables:** In Step 1, you first declare five variables:

   ▪ `MyRecordset` is a `Recordset` object that holds the results of the data pull.

   ▪ `xl` is an object variable that exposes the Excel `Application` object.

   ▪ `xlwkbk` is an object variable that exposes the Excel `Workbooks` object.

   ▪ `xlsheet` is an object variable that exposes the Excel `Worksheet` object.

   ▪ `i` in an integer variable that is used to add column headings.

2. **Starting a new instance of Excel with new Workbook and Worksheet:** Step 2 creates a new instance of Excel, opens a new workbook and adds a new worksheet. Note that you give the new worksheet a name, ''Pivot Table Feed.''

3. **Making Excel visible:** Step 3 makes the instance of Excel visible.

4. **Assigning data to your** `Recordset`**:** Step 4 specifies that your Recordset is read-only and is filled with data from the PvTblFeed table found in the ZalexCorp Restaurant Equipment and Supply.accdb Access database.

5. **Copying the Recordset into Excel:** By the time you reach step 5, the `MyRecordset` object is filled with data from the PvTblFeed table. In Step 5,

you use Excel's `CopyFromRecordset` method to get it out and into your spreadsheet. In this example, you are copying the data onto your newly created sheet starting at cell A2.

6. **Adding column headers:** As you know the `CopyFromRecordset` method does not return column headers or field names. There are several ways to fill in the column headers for a dataset. In Chapter 8, you used an array to fill in the column headers. This example demonstrates how you can enumerate through each field in the Recordset to automatically get the name of each header and enter it into Excel.

7. **Cleaning up the open objects:** This step releases the objects assigned to your variables, reducing the chance of any problems caused by rogue objects that may remain open in memory.

Sending Two Datasets to Two Different Tabs in the Same Workbook

You will sometimes come across a scenario where you have to send two or more datasets to Excel into different tabs. This is as easy as repeating parts of the automation procedure for a different Recordset. The following code sends the PvTblFeed table to a tab called "Pivot Table Feed" and then sends the MainSummary table to another tab in the same the workbook.

```
Function SendMoreThanOneRecordset()

'Step1: Declare the objects and variables you will work with
    Dim MyRecordset As ADODB.Recordset
    Dim xl As Excel.Application
    Dim xlwkbk As Excel.Workbook
    Dim xlsheet As Excel.Worksheet
    Dim i As Integer

'Step 2: Start Excel, then add a workbook and a worksheet
    Set xl = New Excel.Application
    Set xlwkbk = xl.Workbooks.Add
    Set xlsheet = xlwkbk.Worksheets.Add
    xlsheet.Name = "Pivot Table Feed"

'Step3: Make the instance of Excel visible
    xl.Visible = True

'Step 4: Assign a dataset to the recordset object
    Set MyRecordset = New ADODB.Recordset
    MyRecordset.Open "PvTblFeed", CurrentProject.Connection

'Step 5: Copy the records to the active Excel sheet
    With xlsheet
```

```
    xl.Range("A2").CopyFromRecordset MyRecordset
    End With

'Step 6: Add column heading names to the spreadsheet
    For i = 1 To MyRecordset.Fields.Count
    xl.ActiveSheet.Cells(1, i).Value = MyRecordset.Fields(i - 1).Name
    Next i

'Step 7: Close active recordset: Repeat steps 4-6 for new a recordset
    MyRecordset.Close
    MyRecordset.Open "ForecastSummary", CurrentProject.Connection

    Set xlsheet = xlwkbk.Worksheets.Add
    xlsheet.Name = "Forecast Summary"

    With xlsheet
    xl.Range("A2").CopyFromRecordset MyRecordset
    End With

    For i = 1 To MyRecordset.Fields.Count
    xl.ActiveSheet.Cells(1, i).Value = MyRecordset.Fields(i - 1).Name
    Next i

'Step 8: Memory Clean up
    Set MyRecordset = Nothing
    Set xl = Nothing
    Set xlwkbk = Nothing
    Set xlsheet = Nothing

End Function
```

CHECKING FOR RECORD COUNT BEFORE AUTOMATING EXCEL

Often times, the Recordset you are sending to your spreadsheet is a query that may or may not return records. Interestingly enough, you do not receive an error when you use the `CopyFromRecordset` method on an empty Recordset. That means that it is completely possible to automate Excel, create a workbook, and copy no records to it. This can cause problems later, especially if you further your automation of Excel to include building a pivot table, creating a chart, etc.

The quick and easy workaround to this potential problem is to check your Recordset for a record count before doing anything. In Step 3 of the example code that follows, a simple IF statement evaluates the count of records in the Recordset. If the record count is less than 1 (meaning the Recordset is holding 0 records), the procedure terminates. Otherwise, the procedure continues.

(continued)

CHECKING FOR RECORD COUNT BEFORE AUTOMATING EXCEL *(continued)*

```
Function TestRecordCount()

'Step1: Declare the objects and variables you will work with
    Dim MyRecordset As ADODB.Recordset

'Step 2: Start a new recordset
    Set MyRecordset = New ADODB.Recordset
    MyRecordset.Open "Employee_Master", _
    "CurrentProject.Connection"

'Step 3: Check RecordCount
If MyRecordset.RecordCount < 1 Then
    MsgBox ("There are no records to output")
    Set MyRecordset = Nothing
    Exit Function
Else

'Continue with your automation code...
End If

End Function
```

Automating Excel Reports: Without Programming Excel

Excel automation goes beyond getting your data to Excel. With Excel automation, you can have Access dynamically add formatting, set print options, add an AutoFilter, create pivot tables, build charts, and the list goes on.

However, the rub here is there are countless actions you can take after your Access data reaches Excel. Where do you begin to learn how to create a pivot table using VBA, create and format a chart with VBA, or even add an AutoFilter? While it's true there are many resources that can help you learn VBA, the reality is that this kind of a learning process takes trial and error as well as time to build experience working with the Excel object model. Even if programming Excel pivot tables and charts were within the scope of this book, there are enough nuances to Excel programming that any instruction that could fit into one chapter would fall short.

So what is an aspiring analyst to do? After all, the reason you are reading this book is that you need to implement automation now. The answer is to simply let Excel program for you!

In Excel, *macros* are used as a way to record actions that can be played back when needed. When you start recording a macro, Excel automatically generates one or more lines of code for every action you take. After you stop recording, you can open the macro to review, edit, or even copy the generated code. The idea here is after you send Access data to Excel, you can perform some actions on your data while recording a macro, and then copy the macro generated-code into the Access module where you have the automation procedure. The next time you run the automation procedure, the recorded macro actions will run right from Access.

To illustrate this concept, take some time to walk through the following demonstration.

1. In the sample database, execute the `SendRecordset` function in the Module titled "Excel_Automation_2." Once the function finishes running, you should have an Excel spreadsheet that looks similar to the one shown in Figure 16-2.

	A	B	C	D	E	F	G	H	I	J
1	Region	Market	Branch_N	Customer	State	Effective_D	Product_L	Revenue	TransactionCount	
2	MIDWEST	DENVER	201605	JPEASU Cc	CO	12/29/2004	Predictive	184.1868	1	
3	MIDWEST	DENVER	201605	MANROS	CO	2/3/2004	Facility M	1078.793	9	
4	MIDWEST	DENVER	201605	MAULLU C	CO	1/29/2004	Fleet Mai	1879.784	13	
5	MIDWEST	DENVER	201605	MAYSCU C	CO	12/8/2004	Fleet Mai	144.5988	1	
6	MIDWEST	DENVER	201605	MHCKUN	CO	1/8/2004	Predictive	2394.428	13	
7	MIDWEST	DENVER	201605	MOFFAT C	CO	2/26/2004	Facility M	719.1954	6	
8	MIDWEST	DENVER	201605	MUANTE (	CO	2/10/2004	Facility M	479.4636	4	
9	MIDWEST	DENVER	201605	MUANTE (	CO	2/13/2004	Facility M	719.1954	6	
10	MIDWEST	DENVER	201605	MUNTRU (	CO	2/18/2004	Facility M	719.1954	6	
11	MIDWEST	DENVER	201605	MUNTRU (	CO	5/24/2004	Landscapi	914.2172	4	
12	MIDWEST	DENVER	201605	MUUSE Cc	CO	1/16/2004	Predictive	2394.428	13	
13	MIDWEST	DENVER	201605	NULSUN C	CO	1/26/2004	Predictive	2394.428	13	
14	MIDWEST	DENVER	201605	OSPUNF C	CO	2/16/2004	Facility M	479.4636	4	

Figure 16-2: This is the spreadsheet you start with when you run the `SendRecordset` function.

2. In Excel, start a new macro, name it "MyMacro" and click the OK button. At this point, your macro will start recording your actions.

3. Make the following formatting changes:

   1. Click cell A1.

   2. Go up to the Data tab and click the Filter icon.

   3. Select cells A1 through I1 and change the font style to bold.

   4. Select columns A through I, then click the Home tab and select Format ▷ AutoFit Column Width.

   5. Click cell A1

   6. Select the Insert tab and click the pivot table icon. This activates the Create PivotTable dialog box shown in Figure 16-3. Click the OK button to create the pivot table. A new pivot table and a PivotTable Field List appears.

   7. In the PivotTable Field List, select the check boxes next to the following fields: `Region`, `Market`, `Revenue`, and `TransactionCount`. Figure 16-4 illustrates the selections.

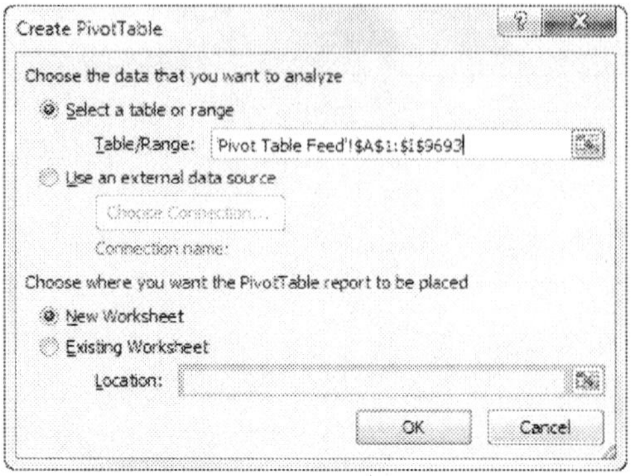

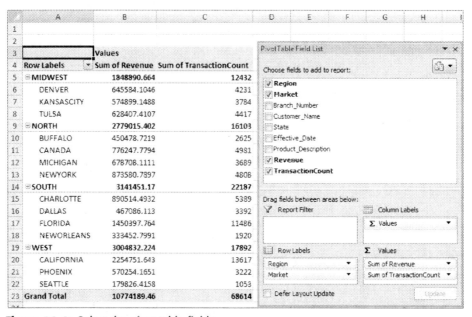

Figure 16-3: Create a new pivot table.

Figure 16-4: Select the pivot table fields.

4. Click cell A1.

5. Stop the macro recording.

6. Now that you have finished recording the necessary actions, you can copy the macro-generated code out of Excel and into Access. In order to do this, click the Developer tab and select Macros. This opens up the Macro dialog box shown in Figure 16-5. Select MyMacro, then select Edit.

7. The code in your macro should look similar to the code shown in Figure 16-6. At this point, all you have to do is select and copy all the code within the Sub procedure (don't include the comments or End Sub).

Figure 16-5: Open your newly created macro in Edit mode to copy to the macro-generated code.

8. Open the "Excel_Automation_2" module in Access and paste the code after the step where you enumerate through the column headings (Step 6) as shown in Figure 16-7.

```
(General)                                                    MyMacro

  Option Explicit

  Sub MyMacro()
  '
  ' MyMacro Macro
  '
      Range("A1").Select
      Selection.AutoFilter
      Range("A1:I1").Select
      Selection.Font.Bold = True
      Columns("A:I").Select
      Selection.Columns.AutoFit
      Range("A1").Select
      Sheets.Add
      ActiveWorkbook.PivotCaches.Create(SourceType:=xlDatabase, SourceData:= _
          "Pivot Table Feed!R1C1:R9693C9", Version:=xlPivotTableVersion12). _
          CreatePivotTable TableDestination:="Sheet5!R3C1", TableName:="PivotTable1" _
          , DefaultVersion:=xlPivotTableVersion12
      Sheets("Sheet5").Select
      Cells(3, 1).Select
      With ActiveSheet.PivotTables("PivotTable1").PivotFields("Region")
          .Orientation = xlRowField
          .Position = 1
      End With
      With ActiveSheet.PivotTables("PivotTable1").PivotFields("Market")
          .Orientation = xlRowField
          .Position = 2
      End With
      ActiveSheet.PivotTables("PivotTable1").AddDataField ActiveSheet.PivotTables( _
          "PivotTable1").PivotFields("Revenue"), "Sum of Revenue", xlSum
      ActiveSheet.PivotTables("PivotTable1").AddDataField ActiveSheet.PivotTables( _
          "PivotTable1").PivotFields("TransactionCount"), "Sum of TransactionCount", _
          xlSum
      Range("A1").Select
  End Sub
```

Figure 16-6: Copy the macro-generated code out of Excel.

```
(General)

        End With

'Step 6: Add column heading names to the spreadsheet
    For i = 1 To MyRecordset.Fields.Count
    xl.ActiveSheet.Cells(1, i).Value = MyRecordset.Fields(i - 1).Name
    Next i

'*****************Start Excel Formatting*****************

    Range("A1").Select
    Selection.AutoFilter
    Range("A1:I1").Select
    Selection.Font.Bold = True
    Columns("A:I").Select
    Selection.Columns.AutoFit
    Range("A1").Select
    Sheets.Add
    ActiveWorkbook.PivotCaches.Create(SourceType:=xlDatabase, SourceData:= _
        "Pivot Table Feed!R1C1:R9693C9", Version:=xlPivotTableVersion12). _
        CreatePivotTable TableDestination:="Sheet5!R3C1", TableName:="PivotTable1" _
        , DefaultVersion:=xlPivotTableVersion12
    Sheets("Sheet5").Select
    Cells(3, 1).Select
    With ActiveSheet.PivotTables("PivotTable1").PivotFields("Region")
        .Orientation = xlRowField
        .Position = 1
    End With
    With ActiveSheet.PivotTables("PivotTable1").PivotFields("Market")
        .Orientation = xlRowField
        .Position = 2
    End With
    ActiveSheet.PivotTables("PivotTable1").AddDataField ActiveSheet.PivotTables( _
        "PivotTable1").PivotFields("Revenue"), "Sum of Revenue", xlSum
    ActiveSheet.PivotTables("PivotTable1").AddDataField ActiveSheet.PivotTables( _
        "PivotTable1").PivotFields("TransactionCount"), "Sum of TransactionCount", _
        xlSum
    Range("A1").Select
```

Figure 16-7: Copy the macro-generated code out of Excel.

TIP Be sure to paste your macro-generated code in a place within your procedure that makes sense. For example, you don't want the procedure to encounter this code before the data has been sent to Excel. Generally, Excel generated code can logically be added directly after the section of code that applies column headings.

Also, notice that in Figure 16-7, there is a clear marker that indicates where the Excel generated code starts. It's good practice to clearly define the point where you are working with Excel generated code. This ensures that you can easily find the section of code in the event you need to replace it, or remove it all together.

9. You're almost done. Now add the appropriate application variable name to each foreign object that is a direct property of that application object. In other words, since the objects and properties in the macro-generated code come from the Excel Object Library, you need to let Access know by prefacing each of these with the name you assigned to the Excel application. For example: `Range("A1").Select` would be edited to `xl.Range("A1").Select` because `xl` is the variable name you assigned

to the Excel application object and `Range` is used as a direct property of the Excel application. In this example, you prefix each one of the following objects with `xl.`: `Range`, `Selection`, `Columns`, `Cells`, `Sheets`, `ActiveWorkbook`, and `ActiveSheet`. Figure 16-8 demonstrates what your code should look like once you have made this change.

```
(General)                                          ▼

'****************'Start Excel Formatting'****************
  xl.Range("A1").Select
   xl.Selection.AutoFilter
   xl.Range("A1:I1").Select
   xl.Selection.Font.Bold = True
   xl.Columns("A:I").Select
   xl.Selection.Columns.AutoFit
   xl.Range("A1").Select
   xl.Sheets.Add
   xl.ActiveWorkbook.PivotCaches.Create(SourceType:=xlDatabase, SourceData:= _
      "Pivot Table Feed!R1C1:R9693C9", Version:=xlPivotTableVersion12). _
      CreatePivotTable TableDestination:="Sheet5!R3C1", TableName:="PivotTable1" _
      , DefaultVersion:=xlPivotTableVersion12
   xl.Sheets("Sheet5").Select
   xl.Cells(3, 1).Select
   With xl.ActiveSheet.PivotTables("PivotTable1").PivotFields("Region")
       .Orientation = xlRowField
       .Position = 1
   End With
   With xl.ActiveSheet.PivotTables("PivotTable1").PivotFields("Market")
       .Orientation = xlRowField
       .Position = 2
   End With
   xl.ActiveSheet.PivotTables("PivotTable1").AddDataField xl.ActiveSheet.PivotTables( _
      "PivotTable1").PivotFields("Revenue"), "Sum of Revenue", xlSum
   xl.ActiveSheet.PivotTables("PivotTable1").AddDataField xl.ActiveSheet.PivotTables( _
      "PivotTable1").PivotFields("TransactionCount"), "Sum of TransactionCount", _
      xlSum
   xl.Range("A1").Select
```

Figure 16-8: Add the `xl.` variable tags you see here in bold font.

Note that you only have to add the application variable name to object and properties that are not being used by an object or property of a higher object. To drive this point home, take these two lines of code for example:

```
xl.Columns("A:I").Select

xl.Selection.Columns.AutoFit
```

Notice that when `Columns` is used as a property of the `Selection` object it is not prefaced with the variable name `xl`.

WARNING Be warned that skipping Step 9 causes you to get these seemingly unpredictable run-time errors:

- Run-time error '1004': Method 'Range' of object '_Global' failed
- Run-time error '91': Object variable or With block variable not set

10. Save your module and test it.

You have just built your first fully automated Excel report! Keep in mind that this is a simple example. The possibilities are as expansive as Excel itself. For example, you could create a chart, create a pivot table, or apply subtotals. Using this method, you can literally create a report purely in VBA and then run it whenever you want.

SUPPRESSING EXCEL'S WARNING AND INFORMATIONAL MESSAGES

When building your automation procedures, you may invoke some actions that require your input. For example, choosing to save a worksheet may invoke a message from Excel asking if you want to overwrite the previously saved file.

The problem with these types of messages is that they interrupt your automated procedures while Excel waits for an answer from you. Given that the purpose of automation is to remove the element of human interaction, this just won't do.

If you want to suppress Excel's warning and informational messages that pop up occasionally, use Excel's `DisplayAlerts` property. The `DisplayAlerts` property is analogous to Access' `SetWarnings` method: It's used to suppress application messages by automatically selecting Yes or OK for the user.

To suppress Excel's alerts, insert the following code before your macro-generated code.

```
xl.DisplayAlerts = False
```

To turn alerts back on, insert the following code after your macro-generated code.

```
xl.DisplayAlerts = True
```

Using Find and Replace to Adjust Macro-Generated Code

In the previous section, you learned that there are Excel objects and properties that you needed to point back to the Excel `Application` object by prefacing them with the name you assigned to the Excel application. For example: `Range("A1").Select` would be edited to `xl.Range("A1").Select` because `xl` is the name you assigned to the Excel `Application` object.

The problem is that this can be quite an ordeal if you have recorded a macro that generated a substantial block of code. It would take a long time to search through the macro-generated code and preface each appropriate object or property. However, there are Excel objects and properties used repeatedly in your macro-generated code. These are `Range`, `ActiveSheet`, `ActiveWorkbook`, `ActiveCell`, `Application`, and `Selection`. The good news is that you can leverage this fact by filtering these objects and properties into the four most commonly used keywords.

The four most common keywords are:

- `Range`
- `Selection`
- `Active`
- `Application`

This is where the Find and Replace functionality can come in handy. With Find and Replace, you can find these keywords and preface them all in one fell swoop. To do this, follow these steps:

1. Select all the macro-generated code in the Visual Basic Editor.

2. Then you select Edit ➪ Replace. This activates the Replace dialog box shown in Figure 16-9.

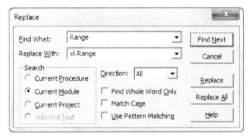

Figure 16-9: Use the find and replace functionality to preface the four most common key words.

3. As you can see, all you have to do is enter each keyword into the Find What drop-down list, and enter the prefaced keyword in the Replace With drop-down list. Keep in mind that depending on your macro-generated code, some of these keywords may not produce any hits, which is OK.

WARNING Notice in Figure 16-9 that there is a search option called Selected Text. This means that any of the Find and Replace functionalities that you apply are limited to the selected text. It is extremely important that you select the macro-generated code and ensure that the Selected Text option is active before you start any Find and Replace procedures. Otherwise, you could inadvertently change code in other parts of your module.

Bear in mind that these keywords only make up the bulk of the objects and properties that may need to be prefaced in your macro-generated code. There are others that you'll need to preface by hand, the most common of which are:

- Columns

- Cells

- Rows

- Sheets

Why can't you preface these using Find and Replace? It's a question of object hierarchy. Often times, these are used as properties of higher objects, which means you would not need to preface them because the higher object is prefaced. Here's an example:

```
xl.Columns("A:I").Select
xl.Selection.Columns.AutoFit
```

Notice that when Columns is used as a property of the Selection object it is not prefaced. Prefacing the Columns, Cells, and Rows properties manually ensures that you don't unintentionally cause an error.

Running an Excel Macro from Access

Admittedly, bringing your Excel macro-generated code into Access and manipulating the code to run in an Access module can be a daunting prospect for some. Fortunately, there is an easier alternative. The alternative is to keep the macro-generated code in Excel and simply fire the macro from Access. That is to say, Access will do nothing more than just call the macro and run it. The following code demonstrates how to fire a macro from Access.

```
Function RunExcelMacro()

'Step1:  Declare the objects you will work with.
    Dim xl As Excel.Application
    Dim xlwkbk As Excel.Workbook

'Step 2:  Start Excel, then open the target workbook.
    Set xl = New Excel.Application
    Set xlwkbk = xl.Workbooks.Open("C:\Book1.xlsm")

'Step 3:  Make Excel visible
    xl.Visible = True

'Step 4:  Run the target macro
    xl.Run "Macro1"

'Step 5:  Close and save the workbook, then close Excel
    xlwkbk.Close (True)
    xl.Quit
```

```
'Step 6:  Memory Clean up.
    Set xl = Nothing
    Set xlwkbk = Nothing

End Function
```

The following outlines what the steps in the code do:

1. **Declaring the necessary objects:** In Step 1, you first declare two variables:

   - xl is an object variable that exposes the Excel Application object.

   - xlwkbk is an object variable that exposes the Excel Workbook object.

2. **Starting a new instance of Excel with a new Workbook and Worksheet:** In Step 2, you create a new instance of Excel and open the target workbook—the workbook that contains the macro you need to run.

3. **Making Excel visible:** Step 3 makes the instance of Excel visible.

4. **Running the target macro:** Step 4 runs the target macro.

5. **Closing and saving the target Workbook:** This step closes and saves the target workbook. The True argument in xlwkbk.Close(True) indicates that you want the workbook saved after the macro has run. If you do not want to save the target workbook, change this argument to False. Also in Step 5, you quit the Excel application, effectively closing the instance of Excel.

6. **Cleaning up open objects:** This steps releases the objects assigned to your variables, reducing the chance of any problems caused by rogue objects that may remain open in memory.

Optimizing Macro-Generated Code

There is no arguing that Excel's Macro Recorder can prove to be an invaluable tool when building an automation procedure. The macro-generated code it provides cannot only get you up and running quickly but also can help you learn some of Excel's programming fundamentals. The one drawback to using macro-generated code, however, is that the code itself is rather inefficient. This is because the macro recorder not only records the functional actions that give your macro its utility, but it also records mouse moves, mouse clicks, mistakes, redundant actions, etc. This leaves you with lots of useless code that has nothing to do with macro's original purpose. Although the impact of this superfluous code is typically negligible, larger automation procedures can take speed and performance hits due to these inefficiencies. In that light, it's generally a good practice to take some time to clean up and optimize your macro-generated code.

Removing Navigation Actions

If you want to enter a formula in a cell within Excel, you have to select that cell first and then enter the formula. Indeed, this is true with most actions; you have to select the cell first and then perform the action. As you are recording a macro, you are moving around and clicking each cell on which you need to perform an action. Meanwhile the macro recorder is generating code for all that navigation you are doing. However, the fact is that in VBA, you rarely have to explicitly select a cell before performing an action on it. Therefore, all that code is superfluous and is not needed. Consider the following macro-generated code:

```
Range("A1:I1").Select
Selection.Font.Bold = True
```

In this example, the macro is selecting a range of cells first and then changing the font style to bold. It's not necessary to select the range first. This code can be changed to read:

```
Range("A1:I1").Font.Bold = True
```

Another version of this type of behavior is the shown in the following code:

```
Range("A20").Activate
ActiveCell.FormulaR1C1 = "=4+4"
```

In this example, a cell is activated and then a formula is entered into the cell. Again, it is not necessary to select the cell before entering the formula. This code can be changed to read:

```
Range("A20").FormulaR1C1 = "=4+4"
```

Navigation code typically makes up a majority of the superfluous entries in your macro-generated code. These are easy to spot and change. Remember these general rules:

- If one line contains the word `Select` and the following line contains `Selection`, you can adjust the code.

- If one line contains the word `Activate` and the following line contains `ActiveCell`, you can adjust the code.

Deleting Code that Specifies Default Settings

Certain actions you take in Excel while recording a macro generate a pre-defined collection of default settings. To demonstrate what this means, open Excel and start recording a macro. Click on any cell and simply change the Font to 12-pitch font. Stop the recording. The code that is generated will look similar to this:

```
Range("A2").Select
With Selection.Font
    .Name = "Calibri"
    .Size = 12
    .Strikethrough = False
    .Superscript = False
    .Subscript = False
    .OutlineFont = False
    .Shadow = False
    .Underline = xlUnderlineStyleNone
    .ThemeColor = xlThemeColorLight1
    .TintAndShade = 0
    .ThemeFont = xlThemeFontNone
End With
```

Remember that all you did was change the font of one cell, but here you have a litany of properties that reiterate default settings. These default settings are unnecessary and can be removed. This macro can and should be adjusted to read:

```
Range("A2").Font.Size = 12
```

TIP You can easily spot the lines of code that represent default setting because they are usually encapsulated within a `With` statement.

Cleaning Up Double Takes and Mistakes

While you are recording a macro, you will inevitably make missteps and, as a result, redo actions once or twice. As you can imagine, the macro recorder will steadily record these actions, not knowing they are mistakes. To illustrate this, look at the following code:

```
Range("D5").Select
Selection.NumberFormat = "$#,##0.00"
Selection.NumberFormat = "$#,##0"
Range("D4").Select
Range("D5").Select
Range("A2").Select
With Selection.Font
    .Name = "Calibri"
    .Size = 12
    .Strikethrough = False
    .Superscript = False
    .Subscript = False
```

```
        .OutlineFont = False
        .Shadow = False
        .Underline = xlUnderlineStyleNone
        .ThemeColor = xlThemeColorLight1
        .TintAndShade = 0
        .ThemeFont = xlThemeFontNone
    End With
    Range("A2").Select
    With Selection.Font
        .Name = "Calibri"
        .Size = 10
        .Strikethrough = False
        .Superscript = False
        .Subscript = False
        .OutlineFont = False
        .Shadow = False
        .Underline = xlUnderlineStyleNone
        .ThemeColor = xlThemeColorLight1
        .TintAndShade = 0
        .ThemeFont = xlThemeFontNone
    End With
    Range("D5").Select
```

Believe it or not, there is only one real action being performed here: Change the number format of cell D5. So why are there so many lines of code? If you look closely, you will see that number formatting has been applied twice, first with two decimal places and then with no decimal places. In addition, the font in Cell A2 was changed to 12-pitch font, then changed back to 10-pitch font. If you remove these missteps, you get a more efficient set of code.

```
    Range("D5").NumberFormat = "$#,##0"
```

TIP When you hit the Undo command while recording a macro, the macro recorder actually erases the lines of code that represent the actions that you are undoing. In that light, make sure you utilize the Undo command before going back to correct your missteps. This ensures you don't record mistakes along with good actions.

Temporarily Disabling Screen Updating

You will notice that while you are running an Excel macro, your screen flickers and changes as each action is performed. This is because Excel's default behavior is to carry out a screen update with every new action. Unfortunately, screen updating has a negative impact on macros. Because the macro has to wait for the screen to update after every action, macro execution is slowed down. Depending on your system memory, this can have a huge impact on performance.

To resolve this issue, you can temporarily disable screen updating by inserting the following code before your macro-generated code:

```
xl.ScreenUpdating = False
```

To turn screen updating back on, insert the following code after your macro-generated code.

```
xl.ScreenUpdating = True
```

NOTE In the code example above, `xl` is the variable name assigned to the Excel Application object. This can be different depending on the variable name you give to the Excel Application object.

Automating Access from Excel

It typically doesn't occur to most Excel users to automate Access using Excel. Indeed, it's difficult for most to think of situations where this would even be necessary. Although there are admittedly few mind-blowing reasons to automate Access from Excel, you may find some of the automation tricks found in this section strangely appealing. Who knows? You may even implement a few of them.

Setting the Required References

You should be familiar with the fact that if you want to work with another object's Object Library, you must set references. In order to work with Access, you must set a reference to the Microsoft Access Object Library as illustrated in Figure 16-10. In addition to the Access Object Library, you will note that there is also a reference set to the Microsoft DAO Object Library. The *DAO* (Data Access Objects) *library* allows you to easily create and manipulate the database objects within Access.

NOTE It's generally best to select the latest version of the Microsoft DAO library available. You will notice that in Figure 16-10, latest version of the Microsoft DAO Object Library is 3.6. Don't be too concerned if you only have earlier versions available; the examples in this chapter will run fine with those earlier version.

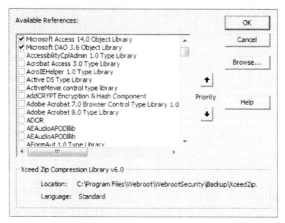

Figure 16-10: When automating Access, you should set a reference to both the Access Object Library and the DAO Object Library.

At this point, open the Excel workbook called Chapter16_SampleFiles.xls installed with the sample files for this book. There you will find the code for the examples in this section. Take some time to review and test out each example.

Running an Access Query from Excel

Here's a nifty technique for those of you who often copy and paste the results of your Access queries to Excel. In this technique, you use DAO to run an Access query in the background and output the results into Excel via a Recordset object.

```
Sub RunAccessQuery()

'Step 1:  Declare your variables
    Dim MyDatabase As DAO.Database
    Dim MyQueryDef As DAO.QueryDef
    Dim MyRecordset As DAO.Recordset
    Dim i As Integer

'Step 2:  Identify the database and query
    Set MyDatabase = DBEngine.OpenDatabase _
    ("C:\OffTheGrid\ZalexCorp Restaurant Equipment and Supply.accdb")
    Set MyQueryDef = MyDatabase.QueryDefs("Revenue by Period")

'Step 3:  Open the query
    Set MyRecordset = MyQueryDef.OpenRecordset

'Step 4:  Clear previous contents
    Sheets("Main").Select
    ActiveSheet.Range("A6:K10000").ClearContents
```

```
'Step 5:  Copy the recordset to Excel
    ActiveSheet.Range("A7").CopyFromRecordset MyRecordset

'Step 6: Add column heading names to the spreadsheet
    For i = 1 To MyRecordset.Fields.Count
    ActiveSheet.Cells(6, i).Value = MyRecordset.Fields(i - 1).Name
    Next i

End Sub
```

The following outlines what the steps in the code do:

1. **Declaring the necessary variables:** In Step 1, you first declare four variables:

   - `MyDatabase` exposes your application via DAO.

   - `MyQueryDef` is a query definition object that exposes the target query.

   - `MyRecordset` is a Recordset object that holds the results of the data pull.

   - `i` is an integer variable that adds column headings.

2. **Setting the target database and target query:** Step 2 specifies the database that holds your target query as well as which query will be run. Assigning the query to a `QueryDef` object allows you to essentially open the query in memory.

3. **Opening the query into a Recordset:** In this step, you literally run the query in memory and output the results into a Recordset. Once the results are in a Recordset, you can use it just as you would any other Recordset.

4. **Clearing contents in the spreadsheet:** This step clears the "Main" worksheet before copying the Recordset. This ensures that all data from the previous pull has been removed before bringing in fresh data.

5. **Copying the Recordset into Excel:** In Step 5, you use Excel's `CopyFromRecordset` method to get the returned dataset into your spreadsheet. In this example, you are copying the data in the `MyRecordset` object onto the sheet called "Main" starting at cell A7.

6. **Adding column headers:** In Step 6, you enumerate through each field in the Recordset to automatically get the name of each header and enter it into Excel.

Running Access Parameter Queries from Excel

An *Access parameter query* is interactive, prompting you for criteria before the query is run. A parameter query is useful when you need to ask a query different questions using different criteria each time it is run. To get a firm understanding of how a parameter query can help you, build query in Figure 16-11. With this query, you want to see the all purchase orders logged during the 200705 system period.

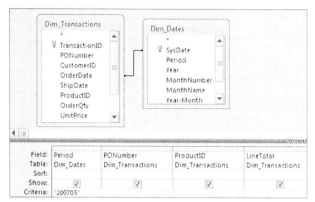

Figure 16-11: This query has a hard-coded criterion for system period.

Although this query gives you what you need, the problem is that the criterion for system period is hard-coded as 200705. That means if you want to analyze revenue for a different period, you essentially have to rebuild the query. Using a parameter query allows you to create a conditional analysis; that is, an analysis based on variables you specify each time you run the query. To create a parameter query, simply replace the hard-coded criteria with text that you have enclosed in square brackets ([ ]), as shown in Figure 16-12.

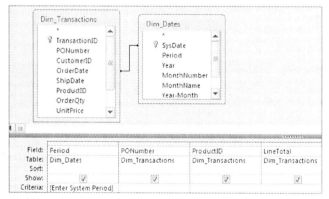

Figure 16-12: To create a parameter query, replace the hard-coded criteria with text enclosed in square brackets [ ].

Running a parameter query forces the Enter Parameter Value dialog box to open and ask for a variable. Note that the text you typed inside the brackets of your parameter appears in the dialog box. At this point, you would simply enter your parameter, as shown in Figure 16-13.

Figure 16-13: Enter your criteria in the Enter Parameter Value dialog box and click OK.

By the way, you are not in any way limited in the number of parameters you can use in your query. When you run this query, you are prompted for both a system period and a product ID, allowing you to dynamically filter on two data points without ever having to rewrite your query.

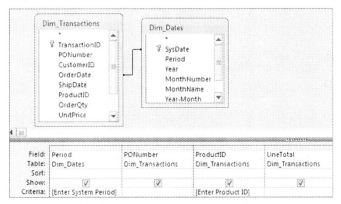

Figure 16-14: You can employ more than one parameter in a query.

The idea behind running an Access parameter query with Excel is simple. Have the user input the parameters on your spreadsheet, then use automation to run the parameter query in memory and output the results to Excel.

In the sample database, you will find a query called MyParameterQuery. A quick look at this query in Design view (Figure 16-15) reveals that this query checks for two parameters: region and business segment.

TIP You will notice that the parameters in Figure 16-15 have been combined with the asterisk wildcard character (*). This useful technique forces all records to be returned if the parameter is left blank. Without the wildcard characters, blank parameters would cause the query to return no records. This trick essentially gives you the option of entering the parameters to filter the records or ignore the parameter to return all records.

Using the wildcard with a parameter also allows users to enter in a partial parameter and still get results. Suppose, for example, that the criterion in your parameter query is:

```
Like [Enter Lastname] & "*"
```

Entering A as the parameter would return all last names that start with the letter *A*.

Or suppose the criterion in your parameter query is:

```
Like "*" & [Enter Lastname] & "*"
```

Entering A would return all last names that contain the letter *A*.

Figure 16-16 illustrates that the ''Chapter16_SampleFiles.xlsm'' workbook has two cells designated as input fields: one for region and one for business segment.

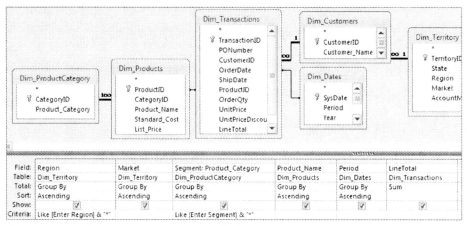

Figure 16-15: The MyParametersQuery asks for two parameters.

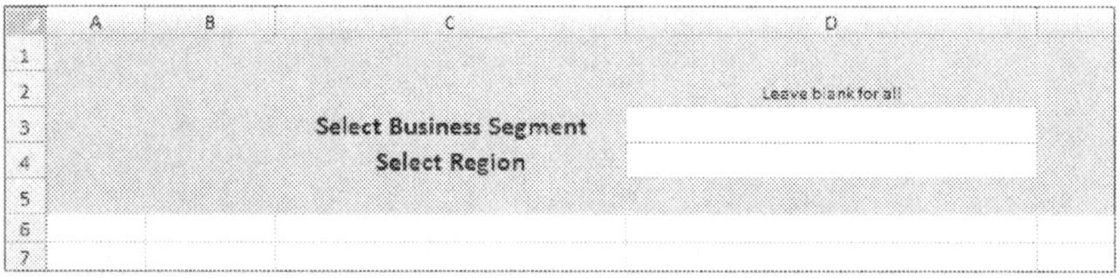

Figure 16-16: The input fields correspond with the parameters in the query called MyParameterQuery.

Take a moment to review the code that brings it all together. This technique allows you to build some interesting reporting solutions with relatively little effort.

```
Sub RunAccessQuery()

'Step 1:  Declare your variables
    Dim MyDatabase As DAO.Database
    Dim MyQueryDef As DAO.QueryDef
    Dim MyRecordset As DAO.Recordset
    Dim i As Integer

'Step 2:  Identify the database and query
    Set MyDatabase = DBEngine.OpenDatabase _
    ("C:\OffTheGrid\ZalexCorp Restaurant Equipment and Supply.accdb")
    Set MyQueryDef = MyDatabase.QueryDefs("MyParameterQuery")

'Step 3:  Define the Parameters
    With MyQueryDef
        .Parameters("[Enter Segment]") = Range("D3").Value
        .Parameters("[Enter Region]") = Range("D4").Value
    End With

'Step 4:  Open the query
    Set MyRecordset = MyQueryDef.OpenRecordset

'Step 5:  Clear previous contents
    Sheets("Main").Select
    ActiveSheet.Range("A6:K10000").ClearContents

'Step 6:  Copy the recordset to Excel
    ActiveSheet.Range("A7").CopyFromRecordset MyRecordset

'Step 7: Add column heading names to the spreadsheet
    For i = 1 To MyRecordset.Fields.Count
    ActiveSheet.Cells(6, i).Value = MyRecordset.Fields(i - 1).Name
    Next i

End Sub
```

The following outlines what the steps in the code do:

1. **Declaring the necessary variables:** For step 1, declare four variables:

   ▪ MyDatabase exposes your application via DAO.

   ▪ MyQueryDef is a query definition object that exposes the target query.

   ▪ MyRecordset is a Recordset object that holds the results of the data pull.

   ▪ i is an integer variable that adds column headings.

2. **Setting the target database and target query:** In Step 2, you specify the database that holds your target query as well as which query will be run.

3. **Define parameters:** In Step 3, you expose the query parameters in order to assign values to each one. As you can see, the name of each parameter matches the parameter name as entered in Query Design view (Figure 16-15). The values assigned to each parameter come from the corresponding input boxes on the Excel spreadsheet (Figure 16-16).

4. **Opening the query into a Recordset:** Step 4 runs the query in memory and outputs the results into a Recordset.

5. **Clearing contents in the Spreadsheet:** Step 5 clears the "Main" worksheet before copying the Recordset, ensuring that all data from the previous pull has been removed before bringing in fresh data.

6. **Copying the Recordset into Excel:** In Step 6, you use Excel's `CopyFromRecordset` method to get the returned dataset into your spreadsheet.

7. **Adding column headers:** In Step 7, you enumerate through each field in the Recordset to automatically get the name of each header and enter it into Excel.

Running an Access Macro from Excel

You can run Access macros from Excel, using automation to fire the macro without opening Access. This technique is not only useful for running those epic macros that involve a multi-step series of 20 queries but can also come in handy for everyday tasks like outputting Access data to an Excel file. For example, the following code fires an Access macro that exports a table to an Excel file, and then opens the file with Excel.

NOTE Keep in mind that Access 2007 and 2010 have security features that may prevent your macros from running. Feel free to review Chapter 6 to learn how to manage macro security.

```
Sub OpenAccessMacro()

'Step 1:  Declare your variables
    Dim AC As Access.Application

'Step 2:  Start Access and open the target database
    Set AC = New Access.Application
    AC.OpenCurrentDatabase ("C:\OffTheGrid\ZalexCorp Restaurant
Equipment and Supply.accdb")
```

```
'Step 3:  Run the target macro, then close Access
    With AC
        .DoCmd.RunMacro "MyMacro"
        .Quit
    End With

  Workbooks.Open "C:\OffTheGrid\MyExcel_Output.xlsx"

End Sub
```

Opening an Access Report from Excel

As you learned in Chapter 11, Access reports allow you to build professional looking reports that have a clean PDF-style look and feel. This example demonstrates how you can open your Access reports right from Excel. The appealing thing about this technique is that you don't see Access at all; the report goes straight to a Word rich-text file!

NOTE It takes a few seconds for Access to output the target report to rich text format. The larger the report, the longer the conversion takes. With very large reports, you may see the hourglass for a few minutes. Ultimately, you can weigh the options and determine your patience threshold.

```
Sub OpenAccessReport()

'Step 1:  Declare your variables
    Dim AC As Access.Application

'Step 2:  Start Access and open the target database
    Set AC = New Access.Application
    AC.OpenCurrentDatabase ("C:\OffTheGrid\ZalexCorp Restaurant
Equipment and Supply.accdb")

'Step 3:  Open the target report as a Word rich text file
    With AC
        .DoCmd.OpenReport "Revenue Report", acViewPreview
        .DoCmd.RunCommand acCmdOutputToRTF
        .Quit
    End With

End Sub
```

Opening an Access Form from Excel

There may be times when you or your clients need to switch focus to an Access form. This example demonstrates how you can open an Access form from Excel.

```
Sub OpenAccessForm()

'Step 1:  Declare your variables
    Dim AC As Access.Application

'Step 2:  Start Access and open the target database
    Set AC = New Access.Application
    AC.OpenCurrentDatabase ("C:\OffTheGrid\ZalexCorp Restaurant
Equipment and Supply.accdb")

'Step 3:  Open the target form and make Access visible
    With AC
        .DoCmd.OpenForm "MainForm", acNormal
        .Visible = True
    End With

End Sub
```

> **NOTE** You will notice that the last few examples you walked through make use of Access' DoCmd object. This object exposes methods that are essentially macro actions. That is to say, if you go to Access and start a new macro, the available actions you will see listed there are the same ones exposed via DoCmd methods. What's the point? The point is that you can perform virtually any action that a macro allows you to perform, simply by using the DoCmd object. This means that you can build a virtual Access macro strictly with VBA.

Compacting an Access Database from Excel

During your integrated processes, you may routinely increase or decrease the number of records and tables in your database. As time goes on, your Access database grows in file size. This is because Access does not release file space. All the space needed for the data you move in and out of your database are held by your Access file, regardless if the data is still there or not. In that light, it's critical that you run Compact and Repair on your Access database regularly. Among other things, running Compact and Repair defragments your database, releasing any unused space and ensuring that your database does not grow to an unmanageable size.

> **NOTE** To manually compact and repair your database in Access 2007, click the Office icon and select Manage ➪ Compact and Repair Database.
>
> To manually compact and repair your database in Access 2010, go to the application ribbon and select File ➪ Info ➪ Compact and Repair Database

Office automation enables you to Compact and Repair your databases right from code. The example outlined in the following code demonstrates how to run Compact and Repair on an Access database directly from Excel.

```
Sub CompactRepairFromExcel()

'Step 1:  Declare your variables
    Dim OriginalFile As String
    Dim BackupFile As String
    Dim TempFile As String

'Step 2:  Identify the target database assign file paths
    OriginalFile = "C:\OffTheGrid\MyDatabase.accdb"
    BackupFile = "C:\ OffTheGrid\MyDatabaseBackup.accdb"
    TempFile = "C:\ OffTheGrid\MyDatabaseTemporary.accdb"

'Step 3:  Make a backup copy of database
    FileCopy OriginalFile, BackupFile

'Step 4:  Perform the compact and repair
    DBEngine.CompactDatabase OriginalFile, TempFile

'Step 5:  Delete the old database
    Kill OriginalFile

'Step 6:  Rename the temporary database to the old database name
    Name TempFile As OriginalFile

End Sub
```

The following outlines what the steps in the code do:

1. **Declaring the necessary variables:** In Step 1, you first declare three string variables that will hold file names.

2. **Assigning file names:** In Step 2, you are assigning each of the string variables a file name.

   - The `OriginalFile` string variable is assigned the file path and name of the target database. This variable will represent your database during the procedure.

   - The `BackupFile` string variable is assigned the file path and name of a backup file you will create during this procedure.

   - The `TempFile` string variable is assigned the file path and name of a temporary file you will create during this procedure.

3. **Making a backup copy of the target database:** In Step 3, you use the `FileCopy` function to make a backup of the `OriginalFile` (the target database). Although this step is not necessary for the Compact and Repair procedure, it's generally a good practice to make a backup of your database before running this level of VBA on it.

4. **Executing the Compact and Repair:** To understand what is going on from this point on, you must understand how Access actually performs Compact and Repair. When you Compact and Repair a database manually, it seems as though Access simply compresses your original database; this is not the case. Access actually creates a second file and essentially copies your original database minus the empty file space. Access then deletes the old file. You need to take the same action with your code.

   In that light, Step 4 executes the Compact and Repair, specifying the original database and specifying the file path of the temporary database.

5. **Deleting the old file:** At this point, you have two copies of your database: the original database, and a second database, which is a copy of your original without the empty file space. Step 5 deletes the original database, leaving you with the copy.

6. **Renaming the temporary file:** In Step 6, you simply rename the temporary file, giving it the name of your original database. This leaves you with a database that is compacted and optimized.

Summary

Both Excel and Access applications have strengths, which you routinely leverage through manual processes. For example, you may routinely crunch data in Access only to bring the results into Excel for presentation. Or, you may send Excel data to Access only to open Access and run a set of queries or output a report. The objective of automation is to take all manual intervention out of these processes by controlling one application with another.

Access data processing lends itself quite nicely to automation. The typical automation scenario is one where you send Access data to Excel, then use Excel automation to build charts, pivot tables, or some other presentation mechanism displaying the data. From Excel, you can use Access automation to fire an Access macro, run Access queries or even open Access reports.

Automation can literally take you out of the processes you have set up, allowing them to run without any human interaction.

CHAPTER 17

Integrating Excel and Access with XML

As intimidating as XML may seem, it is really nothing more than a text file that contains data wrapped in markup (tags that denote structure and meaning). These tags essentially make a text file machine-readable. The term "machine-readable" essentially means that any application or Web-based solution designed to read XML files is able to discern the structure and content of your file.

Because XML is text-based, it is not dependent on a specific application for construction, reading, or editing. This versatility makes XML an excellent integration mechanism.

In this chapter, you gain a solid understanding of the fundamentals of XML. You also get some context for XML functionality in Excel and Access by exploring some of the ways both Excel and Access allow you to work with XML data through the user interface.

Why XML?

Up to this point, you have explored several integration techniques that use well-established technologies that you are sure to feel comfortable with. So the question is: Why XML? Why should you explore a relatively new technology that, frankly, few in the Excel and Access community are using? There are three major benefits to using XML as an integration mechanism.

With XML, you can bypass technologies that you may not feel comfortable with such as MS Query, SQL statements, or ADO. Imagine incorporating external data into your Excel or Access processes without the need to manage database connectivity or use complex SQL statements. And because XML files are nothing more than text files, the process of moving and refreshing data, in most cases, is faster and more streamlined.

Second, XML gives you more flexibility than standard text files. With XML, you can import and use only the columns of data required as opposed to importing the entire text file. You can also import different parts of the XML file to different locations instead of importing the entire block of text into one table.

The third and possibly most attractive reason to use XML is that you can simply "refresh" your XML maps to get new data. With text files, you need to walk through the import process again. Of course, you could write some code to automate the import process, but again, XML allows you to bypass the need for that.

Can you survive without using XML? Sure, you can. However, there are enough attractive possibilities with XML to warrant a closer look.

Understanding XML

Before working with XML functionality, it's important to understand the makeup of an XML document and how its syntactic constructs work. Let's take a moment to explore the fundamental components of a standard XML document.

The XML Declaration

The first line of an XML document is called the *XML declaration*. Look at an example of a typical XML declaration:

```
<?xml version="1.0"? encoding="UTF-8" standalone="Yes"?>
```

The XML declaration typically contains three parts: a version attribute, an optional encoding attribute, and a standalone attribute.

- **Version attribute:** The version attribute tells the processing application that this text file is an XML document.

- **Encoding attribute:** You primarily use the encoding attribute to work around character encoding issues that may be raised when dealing with international characters and those outside of the Unicode/ASCII standard. Since XML documents are inherently Unicode, the encoding attribute is optional if the character encoding used to create the document is UTF-8, UTF16 or ASCII. Indeed, you will find that the character encoding is omitted from many of the XML documents you may encounter.

■ **Standalone attribute:** The standalone attribute tells the processing application whether the document references an external data source. If the document contains no reference to external data sources, it is deemed a standalone, thus having the "Yes" value. Since every XML document is inherently standalone, this attribute is optional for documents that do not reference an external source.

Processing Instructions

As their name implies, processing instructions provide explicit instructions to the processing application. These can be identified by distinctive tags composed of left and right angle brackets coupled with question marks (<?, ?>). These instructions are typically found directly under the XML declaration and can provide any number of directives. For example, the following processing instruction would direct Excel to open the given XML document.

```
<?mso-application progid="Excel.Sheet"?>
```

Comments

Comments allow XML developers to enter plain-language explanation or remarks about the contents of the document. Just as in VBA, where the single quote signifies a comment, XML has its own syntax to denote a comment. Comments in XML begin with the <!-- characters and ends with the --> characters, as in the following example.

```
<!--Document created by Mike Alexander-->
```

Elements

An element is defined by a start tag and an end tag (for example, <MyData> </MyData>). Any data you enter in between the start and end tags makes up the contents of that element. As you can see in the following example, the document begins with <MyTable> and ends with </MyTable>; all the syntax you see in between these tags makes up the content for the MyTable element.

```
<?xml version="1.0"?>
<MyTable>
    <Customer>
        <Quarter>Q1</Quarter>
        <Region>North</Region>
        <Revenue>25000</Revenue>
    </Customer>
</MyTable>
```

The concept of tags is a familiar one if you have worked with HTML. However, unlike HTML, tags in XML are not predefined. That is to say, the text "MyTable" has no predefined utility or meaning. You can change that text to anything and it's all the same to the XML document. Herein you stumble on the beauty of XML: XML allows you to create custom tags, tags to which you give definition and purpose. As long as you adhere to a few basic rules, you can create and describe any number of elements by creating your own custom tags. Here are the basic syntactic rules you must follow when creating elements:

- Every element must have a start tag, represented by left and right angle brackets (<>), as well as a corresponding end tag represented by a left angle bracket, back slash and right angle bracket (</>). Naturally, to avoid errors, you need to use the same syntactical name within the start and end tags.

- Names in XML are case sensitive, so the start and end tags of an element must match in case as well as in syntax. For example, an element defined by the tags `<Data>` `</data>` causes a parsing error. XML is looking for the end tag for `<Data>` as well as the start tag for `</data>`.

You must begin all element names with a letter or an underscore, never a digit or other character. In addition, names that begin with any permutation of *xml* are reserved and cannot be used.

Elements can contain numbers, text, and even other elements. Elements are normally framed in a parent/child hierarchy. For example, in the `MyTable` example, the `Customer` element is a child of the `MyTable` root element. Likewise, the `MyTable` element is the parent of the `Customer` element. Following that logic, the `Quarter`, `Region`, and `Revenue` elements are the children of the `Customer` element. This parent/child hierarchy allows the XML document to describe the arrangement of the data as well as the content. Later in this chapter, you will discover how this parent/child hierarchy is leveraged to programmatically move around in XML documents.

The Root Element

The root element (which is always the top-most element in an XML document) serves as the container for all of the contents within the document. Every XML document must have one (and only one) root element. The `MyTable` element shown in the following example is the *root element* for this particular XML document.

```
<?xml version="1.0"?>
<MyTable>
    <Customer>
```

```
        <Quarter>Q1</Quarter>
        <Region>North</Region>
        <Revenue>25000</Revenue>
    </Customer>
</MyTable>
```

In this example, the root element contains four elements, each one containing its own content.

Attributes

Attributes in XML documents come in two flavors: data attributes and meta-data attributes. Data attributes are used to provide the actual data for an element. For example, the following attributes (name and age) provide the data for the Pet element.

```
<Pet name='Spot' age="4">Dog</Pet>
```

Notice that the age attribute is wrapped in quotes although the value itself is a number. This is because unlike elements, attributes are textual. This means that attributes must be wrapped in either single or double quotes.

Metadata attributes typically provide descriptive information about the contents of elements. For instance, in the following example, the Customer element has an attribute called id which provides that Customer with a unique identifier.

```
<?xml version="1.0"?>
<MyTable>

        <Customer id="1"/>
        <Quarter>Q1</Quarter>
        <Region>North</Region>
        <Revenue>25000</Revenue>

</MyTable>
```

Many new users of XML find the concept of attributes versus elements a bit confusing. After all, you can easily convert most elements to attributes (or vice versa) and the XML document would parse just fine. For example, the Customer id attribute could just as easily be presented in an element as such: <id>1</id >. However, most XML documents adhere to some general rules of thumb when it comes to elements versus attributes:

- ▪ If the content is not an actual data item but is instead a descriptor of the data (record number, index number, unique identifier, and so on), then an attribute is typically used.

- Elements are used for any content that consists of multiple values.

- If there is a chance that the content will expand in structure to include children, elements are typically used.

Namespaces

The idea behind namespaces is simple. Because XML lets developers create and name their own elements and attributes, there is a possibility that a particular name could be used in different contexts. For instance, an XML document may use the name ID to describe both a customer ID and an invoice ID. Namespaces associate overlapping identifiers with *Uniform Resource Identifiers* (*URI*), allowing applications that process XML documents to make a distinction between similar names.

A URI is typically made up of a URL and a relative descriptor. For instance, the following line defines a namespace. As you can image, Xmlns stands for XML namespace.

```
Xmlns="http://www.datapigtechnologies.com/customers"
```

The fact that URLs are used to define namespaces leads many to believe that namespaces point to some sort of online source. URLs provide some semblance of ownership to anyone reading the XML file. The goal of a namespace is merely to create a unique string. So you could technically use something like Xmlns="arbitrary_namespace", although it wouldn't be very useful in identifying ownership or utility.

As you can imagine, using a URL can lead to some fairly long namespace strings. Most XML developers get around this problem by creating namespace prefixes. A prefix is nothing more than an alias for the namespace. For instance, the following namespace uses the prefix dpc. Then the dpc prefix is applied to an attribute.

```
Xmlns:dpc=http://www.datapigtechnologies.com/customers
<Invoice dpc:id="201">
```

Notice that in the example illustrated that follows, the namespace is placed directly into the root element. Any namespace declared within an element automatically applies to all child elements.

```
<?xml version="1.0"?>
<MyTable xmlns="http://www.datapigtechnologies.com/customers">
    <Customer>
```

```
        <Quarter>Q1</Quarter>
        <Region>North</Region>
        <Revenue>25000</Revenue>
    </Customer>
</MyTable>
```

Now you may be wondering why you would use a namespace in a document where there are no duplicate names. This is primarily to avoid overlapping names with other XML documents that may be consumed in the same process or application.

Creating a Simple Reporting Solution with XML

In a reporting solution, you typically have a data layer and a presentation layer. In this section, you will discover how XML can help you easily create a simple reporting solution where Access provides the data and Excel uses the data in some sort of a presentation layer.

Exporting XML Data from Access

Despite the anxiety that some people feel about XML, it's interesting to observe that most of the XML functionality built into Excel and Access requires no programming and little knowledge of databases. That is to say, all the steps you need to create an XML-based reporting solution can be performed using only the user interfaces that come with Excel and Access.

To start the export from Access, follow these steps:

1. Right click the SalesByRegion table found in the sample database and select Export ➪ XML File. This activates the Export-XML File dialog box where you specify the location where you want to save your XML file. As you can see in Figure 17-1, you generally want to specify a directory dedicated to your XML files.

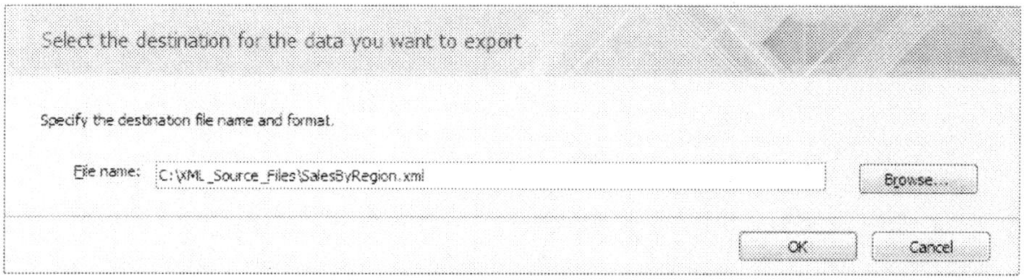

Select the destination for the data you want to export

Specify the destination file name and format.

File name: C:\XML_Source_Files\SalesByRegion.xml   Browse...

OK   Cancel

Figure 17-1: Activate the Export-XML File dialog box and specify a location to save your XML File.

TIP You can also start the export process by highlighting a table in your database, selecting the External Data tab in the ribbon, and then selecting More ⇨ XML File.

2. Clicking the OK button activates the Export XML dialog box illustrated in Figure 17-2. Here, you are given the option of exporting the schema definition and presentation specifications as well as the data. In this example, you only want the XML data exported; therefore, you deselect all but that option in the dialog box.

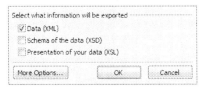

Figure 17-2: Choose to export only the XML file.

NOTE The schema definition exports as an *XSD* (*Extensible Schema Definition*) document, while the presentation specifications export as an *XSL* (*Extensible Stylesheet Language*) document. XSD files dictate the layout and sequencing for the data in an XML document, as well as the data types, and default values for each element and attribute. An XSL file dictates the formatting rules for the document, controlling the way the XML data is presented. The topics of XSD and XSL are focused on areas outside the scope of this chapter, so they're not covered in detail here. If you want to learn more about XSD and XSL, feel free to visit www.w3schools.com, where you can get free tutorials on these topics.

3. Once you click the OK button, your data will be saved to an XML file in the location you specified. Access then gives you the option to save your export process (see Figure 17-3). Here you can save the steps of the export process so you can perform the export at the touch of a button.

4. Simply check that you want to save your export and give your export process a name. As you can see in Figure 17-3, you can even create a task reminder in Outlook!

5. Once your export process is saved, you can call it by clicking the Saved Exports button found on the External Data tab in the ribbon. This activates the Manage Data Tasks dialog box, shown in Figure 17-4, where you can run your export process as often as you need.

As Figure 17-5 illustrates, you can even get fancy and automate your export by calling the saved export via a macro.

TIP Want to export only specific records to XML? Write a query. You can export the results of a query to XML just as you would a table.

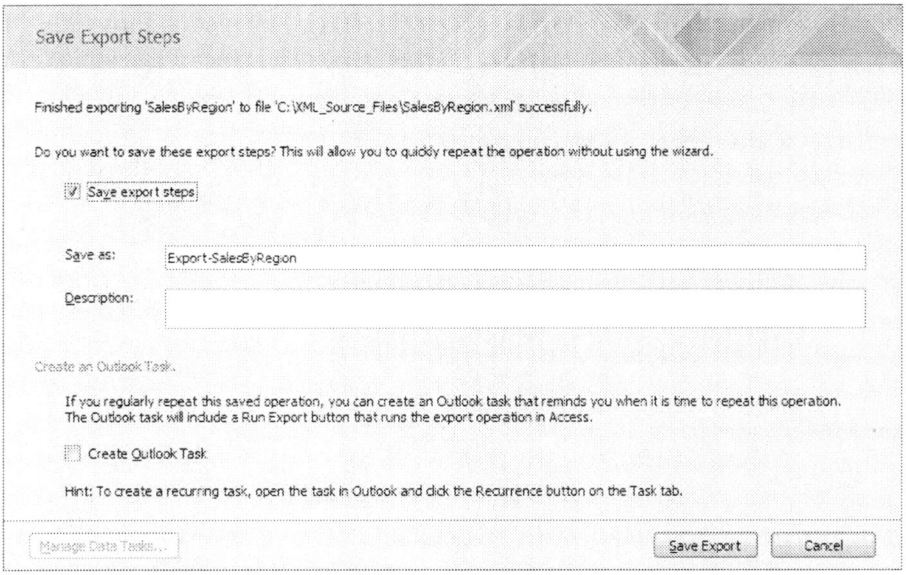

Save Export Steps

Finished exporting 'SalesByRegion' to file 'C:\XML_Source_Files\SalesByRegion.xml' successfully.

Do you want to save these export steps? This will allow you to quickly repeat the operation without using the wizard.

☑ Save export steps

Save as: Export-SalesByRegion

Description:

Create an Outlook Task.

If you regularly repeat this saved operation, you can create an Outlook task that reminds you when it is time to repeat this operation. The Outlook task will include a Run Export button that runs the export operation in Access.

☐ Create Outlook Task

Hint: To create a recurring task, open the task in Outlook and click the Recurrence button on the Task tab.

Manage Data Tasks...   Save Export   Cancel

Figure 17-3: You can choose to save your export process so that you can perform it routinely with the touch of a button.

Saved Imports | Saved Exports

Click to select the saved export to manage.

Export-SalesByRegion   C:\XML_Source_Files\SalesByRegion.xml
                              Click here to edit the description.

To edit the name or description of the saved operation, select the operation and then click the text you want to edit.

Run   Create Outlook Task...   Delete   Close

Figure 17-4: You can rerun your saved export process via the Manage Data Tasks dialog box.

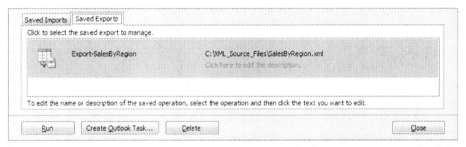

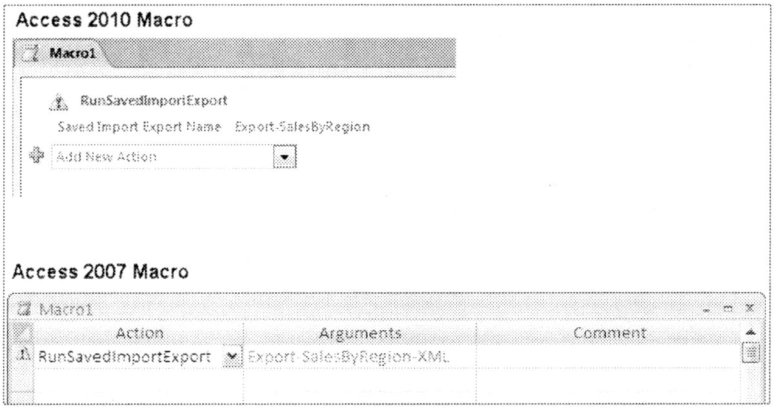

Figure 17-5: You can use the RunSavedImportExport macro action to automate the exporting of your XML data.

Utilize XML Data in Excel

One of the simplest ways to utilize an XML document in Excel is to open it directly. To help demonstrate this, follow these steps:

1. Start Excel and open the SalesByRegion.xml file you just saved. Excel immediately recognizes that the file you are opening is an XML document, so it actives the Open XML dialog box shown in Figure 17-6.

Figure 17-6: Choose to open your XML document as an XML table.

2. Select the As an XML table option and click the OK.

   Because the EmployeeSales.xml file does not have an associated schema file (XSD), Excel infers a schema from our XML document. This means Excel essentially creates an internal schema that will dictate the rules for the document.

   TIP Again, an *XSD* or schema file dictates the layout and sequencing for the data in an XML document, as well as the data types and default values for each element and attribute.

   From here, Excel automatically creates an XML list, mapping a range of cells to the elements in the source XML document (see Figure 17-7).

   NOTE You will note in Figure 17-7 that Access has included a field called "generated," specifying the date and time the XML extract was created. You can safely delete this column if it does not suit your needs.

3. So now what? Well, you can use this data as if it were a normal range. You can create a pivot table report, build charts, apply some fancy conditional formatting, and so on. The nifty thing about this setup, however, is that these cells are linked back to the XML document and can be refreshed with the latest data by right-clicking inside the XML list and selecting Refresh XML Data!

4. To test out the refresh function, go back to Access and add a few records to the SalesByRegion table, as demonstrated in Figure 17-8.

5. Re-export the SalesByRegion XML file. If you saved your export process, you can simply call it by clicking the Saved Exports button found on the External Data tab in the Ribbon. If you did not save your export process,

you have to go through the steps of exporting your XML file. Either way, the idea is to replace the previously exported SalesByRegion.xml file. Therefore, you need to save your export in the exact same file path you used previously.

6. Once you have updated your XML document, you can return to your Excel file and refresh the XML list. As you can see in Figure 17-9, the newly added records are included in the mapped range.

	A	B	C	D	E
1	generated	Market	SalesPeriod	Revenue	UnitsSold
2	10/18/2009 11:36	Asia	P01	301051.0857	893
3	10/18/2009 11:36	Australia	P01	311228.1714	875
4	10/18/2009 11:36	Northern Europe	P01	744090.6286	1921
5	10/18/2009 11:36	South America	P01	346466.0571	1001
6	10/18/2009 11:36	Southern Europe	P01	461854.8571	1253
7	10/18/2009 11:36	United Kingdom	P01	845890.5143	2182
8	10/18/2009 11:36	United States	P01	519995.7143	1420
9	10/18/2009 11:36	Asia	P02	540548.0571	1508
10	10/18/2009 11:36	Australia	P02	500139.5429	1442
11	10/18/2009 11:36	Northern Europe	P02	1439830.914	3661
12	10/18/2009 11:36	South America	P02	474503.6571	1329
13	10/18/2009 11:36	Southern Europe	P02	904641.7714	2490

Figure 17-7: Your XML data automatically maps to your workbook.

Market	SalesPeriod	Revenue	UnitsSold
Asia	P07	$100,000	100
Australia	P07	$100,000	100
Northern Europe	P07	$100,000	100
South America	P07	$100,000	100
Southern Europe	P07	$100,000	100
United Kingdom	P07	$100,000	100
United States	P07	$100,000	100
*			

Figure 17-8: Add another period's worth of records to the SalesByRegion table.

	A	B	C	D	E
1	generated	Market	SalesPeriod	Revenue	UnitsSold
42	10/18/2009 11:48	United Kingdom	P06	1064273.2	2714
43	10/18/2009 11:48	United States	P06	642634.6857	1752
44	10/18/2009 11:48	Asia	P07	100000	100
45	10/18/2009 11:48	Australia	P07	100000	100
46	10/18/2009 11:48	Northern Europe	P07	100000	100
47	10/18/2009 11:48	South America	P07	100000	100
48	10/18/2009 11:48	Southern Europe	P07	100000	100
49	10/18/2009 11:48	United Kingdom	P07	100000	100
50	10/18/2009 11:48	United States	P07	100000	100

Figure 17-9: Refreshing the XML list includes updates to your Excel file with fresh data.

Take a moment now to think about what XML allows you to do. Imagine building an Excel-based reporting system where all data that feeds your pivot tables and charts link back to XML files on a network server. Imagine that you can update those XML files on a nightly basis using an automated Access process. In addition, you could design your client's workbooks to automatically refresh on open. Moreover, remember that you are essentially working with a text file, so your clients do not have to worry about server drivers, passwords, and the like.

> **TIP** If you are interested in programming XML in Excel, feel free to check out *Excel 2007 VBA Programmer's Reference*, **published by Wiley, ISBN: 978-0-470-04643-2.**

Creating a Data Entry Process Using XML

In many data entry processes, Excel is used as the interface to enter the data and then the data is sent to an Access database to be stored and analyzed. In this section, you will discover how XML can help simplify these sorts of processes as well.

The general idea in this exercise is to create a data entry template in Access and convert that template to an XML file. Then you use that XML file to create a data entry form in Excel that can be completed and exported back out to XML. The final step is to pick up the XML with Access and import it into a source table.

Creating the Data Entry Schema in Access

Start the process by building an Access table that will generate the base XML and the schema file. You can also use this table to capture the results of your data entry exercise. Figure 17-10 illustrates the table that you'll use in this example. Save this table as "DataEntry."

> **NOTE** What's all this talk about a schema file? Well, way back in Figure 17-2, remember that you chose to only export the XML data, not the schema or presentation specifications. In this example, you tell Access to create the schema file. Why? Doing so ensures that Access provides Excel with the information it needs to map the empty fields to your worksheet.

Once you have created the source table, you can export an XML file from the source table using the same process outlined in Figures 17-1 through 17-3 earlier in this chapter, with one exception. In the step highlighted in Figure 17-2, you need to tell Access to create the XSD file. Figure 17-11 illustrates what the Export XML dialog box should look like when both XML and XSD are selected.

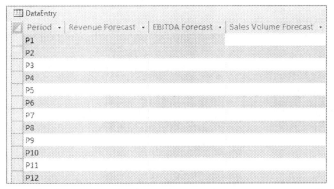

Figure 17-10: Build the Access table shown here and save as "DataEntry."

Figure 17-11: Tell Access to create both the XML and XSD files.

Setting up the Data Entry Form in Excel

Start Excel and open the DataEntry.xml file you saved in the previous section. Excel immediately recognizes that the file you are opening is an XML document, activating the Open XML dialog box shown in Figure 17-12. Select the As an XML table option and click OK.

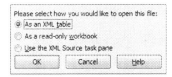

Figure 17-12: Choose to open your XML document as an XML table.

Note that Access has included a field called "generated" specifying the date and time the XML extract was created (see Figure 17-13). You need to delete this column in order to export your results back into XML.

	A	B	C	D	E
1	generated ▼	Period ▼	Revenue Forecast ▼	EBITDA Forecast ▼	Sales Volume Forecast ▼
2	10/18/2009 11:56	P1			
3	10/18/2009 11:56	P2			
4	10/18/2009 11:56	P3			
5	10/18/2009 11:56	P4			
6	10/18/2009 11:56	P5			
7	10/18/2009 11:56	P6			
8	10/18/2009 11:56	P7			
9	10/18/2009 11:56	P8			
10	10/18/2009 11:56	P9			
11	10/18/2009 11:56	P10			
12	10/18/2009 11:56	P11			
13	10/18/2009 11:56	P12			

Figure 17-13: Delete the "generated" field.

Obviously, the idea is to distribute the data entry form and have your users complete it. So at this point, you should take some time to format your data entry form, making it easy to work with as shown in Figure 17-14.

	A	B	C	D
1		**Forecast Entry Portal**		
2		Instructions: Enter your forecasts for each measure specified		
3				
4	Period ▼	Revenue Forecast ▼	EBITDA Forecast ▼	Sales Volume Forecast ▼
5	P1			
6	P2			
7	P3			
8	P4			
9	P5			
10	P6			
11	P7			
12	P8			
13	P9			
14	P10			
15	P11			
16	P12			

Figure 17-14: Take a moment to format your data entry form.

Exporting Results from Excel to XML

So how do you get the data back into Access? Once the data entry form is completed, Excel can export the data back into an XML file and save that file to a specified location. To test this, fill out your data entry form and right click anywhere inside the list. This pulls up a context menu where you will select XML ⇨ Export, as demonstrated in Figure 17-15.

Excel asks you to specify the file path of the exported XML. In this example, you replace the DataEntry.xml file you have saved (see Figure 17-16).

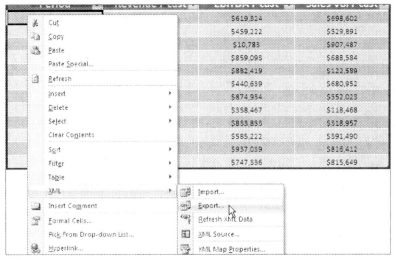

Figure 17-15: Export the data in your list back into an XML file.

Figure 17-16: Replace the DataEntry.xml file you previously saved.

TIP Record a macro to capture the process of exporting the data in your XML list to an XML file path. Once recoded, you can assign the macro to a button, allowing your users to export their results at the click of a button.

Getting the Results Back into Access

Once you have an XML file with the results, all Access has to do is find the file and import it. Start by selecting the External Data tab in the ribbon. From there, select XML File under the Import group as illustrated in Figure 17-17.

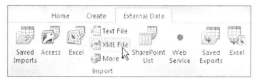

Figure 17-17: Select XML File from the Import group.

This activates the Get External Data-XML File dialog box (see Figure 17-18), where you're asked to specify the file path of the XML file you want to import.

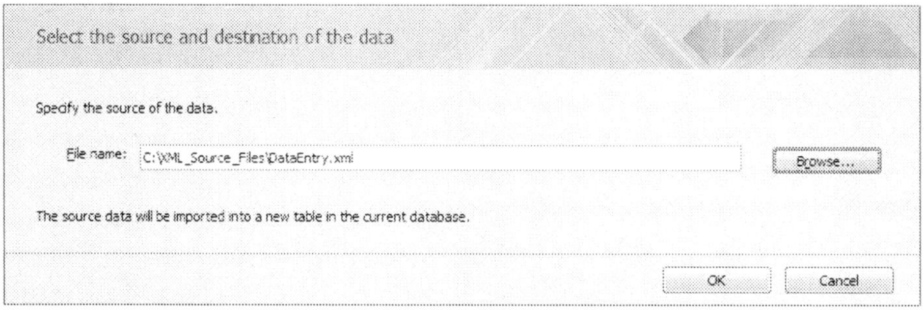

Select the source and destination of the data

Specify the source of the data.

File name: C:\XML_Source_Files\DataEntry.xml   Browse...

The source data will be imported into a new table in the current database.

OK   Cancel

Figure 17-18: Specify the file path of the XML file to be imported.

When you click OK, the Import XML dialog box allows you to determine how the XML data is imported. As you can see here in Figure 17-19, you can choose to import only the XML structure, both the structure and the data, or you can choose to append only the data to an existing table. Since you have already created a table to capture the data, you will select the last option (Append Data to Existing Table).

⊟ Tables
  ⊞ DataEntry

OK

Cancel

Help

Transform...

Import Options
○ Structure Only
○ Structure and Data
⦿ Append Data to Existing Table(s)

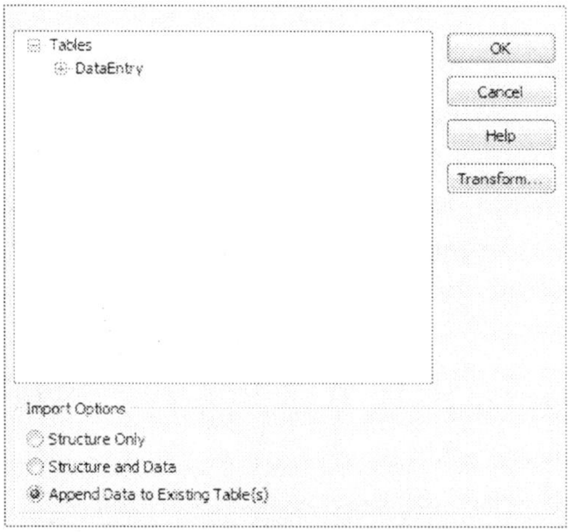

Figure 17-19: Append the data to the existing table DataEntry.

After a few clicks, your DataEntry table is updated with the data from the XML file (Figure 17-19).

Again, no data connections, no MS Query, and no programming are needed. Simply passing XML files between Excel and Access allows you to integrate data between the two programs.

WHERE TO GO FROM HERE

The goal of this chapter is obviously not to make you an expert XML developer. Rather, the goal is to give you a solid understanding of the aspects of XML you'll need to be familiar with when working with XML in Excel and Access.

There are plenty of resources that will expand on the techniques found here. So, if the topic of using XML in your Excel and Access processes has captured your imagination, feel free to search these out.

- www.w3shcools.com: This site gives you some free tutorials on XML and other technologies such as XSD, Xpath, and so on.

- *Powering Office 2003 with XML* (ISBN: 0764541226): Don't let that fact that this book covers Office 2003 deter you. Although the Excel and Access 2007 come with new interfaces, the XML functionality in both these programs remains virtually unchanged. Many of the techniques and exercises found in here work nicely with Office 2007.

Summary

An XML document is little more than a text file that contains data wrapped in tags that denote structure and meaning. These tags essentially make a text file machine-readable, which means that any application designed to read XML files will be able to discern the structure and content of the XML document. Because XML is text-based, XML is not dependent on a specific application for construction, reading, or editing. This versatility makes XML an excellent integration mechanism.

With XML, you can bypass those technologies that you may not feel comfortable with such as MS Query, SQL statements, or ADO. You can incorporate external data into your Excel or Access processes without the need to manage database connectivity or use complex SQL statements.

Despite the anxiety that some people feel about XML, most of the XML functionality built into Excel and Access requires no programming and little knowledge of databases. That is to say, all of the steps you need to create an

XML-based reporting solution can be performed using only the user interfaces that come with Excel and Access. For example, you can open an XML file directly with Excel. Excel will immediately recognize that the file you are opening is an XML document, so it will active the user-friendly Open XML dialog box.

The exercises in this chapter are very basic examples that use only a small fraction of the power of XML. Incorporating a little creative thinking and a handful of code via Macros or VBA will allow you to create relatively robust XML-based processes that integrate Excel and Access quite nicely.

CHAPTER 18

Integrating Excel and Other Office Applications

Every data-oriented process has an application flow, a succession of applications that take the data from creation to end user. Sometimes only one application touches a dataset, such as when you create a report and present it in Excel. In many cases, however, data is moved from a database such as Access, is analyzed and aggregated in Excel, and is then distributed via a Word document, PowerPoint presentation, or even email.

As you know, the focus of this book has been on the integration of Excel and Access. However, it is worth looking at how Excel integrates with some other Office applications. In this chapter, you will do just that, learning how you can integrate Excel with some of the other applications in the Microsoft Office Suite.

NOTE All the code in this chapter is in the Chapter18_SampleFile.xlsm file you downloaded with the sample files for this book.

Integrating Excel with Microsoft Word

It's not unusual to see a Word document that contains a table that originated in Excel. In most cases, that table was simply copied and pasted directly into Word. While this is indeed a valid form of integration, there are countless ways to integrate Excel and Word that go beyond copying and pasting data. This section offers a few examples, demonstrating different techniques you can leverage to integrate Excel and Word.

Creating a Dynamic Link to an Excel Table

How many times have you copied and pasted the same Excel table into Word, only because the data changed? There is a better way. You can create a *dynamic link* to your Excel data, allowing your Word document to pick up changes to the table automatically.

Linking an Excel Table to Word

When you copy and paste a range, you are simply creating a picture of the range. However, when you create a link to a range, Word stores the location information to your source field and then displays a representation of the linked data. The net effect is that when the data in your source file changes, Word updates its representation of the data to reflect the changes. To test this concept of linking to an Excel range, take a moment to walk through an example.

1. Open the Chapter18_SampleFile.xlsm file and go to the Revenue Table tab. Select and copy the range of cells shown here in Figure 18-1.

	A	B	C	D	E
1	Market	SalesPeriod	Revenue	UnitsSold	Dollar Per Unit
2	United States	P01	$519,995.71	1420.00	$366.19
3	United States	P02	$918,489.77	2495.00	$368.13
4	United States	P03	$447,976.91	1237.00	$362.15
5	United States	P04	$111,111.00	1915.00	$58.02
6	United States	P05	$762,330.23	2066.00	$368.99
7	United States	P06	$447,976.91	1420.00	$315.48
8					
9					

Contact List │ Revenue Table │ Side Data

Figure 18-1: Copy your range of cells.

2. Open a Word document and place your cursor where you want to display the linked table. Go up to the Home tab in Word and select Paste ⇨ Paste Special as demonstrated in Figure 18-2.

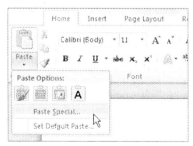

Figure 18-2: Select Paste Special from the Home tab in Word.

3. In the Paste Special dialog box, illustrated in Figure 18-3, select the Paste link option and choose Microsoft Excel Worksheet from the list of document types.

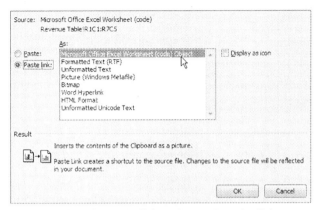

Figure 18-3: Be sure to select the Paste link option and set the link as an Excel Workbook.

4. Click the OK button to apply the link. At this point, you have the table linked to your Excel file (Figure 18-4).

Market	SalesPeriod	Revenue	UnitsSold	Dollar Per Unit
United States	P01	$519,995.71	1420.00	$366.19
United States	P02	$918,489.77	2495.00	$368.13
United States	P03	$447,976.91	1237.00	$362.15
United States	P04	$111,111.00	1915.00	$58.02
United States	P05	$762,330.23	2066.00	$368.99
United States	P06	$447,976.91	1420.00	$315.48

Figure 18-4: Your linked table is ready.

5. Open your Excel file and change some data as demonstrated in Figure 18-5.

	A	B	C	D	E
1	Market	SalesPeriod	Revenue	UnitsSold	Dollar Per Unit
2	United States	P01	$519,995.71	1420.00	$366.19
3	United States	P02	$918,489.77	2495.00	$368.13
4	United States	P03	$447,976.91	1237.00	$362.15
5	United States	P04	$4,444,444.00	1915.00	$2,320.86
6	United States	P05	$762,330.23	2066.00	$368.99
7	United States	P06	$447,976.91	1420.00	$315.48
8					
9					

| ⇤ ◂ ▸ ⇥ | Contact List | Revenue Table | Slide Data |

Figure 18-5: Make changes to the source Excel range.

6. Upon returning to Word, you will see that your linked table automatically captured the changes (see Figure 18-6)!

Market	SalesPeriod	Revenue	UnitsSold	Dollar Per Unit
United States	P01	$519,995.71	1420.00	$366.19
United States	P02	$918,489.77	2495.00	$368.13
United States	P03	$447,976.91	1237.00	$362.15
United States	P04	$4,444,444.00	1915.00	$2,320.86
United States	P05	$762,330.23	2066.00	$368.99
United States	P06	$447,976.91	1420.00	$315.48

Figure 18-6: Word automatically captured the changes.

Preventing the Link from Automatically Updating

Word automatically captured the changes here because both the Word file and the source Excel file were open. Close and save both files and then open Word again. This time you will see the message shown here in Figure 18-7. Clicking the Yes button will refresh the link.

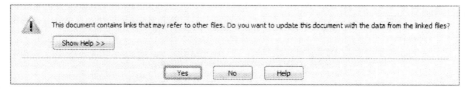

This document contains links that may refer to other files. Do you want to update this document with the data from the linked files?

Show Help >>

Yes   No   Help

Figure 18-7: Click Yes to refresh the link.

There may be situations where getting the message you see in Figure 18-7 is not ideal. For example, if you are distributing this document, you may not want your clients to see this message. Also, you may have a linked table that contains data that doesn't change that often, so there's no need for Word to automatically refresh on every open. In these situations, you may want to specify that you will always refresh the link manually. That is to say, you don't want Word to automatically try to refresh the link:

1. Right-click the linked table and select Linked Worksheet Object ⇨ Links. This activates the Links dialog box illustrated in Figure 18-8.

2. As you can see, the idea here is to choose the target source file from the Source File list and select the Manual update option.

3. To manually refresh the link at any time, simply right click the linked table and select Update Link as demonstrated in Figure 18-9.

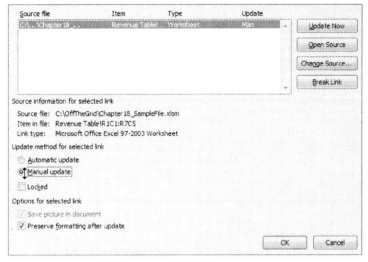

Figure 18-8: Tell Word that you will always refresh manually.

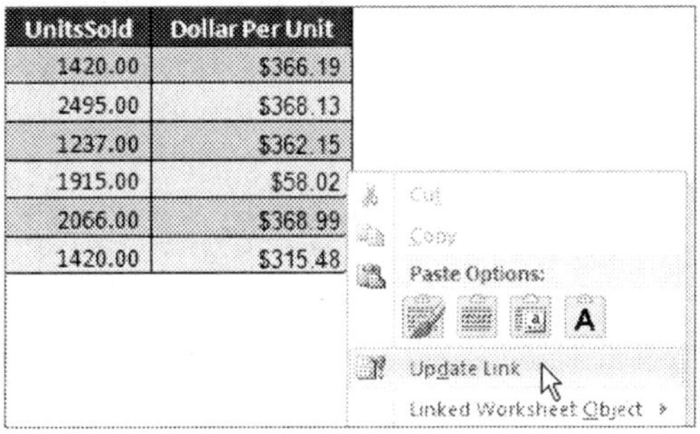

UnitsSold	Dollar Per Unit
1420.00	$366.19
2495.00	$368.13
1237.00	$362.15
1915.00	$58.02
2066.00	$368.99
1420.00	$315.48

Figure 18-9: You can manually refresh the link at any time.

Getting Excel Data to a Word Document Using Automation

If you're more of the automation type, here is an example of how you can copy an Excel range into a Word document. The idea here is that instead of linking a table, you can create your document on the fly.

To set up for a process like this, you must have a template Word document already created. In that document, create a bookmark tagging the location where you want your Excel data to be copied.

To create a bookmark in a Word document, place your cursor where you want the bookmark, select the Insert tab, and select Bookmark (found under the Links group). This activates the Bookmark dialog box, illustrated in Figure 18-10. Here, you assign a name for your bookmark and click the Add button.

Figure 18-10: Name your bookmark and click Add.

In the sample files, you will find a document called PasteTable.docx. This document is a simple template that contains one bookmark called DataTable-Here. In the following example code, you copy a range to that PasteTable.docx template, using the DataTableHere bookmark to specify where to paste the copied range.

> **NOTE** This code is designed to run from Excel. Therefore, you need to set a reference to the Microsoft Word Object Library. To do so, open the Visual Basic Editor in Excel and select Tools ⇨ References. The Reference dialog box will activate. Scroll down until you find the entry "Microsoft Word *XX* Object Library," where the *XX* is your version of Word. Place a check in the checkbox next to the entry.

```
Sub PasteExcelTableIntoWord()

'Step 1:  Declare your variables
    Dim MyRange As Excel.Range
    Dim wd As Word.Application
    Dim wdDoc As Word.Document
    Dim WdRange As Word.Range

'Step 2:  Copy the defined range
    Sheets("Revenue Table").Range("A1:E7").Copy

'Step 3:  Open the target Word document
    Set wd = New Word.Application
    Set wdDoc = wd.Documents.Open("C:\OffTheGrid\PasteTable.docx")
    wd.Visible = True
```

```
'Step 4:  Set focus on the target bookmark
    Set WdRange = wdDoc.Bookmarks("DataTableHere").Range

'Step 5:  Delete the old table and paste new
    On Error Resume Next
    WdRange.Tables(1).Delete
    WdRange.Paste 'paste in the table

'Step 6:  Adjust column widths
    WdRange.Tables(1).Columns.SetWidth _
    (MyRange.Width / MyRange.Columns.Count), wdAdjustSameWidth

'Step 7:  Reinsert the bookmark
    wdDoc.Bookmarks.Add "DataTableHere", WdRange

'Step 8:  Memory cleanup
    Set wd = Nothing
    Set wdDoc = Nothing
    Set WdRange = Nothing

End Sub
```

The following outlines what the steps in the code do:

1. **Declaring the necessary variables:** In Step 1, you first declare four variables:

   ▪ MyRange contains the target Excel range you want copied.

   ▪ wd is an object variable that exposes the Word Application object.

   ▪ wdDoc is an object variable that exposes the Word Document object.

   ▪ wdRange is an object variable that exposes the Word Range object.

2. **Copying the Excel range:** Step 2 copies a range from the Revenue Table worksheet. In this example, the range is hard-coded, but you can always make this range into something more variable.

3. **Opening the target Word document:** In Step 3, you are opening an existing target Word document that will serve as your template. Note that you are setting the Visible property of the Word application to True. This will ensure that you can see the action in Word as the code runs.

4. **Selecting the target bookmark:** In Step 4, you use Word's Range object to set focus on the target bookmark. This essentially selects the bookmark as a range, allowing you to take actions in that range.

5. **Deleting the old table and paste the new table:** In Step 5, you delete any table that may exist within the bookmark; then you paste the copied Excel range. If you don't delete any existing tables first, the copied range will be appended to the existing data.

6. **Adjusting column widths:** When pasting an Excel range in to a Word document, the column widths don't always come out clean. Step 6 fixes this issue by adjusting the column widths. Here, each column's width is set to a number that equals the total width of the table divided by the number of columns in the table.

7. **Reinserting the bookmarks:** When you paste your Excel range to the target bookmark, you essentially overwrite the bookmark. In Step 7, you re-create the bookmark to ensure that the next time you run this code, the bookmark is there.

8. **Cleaning up the open objects:** In Step 8, you release the objects assigned to your variables, reducing the chance of any problems caused by rogue objects that may remain open in memory.

Creating a Word Mail Merge Document

One of the most requested forms of integration with Word is the mail merge. In most cases, *mail merge* refers to the process of creating one letter or document for each customer in a list of customers. For example, suppose you had a list of customers and you wanted to compose a letter to each customer. With mail merge, you can write the body of the letter one time and then run the Mail Merge feature in Word to automatically create a letter for each customer, affixing the appropriate address, name, and other information to each letter.

To create your first mail-merge process, walk through this next example.

1. Although it's not necessary, it's typically a good idea to create a template for your mail merge document. Creating a *template* beforehand allows you take some time in constructing and formatting your letter or document. Figure 18-11 shows the MyTemplate.docx file found in the sample files for this book. Open this file.

2. Click the Mailings tab in Word and click Select Recipients ⇨ Use Existing List (Figure 18-12). This activates a dialog box asking you to select your data source. Find and open C:\OffTheGrid\MyContacts.xlsx.

3. Once you open an existing list of resources, you see the dialog box illustrated in Figure 18-13. The most notable aspect of this step is that you can specify whether the file you are using as your list of recipients has a header row. That is to say, the first row of the dataset is dedicated to column headers.

Allow me to personally thank you for expressing interest in our services. In response to your inquiry, we have provided a list of our product offerings along with an initial quote. I'm confident you will find our pricing to be extremely competitive.

Product Number	Product Description	Quote
16000	Facility Maintenance and Repair	$132.58
30300	Fleet Maintenance	$169.92
70700	Predictive Maintenance/Preventative Maintenance	$220.20
81150	Cleaning & Housekeeping Services	$581.62
87000	Landscaping/Grounds Care	$232.52
90830	Green Plants and Foliage Care	$189.52

Feel free to contact me with any questions you may have. I am very much looking forward to working, and hope to hear from you soon.

Kind Regards,

Mike Alexander
Managing Director,
Zalexcorp Integrated Facility Services

Figure 18-11: Open your document template.

Figure 18-12: Specify the location of your list of recipients.

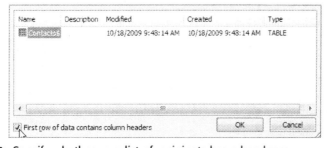

Figure 18-13: Specify whether your list of recipients has a header row.

4. Go back to the Mailings tab in Word and select the Address Block command button (found under the Write & Insert Fields group). This activates the dialog box shown here in Figure 18-14. Here, you specify how you want your address block to be compiled. Word takes all the components that make up an address and compiles them into a standard address format. Word typically does a good job at getting this right the first time; however, you can configure the address block if needed.

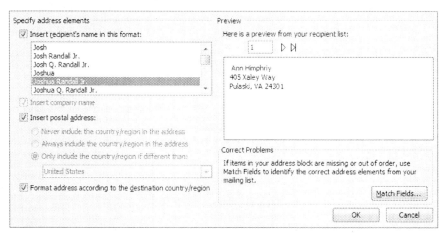

Figure 18-14: Configure the format of the address block.

5. At this point, you will see a marker in your document called Address Block (Figure 18-15). You can move this tag to the most appropriate location.

«AddressBlock»

Allow me to personally thank you for expressing interest in our services. In response to your inquiry, we have provided a list of our product offerings along with an initial quote. I'm confident you will find our pricing to be extremely competitive.

Product Number	Product Description	Quote
16000	Facility Maintenance and Repair	$132.58
30300	Fleet Maintenance	$169.92
70700	Predictive Maintenance/Preventative Maintenance	$220.20
81150	Cleaning & Housekeeping Services	$581.62
87000	Landscaping/Grounds Care	$232.52
90830	Green Plants and Foliage Care	$189.52

Figure 18-15: An address block marker defines where the address block is placed.

6. Go back to the Mailings tab in Word and select the Greeting Line command button (you can find this under the Write & Insert Field group). This activates the dialog box shown here in Figure 18-16. Here, you specify how you want your greetings to be configured.

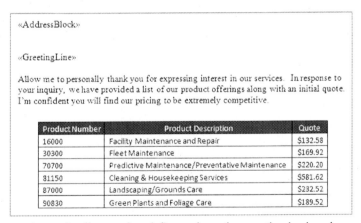

Figure 18-16: Configure the format of the greeting line.

7. At this point, you will see an additional marker in your document called Greeting Line (Figure 18-17). Again, you can move this tag to the location that is most appropriate.

«AddressBlock»

«GreetingLine»

Allow me to personally thank you for expressing interest in our services. In response to your inquiry, we have provided a list of our product offerings along with an initial quote. I'm confident you will find our pricing to be extremely competitive.

Product Number	Product Description	Quote
16000	Facility Maintenance and Repair	$132.58
30300	Fleet Maintenance	$169.92
70700	Predictive Maintenance/Preventative Maintenance	$220.20
81150	Cleaning & Housekeeping Services	$581.62
87000	Landscaping/Grounds Care	$232.52
90830	Green Plants and Foliage Care	$189.52

Figure 18-17: A greeting line marker defines where the greeting is placed.

8. Go back to the Mailings tab and select the Finish and Merge command button (Figure 18-18). As you can see, you can choose to edit the documents, print the documents, or send each document via email. In this case, select Edit Individual Documents.

Figure 18-18: Activate the mail merge and choose to edit the documents.

9. After you indicated the records you want, you'll see a set of Word documents that contain your original template with personalized contact information for each person in your Excel contacts list (Figure 18-19).

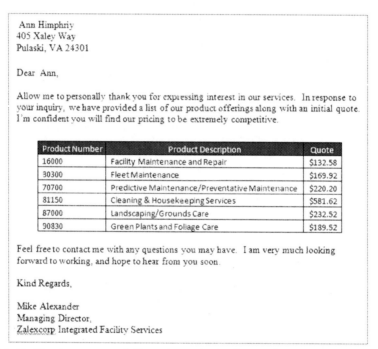

Ann Himphriy
405 Xaley Way
Pulaski, VA 24301

Dear Ann,

Allow me to personally thank you for expressing interest in our services. In response to your inquiry, we have provided a list of our product offerings along with an initial quote. I'm confident you will find our pricing to be extremely competitive.

Product Number	Product Description	Quote
16000	Facility Maintenance and Repair	$132.58
30300	Fleet Maintenance	$169.92
70700	Predictive Maintenance/Preventative Maintenance	$220.20
81150	Cleaning & Housekeeping Services	$581.62
87000	Landscaping/Grounds Care	$232.52
90830	Green Plants and Foliage Care	$189.52

Feel free to contact me with any questions you may have. I am very much looking forward to working, and hope to hear from you soon.

Kind Regards,

Mike Alexander
Managing Director,
Zalexcorp Integrated Facility Services

Figure 18-19: You have successfully performed your first mail merge!

Simulating the Word Mail Merge Function from Excel

For you automation buffs, you can also simulate the Word Mail Merge function from Excel. The idea is relatively simple. You start with a template that contains bookmarks identifying where each element of contact information will go.

NOTE You can open the MailMerge.docx document (found in the sample files for this book) to take a peek at the template. However, you'll have to open the Chapter18_SampleFile.xlsm file to run the code example demonstrated here.

With the template set to go, the idea for the following code is to simply loop through each contact in your contact list, assigning the component pieces of their contact information to the respective bookmarks.

```
Private Sub MailMergeWithExcel()

'Step 1:  Declare your variables
    Dim wd As Word.Application
    Dim wdDoc As Word.Document
    Dim MyRange As Excel.Range
    Dim MyCell As Excel.Range
    Dim txtAddress As String
    Dim txtCity As String
    Dim txtState As String
    Dim txtPostalCode As String
    Dim txtFname As String
    Dim txtFullname As String

'Step 2:  Start Word and add a new document
    Set wd = New Word.Application
    Set wdDoc = wd.Documents.Add
    wd.Visible = True

'Step 3:  Set the range of your contact list
    Set MyRange = Sheets("Contact List").Range("A2:A21")

'Step 4:  Start the loop through each cell
    For Each MyCell In MyRange.Cells

'Step 5:  Assign values to each component of the letter
    txtAddress = MyCell.Value
    txtCity = MyCell.Offset(, 1).Value
    txtState = MyCell.Offset(, 2).Value
    txtPostalCode = MyCell.Offset(, 3).Value
    txtFname = MyCell.Offset(, 5).Value
    txtFullname = MyCell.Offset(, 6).Value

'Step 6:Insert the structure of your template document
    wd.Selection.InsertFile "C:\OffTheGrid\MailMerge.docx"

'Step 7:  Fill each relevant bookmark with its respective value
    wd.Selection.Goto What:=wdGoToBookmark, Name:="Customer"
    wd.Selection.TypeText Text:=txtFullname
```

```
    wd.Selection.Goto What:=wdGoToBookmark, Name:="Address"
    wd.Selection.TypeText Text:=txtAddress

    wd.Selection.Goto What:=wdGoToBookmark, Name:="City"
    wd.Selection.TypeText Text:=txtCity

    wd.Selection.Goto What:=wdGoToBookmark, Name:="State"
    wd.Selection.TypeText Text:=txtState

    wd.Selection.Goto What:=wdGoToBookmark, Name:="Zip"
    wd.Selection.TypeText Text:=txtPostalCode

    wd.Selection.Goto What:=wdGoToBookmark, Name:="FirstName"
    wd.Selection.TypeText Text:=txtFname

'Step 8:  Clear any remaining bookmarks
    On Error Resume Next
    wdDoc.Bookmarks("Address").Delete
    wdDoc.Bookmarks("Customer").Delete
    wdDoc.Bookmarks("City").Delete
    wdDoc.Bookmarks("State").Delete
    wdDoc.Bookmarks("FirstName").Delete
    wdDoc.Bookmarks("Zip").Delete
    On Error GoTo 0
'Step 9:  Go to the end, insert new page, and start with the next cell
    wd.Selection.EndKey Unit:=wdStory
    wd.Selection.InsertBreak Type:=wdPageBreak
    Next MyCell

'Step 10:  Set cursor to beginning and clean up memory
    wd.Selection.HomeKey Unit:=wdStory
    wd.Activate
    Set wd = Nothing
    Set wdDoc = Nothing

End Sub
```

The following outlines what the steps in the code do:

1. **Declaring the necessary variables:** In Step 1, you first declare four variables:

   ▪ wd is an object variable that exposes the Word Application object.

   ▪ wdDoc is an object variable that exposes the Word Document object.

   ▪ MyRange contains the range defining the contact list.

   ▪ MyCell passes cell values into the string variables.

   Then you declare six string variables. Each of the string variables will hold a component piece of information for each contact in the contact list.

2. **Opening Word and starting a new document:** Step 2 opens Word with a blank document. Note that you're setting the `Visible` property of the Word application to `True`. This ensures that you can see the action in Word as the code runs.

3. **Setting the range of the contact list:** Step 3 defines each contact in the contact list. Note that this range only selects the first column in the contacts table. This is because each cell in the range must be passed individually to string variables. Selecting only the first column gives you one cell per row. From that one cell, you can easily adjust your cursor to the right or left to capture the cells around it. The idea is that if you move to the right one space, you get the value of the next field in that row. If you move to the right two spaces, you get the value of that field, and so on.

4. **Starting looping through each contact:** Step 4 starts the loop through each contact as defined in the range set in Step 3.

5. **Assigning values to each component piece of the contact's information:** In Step 5, you use Excel's `Offset` method to capture the value of each field in a particular row. You start with the range defined in Step 3 (the first column in the list of contacts). You then use `Offset` to move your cursor a certain number of columns to the right to capture the data each relevant field. As each field is covered, you assign their values to the appropriate string variable.

6. **Inserting the structure of your template:** In Step 6, you insert your existing template into the empty document in Word. This is tantamount to copying the structure of your template and pasting it into a blank document.

7. **Assigning values to the bookmarks:** In Step 7, you assign the value of each string variable to its respective bookmark. As you can see in the code, you simply select the bookmark by name, and then change the text to equal the value of the assigned string variable.

8. **Deleting bookmarks:** The goal in Step 8 is to remove any stray bookmarks. If any bookmarks linger, you will get duplicate bookmarks as the procedure loops through each cell.

9. **Inserting a new document and looping to next contact:** At this point in the code, you have created a document for one contact in your list of contacts. The idea now is to create a new blank document so that you can perform the same procedure for the next contact.

   Inserting a page break effectively creates the blank document. You then loop back to Step 5 where you pick up the contact information for the next row in the list. Then at Step 6, you insert the blank template (complete with bookmarks) into the new page. Finally, you assign values to the bookmarks and clean up. The `For...Next` loop ensures that this cycle is repeated for each row in your contact list

10. **Cleaning up the open objects:** In Step 10, you release the objects assigned to your variables, reducing the chance of any problems caused by rogue objects that may remain open in memory.

Integrating Excel with PowerPoint

It's been said that up to 50 percent of PowerPoint presentations contain data that has been copied straight out of Excel. This is not difficult to believe. It's often much easier to analyze and create charts and data views in Excel than in PowerPoint. Once you create those charts and data views, why *wouldn't* you simply copy them into PowerPoint? The time and effort saved by copying directly from Excel is too good to pass up.

This section offers up a few techniques that can help you automate the process of getting your Excel data into PowerPoint.

Creating a PowerPoint Slide with a Title

To help get a few fundamentals down, let's start simple and automate the creation of a PowerPoint presentation containing one slide with a title. The idea here is that you place this code into an Excel module and run it directly from Excel.

NOTE Keep in mind that because this code is run from Excel, you need to set a reference to the Microsoft PowerPoint Object Library. Again, you can set the reference by opening the Visual Basic Editor in Excel and selecting Tools ⇨ References. Scroll down until you find the entry "Microsoft PowerPoint *XX* Object Library," where the *XX* is your version of PowerPoint. Place a check in the checkbox next to the entry.

```
Sub CreatePowerPointSlideWithTitle()

  'Step 1:  Declare variables
     Dim PP As PowerPoint.Application
     Dim PPPres As PowerPoint.Presentation
     Dim PPSlide As PowerPoint.Slide
     Dim SlideTitle As String

  'Step 2:  Open PowerPoint and create new presentation
     Set PP = New PowerPoint.Application
```

```
    Set PPPres = PP.Presentations.Add
    PP.Visible = True

'Step 3:  Add new slide as slide 1 and set focus to it
    Set PPSlide = PPPres.Slides.Add(1, ppLayoutTitleOnly)
    PPSlide.Select

'Step 4:  Add the title to the slide
    SlideTitle = "My First PowerPoint Slide"
    PPSlide.Shapes.Title.TextFrame.TextRange.Text = SlideTitle

'Step 5:  See the presentation
    PP.Activate

'Step 6:  Memory Cleanup
    Set PPSlide = Nothing
    Set PPPres = Nothing
    Set PP = Nothing

End sub
```

The following outlines what the steps in the code do:

1. **Declaring the necessary variables:** In Step 1, you first declare four variables:

   - PP is an object variable that exposes the PowerPoint Application object.

   - PPPres is an object variable that exposes the PowerPoint Presentation object.

   - PPSlide is an object variable that exposes the PowerPoint Slide object.

   - SlideTitle is a string variable used to pass the text for the slide title.

2. **Opening PowerPoint and start a new presentation:** Step 2 opens PowerPoint with an empty presentation. Note that you are setting the Visible property of the PowerPoint application to True. This ensures that you can see the action as the code runs.

3. **Adding a new slide:** In Step 3, you add a new slide to the presentation using the Add method of Slide object. Notice that when you add a new slide, you'll need to provide two arguments: the index number for the slide and the layout option for the slide. Since this is the first slide in the presentation, the index number is 1. The default layout option allows you to specify which one of PowerPoint's many layout options you want to apply to your slide. When you're automating PowerPoint, it's generally best to use either ppLayoutTitleOnly (when you want a title in your presentation) or ppLayoutBlank (when you don't need a title in your presentation).

4. **Adding the title to the slide:** In Step 4, you store the text for the title in a string variable and pass that variable to PowerPoint to apply text to the title text frame.

5. **Saving the presentation:** Step 5 uses the `Activate` method to set the focus on PowerPoint, ensuring that is comes into view when the code is done running.

6. **Cleaning up the open objects:** In Step 6, you release the objects assigned to your variables, reducing the chance of any problems caused by rogue objects that may remain open in memory.

Copying a Range of Cells to a Presentation

Now that you have a good sense of the basic code that creates a PowerPoint presentation, you should try adding some utility and actually copy a range from Excel into a PowerPoint presentation. In the following code, you copy a range from the Chapter18_SampleFile.xlsm file and paste that range to a slide in a newly created PowerPoint presentation.

```
Sub CopyRangeToPresentation ()

'Step 1:  Declare your variables
    Dim PP As PowerPoint.Application
    Dim PPPres As PowerPoint.Presentation
    Dim PPSlide As PowerPoint.Slide
    Dim SlideTitle As String

'Step 2:  Open PowerPoint and create new presentation
    Set PP = New PowerPoint.Application
    Set PPPres = PP.Presentations.Add
    PP.Visible = True

'Step 3:  Add new slide as slide 1 and set focus to it
    Set PPSlide = PPPres.Slides.Add(1, ppLayoutTitleOnly)
    PPSlide.Select

'Step 4:  Copy the range as a picture
    Sheets("Slide Data").Range("A1:J28").CopyPicture _
    Appearance:=xlScreen, Format:=xlPicture

'Step 5:  Paste the picture and adjust its position
    PPSlide.Shapes.Paste.Select
    PP.ActiveWindow.Selection.ShapeRange.Align msoAlignCenters, True
    PP.ActiveWindow.Selection.ShapeRange.Align msoAlignMiddles, True

'Step 6:  Add the title to the slide
```

```
        SlideTitle = "My First PowerPoint Slide"
        PPSlide.Shapes.Title.TextFrame.TextRange.Text = SlideTitle

    'Step 7:  Memory Cleanup
        PP.Activate
        Set PPSlide = Nothing
        Set PPPres = Nothing
        Set PP = Nothing


    End sub
```

1. **Declaring the necessary variables:** In Step 1, you first declare four variables:

   - PP is an object variable that exposes the PowerPoint Application object.

   - PPPres is an object variable that exposes the PowerPoint Presentation object.

   - PPSlide is an object variable that exposes the PowerPoint Slide object.

   - SlideTitle is a string variable that passes the text for the slide title.

2. **Opening PowerPoint and start a new presentation:** Step 2 opens Power-Point with an empty presentation. Note that you're setting the Visible property of the PowerPoint application to True. This ensures that you can see the action as the code runs.

3. **Adding a new slide and setting focus to it:** In Step 3, you add a new slide to the presentation using the Add method of Slide object. Note that you're using the ppLayoutTitleOnly attribute, ensuring your slide is created with a title text frame. You then take an extra step here and actually set focus on the slide. That is to say, you explicitly tell PowerPoint to select this slide, making it active.

4. **Copying your range as a picture:** In Step 4, use the CopyPicture method to copy the target range as a picture. The range you're copying here is A1 to J28 in the Slide Data tab.

5. **Pasting the picture into the presentation:** Step 5 pastes the picture into the active slide and centers the picture both horizontally and vertically.

6. **Adding the title to the slide:** In Step 6, you store the text for the title in a string variable and then pass that variable to PowerPoint to apply text to the title text frame.

7. **Cleaning up the open objects:** In Step 7, you release the objects assigned to your variables, reducing the chance of any problems caused by rogue objects that may remain open in memory.

Sending All Excel Charts to the Presentation

It's not uncommon to see multiple charts on one worksheet. For example, open the `Chapter18_SampleFile.xlsm` sample file and go to the Slide Data tab. There, you will see a worksheet that contains multiple charts, one for each Region. The idea here is that you can automate the process of copying each one of these charts into its own slide.

The example code that follows does just that. In this code, you loop through each chart in the specified worksheet, copying each and pasting it into its own slide in PowerPoint.

```
Sub CopyAllChartsToPresentation()

'Step 1:  Declare your variables
    Dim PP As PowerPoint.Application
    Dim PPPres As PowerPoint.Presentation
    Dim PPSlide As PowerPoint.Slide
    Dim PPSlideCount As Long
    Dim i As Integer

'Step 2:  Check for charts; exit if no charts exist
    Sheets("Slide Data").Select
    If ActiveSheet.ChartObjects.Count < 1 Then
    MsgBox "No charts existing the active sheet"
    Exit Sub
    End If

'Step 3:  Open PowerPoint and create new presentation
    Set PP = New PowerPoint.Application
    Set PPPres = PP.Presentations.Add
    PP.Visible = True

'Step 4:  Start the loop based on chart count
    For i = 1 To ActiveSheet.ChartObjects.Count

'Step 5:  Copy the chart as a picture
    ActiveSheet.ChartObjects(i).Chart.CopyPicture _
    Size:=xlScreen, Format:=xlPicture
    Application.Wait (Now + TimeValue("0:00:1"))

'Step 6:  Count slides and add new slide as next available slide number
    PPSlideCount = PPPres.Slides.Count
    Set PPSlide = PPPres.Slides.Add(PPSlideCount + 1, ppLayoutBlank)
    PPSlide.Select

'Step 7:  Paste the picture and adjust its position; Go to next chart
    PPSlide.Shapes.Paste.Select
    PP.ActiveWindow.Selection.ShapeRange.Align msoAlignCenters, True
```

```
      PP.ActiveWindow.Selection.ShapeRange.Align msoAlignMiddles, True
      Next i

'Step 8:  Memory Cleanup
      Set PPSlide = Nothing
      Set PPPres = Nothing
      Set PP = Nothing

End Sub
```

The following outlines what the steps in the code do:

1. **Declaring the necessary variables:** In Step 1, you first declare four variables:

   - PP is an object variable that exposes the PowerPoint Application object.

   - PPPres is an object variable that exposes the PowerPoint Presentation object.

   - PPSlide is an object variable that exposes the PowerPoint Slide object.

   - PPSlideCount is numeric variable that helps keep track of which slide is the target slide. i is a counter to help loop through the charts in the worksheet.

2. **Checking for charts:** Step 2 is an administrative check to ensure there are actually charts in the specified worksheet. If no charts are found, you exit the procedure with no further action.

3. **Opening PowerPoint and starting a new presentation:** Step 3 opens PowerPoint with an empty presentation. Note that you're setting the Visible property of the PowerPoint application to True. This ensures that you can see the action as the code runs.

4. **Starting looping through the charts:** In Step 4, you establish how many times you will loop through the procedure by capturing the number of charts in the worksheet. In other words, if you have five charts in the worksheet, you loop five times. You start the loop with 1 and keep looping through the procedure until you hit the number of charts in the worksheet. The variable i ultimately represents the chart number you are currently on.

5. **Copying your chart as a picture:** In Step 5, use the CopyPicture method to copy the chart as a picture. The variable i passes the actual chart number you are currently working with. The Application.Wait method, here, tells the macro to pause for a second, allowing the clipboard to catch up with all the copying going on.

6. **Count the slides and adding a new slide at the next available index:**
   In Step 6, you add a new slide to the presentation using the `Add` method
   of the `Slide` object. You will notice that you are using `SlideCount+1` to
   specify the index number of the added slide. Because you are looping
   through an unknown number of charts, you can't hard-code the index
   number for each slide. Using `SlideCount+1` allows you to dynamically
   assign the next available number as the slide index.

   Also note that you are using `ppLayoutBlank`, which ensures that the
   newly created slides start with a blank layout. You then take an extra step
   here and actually set focus on the slide. That is to say, you explicitly tell
   PowerPoint to select this slide, making it active.

7. **Pasting the chart into the presentation and moving to next chart:**
   Step 7 pastes the picture into the active slide, centers the picture both
   horizontally and vertically and then moves to the next chart.

8. **Cleaning up the open objects:** In Step 8, you release the objects assigned
   to your variables, reducing the chance of any problems caused by rouge
   objects that may remain open in memory.

Converting a Workbook into a PowerPoint Presentation

This last example takes the concept of using Excel data in PowerPoint to the
extreme. Open the sample workbook called `WorkbooktoPowerpoint.xlsm`. In
this workbook, you notice that each worksheet contains its own data about a
region—almost like each worksheet has its own separate slide, which provides
information on a particular region.

The idea here is that you can build a workbook in such a way that it mimics
a PowerPoint presentation; the workbook is the presentation itself and each
worksheet becomes a slide in the presentation. Once you do that, you can
easily convert that workbook into an actual PowerPoint presentation using a
bit of automation.

With this technique, you can build entire presentations in Excel where you
have better analytical and automation tools. Then you can simply convert the
Excel version of your presentation to a PowerPoint presentation.

The following code will convert the sheets of an Excel workbook to a
PowerPoint presentation.

```
Sub WorkbooktoPowerPoint()

'Step 1:  Declare your variables
    Dim pp As PowerPoint.Application
    Dim PPPres As PowerPoint.Presentation
    Dim PPSlide As PowerPoint.Slide
    Dim xlwksht As Excel.Worksheet
```

```
        Dim MyRange As String
        Dim MyTitle As String
        Dim Slidecount As Long


 'Step 2:  Open PowerPoint, add a new presentation and make visible
        Set pp = New PowerPoint.Application
        Set PPPres = pp.Presentations.Add
        pp.Visible = True


 'Step 3:  Set the ranges for your data and title
        MyRange = "A1:I27"

 'Step 4:  Start the loop through each worksheet
        For Each xlwksht In ActiveWorkbook.Worksheets
        xlwksht.Select
        Application.Wait (Now + TimeValue("0:00:1"))
        MyTitle = xlwksht.Range("20").Value

 'Step 5:  Copy the range as picture
        xlwksht.Range(MyRange).CopyPicture _
        Appearance:=xlScreen, Format:=xlPicture

 'Step 6:  Count slides and add new slide as next available slide number
        SlideCount = PPPres.Slides.Count
        Set PPSlide = PPPres.Slides.Add(SlideCount + 1, ppLayoutTitleOnly)
        PPSlide.Select

 'Step 7:  Paste the picture and adjust its position
        PPSlide.Shapes.Paste.Select
        pp.ActiveWindow.Selection.ShapeRange.Align msoAlignCenters, True
        pp.ActiveWindow.Selection.ShapeRange.Top = 100

 'Step 8:  Add the title to the slide then move to next worksheet
        PPSlide.Shapes.Title.TextFrame.TextRange.Text = MyTitle
        Next xlwksht

 'Step 9:  Memory Cleanup
        pp.Activate
        Set PPSlide = Nothing
        Set PPPres = Nothing
        Set pp = Nothing


 End Sub
```

The following outlines what the steps in the code do:

1. **Declaring the necessary variables:** In Step 1, you first declare six variables:

   ▪ PP is an object variable that exposes the PowerPoint Application object.

- PPPres is an object variable that exposes the PowerPoint Presentation object.

- PPSlide is an object variable that exposes the PowerPoint Slide object.

- xlwksht is an object variable that exposes the Worksheet object.

- MyRange is a string variable that stores and passes a range name as a string.

- MyTitle is a string variable that stores and passes a title for each slide.

- PPSlideCount is numeric variable that helps keep track of which slide is the target slide.

2. **Opening PowerPoint and start a new presentation:** Step 2 opens Power-Point with an empty presentation. Note that you're setting the Visible property of the PowerPoint application to True. This ensures that you can see the action as the code runs.

3. **Setting the ranges for your data and title:** In Step 3, fill the MyRange variable with a string representing the range you want to capture as the slide content.

4. **Starting a loop through the charts:** In Step 4, you start the loop through each worksheet in the workbook. The loop stops when all worksheets have been looped through. Note that you're using the Application.Wait method, telling the macro to pause for a second. This allows the chart to render completely before the range is copied. While you loop, you fill the MyTitle variable with the value of cell C20. This value becomes the title for the slide.

5. **Copying your range as a picture:** In Step 5, use the CopyPicture method to copy your specified range as a picture.

6. **Count the slides and add a new slide at the next available index:** In Step 6, you add a new slide to the presentation using the Add method of the Slide object. Notice that you are using SlideCount+1 to specify the index number of the added slide. Using SlideCount+1 allows you to dynamically assign the next available number as the slide index. Note that you are using the ppLayoutTitleOnly, ensuring your slide is created with a title text frame.

7. **Pasting the chart into the presentation and moving to next chart:** Step 7 pastes the picture into the active slide, centers the picture horizontally, and adjusts the picture vertically 100 pixels from the top margin.

8. **Adding the title to the slide:** Step 8 passes the MyTitle variable to apply text to the title text frame.

9. **Cleaning up the open objects:** In Step 9, you release the objects assigned to your variables, reducing the chance of any problems caused by rogue objects that may remain open in memory.

Integrating Excel and Outlook

Did you know that you integrate Excel and Outlook every day? It's true. If you sent or received an Excel workbook through Outlook, you've integrated the two programs, albeit manually. In this section, you will discover a few examples of how to integrate Excel and Outlook in a more automated fashion.

Mailing the Active Workbook

The most fundamental Outlook task you can perform through automation is sending an email. In the example that follows code, the active workbook is sent to two email recipients as an attachment.

NOTE Keep in mind that because this code is run from Excel, you need to set a reference to the Microsoft Outlook Object Library. Again, you can set the reference by opening the Visual Basic Editor in Excel and selecting Tools ➪ References. Scroll down until you find the entry "Microsoft Outlook *XX* Object Library," where the *XX* is your version of Outlook. Place a check in the checkbox next to the entry.

```
Sub Mail_workbook_Outlook()
'Step 1:  Declare your variables
    Dim OLApp As Outlook.Application
    Dim OLMail As Object

'Step 2:  Open Outlook start a new mail item
    Set OLApp = New Outlook.Application
    Set OLMail = OLApp.CreateItem(0)
    OLApp.Session.Logon

'Step 3:  Build your mail item and send
    With OLMail
    .To = "admin@datapigtechnologies.com; mike@datapigtechnologies.com"
    .CC = ""
    .BCC = ""
    .Subject = "This is the Subject line"
    .Body = "Hi there"
    .Attachments.Add ActiveWorkbook.Fullname
    .Send
    End With
```

```
'Step 4:  Memory cleanup
    Set OLMail = Nothing
    Set OLApp = Nothing

End Sub
```

The following outlines what the steps in the code do:

1. **Declaring the necessary variables:** In Step 1, you first declare two variables:

   - `OLApp` is an object variable that exposes the Outlook `Application` object.

   - `OLMail` is an object variable that holds a mail item.

2. **Open Outlook and start a new session:** In Step 2, you activate Outlook and start a new session. Note that you'll use OLApp.Session.Logon to log on to the current MAPI session with default credentials. You also create a mail item. This is equivalent to selecting the New Message button in Outlook.

3. **Build your mail item and send:** In Step 3, you build the profile of your mail item. This includes the `To` recipients, the `CC` recipients, the `BCC` recipients, the `Subject`, the `Body`, and the `Attachments`. Note that you enter the recipients in quotes, and you separate recipients using a semicolon.

   The standard syntax for an attachment is as follows:

   ```
   .Attachments.Add "File Path"
   ```

   Here, in the previous code, you specify the current workbook's file path with the syntax: `ActiveWorkbook.Fullname`. This sets the current workbook as the attachment for the email. When the message is built, you use the `Send` method to send the email.

4. **Clean up the open objects:** It is generally good practice to release the objects assigned to your variables. This reduces the chance of any problems caused by rogue objects that may remain open in memory. As you can see in the code, you simply set variable to `Nothing`.

> **NOTE** Your workbook must be saved before running the preceding code. You cannot attach an unsaved workbook to an email.

Mailing a Specific Range

You can imagine that you may not always want to send your entire workbook through email. The following example code demonstrates how you would send a specific range of data rather than the entire workbook.

```
Sub Mail_Range()
'Step 1:  Declare your variables
    Dim OLApp As Outlook.Application
    Dim OLMail As Object

'Step 2:  Copy range, paste to new workbook, and save it
    Sheets("Revenue Table").Range("A1:K50").Copy
    Workbooks.Add
    Range("A1").PasteSpecial xlPasteValues
    Range("A1").PasteSpecial xlPasteFormats
    ActiveWorkbook.SaveAs "C:\OffTheGrid\Excel_to_be_Mailed.xls"

'Step 3:  Open Outlook start a new mail item
    Set OLApp = New Outlook.Application
    Set OLMail = OLApp.CreateItem(0)
    OLApp.Session.Logon

'Step 4:  Build your mail item and send
    With OLMail
    .To = "admin@datapigtechnologies.com; mike@datapigtechnologies.com"
    .CC = ""
    .BCC = ""
    .Subject = "This is the Subject line"
    .Body = "Hi there"
    .Attachments.Add ("C:\OffTheGrid\Excel_to_be_Mailed.xls")
    .Send
    End With

'Step 5:  Delete the temporary Excel file
    ActiveWorkbook.Close SaveChanges:=True
    Kill "C:\Excel_to_be_Mailed.xls"

'Step 6:  Memory cleanup
    Set OLMail = Nothing
    Set OLApp = Nothing

End Sub
```

The following outlines what the steps in the code do:

1. **Declaring the necessary variables:** In Step 1, you first declare two variables:

   ▪ OLApp is an object variable that exposes the Outlook Application object.

   ▪ OLMail.is an object variable that holds a mail item.

2. **Copy the desired range to a temporary Excel file:** In Step 2, you copy a specified range and paste the values and formats to a temporary Excel file. You then save that temporary file, giving it a file path and file name.

3. **Open Outlook and start a new session:** In Step 3, you activate Outlook and start a new session. Note that you'll use OLApp.Session.Logon to log on to the current MAPI session with default credentials. You'll also create a mail item. This is equivalent to selecting the New Message button in Outlook.

4. **Build your mail item and send:** In Step 4, you build the profile of your mail item. This includes the To recipients, the CC recipients, the BCC recipients, the Subject, the Body, and the Attachments. Note that you enter the recipients in quotes, and you separate recipients using a semicolon.

   Here in Step 4, you specify your newly created temporary Excel file path as the attachment for the email. When the message is built, you use the Send method to send the email.

5. **Delete the temporary Excel file:** You don't want to leave temporary files hanging out there, so once the email has been sent, you delete the temporary Excel file you created.

6. **Clean up the open objects:** It is generally good practice to release the objects assigned to your variables. This reduces the chance of any problems caused by rogue objects that may remain open in memory. As you can see in the code, you simply set variable to Nothing.

Mailing to All Email Addresses in Your Contact List

Ever need to send out a mass mailing such as a newsletter or a memo? Instead of manually entering your contacts' email addresses, you can run the following code. In this code, you send out one email, automatically adding all the email addresses in your contact list to your email.

```
Sub Mail_To_All_Contacts()
'Step 1:  Declare your variables
    Dim OLApp As Outlook.Application
    Dim OLMail As Object
    Dim MyCell As Range
    Dim MyContacts As Range

'Step 2:  Define the range to loop through
    Set MyContacts = Sheets("Contact List").Range("H2:H21")

'Step 3:  Open Outlook
    Set OLApp = New Outlook.Application
    Set OLMail = OLApp.CreateItem(0)
    OLApp.Session.Logon

'Step 4:  Add each address in the contact list
    With OLMail
```

```
        .BCC = " "
         For Each MyCell In MyContacts
            .BCC = .BCC & MyCell.Value & ";"
         Next MyCell
        .Subject = "Chapter 18 Sample Email"
        .Body = "Sample file is attached"
        .Attachments.Add ActiveWorkbook.Fullname
        .Send
    End With

'Step 5:  Memory cleanup
    Set OLMail = Nothing
    Set OLApp = Nothing

End sub
```

The following outlines what the steps in the code do:

1. **Declaring the necessary variables:** In Step 1, you first declare four variables:

   - OLApp is an object variable that exposes the Outlook Application object.

   - OLMail is an object variable that holds a mail item.

   - MyCell is an object variable that holds an Excel range.

   - MyContacts is an object variable that holds an Excel range.

2. **Define the target range:** In Step 2, you point to the MyContacts variable to the range of cells that contains your email addresses. This is the range of cells through which you'll loop to add email addresses to your email.

3. **Open Outlook and start a new session:** In Step 3, you activate outlook and start a new session. Note that you'll use OLApp.Session.Logon to log on to the current MAPI session with default credentials. You'll also create a mail item. This is equivalent to selecting the New Message button in Outlook.

4. **Add each address in your contact list:** In Step 4, you build the profile of your mail item. Note that you loop through each cell in the MyContacts range and add the contents (which are email addresses) to the BCC. Here, you are using the BCC property instead of To or CC so that each recipient gets an email that looks as though it was sent only to him. He will not be able to see the other email addresses, as they have been sent with BCC (Blind Courtesy Copy).

5. **Clean up the open objects:** It is generally good practice to release the objects assigned to your variables. This reduces the chance of any problems caused by rogue objects that may remain open in memory. As you can see in the code, you simply set variable to Nothing.

Saving All Attachments in a Folder

You may often find that certain processes lend themselves to the exchange of data via email. For example, you may send a budget template out for each branch manager to fill out and send back to you via email. Well, if there are 150 branch members, it could be a bit of a pain to bring down all those email attachments.

The code that follows demonstrates one solution to this problem. In this code, you use automation to search for all attachments in your inbox and save them to a specified folder.

```
Sub SaveAttachments()
'Step 1:  Declare your variables
    Dim ns As Namespace
    Dim MyInbox As MAPIFolder
    Dim MItem As MailItem
    Dim Atmt As Attachment
    Dim FileName As String

'Step 2:  Set a reference to your inbox
    Set ns = GetNamespace("MAPI")
    Set MyInbox = ns.GetDefaultFolder(olFolderInbox)

'Step 3:  Check for messages in your inbox; exit if none
    If MyInbox.Items.Count = 0 Then
    MsgBox "No messages in folder."
    Exit Sub
    End If

'Step 4:  Create directory to hold attachments
    On Error Resume Next
    MkDir "C:\OffTheGrid\MyAttachments\"

'Step 5:  Start to loop through each mail item
    For Each MItem In MyInbox.Items

'Step 6:  Save each attachement then go to the next attachment
    For Each Atmt In MItem.Attachments
    FileName = "C:\OffTheGrid\MyAttachments\" & Atmt.FileName
    Atmt.SaveAsFile FileName
    Next Atmt

'Step 7:  Move to the next mail item
    Next MItem
End Sub
```

The following outlines what the steps in the code do:

1. **Declaring the necessary variables:** In Step 1, you first declare five variables:

   - ns is an object that exposes the MAPI namespace.

   - MyInbox exposes the target mail folder.

   - MItem exposes the properties of a mail item.

   - Atmt is an object variable that holds an Attachment object.

   - FileName is a string variable that holds the name of the attachment.

2. **Point to your Inbox:** In Step 2, you set the MyInbox variable to point to the inbox for your default mail client.

3. **Check for messages:** In Step 3, you perform a quick check to make sure there are actually messages in your inbox. If there are no messages, you exit the procedure with a message box telling you there are no messages.

4. **Create directory to hold attachments:** In Step 4, you create a directory to hold the attachments you find. Although you could use an existing directory, it's generally best to use a directory dedicated specifically for the attachments you bring down. Here, you are creating that directory on the fly. Note you are using On Error Resume Next. This ensures the code does not error out if the directory you are trying to create already exists.

5. **Start the loop:** In Step 5, you start the loop through each mail item in the target mail folder.

6. **Loop through all attachments in each mail item:** Step 6 ensures that each mail item you loop through is checked for attachments. As you loop, you will save each attachment you find into the specified directory you created.

7. **Move to next mail item:** Step 7 loops back to Step 5 until there are no more mail items to go through.

8. **Clean up the open objects:** It is generally good practice to release the objects assigned to your variables. This reduces the chance of any problems caused by rogue objects that may remain open in memory. As you can see in the code, you simply set variable to Nothing.

Saving Certain Attachments to a Folder

In the previous procedure, you use automation to search for all attachments in your inbox and save them to a specified folder. However, you'll more likely only want to save certain attachments. That is to say, those attachments attached to emails that contain a certain subject, for example. In the following example code, you get a demonstration of how to check for certain syntax and selectively bring down attachments.

```
Sub SaveCertainAttachments()

'Step 1:  Declare your variables
    Dim ns As Namespace
    Dim MyInbox As MAPIFolder
    Dim MItem As Object
    Dim Atmt As Attachment
    Dim FileName As String
    Dim i As Integer

'Step 2:  Set a reference to your inbox
    Set ns = GetNamespace("MAPI")
    Set MyInbox = ns.GetDefaultFolder(olFolderInbox)

'Step 3:  Check for messages in your inbox; exit if none
    If MyInbox.Items.Count = 0 Then
    MsgBox "No messages in folder."
    Exit Sub
    End If

'Step 4:  Create directory to hold attachments
    On Error Resume Next
    MkDir "C:\OffTheGrid\MyAttachments\"

'Step 5:  Start to loop through each mail item
    For Each MItem In MyInbox.Items

'Step 6:  Check for the words Data Submission in Subject line
    If InStr(1, MItem.Subject, "Data Submission") < 1 Then
    GoTo SkipIt
    End If

'Step 7:  Save each with a log number; go to the next attachment
    i = 0
    For Each Atmt In MItem.Attachments
    FileName = _
    "C:\OffTheGrid\MyAttachments\Attachment-" & i & "-" & Atmt.FileName
    Atmt.SaveAsFile FileName
    i = i + 1
    Next Atmt

'Step 8:  Move to the next mail item
SkipIt:
    Next MItem
```

```
'Step 9:  Memory cleanup
    Set ns = Nothing
    Set MyInbox = Nothing
End Sub
```

The following outlines what the steps in the code do:

1. **Declaring the necessary variables:** In Step 1, you first declare six variables:

   - `ns` is an object that exposes the `MAPI` namespace.
   - `MyInbox` exposes the target mail folder.
   - `MItem` exposes the properties of a mail item.
   - `Atmt` is an object variable that holds an `Attachment` object.
   - `FileName` is a string variable that holds the name of the attachment.
   - `i` is an integer variable that ensures each attachment is saved as a unique name.

2. **Point to your inbox:** In Step 2, you set the `MyInbox` variable to point to the inbox for your default mail client.

3. **Check for messages:** In Step 3, you perform a quick check to make sure there are actually messages in your inbox. If there are no messages, you exit the procedure with a message box telling you there are no messages.

4. **Create directory to hold attachments:** In Step 4, you create a directory to hold the attachments you find. Note you are using `On Error Resume Next`. This ensures the code does not error out if the directory you are trying to create already exists.

5. **Start the loop:** In Step 5, you start the loop through each mail item in the target mail folder.

6. **Check for the correct key words in the Subject line:** In Step 6, you use the `Instr` function to check if the string "Data Submission" is in the Subject line of the email. If that string does not exist, then you are not interested in the attachment there. Therefore, you force the code to go to the `SkipIt` reference (in Step 8). Because the line of code immediately following the `SkipIt` reference is essentially a "move next" command, this has the effect of telling the procedure to move to the next mail item.

7. **Loop through all attachments in each mail item:** Step 7 loops through all the attachments and saves each one into the specified directory you created. Note that you are adding a running integer to the name of each attachment. This is to ensure that each attachment is saved as a unique name, helping you to avoid overwriting attachments.

8. **Move to next mail item:** Step 8 loops back to Step 5 until there are no more mail items to go through.

9. **Clean up the open objects:** It is generally good practice to release the objects assigned to your variables. This reduces the chance of any problems caused by rogue objects that may remain open in memory. As you can see in the code, you simply set the variable to `Nothing`.

Summary

Excel data has a way of touching every application in the Office suite. Excel data is often distributed via a Word document, displayed through a PowerPoint presentation and even shared using Outlook. Although Access is the most well suited to integrate with Excel, these other Office applications also have the ability to integrate with Excel. You can use Excel and Word to create a Mail Merge document. You can automate the creation of an entire PowerPoint presentation directly from an Excel workbook. You can send mass emails through outlook, using nothing more than a list of email addresses in Excel. Use the techniques you learned in this chapter to think about some of the ways you can integrate Excel with the other applications in Office.

Part

VI

Appendixes

In This Part

Access VBA Fundamentals

If you haven't worked much with VBA, you may want to brush up on some of the basics before tackling the later chapters in this book (Chapters 14–18). The purpose of this appendix is to provide a high-level overview of some of the fundamental concepts and techniques demonstrated in the latter chapters. Bear in mind that because the focus of this book is data analysis, this appendix provides only an introductory look at VBA. If you are interested in an in-depth look at programming Access VBA, consider picking up one of the following titles:

Beginning Access 2007 VBA, by Denise Gosnell (ISBN: 0-470-04684-8)

Access 2007 VBA Programming For Dummies, by Alan Simpson (ISBN: 0-470-04653-8)

These books offer a solid introduction to VBA that is ideal for novice Access programmers.

Covering the Basics in 10 Steps

There is no better way to learn than hands-on experience. So instead of reading paragraph after paragraph of terms and definitions, you will cover some of the basics of VBA in 10 steps!

Step 1: Creating a Standard Module

Have you ever found code on the Internet that you could supposedly copy and paste into Access to do something wonderful, but you didn't know where to paste it? Well, knowing where to put your code is the first step in programming. In Access, VBA code is contained in a *module*.

Here are the types of modules you can use:

- **Standard Modules:** This type is the most common, letting you store code you can use anywhere within your database.

- **Form and Report Modules:** These types of modules store code that you can only use within the form or report to which they belong.

- **Class Modules:** These modules are for hardcore programmers who want to create and define their own custom objects.

To create a module, do the following:

1. Start a new standard module by going to the application ribbon and selecting the Create tab.

2. From there, select the Macro dropdown menu, and then select Module if you are using Access 2007. If you are using Access 2010, the Module button is directly on the Ribbon.

At this point, your screen should look similar to Figure A-1.

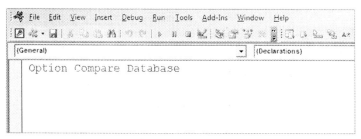

Figure A-1: A module is the container that will hold your code and expose it to other parts of your database.

Step 2: Creating a Function

A *function* is a set of instructions that returns a value. You can think of a function as a defined task that contains the individual actions that Access needs to perform to reach an answer or goal.

To create a function, go to the first empty line and type:

```
Function MyFirstFunction
```

This creates a new function named `MyFirstFunction`. After you press Enter on your keyboard, Access adds a few things to your code. As you can see in Figure A-2, a set of parentheses and the words ''End Function'' are added automatically.

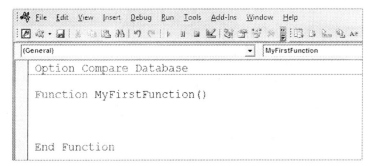

Figure A-2: Create a function that will provide the steps for your task.

Step 3: Giving Your Function Purpose with a Procedure

A function's utility and purpose in life is defined in large part by its procedures. *Procedures* (sometimes called *routines*) are the actions Access takes to accomplish an objective.

For your first procedure, follow these steps:

1. Call a message box. Type **MsgBox** within the function:

```
Function MyFirstFunction()
MsgBox
End Function
```

2. After you press the space key on your keyboard, you see a tool-tip popup, shown in Figure A-3, which shows you the valid arguments for `MsgBox`. This useful functionality, called *IntelliSense* is a kind of cheat sheet that allows you to quickly grasp the methods, properties, and arguments involved in the object or function you are working with. IntelliSense is typically activated when you enter an object or a function and then follow it with a space, open parenthesis, period, or equal sign.

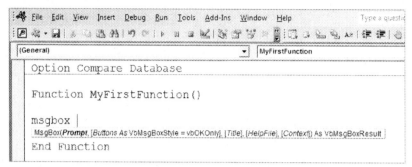

Figure A-3: Intellisense is an invaluable tool when working with VBA.

3. Finish the `MsgBox` function by typing **I am blank years old**. At this point, your function should look like the one shown in Figure A-4.

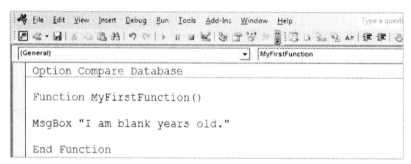

Figure A-4: Your function is ready to play.

Step 4: Testing Your Function

To test your function, simply place your cursor anywhere inside the function and press the F5 key on your key board. If all goes well, you should see the message box shown in Figure A-5.

Figure A-5: You have successfully written your first function!

Step 5: Declaring a Variable

A *variable* is a kind of placeholder for a data type. When you declare a variable, you are telling Access to set aside memory to store a value. The amount of memory allocated depends on the data type.

> **TIP** To get a list of the data types available to you along with the amount of memory that each data type requires, activate Access's Help System and enter **Data Type Summary** in the Search for: input box.

Your next question should be, "How do I know which data type to use?" The data type itself depends on what you are trying to accomplish with the variable. For example, in this scenario, you want to declare a variable that will capture your age. Because age is a number, you use the `Integer` data type.

To declare a variable, you must use a `Dim` statement. `Dim`, short for dimension, explicitly lets Access know that you are declaring a variable. It is good programming practice to declare all your variables before you start your procedure.

Declare a new variable called `MyAge` as an `Integer` data type:

```
Function MyFirstFunction()
Dim MyAge as Integer
MsgBox "I am blank years old."
End Function
```

Step 6: Assigning a Value to a Variable

Once you have memory set aside for a variable, you can assign a value to it. To assign a value to a variable, simply indicate the value to which it is equal. Here are some examples:

- **MyVariable = 1:** This assigns a 1 to the variable called MyVariable.
- **MyVariable = "Access":** This assigns the word "Access" to MyVariable.
- **MyVariable = [Forms]![MainForm].[TextBox1]:** This sets the value of MyVariable to equal the value in the TextBox1 control in the form called MainForm.
- **MyVariable = InputBox("User Input"):** This sets the value of MyVariable to equal the value of a user's input using an InputBox.

In this scenario, you will use an InputBox to capture an age from a user and then pass that age to the MyAge variable. You will then pass the MyAge variable to the message box. You can see the distinct flow of information from a user to an Access message box. Your code should look similar to the code shown here.

```
Function MyFirstFunction()
Dim MyAge as Integer
MyAge = InputBox("Enter your Age")
MsgBox "I am " & MyAge & " years old."
End Function
```

NOTE The MsgBox is broken into three sections separated by ampersands (&):

- "I am " (The first two words in the message)
- MyAge (The variable that will return your age)
- " years old." (The last two words in the message)

Go ahead and test your function. To do so, place your cursor anywhere inside the function and hit the F5 key on your keyboard. If you do everything correctly, you should see an input dialog box, shown in Figure A-6, asking you for your age.

Figure A-6: This InputBox will capture your age and pass it to the MyAge variable.

Step 7: Compiling Your Newly Created Function

You should get into the habit of compiling your code after you create it. Compiling has two major benefits. First, when you compile a procedure, Access checks your code for errors. Second, Access translates your code from the text you can read and understand to a machine language that your computer can understand. To compile your code, go to the application menu and select Debug ⇨ Compile *xxxx* (where *xxxx* is the name of your project).

Step 8: Saving Your Newly Created Function

Now that you have built your first function, you should save it. Go to the application menu and select File ⇨ Save *xxxx* (where *xxxx* is the name of your project).

If your module is new, a dialog box activates, asking you to give your module a name. Keep the debapp01fult name (Module1) and click OK. Close your module and look in the Navigation Pane shown in Figure A-7 to see it in the Modules collection.

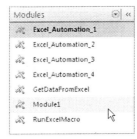

Figure A-7: Once you save a module, you can see it in the Database Window in the Modules collection.

Step 9: Running Your Function in a Macro

The benefit of building your VBA procedures in standard modules is that you can run them from anywhere within your database. For example, you can run your newly created function in a macro by simply calling your function using the RunCode macro action.

Create a new macro and add the RunCode macro action. The function name you are calling is MyFirstFunction(). When your Macro window looks like the one shown in Figure A-8, save the macro and run it.

Figure A-8: You can run your VBA as part of a macro process.

If you are running Access 2007, your Macro window will look like Figure A-9.

Action	Arguments
RunCode	MyFirstFunction()
	Action Arguments
Function Name	MyFirstFunction()

Figure A-9: Running the macro in Access 2007.

Step 10: Running Your Function from a Form

You can also call your functions from a form. Start by creating a new form. You can do this by selecting Blank Form on the Create tab, as demonstrated in Figure A-10.

Figure A-10: Start a new form in Design view.

On the Design tab, select View ⇨ Design View. This activates the toolbox shown in Figure A-11. Select Button and then click anywhere on your form. This places a command button on your form.

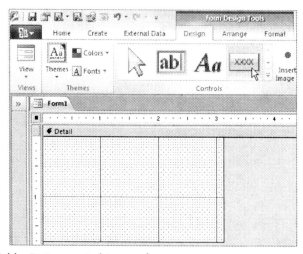

Figure A-11: Add a Button control to your form.

NOTE If the Command Button Wizard activates, click Cancel to close it. You do not need that wizard for this exercise.

Right-click your newly created command button and select Build Event. This activates the Choose Builder dialog box. Select Code Builder, and you are taken to the form module, shown in Figure A-12. A form module serves as a container for event procedures managed and executed by the form or its controls.

Figure A-12: Create a new event using the code builder.

Access is an event-driven environment, which means that procedures are executed with the occurrence of certain events. For example, in Figure A-12, you will notice the procedure's name is Command0_Click(). This means that you are building a procedure for the button you added—which happens to be named Command0, and this procedure will fire when the control is clicked. You can execute your function from here by calling it. Figure A-13 demonstrates how this is done.

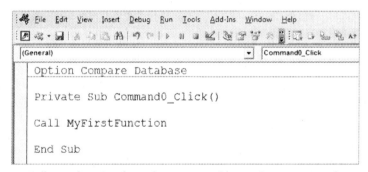

Figure A-13: Call your function from the command button's event procedure.

Now you can close the VBA editor (File ⇨ Close and return to Microsoft Access) and switch to Form View by going to the application menu and selecting View ⇨ Form View. Click your command button to fire your function.

Letting Access Teach You VBA

One of the most beneficial functionalities in Access is the ability to convert a macro to VBA code. To demonstrate how this is done, click Macros in the Database Window and highlight the TopTenB_Child macro, as shown in Figure A-14.

Figure A-14: Highlight the macro you want to convert.

Go to the application menu and select the File ⇨ Save As. This activates the Save As dialog box. In Access 2007, the selection path is Office Icon ⇨ Save As.

This activates the Save As dialog box. Here, you can indicate that you want to save this macro as a module and then name the module. Figure A-15 demonstrates how to fill in this dialog box.

Figure A-15: Indicate that you want to save this macro as a module and then name the module.

Next, the dialog box shown in Figure A-16 gives you the options of adding comments and error handling to the converted VBA. In this case, you want both, so simply click the Convert button.

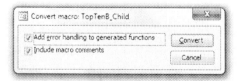

Figure A-16: Tell Access to add comments and include error handling.

When the conversion is complete, select Modules in the Database window and click the module named Converted Macro: TopTenB_Child, as shown in Figure A-17.

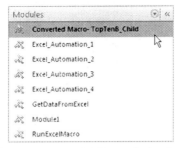

Figure A-17: You can find your converted VBA code in the Modules collection of the Database window.

As you can see in Figure A-18, Access has converted all the macro actions in the TopTenB_Child macro to a VBA function complete with comments and error handling.

```
 File   Edit   View   Insert   Debug   Run   Tools   Add-Ins   Window   Help          Type a question for help

(General)                                              TopTenB_Child

Function TopTenB_Child()
On Error GoTo TopTenB_Child_Err

    If (DCount("[Market]", "[LoopList]") > 0) Then
        ' Condition Check
        Beep
        ' Turn Warnings Off
        DoCmd.SetWarnings False
        ' Open the TopTen_Step3 Query
        DoCmd.OpenQuery "TopTen_Step3", acViewNormal, acEdit
        ' Open the TopTen_Step4 Query
        DoCmd.OpenQuery "TopTen_Step4", acViewNormal, acEdit
        ' Loop if there are markets left in the LoopList table
        DoCmd.RunMacro "TopTenB_Child", , ""
    End If
    ' Delete LoopList table
    DoCmd.DeleteObject acTable, "LoopList"
    ' Turn Warnings Back on
    DoCmd.SetWarnings True
    ' Message box
    Beep
    MsgBox "Top Ten Customers by Market can now be found in the
    ' Stop All Action
    Exit Function
```

Figure A-18: Your macro has been converted to a VBA function!

Keep in mind that this is not just a cool way to get out of writing code. This is a personal tutor! Look at Figure A-18 again. With this one converted macro, you get a firsthand look at how an If statement works, how to call queries from code, how to call macros from code, and how to handle errors. You can create a wide variety of macros and then convert them to VBA to learn about the syntax used for each action and to experiment by adding your own functionality to them. For many Access developers, this was the first step to long programming careers.

Understanding and Using SQL

SQL (Structured Query Language), commonly pronounced "sequel," is the language relational database management systems such as Access use to perform their various tasks. To tell Access to perform any kind of query, you must convey your instructions in SQL. Don't panic; the truth is that you have already been building and using SQL statements without knowing it.

Here, you will discover the role that SQL plays in your dealings with Access and learn how to understand the SQL statements generated when building queries. You will also explore some of the advanced actions you can take with SQL statements, allowing you to accomplish actions that go beyond the Access user interface. The basics you learn here will lay the foundation for your ability to perform the advanced techniques you will encounter throughout this book.

Understanding Basic SQL

A major reason your exposure to SQL is limited is that Access is more user-friendly than most people give it credit for being. The fact is that Access performs a majority of its actions in user-friendly environments that hide the real grunt work that goes on behind the scenes.

For a demonstration of this, follow these steps:

1. In Design view, build the query you see in Figure B-1. In this relatively simple query, you are asking for the sum of revenue by period.

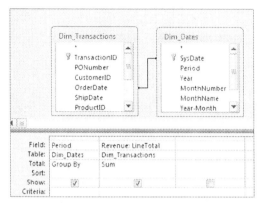

Figure B-1: Build this relatively simple query in Design view.

2. Go up to the Design tab on the application ribbon and select View ⇨ SQL View. Access will switch from Design view to the view you see in Figure B-2.

```
SELECT Dim_Dates.Period, Sum(Dim_Transactions.LineTotal) AS Revenue
FROM Dim_Dates INNER JOIN Dim_Transactions ON Dim_Dates.SysDate = Dim_Transactions.OrderDate
GROUP BY Dim_Dates.Period;
```

Figure B-2: You can get to SQL view by selecting View ⇨ SQL View.

As you can see in Figure B-2, while you were busy designing your query in Design view, Access was diligently creating the SQL statement that will allow the query to run. This example shows that with the user-friendly interface provided by Access, you don't necessarily need to know the SQL behind each query. The question now becomes this: If you can run queries just fine without knowing SQL, why bother to learn it?

Admittedly, the convenient query interface provided by Access does make it a bit tempting to go through life not really understanding SQL. However, if you want to harness the real power of data analysis with Access, it is important to understand the fundamentals of SQL. Throughout this appendix, you will get a solid understanding of SQL as well as insights into some techniques that leverage it to enhance your data analysis.

The SELECT Statement

The SELECT statement, the cornerstone of SQL, enables you to retrieve records from a dataset. The basic syntax of a SELECT statement is:

```
SELECT column_name(s)
FROM table_name
```

The SELECT statement is most often used with a FROM clause. The FROM clause indentifies the table or tables that make up the source for the data.

Try this:

1. Start a new query in Design view.

2. Close the Show Table dialog box (if it is open).

3. Go to the Design tab on the application ribbon and select View ⇨ SQL view.

4. In the SQL view, type the SELECT statement shown in Figure B-3, and then run the query by selecting Run in the Design tab of the ribbon.

Figure B-3: A basic SELECT statement in SQL view.

Congratulations! You have just written your first query manually.

NOTE You may notice that the SQL statement automatically created by Access in Figure B-2 has a semicolon at the end of it. This semicolon is not required for Access to run the query. The semicolon is a standard way to end a SQL statement and is required by some database programs. However, it is not necessary to end your SQL statements with a semicolon in Access, as Access will automatically add it when the query compiles.

Selecting Specific Columns

You can retrieve specific columns from your dataset by explicitly defining the columns in your SELECT statement, as follows:

```
SELECT AccountManagerID, FullName, [Email Address]
FROM Dim_AccountManagers
```

WARNING Any column in your database that has a name that includes spaces or a non-alphanumeric character must be enclosed within brackets ([ ]) in your SQL statement. For example, the SQL statement selecting data from a column called Email Address would be referred to as [Email Address].

Selecting All Columns

Using the wildcard (*) allows you to select all columns from a dataset without having to define every column explicitly.

```
SELECT *
FROM Dim_AccountManagers
```

The WHERE Clause

You can use the WHERE clause in a SELECT statement to filter your dataset and conditionally select specific records. The WHERE clause is always used in combination with an operator such as: = (equal), <> (not equal), > (greater than), < (less than), >= (greater than or equal to), <= (less than or equal to), BETWEEN (within general range).

The following SQL statement retrieves only those employees whose last name is Winston:

```
SELECT AccountManagerID, [Last Name], [First Name]
FROM Dim_AccountManagers
WHERE [Last Name] = "Winston"
```

And this SQL statement retrieves only those employees whose hire date is later than May 16, 2007:

```
SELECT AccountManagerID, [Last Name], [First Name]
FROM Dim_AccountManagers
WHERE HireDate > #5/16/2007#
```

NOTE Notice in the preceding two examples that the word Winston is wrapped in quotes ("Winston") and the date 5/16/2004 is wrapped in the number signs (#5/16/2007#). When referring to a text value in a SQL statement, you must place quotes around the value, while referring to a date requires you use the numbers signs.

Making Sense of Joins

You will often need to build queries that require two or more related tables be joined to achieve the desired results. For example, you may want to join an employee table to a transaction table in order create a report that contains both transaction details and information on the employees who logged those transactions. The type of join you use determines the records outputted.

Inner Joins

An *inner join* operation tells Access to select only those records from both tables that have matching values. Records with values in the joined field that do not appear in both tables are omitted from the query results. Figure B-4 represents the inner join operation visually.

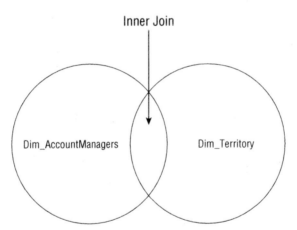

Figure B-4: An inner join operation only selects the records that match values in both tables. The arrows point to the records included in the results.

The following SQL statement selects only those records where the employee numbers in the AccountManagerID field are in both the Dim_AccountManagers table and the Dim_Territory table.

```
SELECT Region, Market, Dim_AccountManagers.AccountManagerID, FullName
FROM Dim_AccountManagers INNER JOIN Dim_Territory
ON Dim_AccountManagers.AccountManagerID = Dim_Territory.AccountManagerID
```

Outer Joins

An *outer join* operation tells Access to select all the records from one table and only the records from a second table with matching values in the joined field. There are two types of outer joins: left joins and right joins.

A *left join* operation (sometimes called an *outer left join*) tells Access to select all the records from the first table regardless of matching and only those records from the second table that have matching values in the joined field. Figure B-5 represents the left join operation visually.

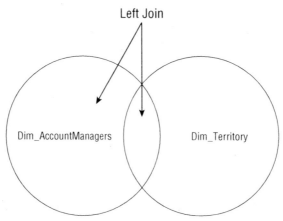

Figure B-5: A left join operation selects all records from the first table and only those records from the second table with matching values in both tables. The arrows point to the records included in the results.

This SQL statement selects all records from the Dim_AccountManagers table and only those records in the Dim_Territory table where values for the AccountManagerID field exist in the Dim_AccountManagers table.

```
SELECT Region, Market, Dim_AccountManagers.AccountManagerID, FullName
FROM Dim_AccountManagers LEFT JOIN Dim_Territory
ON Dim_AccountManagers.AccountManagerID =
Dim_Territory.AccountManagerID
```

A right join operation (sometimes called an *outer right join*) tells Access to select all the records from the second table regardless of matching, and only those records from the first table that have matching values in the joined field (see Figure B-6).

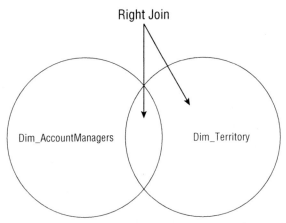

Figure B-6: A right join operation selects all records from the second table and only those records from the first table with matching values in both tables. The arrows point to the records that are included in the results.

This SQL statement selects all records from the Dim_Territory table and only those records in the Dim_AccountManagers table where values for the AccountManagerID field exist in the Dim_Territory table.

```
SELECT Region, Market, Dim_AccountManagers.AccountManagerID, FullName
FROM Dim_AccountManagers RIGHT JOIN Dim_Territory
ON Dim_AccountManagers.AccountManagerID =
Dim_Territory.AccountManagerID
```

TIP Notice that in the preceding join statements, table names are listed before each column name separated by a dot (for example, Dim_AccountManager .AccountManagerID). When you are building a SQL statement for a query that utilizes multiple tables, it is generally a good practice to refer to the table names as well as field names in order to avoid confusion and errors. Access does this for all queries automatically.

Getting Fancy with Advanced SQL Statements

You will soon realize that the SQL language itself is a quite versatile, allowing you to go far beyond basic SELECT, FROM, WHERE statements. In this section, you will explore some of the advanced actions you can accomplish with SQL.

Expanding Your Search with the Like Operator

By itself, the `Like` operator is no different from the equal (=) operator. For instance, these two SQL statements will return the same number of records:

```
SELECT AccountManagerID, [Last Name], [First Name]
FROM Dim_AccountManagers
WHERE [Last Name] = "Winston"
SELECT AccountManagerID, [Last Name], [First Name]
FROM Dim_AccountManagers
WHERE [Last Name] Like "Winston"
```

The `Like` operator is typically used with wildcard characters to expand the scope of your search to include any record that matches a pattern. The wildcard characters valid in Access are shown in Table B-1.

Table B-1: Wildcard Characters Used with the Like Operator

WILDCARD CHARACTERS	DESCRIPTION	PURPOSE
*	Asterisk	Represents any number and type characters
?	Question mark	Represents any single character
#	Pound or hash symbol	Represents any single digit
[]	Brackets	Allow you to pass a single character or an array of characters to the `Like` operator. Any values matching the character values within the brackets will be included in the results.
[!]	The brackets with an embedded exclamation point	Allow you to pass a single character or an array of characters to the `Like` operator. Any values matching the character values following the exclamation point are excluded from the results.

Listed in Table B-2 are some example SQL statements that use the `Like` operator to select different records from the same table column.

Selecting Unique Values and Rows without Grouping

The `DISTINCT` predicate enables you to retrieve only unique values from the selected fields in your dataset. For example, the following SQL statement

Table B-2: Selection Methods using the Like Operator

WILDCARD CHARACTER(S) USED	SQL STATEMENT EXAMPLE	RESULT
*	SELECT Field1 FROM Table1 WHERE Field1 Like "A*"	Selects all records where Field1 starts with the letter "A"
*	SELECT Field1 FROM Table1 WHERE Field1 Like "*A*"	Selects all records where Field1 includes the letter "A"
?	SELECT Field1 FROM Table1 WHERE Field1 Like "???"	Selects all records where the length of Field1 is three characters long
?	SELECT Field1 FROM Table1 WHERE Field1 Like "B??"	Selects all records where Field1 is a three-letter word that starts with "B"
#	SELECT Field1 FROM Table1 WHERE Field1 Like "###"	Selects all records where Field1 is a number that is exactly three digits long
#	SELECT Field1 FROM Table1 WHERE Field1 Like "A#A"	Selects all records where the value in Field1 is a three-character value that starts with "A," contains one digit, and ends with "A"
#, *	SELECT Field1 FROM Table1 WHERE Field1 Like "A#*"	Selects all records where Field1 begins with "A" any digit length.
[], *	SELECT Field1 FROM Table1 WHERE Field1 Like "*[$%!*/]*"	Selects all records where Field1 includes any one of the special characters shown in the SQL statement
[!], *	SELECT Field1 FROM Table1 WHERE Field1 Like "*[!a-z]*"	Selects all records where the value of Field1 is *not* a a string consisting of only characters from a-z
[!], *	SELECT Field1 FROM Table1 WHERE Field1 Like "*[!0-9]*"	Selects all records where the value of Field1 is a text value

selects only unique job titles from the Dim_AccountManagers table, resulting in six records:

```
SELECT DISTINCT AccountManagerID
FROM Dim_AccountManagers
```

If your SQL statement selects more than one field, the combination of values from all fields must be unique for a given record to be included in the results.

Using SELECT DISTINCT is different from using GROUP BY or an aggregate query. There is no grouping going on here; Access is simply running through the records and retrieving the unique values. To see how GROUP BY compares to SELECT DISTINCT, read the following sections.

If you require that the entire row be unique, you could use the DISTINCTROW predicate. The DISTINCTROW predicate enables you to retrieve only those records for which the entire row is unique. That is to say, the combination of all values in the selected fields does not match any other record in the returned dataset. You would use the DISTINCTROW predicate just as you would in a SELECT DISTINCT clause.

```
SELECT DISTINCTROW AccountManagerID
FROM Dim_AccountManagers
```

Grouping and Aggregating with the GROUP BY Clause

The GROUP BY clause makes is possible to aggregate records in your dataset by column values. When you create an aggregate query in Design view, you are essentially using the GROUP BY clause. The following SQL statement groups the Market field and gives you the count of states in each market:

```
SELECT Market, Count(State)
FROM Dim_Territory
GROUP BY Market
```

The HAVING Clause

When you are using the GROUP BY clause, you cannot specify criteria using the WHERE clause. Instead, you need to use the HAVING clause. This SQL statement groups the Market field and only gives you the count of states in the Dallas market:

```
SELECT Market, Count(State)
FROM Dim_Territory
GROUP BY Market
HAVING Market = "Dallas"
```

Setting Sort Order with the ORDER BY Clause

The ORDER BY clause enables you to sort data by a specified field. The default sort order is ascending; therefore, sorting your fields in ascending order requires no explicit instruction. The following SQL statement sorts the resulting records in by Last Name ascending, then First Name ascending:

```
SELECT AccountManagerID, [Last Name], [First Name]
FROM Dim_AccountManagers
ORDER BY [Last Name], [First Name]
```

To sort in descending order, you must use the DESC reserved word after each column you want sorted in descending order. The following SQL statement sorts the resulting records in by Last Name descending, then First Name ascending:

```
SELECT AccountManagerID, [Last Name], [First Name]
FROM Dim_AccountManagers
ORDER BY [Last Name] DESC, [First Name]
```

Creating Aliases with the AS Clause

The AS clause enables you to assign aliases to your columns and tables. There are generally two reasons you would want to use aliases: Either you want to make column or table names shorter and easier to read, or you are working with multiple instances of the same table and you need a way to refer to one instance or the other.

Creating a Column Alias

The following SQL statement groups the Market field and gives you the count of states in each market. In addition, the alias State Count has been given to the column containing the count of states by including the AS clause.

```
SELECT Market, Count(State) AS [State Count]
FROM Dim_Territory
GROUP BY Market
HAVING Market = "Dallas"
```

Creating a Table Alias

This SQL statement gives the Dim_AccountManagers the alias "MyTable."

```
SELECT AccountManagerID, [Last Name], [First Name]
FROM Dim_AccountManagers AS MyTable
WHERE MyTable.[Last Name] Like "L*"
```

SELECT TOP and SELECT TOP PERCENT

When you run a SELECT query, you are retrieving all records that meet your definitions and criteria. When you run the SELECT TOP statement, or a top values query, you are telling Access to filter your returned dataset to show only a specific number of records.

Top Values Queries Explained

To get a clear understanding of what the SELECT TOP statement does, follow these steps:

1. Build the aggregate query shown in Figure B-7.

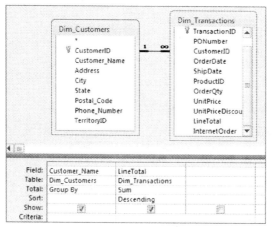

Figure B-7: Build this aggregate query in Design view. Note that the query is sorted descending on the Sum of LineTotal.

2. Right-click the grey area above the white query grid and then select Properties. This activates the Property Sheet dialog box shown in Figure B-8. In the Property Sheet dialog, change the Top Values property to 25.

3. As you can see in Figure B-9, after you run this query, only the customers that fall into the top 25 by sum of revenue are returned. If you want the bottom 25 customers, simply change the sort order of the LineTotal field to ascending.

SELECT TOP

The SELECT TOP statement is easy to spot. This is the same query used to run the results in Figure B-9.

```
SELECT TOP 25 Customer_Name, Sum(LineTotal) AS SumOfLineTotal
FROM Dim_Customers INNER JOIN Dim_Transactions
ON Dim_Customers.CustomerID =
Dim_Transactions.CustomerID
GROUP BY Customer_Name
ORDER BY Sum(LineTotal) DESC
```

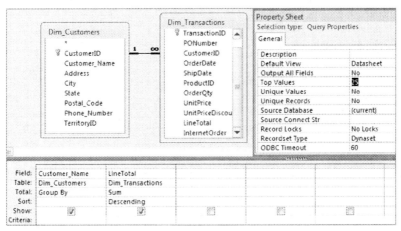

Figure B-8: Change the Top Values property to 25.

Customer_Name ▾	SumOfLineTotal ▾
SUASHU Corp.	$2,738,933.20
GUPDYU Corp.	$2,062,418.05
CATYOF Corp.	$2,007,139.00
SCULOS Corp.	$1,374,781.70
WHATLU Corp.	$1,357,050.30
MADOSM Corp.	$1,282,750.00
USANGE Corp.	$1,226,356.55
CORULA Corp.	$1,201,995.95
RADASS Corp.	$1,198,185.00
SMEAS Corp.	$1,191,758.00
GRECUW Corp.	$1,187,312.80
AVAATA Corp.	$1,174,196.45
ZUQHYR Corp.	$1,173,088.50
ANATUD Corp.	$1,093,389.95
THEMOG Corp.	$1,087,385.00
BASHUQ Corp.	$1,081,070.55
ATLANT Corp.	$1,077,585.85
CUGGAN Corp.	$1,071,389.30
WORUTC Corp.	$1,068,895.55
EBANAU Corp.	$1,025,716.70
USLAND Corp.	$1,005,005.95
QAAKUY Corp.	$996,152.20
MUUZEO Corp.	$946,096.70
CUANTY Corp.	$937,880.00
SUASHF Corp.	$912,274.15

Figure B-9: Running the query gives you the top 25 customers by revenue.

Bear in mind that you don't have to be working with totals or currency to use a top values query. In the following SQL statement, you are returning the ten account managers that have the earliest hire date in the company, effectively producing a seniority report:

```
SELECT Top 10 AccountManagerID, [Last Name], [First Name]
FROM Dim_AccountManagers
ORDER BY HireDate ASC
```

SELECT TOP PERCENT

The SELECT TOP PERCENT statement works in exactly the same way as SELECT TOP except the records returned in a SELECT TOP PERCENT statement represent the *Nth* percent of total records rather than the *Nth* number of records. For example, the following SQL statement will return the top 25 percent of records by revenue:

```
SELECT TOP 25 PERCENT Customer_Name, Sum(LineTotal) AS SumOfLineTotal
FROM Dim_Customers INNER JOIN Dim_Transactions ON
Dim_Customers.CustomerID =
Dim_Transactions.CustomerID
GROUP BY Customer_Name
ORDER BY Sum(LineTotal) DESC
```

NOTE Keep in mind that SELECT TOP PERCENT statements only give you the top or bottom percent of the total number of records in the returned dataset, not the percent of the total value in your records. For example, the preceding SQL statement does not give you only those records that make up 25 percent of the total value in the LineTotal field. It gives you the top 25 percent of total records in the queried dataset.

Performing Action Queries via SQL Statements

You may not have thought about it before, but when you build an action query, you are building a SQL statement that is specific to that action. These SQL statements make it possible for you to go beyond just selecting records.

Make-Table Queries Translated

Make-Table queries use the SELECT...INTO statement to make a hard-coded table that contains the results of your query. The following example first selects account manager number, last name, and first name and then creates a new table called Employees:

```
SELECT AccountManagerID, [Last Name], [First Name] INTO Employees
FROM Dim_AccountManagers
```

Append Queries Translated

Append queries use the INSERT INTO statement to insert new rows into a specified table. The following example will insert new rows into the Employees table from the Dim_AccountManagers table:

```
INSERT INTO Employees (AccountManagerID, [Last Name],
[First Name])
SELECT AccountManagerID, [Last Name], [First Name]
FROM Dim_AccountManagers
```

Update Queries Translated

Update queries use the UPDATE statement in conjunction with SET in order to modify the data in a dataset. This example updates the List_Price field in the Dim_Products table to increase prices by 10 percent.

```
UPDATE Dim_Products SET List_Price = List_Price*1.1
```

Delete Queries Translated

Delete queries use the DELETE statement to delete rows in a dataset. In the example here, you are deleting all rows from the Employees.

```
DELETE *
FROM Employees
```

Creating Crosstabs with the TRANSFORM Statement

The TRANSFORM statement allows the creation of a Crosstab dataset that displays data in a compact view. The TRANSFORM statement requires three main components to work:

- The field to be aggregated
- The SELECT statement that determines the row content for the crosstab
- The field that makes up the column of the crosstab (the "pivot field")

The syntax is as follows:

```
TRANSFORM Aggregated_Field
SELECT Field1, Field2 FROM Table1 GROUP BY Field1, Field2
PIVOT Pivot_Field
```

For example, the following statement creates a crosstab that shows region and market on the rows and products on the columns, with revenue in the center of the crosstab.

```
TRANSFORM Sum(Revenue) AS SumOfRevenue
SELECT Region, Market
FROM PvTblFeed
GROUP BY Region, Market
PIVOT Product_Description
```

Using SQL Specific Queries

SQL specific queries are essentially action queries that cannot be run through Access' query grid. These queries must be run either in SQL view or via code (macro or VBA). Several types of SQL Specific queries perform a specific action. This section introduces a few of these queries, focusing on those that you can use in Access to shape and configure data tables.

Merging Datasets with the UNION Operator

The UNION operator is used to merge two compatible SQL statements to produce one read-only dataset. For example, the following Select statement produces a dataset (Figure B-10) that shows revenue by region and market.

```
SELECT Region, Market, Sum(Revenue) AS Sales
FROM PvTblFeed
GROUP BY Region, Market
```

Region ▾	Market ▾	Sales ▾
MIDWEST	DENVER	$645,584.10
MIDWEST	KANSASCITY	$574,899.15
MIDWEST	TULSA	$628,407.41
NORTH	BUFFALO	$450,478.72
NORTH	CANADA	$776,247.78
NORTH	MICHIGAN	$678,708.11
NORTH	NEWYORK	$873,580.79
SOUTH	CHARLOTTE	$890,514.49
SOUTH	DALLAS	$467,086.11
SOUTH	FLORIDA	$1,450,397.76
SOUTH	NEWORLEANS	$333,452.80
WEST	CALIFORNIA	$2,254,751.64

Figure B-10: This dataset shows revenue by Region and Market.

A second Select statement produces a separate dataset (Figure B-11) that shows total revenue by region.

```
SELECT Region, "Total" AS [Market], Sum(Revenue) AS Sales
FROM PvTblFeed
GROUP BY Region
```

Region ▾	Market ▾	Sales ▾
MIDWEST	Total	$1,848,890.66
NORTH	Total	$2,779,015.40
SOUTH	Total	$3,141,451.17
WEST	Total	$3,004,832.22

Figure B-11: This dataset shows total revenue by region

The idea is to bring these two datasets together to create an analysis that will show detail and totals all in one table. The UNION operator is ideal for this type of work, merging the results of the two Select statements. To use the UNION operator, simply start a new query in SQL view and enter the following syntax:

```
SELECT Region, Market, Sum(Revenue) AS Sales
FROM PvTblFeed
GROUP BY Region, Market
UNION
SELECT Region, "Total" AS [Market], Sum(Revenue) AS Sales
FROM PvTblFeed
GROUP BY Region
```

As you can see, the preceding statement is nothing more than the two SQL statements brought together with a Union operator. When the two are merged (Figure B-12), the result is a dataset that shows both details and totals in one table!

> **NOTE** When a union query is run, Access matches the columns from both datasets by their position in the SELECT statement. That means two things: your SELECT statements must have the same number of columns, and the columns in both statements should, in most cases, be in the same order.

Region ▾	Market ▾	Sales ▾
MIDWEST	DENVER	$645,584.10
MIDWEST	KANSASCITY	$574,899.15
MIDWEST	Total	$1,848,890.66
MIDWEST	TULSA	$623,407.41
NORTH	BUFFALO	$450,478.72
NORTH	CANADA	$776,247.78
NORTH	MICHIGAN	$678,708.11
NORTH	NEWYORK	$873,580.79
NORTH	Total	$2,779,015.40
SOUTH	CHARLOTTE	$890,514.49
SOUTH	DALLAS	$467,086.11
SOUTH	FLORIDA	$1,450,397.76
SOUTH	NEWORLEANS	$333,452.80
SOUTH	Total	$3,141,451.17
WEST	CALIFORNIA	$2,254,751.64
WEST	PHOENIX	$570,254.17
WEST	SEATTLE	$179,826.42
WEST	Total	$3,004,832.22

Figure B-12: The two datasets have now been combined to create a report that provides summary and detail data.

Creating a Table with the CREATE TABLE Statement

Often in your analytical processes, you will need to create a temporary table in order to group, manipulate, or simply hold data. The CREATE TABLE statement allows you to do just that with one SQL specific query.

Unlike a Make-Table query, the CREATE TABLE statement is designed to create only the structure or schema of a table. No records are ever returned with a CREATE TABLE statement. This statement allows you to strategically create an empty table at any point in your analytical process.

The basic syntax for a CREATE TABLE statement is as follows:

```
CREATE TABLE TableName
(<Field1Name> Type(<Field Size>), <Field2Name> Type(<Field Size>))
```

To use the CREATE TABLE statement, simply start a new query in SQL view and define the structure for your table.

In the following example, a new table called TempLog is created with three fields. The first field is a Text field that can accept 50 characters, the second field is a Text field that can accept 150 characters, and the third field is a Date field.

```
CREATE TABLE TempLog
([User] Text(50), [Description] Text, [LogDate] Date)
```

NOTE You will notice that in the preceding example, no field size is specified for the second text column. If the field size is omitted, Access will use the default field size specified for the database.

Manipulating Columns with the ALTER TABLE Statement

The ALTER TABLE statement provides some additional methods of altering the structure of a table behind the scenes. There are several clauses you can use with the ALTER TABLE statement, four of which are quite useful in Access data analysis: ADD, ALTER COLUMN, DROP COLUMN, and ADD CONSTRAINT.

NOTE The ALTER TABLE statement, along with its various clauses, is used much less frequently than the SQL statements mentioned earlier in this appendix. However, the ALTER TABLE statement comes in handy when your analytical processes require you to change the structure of tables on the fly, helping you avoid any manual manipulations that may have to be done.

It should be noted that there is no way to undo any actions performed using an ALTER TABLE statement. This fact obviously calls for some caution when using these statements.

Adding a Column with the ADD Clause

As the name implies, the ADD clause enables you to add a column to an existing table. The basic syntax is as follows:

```
ALTER TABLE <TableName>
ADD <ColumnName> Type(<Field Size>)
```

To use the ADD statement, simply start a new query in SQL view and define the structure for your new column. For instance, running the example statement shown here creates a new column called SupervisorPhone, which is added to a table called TempLog.

```
ALTER TABLE TempLog
ADD SupervisorPhone Text(10)
```

Altering a Column with the ALTER COLUMN Clause

When using the ALTER COLUMN clause, you specify an existing column in an existing table to work edit. You primarily use this clause to change the data type and field size of a given column. The basic syntax is as follows:

```
ALTER TABLE <TableName>
ALTER COLUMN <ColumnName> Type(<Field Size>)
```

To use the ALTER COLUMN statement, simply start a new query in SQL view and define changes for the column in question. For instance, the example statement shown here changes the field size of the SupervisorPhone field.

```
ALTER TABLE TempLog
ALTER COLUMN SupervisorPhone Text(13)
```

Deleting a Column with the DROP COLUMN Clause

The DROP COLUMN clause enables you to delete a given column from an existing table. The basic syntax is as follows:

```
ALTER TABLE <TableName>
DROP COLUMN <ColumnName>
```

To use the DROP COLUMN statement, simply start a new query in SQL view and define which column you want to delete. For instance, running the example statement shown here deletes the column called SupervisorPhone from the TempLog table.

```
ALTER TABLE TempLog
DROP COLUMN SupervisorPhone
```

Dynamically Adding Primary Keys with the ADD CONSTRAINT Clause

For many analysts, Access serves as an easy-to-use ETL (Extract, Transform, Load) tool. That is, Access allows us to extract data from many sources, then reformat and cleanse that data into consolidated tables. Many analysts also automate ETL processes with the use of macros that fire a series of queries. This works quite well in most cases.

There are, however, instances where an ETL process requires primary keys be added to temporary tables in order to keep data normalized during processing. In these situations, most people do one of two things. They stop the macro in the middle of processing to manually add the required primary keys. Or they create a permanent table solely for the purpose of holding a table where the primary keys are already set.

There is a third option. The ADD CONSTRAINT clause allows you to dynamically create the primary keys. The basic syntax is as follows:

```
ALTER TABLE <TableName>
ADD CONSTRAINT CONSTRAINTNAME PRIMARY KEY (<Field Name>)
```

To use the ADD CONSTRAINT clause, simply start a new query in SQL view and define the new primary key you are implementing. For instance, the example statement shown here applies a compound key to three fields in the TempLog table.

```
ALTER TABLE TempLog
ADD CONSTRAINT CONSTRAINTNAME PRIMARY KEY (User, Description, LogDate)
```

Query Performance, Database Corruption, and Other Thoughts

One of the most important aspects of analyzing data with Access is keeping your database healthy. In this chapter, you will learn some of the best practices around building and maintaining your database, ensuring that it runs efficiently and error free. In addition, this chapter will teach you best ways to get help in Access when you need a push in the right direction.

Optimizing Query Performance

When you are analyzing a few thousand records, query performance is not an issue. Analytical processes run quickly and smoothly with few problems. However, when you are moving and crunching hundreds of thousands of records, performance becomes a huge issue. There is no getting around the fact that the larger the volume of data, the slower your queries will run. Even so, there are steps you can take to optimize query performance and reduce the time it takes to run your large analytical processes.

Understanding Access's Query Optimizer

Most relational database programs have a built-in optimizer to ensure efficient performance, even in the face of large volumes of data. Access also has a built-in query optimizer. Have you ever noticed that when you build a query, close it, and then open it again, Access sometimes shuffles your criteria and expressions? This is because of its built-in query optimizer.

The query optimizer is charged with the task of establishing a query execution strategy. The query execution strategy is a set of instructions given to the Microsoft Access database engine (ACE) that tells it how to run the query in the quickest, most cost-effective way possible. Access's query optimizer bases its query execution strategy on the following factors:

- The size of the tables used in the query
- Whether indexes exist in the tables used in the query
- The number of tables and joins used in the query
- The presence and scope of criteria or expressions used in the query

This execution strategy is created when the query is first run, and it is recompiled each time you save a query or compact your database. Once a query execution strategy has been established, the ACE database engine simply refers to it each time the query is run, effectively optimizing the execution of the query.

Steps You Can Take to Optimize Query Performance

You've heard the phrase "garbage in, garbage out," referring to the fact that the results you get out of a database are only as good as the data you put in. This concept also applies to Access's query optimizer. Since Access's optimization functionality largely depends on the makeup and utility of your tables and queries, poorly designed tables and queries can limit the effectiveness of Access's query optimizer. To that end, there are actions you can take to help maximize query optimization.

Normalizing Your Database Design

Many users who are new to Access build one large flat table and call it a database. This structure seems attractive because you don't have to deal with joins and you only have to reference one table when you build your queries. However, as the volume of data grows in a structure such as this one, query performance will take a nosedive.

When you normalize your database to take on a relational structure, you break up your data into several smaller tables. This has two effects. First, you inherently remove redundant data, giving your query less data to scan. Second, you can query only the tables that contain the information you need, preventing the need to scan your entire database each time you run a query.

Using Indexes on Appropriate Fields

Imagine that you have a file cabinet that contains 1,000 records that are not alphabetized. How long do you think it would take to pull out all the records that start with "S"? You would definitely have an easier time pulling out records in an alphabetized filing system. Indexing fields in an Access table is analogous to alphabetizing records in a file cabinet.

When you run a query where you are sorting and filtering on a field that has not been indexed, Access has to scan and read the entire dataset before returning any results. As you can imagine, on large datasets, this can take a very long time. By contrast, queries that sort and filter on fields that have been indexed run much more quickly because Access uses the index to check positions and restrictions.

You can create an index on a field in a table by going into the table's design view and adjusting the Indexed property. Figure C-1 demonstrates this process.

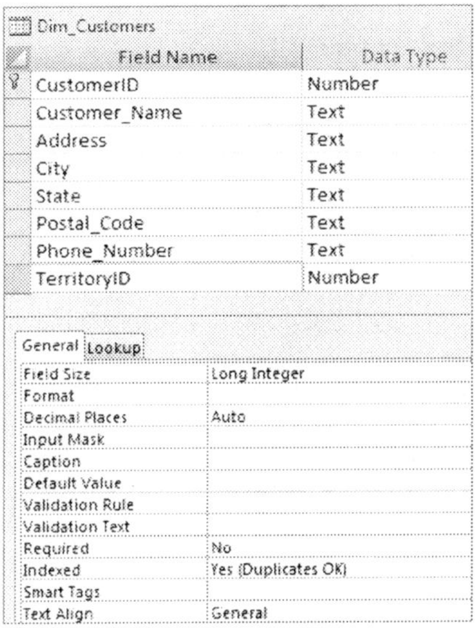

Figure C-1: Create an index by changing the Indexed property.

NOTE Fields tagged as primary keys are already indexed. You can index fields that have duplicate values by setting the Indexed property of the field to Yes (Duplicates OK). Each table in your database can have up to 32 separate indexes.

Now before you go out and start creating an index on every field in your database, there is one caveat to indexing. Although indexes do speed up select queries dramatically, they significantly slow down action queries such as Update, Delete, and Append. This is because when you run an action query on indexed fields, Access has to update each index in addition to the changing the actual table. To that end, it's important that you limit the fields that you index. A best practice is to limit your indexes to the following types of fields:

- Fields where you will routinely filter values using criteria
- Fields you anticipate using as joins on other tables
- Fields where you anticipate sorting values regularly

TIP Feel free to visit Chapter 2, to get a refresher on indexes.

Optimizing by Improving Query Design

You would be surprised how a few simple choices in query design can improve the performance of your queries. Take a moment to review some of the actions you can take to speed up your queries and optimize your analytical processes.

- Avoid sorting or filtering fields that are not indexed.
- Avoid building queries that select "*" from a table. For example, **SELECT * FROM MyTable**. This forces Access to look up the field names from the system tables every time the query is run.
- When creating a totals query, include only the fields needed to achieve the query's goal. The more fields you include in the GROUP BY clause, the longer the query will take to execute.
- Sometimes you need to include fields in your query design only to set criteria against them. Fields that are not needed in the final results should be set to "not shown." In other words, remove the check from the checkbox in the Show row of the query design grid.
- Avoid using open-ended ranges such as > or <. Instead, use the Between ... And statement.
- Use smaller temporary tables in your analytical processes instead of your large core tables. For example, instead of joining two large tables together, consider creating smaller temporary tables limited only to the relevant records and then joining those two. You will often find that your processes will run faster even with the extra steps of creating and deleting temporary tables.
- Use fixed column headings in Crosstab queries whenever possible. This way, Access does not have to take the extra step of establishing column headings in your Crosstab queries.
- Avoid using calculated fields in subqueries or domain aggregate functions, because they already come with an inherent performance hit. Using calculated fields in them compounds your query's performance loss considerably.

NOTE Subqueries and domain aggregate queries are discussed in detail in Chapter 7.

Compacting and Repairing Your Database Regularly

Over time, your database will change due to the rigors of daily operation. The number of tables may have increased or decreased; you may have added and removed several temporary tables and queries; you may have abnormally closed the database once or twice; and the list goes on. All this action may change your table statistics, leaving your previously compiled queries with inaccurate query execution plans. When you compact and repair your database, you force Access to regenerate table statistics and re-optimize your queries so that they will recompile the next time you execute the query. This ensures that Access will run your queries using the most accurate and efficient query execution plans.

TIP You can set your database to automatically compact and repair each time you close it by doing the following:

1. Click the Office icon on the upper left-hand corner of the Ribbon.
2. Click the Access Options button. This will activate the Access Options dialog box.
3. Once in the Access Options dialog box, select Current Database to display the configuration settings for the current database. Here you will see the Compact on Close setting.
4. Place a check next to Compact on Close and click the OK button to confirm the change.

Handling Database Corruption

Corruption is a state where an error occurs in your Access database and causes unpredictable behavior or, in worst-case scenarios, renders your database unusable. To understand why corruption happens, you need to understand how the ACE database engine manages data.

ACE administers your data in a series of blocks, each consisting of 4,096 bytes of data. When you see a table in a database, you see it as a solid object, but it's actually made of blocks of data. Depending on the size the table, a table can be made of one block of data or many blocks that point to each other. Most corruption is caused by errors that occur when writing to one or more of these blocks. In fact, small-scale corruption happens all the time; you just don't know it, because ACE usually resolves these corruption issues during the course of reading and writing data. However, sometimes ACE cannot resolve issues on its own. In these cases, the database is corrupted.

Signs and Symptoms of a Corrupted Database

There are many reasons why a database becomes corrupted. The database may have encountered errors while writing data, table definitions may have degraded over time, some VBA code or macro may have caused a fatal error, and the list goes on. The point is that because corruption can be caused by a wide range of nebulous issues, the signs and symptoms of a corrupted database are just as expansive and just as nebulous. You'll never see a message explicitly stating that your database is corrupt. So how do you know if your database is?

Databases that fall victim to corruption can generally be separated into two categories: those that you can open and work with and those that do not open at all.

Watching for Corruption in Seemingly Normal Databases

The dangerous thing about corrupted databases that are still usable is that you may never know you are working with a corrupted database. It can be quite difficult to spot the signs of this type of corruption. There are, however, some reasonably clear indicators that strongly suggest corruption:

- You get an error message stating "Invalid field data type" when trying to open a table in either data view or design view or when viewing the relationships window.

- You get an error message stating "Could not find field Description" when trying to compact and repair the database.

- When you try to open a table, a query, a form, a report, or a data access page, you get one of the following messages:

  - "MSAccess can't open the table in datasheet view"

  - "Record is deleted"

  - "Unable to carry out the command"

  - "There was an error executing the command"

- You get an error message stating, "Table 'TempMSysAccessObjects' already exists" when trying to compact and repair the database.

- Nothing happens when you try to open or delete a linked table.

- Access unexpectedly closes and then tries to send an error report.

- You get an error message *falsely* stating that "The changes you requested to the table were not successful because they would create duplicate values in the index, primary key, or relationship."

- #DELETED# starts appearing in your tables.

- Access starts to drop records randomly.

- You get an error message stating "Invalid argument" when clicking on a record.

- All fields for a specific record show #Error when you run a query against that record or view it in a form.

Common Errors Associated with Database Corruption

The problem with database corruption is that a wide range of nebulous issues can cause it. Therefore, you will rarely see a message explicitly stating that your database is corrupt. However, the errors listed here in Table C-1 are key indicators that point to the possibility that your database is corrupt.

Table C-1: Errors Commonly Associated with Database Corruption

ERROR	DESCRIPTION
2239	<Database Name> has detected that this database is in an inconsistent state, and cannot attempt to recover the database because the file is read-only. To allow Access to recover the database, close the database and set the file to read/write, and then open the database.
2572	This database is in an unexpected state and <Database Name> cannot open it. This database has been converted from a prior version of <Database Name> by using the DAO CompactDatabase method instead of the Convert Database command (click the Microsoft Office Button and then click Convert). Converting by using the DAO CompactDatabase method has left the database in a partially converted state. If you have a copy of the database in its original format, click the Microsoft Office button and then click Convert to convert it. If the original database is no longer available, create a new database and import your tables and queries to preserve your data and try again. Your other database objects cannot be recovered.
3011	The Microsoft Office Access database engine could not find the object <Object Name>. Make sure the object exists and that you spell its name and the path name correctly.
3019	Operation invalid without a current index.
3033	You do not have the necessary permissions to use the <Object Name> object. Have your system administrator or the person who created this object establish the appropriate permissions for you.
3045	Could not use <File Name>; file already in use.
3049	Cannot open database <Database Name>. It may not be a database that your application recognizes, or the file may be corrupt.
3051	The Microsoft Office Access database engine cannot open or write to the file <File Name>. It is already opened exclusively by another user, or you need permission to view and write its data.

Continued

Table C-1: *(continued)*

ERROR	DESCRIPTION
3078	The Microsoft Office Access database engine cannot find the input table or query <Query Name>. Make sure it exists and that its name is spelled correctly.
3197	The Microsoft Office Access database engine stopped the process because you and another user are attempting to change the same data at the same time.
3340	Query <Query Name> is corrupt.
3343	Unrecognized database format <Object Name>.
3428	A problem occurred in your database. Correct the problem by repairing and compacting the database.
3626	The operation failed. There are too many indexes on table <Table Name>. Delete some of the indexes on the table and try the operation again.
3734	The database has been placed in a state by user <User Name> on machine <Machine Name> that prevents it from being opened or locked.
3800	<Name> is not an index in this table.
7801	This database is in an unrecognized format. The database may have been created with a later version of <Database Name> than the one you are using. Upgrade your version of <Database Name> to the current one, then open this database.
29063	The Visual Basic for Applications project in the database is corrupt.
29072	<Database Name> has detected corruption in this file. To try to repair the corruption, first make a backup copy of the file. Click the Microsoft Office Button, point to Manage and then click Compact and Repair Database. If you are currently trying to repair this corruption, you need to recreate this file or restore it from a previous backup.

Recovering a Corrupted Database

If you have determined that your database is indeed corrupt, there are actions you can take to attempt recovery. Keep in mind that your ability to fix a corrupted database depends on the nature and extent of the corruption. The idea is to follow these steps until your issue is resolved.

1. **Make a backup copy of the corrupt database.** Any recovery attempts come with the possibility of permanently disabling the database. You will definitely want a backup in case this happens.

2. **Try working in another environment.** Try opening and using the database on several local machines (especially if you are working with

the database through a network). If this resolves your issue, the problem is probably not corruption. Look for other hardware or software issues.

3. **Delete the .laccdb file associated with the database.** When you open an Access database, an .laccdb file is created. This file is the mechanism that allows for multi-user operations. Deleting the associated .laccdb file will ensure that no rogue instances of the database are left hanging around. If you cannot delete the file, use the windows task manager and end all instances of MSAccess and/or any other process that could be logged into the database. In some cases, this action can actually resolve your issue.

4. **Import your database into a fresh .accdb file.** Start a new database and attempt to import your tables, queries, forms, reports, macros, data access pages, and modules from the corrupted database. In most cases, all of your data and code can be salvaged using this method.

5. **Restore the database from a previously backed up version.** If you have a backup of your database, you may want to use it to help restore some of the data you have lost.

6. **Use an Access Repair Service.** The last resort is to use an Access repair service. These services use specialized software to restore databases; with a success rate close to 99 percent. This will cost you between $50 and $200, depending on the company you use and the complexity of your issue. You can find a plethora of these services by entering **corrupt Access database** into any of the major search engines.

Steps You Can Take to Prevent Database Corruption

Unfortunately, there isn't a clear set of warnings alerting you that your database is on the verge of corruption. By the time you know that you have a corrupted database, it's too late. In that light, remember that preparation is a lot better that desperation. Get into the habit of taking a few simple measures that will minimize the chance of corruption and prepare you for the event of a corrupted database.

Backing Up Your Database on a Regular Basis

Having a backup of your database is like having a spare tire. There is no better safeguard against losing data than having a spare copy of it stored away. When you choose a backup plan, you will want to consider two things: when and where. When should you back up your database? You will want to choose a backup schedule that directly relates to your threshold of data loss. For example, if you cannot lose more than one day of data, make a backup of your database every day. If daily backups are excessive, make a weekly backup. Where should you back up you database? You will want to choose a location that is safe, accessible, and not in the same folder as your working database.

Compacting and Repairing Your Database on a Regular Basis

There are certain things that happen through the natural course of using a database. For example, the data blocks in the database become fragmented, the table statistics become outmoded, and the database grows. Although none of these occurrences directly lead to a corrupt database, they can contribute to one if left unchecked. Many Access users think that the compact and repair utility simply releases disk space, but several important actions are performed with a compact and repair procedure.

The compact and repair utility:

- Reclaims disk space and ensures the prevention of database bloat.
- Defragments the blocks of data that make up table pages, improving performance and making efficient use of the read ahead cache.
- Resets AutoNumber fields, ensuring that the next value allocated will be one more than the highest value in the remaining records.
- Regenerates table statistics used by the query optimizer to create query execution strategies.
- Flags all queries, indicating a recompile the next time the query is executed.

These actions can play a big part in keeping your database streamlined and efficient. You can set your database to automatically compact and repair each time you close it. To do this, follow these steps:

1. Click the Office Icon in the upper left-hand corner of the Ribbon.
2. Click the Access Options button. This activates the Access Options dialog box.
3. Once in the Access Options dialog box, select Current Database to display the configuration settings for the current database. Here you see the Compact on Close setting.
4. Place a check next to Compact on Close and click the OK button to confirm the change.

Avoiding Interruption of Service While Writing to Your Database

The most common cause of corruption is interruption while writing to your database. Interrupted write processes can lead to a host of issues, from incomplete table definitions to lost indexes. In that vein, be sure to avoid any type of abnormal or abrupt termination of Access. Following these general guidelines will help you avoid corruption due to interrupted processes:

- Always wait until all queries, macros, and procedures have completed execution before closing Access.
- Avoid using the Task Manager to shut down Access.
- Never place your Access database on a file server that is regularly shut down or rebooted.
- Avoid power loss while working with your database. If your database is on a file server, make sure the server has protection against power surges or power outages.

Never Working with a Database from Removable Media

When you work with an Access database, additional disk space is needed for the .laccdb file and for the normal database bloat that comes with using Access. If you open an Access database on removable media such as a memory stick or a ZIP disk, you run the risk of corruption due to disk space errors. Generally, a good practice is to copy the database to your hard drive, work with the database there, and then copy it back to the removable media when you are done.

Getting Help in Access

As you experiment with new functions and tools in Access, you may sometimes need a little help or a simple push in the right direction. The first place you should look is Access's Help system. It is true that the Help system in Access has its flaws. To a new user, the Access Help system may seem like a clunky add-in that returns a perplexing list of topics that has nothing to do with the original search topic. The truth is, however, that once you learn how to use the Access Help system effectively, it is often the fastest and easiest way to get help on a topic. The following sections contain some tips that will help you get the most out of Access's help system.

Location Matters When Asking for Help

You may remember the Help system in Access 97 being a lot more user-friendly and more effective than newer versions of Access. Rest assured that you are not just imagining it. The fact is that the Microsoft did fundamentally change the mechanics of the Access Help system. In Access 97, when you entered a key word into the search index, Access did a kind of global search, throwing your search criteria against all the topics within Access.

In the later versions of Access, however, there are actually two Help systems: one providing help on Access features and another on VBA programming topics. Instead of doing a global search with your criteria, Access throws your search criteria only against the Help system relevant to your current location. This means that the help you get is determined by the area of Access in which you are working. In that vein, if you require help on a topic that involves VBA programming, you will need to be in the VBA Editor while performing your search. On the other hand, if you need help on building a query, it's best to be in the query design view. This will ensure that your keyword search is performed on the correct Help system.

Online Help Is Better than Offline Help

When you search for help on a topic, Access checks to see if there is an Internet connection available. If there is, Access returns help results based on online content from Microsoft's site. If no Internet connection is available, Access uses the help files locally stored with Microsoft Office. One way to maximize the help you are getting in Access is to use the online help. Online help is generally better than offline help because the content you find online is often more detailed, and it includes updated information as well as links to other resources not available offline.

Diversifying your Knowledgebase with Online Resources

Familiarize yourself with a handful of Web sites and forums dedicated to Access. These resources can serve as supplemental help, not only for basic Access topics, but for also giving you situation-specific tips and tricks. Table C-2 gives some sites that should get you started. These sites are free to use and are particularly helpful when you need an extra push in the right direction.

Access topics and general help	www.allenbrowne.com www.mvps.org/access/
Access tutorials and samples	www.fontstuff.com www.datapigtechnologies.com
Access discussion groups and forums	www.microsoft.com/office/community/en-us/default.mspx www.utteraccess.com

Data Analyst's Function Reference

The list outlined here is designed to provide a solid reference to the functions that are most relevant to the realm of data analysis. Several of these functions have been covered in detail throughout the chapters in this book.

TIP You can learn more about the functions that have not been covered here by using the Access help system.

Abs

Abs is a math function that returns a value that represents the absolute value of the number. That is, the magnitude of the number without the positive or negative sign. For example, Abs(-5) would return 5.

Syntax

Abs(number)

Argument

Number (required)

This is the numeric expression you are evaluating. In a query environment, you can use the name of a field to specify that you are evaluating all the row values of that field.

Asc

Asc is a conversion function used to convert a string to its Ascii code. For example, Asc("A") would return 65 because 65 is the Ascii code for the uppercase letter A. If you pass a whole word to the Asc function, it will only return the Ascii code for the first letter of the word.

Syntax

`Asc(String)`

Argument

`String` (required)	This is the string you are evaluating. If the string you are passing to the function contains no characters, the function will fail and produce a runtime error.

Atn

Atn is a math function that allows you to calculate the arctangent of a number.

Syntax

`Atn(number)`

Argument

Number (required)	This is the numeric expression you are evaluating.

Choose

The Choose function is a program flow function that allows you to return a value from a list of choices based on a given position. For instance: Choose(3, "Microsoft", "Access", "Data", "Analysis") would return "Data" This is because word "Data" is in the third position in the list of values.

Syntax

`Choose(PositionNumber, List of Values Separated by Commas)`

Arguments

`PositionNumber` (required)	This is the numeric expression or field that results in a value between 1 and the number of available choices. If this argument's value is less than 1 or greater than the number of choices in the function, a Null value will be returned.
List of Values Separated by Commas (required)	This is a variant expression that contains a list of one or more values.

Chr

Chr is a conversion function used to convert an Ascii code to a string. For example, Chr(65) would return "A".

Syntax

Chr(Number)

Arguments

Number **(required)**	This is the number value that represents an Ascii character code. If the number you are passing to the function is not a valid Ascii character code, the function will fail and produce a runtime error.

Cos

The Cos function is a math function that allows you to calculate the cosine of an angle.

Syntax

Cos(number)

Arguments

Number **(required)**	This is the numeric expression that represents an angle in radians.

Date

The Date function returns today's date based on your PC's current system date. The Date function is key to performing any analysis that involves a time comparison in relation to today's date. There are no required arguments for this function; to use it, simply enter: Date().

DateAdd

The DateAdd function returns a date to which a specified interval has been added. In other words, the DateAdd function allows you calculate a date by adding 30 days to it, subtracting 3 weeks from it, adding 4 months to it, or so on.
For example:

- DateAdd("ww",1,#11/30/2004#): adds 1 week, returning 12/7/2004
- DateAdd("m",2,#11/30/2004#): adds 2 months, returning 1/30/2005
- DateAdd("yyyy",-1,#11/30/2004#): subtracts 1 year, returning 11/30/2003

Table continued on following page

Syntax

```
DateAdd(Interval, Number, Date)
```

Arguments

`Interval` (required)	This is the interval of time that you want to use. The intervals available are:

- "yyyy"- Year
- "q" - Quarter
- "m" - Month
- "y" - Day of year
- "d" - Day
- "w" - Weekday
- "ww" - Week
- "h" - Hour
- "n" - Minute
- "s" - Second

`Number` (required)	This is the number of intervals to add. A positive number will return a date in the future, while a negative number will return a date in the past.
`Date` (required)	This is the date value with which you are working. In a query environment, you can use the name of a field to specify that you are evaluating all the row values of that field.

DateDiff

The DateDiff function returns the difference between two dates based on a specified time interval. For example, DateDiff('yyyy', #5/16/1972#, #5/16/2005#) returns 33 because there is a difference of 33 years between the two dates.

Syntax

```
DateDiff(Interval, Date1, Date2, FirstDayOfTheWeek,
FirstWeekOfTheYear)
```

Arguments

Interval (required)	This is the interval of time that you want to use. The intervals available are:

- yyyy" - Year
- "q" - Quarter

- "m" - Month
- "y" - Day of year
- "d" - Day
- "w" - Weekday
- "ww" - Week
- "h" - Hour
- "n" - Minute
- "s" - Second

Date1 (required)	This is one of the two dates you want to calculate the difference between. In a query environment, you can use the name of a field to specify that you are evaluating all the row values of that field.
Date2 (required)	This is one of the two dates you want to calculate the difference between. In a query environment, you can use the name of a field to specify that you are evaluating all the row values of that field.
FirstDayOfTheWeek (optional)	This specifies which day you want to count as the first day of the week. Enter 1 in this argument to make the first day Sunday, 2 for Monday, 3 for Tuesday, and so on. If this argument is omitted, the first day is a Sunday by default.
FirstWeekOfTheYear (optional)	This specifies the first week of the year. In most cases, you would omit this argument. This uses the first week that includes January 1 as the default. However, you can alter this setting by using one of the following values.

- 0 - Use the NLS(National Language Support) API setting.
- 1 - Use the first week that includes January 1.
- 2 - Use the first week that has at least four days.
- 3 - Use the first week that has seven days.

DatePart

The DatePart function allows you to evaluate a date and return a specific interval of time represented in that date. For example, DatePart("q",#6/4/2004#) returns 2 (as in second quarter), the quarter represented in that date.

Syntax

```
DatePart(Interval, ValidDate, FirstDayOfTheWeek,
FirstWeekOfTheYear)
```

Arguments

`Interval` (required)	This is the interval of time want to use. The intervals available are: ▪ "yyyy" - Year ▪ "q" - Quarter ▪ "m" - Month ▪ "y" - Day of year ▪ "d" - Day ▪ "w" - Weekday ▪ "ww" - Week ▪ "h" - Hour ▪ "n" - Minute ▪ "s" - Second
`ValidDate` (required)	This is the date value with which you are working. In a query environment, you can use the name of a field to specify that you are evaluating all the row values of that field.
`FirstDayOfTheWeek` (optional)	This specifies which day you want to count as the first day of the week. Enter 1 in this argument to make the first day Sunday, 2 for Monday, 3 for Tuesday, and so on. If this argument is omitted, the first day is a Sunday by default.
`FirstWeekOfTheYear` (optional)	This specifies the first week of the year. In most cases, you would omit this argument. This uses the first week that includes January 1 as the default. However, you

can alter this setting by using one of the
following values.

- 0 - Use the NLS API setting.

- 1 - Use the first week that includes January 1.

- 2 - Use the first week that has at least four days.

- 3 - Use the first week that has seven days.

DateSerial

The DateSerial function allows you to construct a date value by combining given
year, month, and day components. This function is perfect for converting disparate
values that, together represent a date, into an actual date. For example,
DateSerial(2004, 4, 3) would return April 3, 2004.

Syntax

`DateSerial(Year, Month, Day)`

Arguments

Year (required)   Any number or numeric expression from
                                   100 to 9999

Month (required)   Any number or numeric expression

Day (required)   Any number or numeric expression

DateValue

The DateValue function allows you to convert any string or expression that
represents a valid date, time, or both into a date value. For Example,
DateValue("October 31, 2004") would return 10/31/2004.

Syntax

`DateValue(Expression)`

Arguments

Expression (required)   Any string or valid expression that can
                                   represent a valid date, time, or both

Day

Day is a conversion function that converts a valid date to a number from 1 to 31, representing the day of the month for a given date. For example, Day(#5/16/1972#) would return 16.

Syntax

Day(ValidDate)

Arguments

ValidDate (required)

This is any value that can represent a valid date. In a query environment, you can use the name of a field to specify that you are evaluating all the row values of that field.

DDB

DDB is a financial function that calculates the depreciation of an asset for a specific period using the double-declining balance method or another specified method.

Syntax

DDB(Cost, Salvage, Life, Period, Factor)

Arguments

Cost (required)

This is the initial cost of the asset; must be a positive number.

Salvage (required)

This is the value of the asset at the end of its useful life; must be a positive number.

Life (required)

This is the length of the useful life of the asset.

Period (required)

This is the period for which asset depreciation is calculated.

Factor (optional)

This is the rate at which the balance declines. The default setting for this argument is the double-declining method (a factor of 2).

Domain Aggregate Functions

Domain aggregate functions allow you to extract and aggregate statistical information from an entire dataset (a domain). These functions differ from an Aggregate query in that an Aggregate query will group data before evaluating the values, while a domain aggregate function will evaluate the values for the entire dataset. There are 12 different domain aggregate functions, but they all have the same Syntax.

Syntax

`("Field Name]","[Dataset Name]", "[Criteria]")`

Arguments

`Field Name` (required)	This expression identifies the field containing the data with which you are working. This argument must be in quotes.
`Dataset Name` (required)	This expression identifies the table or query you are working with; also known as the domain. This argument must be in quotes.
`Criteria` (optional)	This expression is used to restrict the range of data on which the domain aggregate function is performed. If omitted, the domain aggregate function is performed against the entire dataset. This argument must be in quotes.

Additional Remarks

The 12 different domain aggregate functions are:

`DSum`	The DSum function returns the total sum value of a specified field in the domain. *DSum("[Sales_Amount]", "[TransactionMaster]")* would give you the total sum of sales amount in the TransactionMaster table.
`DAvg`	The DAvg function returns the average value of a specified field in the domain. *DAvg("[Sales_Amount]", "[TransactionMaster]")* would give you the average sales amount in the TransactionMaster table.

Table continued on following page

DCount	The DCount function returns the total number of records in the domain. *DCount("*",* *"[TransactionMaster]")* would give you the total number of records in the TransactionMaster table.
DLookup	The DLookup function returns the first value of a specified field that matches the criteria you define within the DLookup function. If you don't supply criteria, the DLookup function returns a random value in the domain. DLookup functions are particularly useful when you need to retrieve a value from an outside dataset. *DLookUp("[Last_Name]",* *"[Employee_* *Master]",* *"[Employee_Number]=* *'42620'")* would return the value in the Last_Name field of the record where the Employee_Number is '42620'.
DMin, DMax	The DMin and DMax would return the minimum and maximum values in the domain respectively. *DMin("[Sales_Amount]",* *"[TransactionMaster]")* would return the lowest sales amount in the Transactionmaster, while *DMin("[Sales_Amount]",* *"[TransactionMaster]")* would return the highest.
DFirst, DLast	The DFirst and DLast would return the first and last values in the domain respectively. *DFirst("[Sales_Amount]",* *"[TransactionMaster]")* would return the first sales amount in the Transactionmaster while *DLast("[Sales_Amount]",* *"[TransactionMaster]")* would return the last.
DStdev, Dstdevp, DVar, Dvarp	You can use the DStdev and the DStdevp to return the standard deviation across a population sample and a population, respectively. The Dvar and the Dvarp similarly returns the variance across a population sample and a population, respectively.

Exp

Exp is a math function that raises the base of natural logarithm's (2.718282) number to a power you specify.

Syntax

Exp(Number)

Arguments

Number (required)	This is the numeric expression used as the power to raise 2.718282.

FormatCurrency

FormatCurrency is a conversion function that converts an expression to a currency using the currency symbol defined by your computer's regional settings.

Syntax

FormatCurrency(Number,TrailingDigits,LeadingDigits, NegativeParens,Group)

Arguments

Number (required)	This is the number value you want to convert. In a query environment, you can use the name of a field to specify that you are evaluating all the row values of that field.
TrailingDigits (optional)	This is the number of digits to the right of the decimal you want displayed.
LeadingDigits (optional)	This indicates whether a leading zero is displayed for fractional values. The settings for this argument are -1 for True, 0 for False, or -2 to use the computer's regional/default settings.
NegativeParens (optional)	This specifies if negative values should be wrapped in parentheses. The settings for this argument are -1 for True, 0 for False, or -2 to use the computer's regional settings FormatNumber.
Group (optional)	This indicates whether or not numbers are grouped using the group delimiter specified in the computer's regional settings. The settings for this argument are -1 for True, 0 for False, or -2 to use the computer's regional settings.

FormatDateTime

The FormatDateTime function is a conversion function that converts an expression to a date or time.

Syntax

```
FormatDateTime(Date,NamedFormat)
```

Arguments

`Date` (required)

This is the date/time expression you want to convert. In a query environment, you can use the name of a field to specify that you are evaluating all the row values of that field.

`NamedFormat` (optional)

This is the format code specifying the date/time format you would like to use. The settings for this argument are as follows:

- 0 - Display date as a short date and time as a long time.
- 1 - Display a date using the long date format specified in your computer's regional settings.
- 2 - Display a date using the short date format specified in your computer's regional settings.
- 3 - Display a time using the time format specified in your computer's regional settings.
- 4 - Display a time using the 24-hour format (hh:mm).

FormatNumber

FormatNumber is a conversion function that converts a numeric expression to a formatted number.

Syntax

```
FormatNumber(Number,TrailingDigits,LeadingDigits,
NegativeParens,Group)
```

Arguments

Number (required)	This is the number value you want to convert. In a query environment, you can use the name of a field to specify that you are evaluating all the row values of that field.
TrailingDigits (optional)	This is the number of digits to the right of the decimal you want displayed.
LeadingDigits (optional)	This indicates whether a leading zero is displayed for fractional values. The settings for this argument are -1 for True, 0 for False, or -2 to use the computer's regional/default settings.
NegativeParens (optional)	This specifies whether negative values should be wrapped in parentheses. The settings for this argument are -1 for True, 0 for False, or -2 to use the computer's regional settings.
Group (optional)	This indicates whether or not numbers are grouped using the group delimiter specified in the computer's regional settings. The settings for this argument are -1 for True, 0 for False, or -2 to use the computer's regional settings.

FormatPercent

FormatPercent is a conversion function that converts a numeric expression to a formatted percentage with a trailing percent (%) character.

Syntax

```
FormatPercent(Number,TrailingDigits,LeadingDigits,
NegativeParens,Group)
```

Arguments

Number (required)	This is the number value you want to convert. In a query environment, you can use the name of a field to specify that you are evaluating all the row values of that field.

Table continued on following page

TrailingDigits (optional)	This is the number of digits to the right of the decimal you want displayed.
LeadingDigits (optional)	This indicates whether a leading zero is displayed for fractional values. The settings for this argument are 1 for True, 0 for False, or 2 to use the computer's regional settings.
NegativeParens (optional)	This specifies if negative values should be wrapped in parentheses. The settings for this argument are 1 for True, 0 for False, or 2 to use the computer's regional settings.
Group (optional)	This indicates whether or not numbers are grouped using the group delimiter specified in the computer's regional settings. The settings for this argument are 1 for True, 0 for False, or 2 to use the computer's regional settings.

FV

FV is a financial function that allows you to calculate an annuity's future value. An annuity is a series of fixed cash payments normally made against a loan over a period of time.

Syntax

FV(Rate, PaymentPeriods, PaymentAmount, PresentValue, Type)

Arguments

Rate (required)	This is the stated interest rate per period.
PaymentPeriods (required)	This is the total number of payment periods in the annuity.
PaymentAmount (required)	This is the payment amount, usually consisting of principal and interest.
PresentValue (optional)	This is the present value of future payments. If omitted, 0 is assumed.
Type (optional)	This argument specifies when payments are due. A value of 0 means that payments are due at the end of the payment period, while a value of 1 means that payments are due at the beginning of the payment period. If omitted, 0 is assumed.

Hour

Hour is a conversion function that converts a valid time to a number from 0 to 23, representing the hour of the day. For example, Hour(#9:30:00 PM#) would return 21.

Syntax

Hour(ValidTime)

Arguments

ValidTime (required)	This is any combination of values that can represent valid time. In a query environment, you can use the name of a field to specify that you are evaluating all the row values of that field.

IIf

IIf is a program flow function allows you to create an If ... Then ... Else statement, returning one value if a condition evaluates to true, and another value if it evaluates to false.

Syntax

IIf(Expression, TrueAnswer, FalseAnswer)

Arguments

Expression (required)	This is the expression you want to evaluate.
TrueAnswer (required)	This is the value to return if the expression is true.
FalseAnswer (required)	This is the value to return if the expression is false.

InStr

InStr is a text function that searches for a specified string in another string and returns its position number. For example: InStr("Alexander, Mike","x") would return 4 because the "x" is character number 4 in this string.

Syntax

InStr(Start, SearchString, FindString, Compare)

Table continued on following page

Arguments

Start (optional)	This is the character number to start the search; default is 1.
SearchString (required)	This is the string to be searched.
FindString (required)	This is the string to search for.
Compare (optional)	This specifies the type of string comparison.

Additional Remarks

The Compare argument can have the following values:

-1	Performs a comparison using the setting of the Option Compare statement
0	Performs a binary comparison
1	Performs a textual comparison
2	(Microsoft Access only) Performs a comparison based on information in your database

InStrRev

InStrRev is a text function that searches for a specified string in another string and returns its position number from the end of the string.

Syntax

```
InstrRev(SearchString, FindString, Start, Compare)
```

Arguments

SearchString (required)	This is the string to be searched.
FindString (required)	This is the string to search for.
Start (optional)	This is character number to start the search; default is 1.
Compare (optional)	This specifies the type of string comparison.

Additional Remarks

The Compare argument can have the following values:

-1	Performs a comparison using the setting of the Option Compare statement
0	Performs a binary comparison
1	Performs a textual comparison
2	(Microsoft Access only) Performs a comparison based on information in your database

IPmt

IPmt is a financial function that allows you to calculate the interest paid within a specified period during the life of an annuity. An annuity is a series of fixed cash payments normally made against a loan over a period of time.

Syntax

```
IPmt(Rate, Period, PaymentPeriods, PresentValue, FutureValue,
Type)
```

Arguments

Rate (required)	This is the average interest rate per period.
Period (required)	This is the specified payment period in question.
PaymentPeriods (required)	This is the total number of payment periods in the annuity.
PresentValue (required)	This is the present value of future payments.
FutureValue (optional)	This is the future value or final balance on a loan or an investment upon making the last payment. If omitted, 0 is assumed.
Type (optional)	This argument specifies when payments are due. A value of 0 means that payments are due at the end of the payment period, while a value of 1 means that payments are due at the beginning of the payment period. If omitted, 0 is assumed.

IRR

IRR is a financial function that calculates the internal rate of return based on serial cash flow, payments, and receipts.

Syntax

```
IRR(IncomeValues, Guess)
```

Arguments

IncomeValues (required)	These values make up an array that represents the periodic cash flow values. Within this array, there must be at least one negative number and one positive number.
Guess (optional)	This argument allows you to estimate the percent of total investment that will be returned. If this omitted, 10 percent is used.

IsError

IsError is an inspection function that determines if an expression evaluates as an error. This function returns a True or False answer.

Syntax

IsError(Expression)

Arguments

Expression (required)   This is any value or expression. In a query environment, you can use the name of a field to specify that you are evaluating all the row values of that field.

IsNull

IsNull is an inspection function that determines whether a value contains no valid data. This function returns a True or False answer.

Syntax

IsNull(Expression)

Arguments

Expression (required)   This is any value or expression. In a query environment, you can use the name of a field to specify that you are evaluating all the row values of that field.

IsNumeric

IsNumeric is an inspection function that determines whether an expression evaluates as a numeric value. This function returns a True or False answer.

Syntax

IsNumeric(Expression)

Arguments

Expression (required)   This is any value or expression. In a query environment, you can use the name of a field to specify that you are evaluating all the row values of that field.

LCase

The LCase function converts a string to lowercase letters.

Syntax

`LCase(String)`

Arguments

`String` (required)	This is the string to be converted. In a query environment, you can use the name of a field to specify that you are converting all the row values of that field.

Left

The Left function returns a specified number of characters starting from the left - most character of the string. For example, Left("Nowhere", 3) would return "Now".

Syntax

`Left(String, NumberOfCharacters)`

Arguments

String (required)	This is the string to be evaluated. In a query environment, you can use the name of a field to specify that you are evaluating all the row values of that field.
`NumberofCharacters` (required)	This is the number of characters you want returned. If this argument is greater than or equal to the number of characters in string, the entire string is returned.

Len

The Len function returns a number identifying the number of characters in a given string. This function is quite useful when you need to dynamically determine the length of a string. For instance, Len("Alexander") would return 9.

Syntax

`Len(String or Variable)`

Arguments

`String or Variable` (required)	This is the string or variable to be evaluated. In a query environment, you can use the name of a field to specify that you are evaluating all the row values of that field.

Log

The Log function is a math function that calculates the natural logarithm of a number.

Syntax

`Log(Number)`

Arguments

`Number` (required)

This is the numeric expression that is to be evaluated; must be greater than zero.

Mid

The Mid function returns a specified number of characters starting from a specified character position. The required Syntax for the Mid Function are: The text you are evaluating, the starting position, and the number of characters you want returned. For example: Mid("Lonely", 2, 3) captures three characters starting from character number 2 in the string, returning "one" .

Syntax

`Mid(String, StartPosition, NumberOfCharacters)`

Arguments

`String` (required)

This is the string to be evaluated. In a query environment, you can use the name of a field to specify that you are evaluating all the row values of that field.

`StartPosition` (required)

This is the position number of the character you want to start your capture.

`NumberofCharacters` (required)

This is the number of characters you want returned. If this argument is greater than or equal to the number of characters in string, the entire string is returned.

Minute

The Minute function converts a valid time to a number from 0 to 59, representing the minute of the hour. For example, Minute(#9:30:00 PM#) would return 30.

Syntax

`Minute(ValidTime)`

Arguments

ValidTime (required) | This is any combination of values that can represent valid time. In a query environment, you can use the name of a field to specify that you are evaluating all the row values of that field

MIRR

MIRR is a financial function that calculates the internal rate of return based on serial cash flow, payments, and receipts financed at different rates.

Syntax

```
MIRR(IncomeValues, FinanceRate, ReinvestRate)
```

Arguments

IncomeValues (required) | These values make up an array that represents the periodic cash flow values. Within this array, there must be at least one negative number and one positive number.

FinanceRate (required) | This is the interest rate paid as the cost of investing. The values of this argument must be represented as decimal values.

ReinvestRate (required) | This is the interest rate received on gains from cash reinvestment. The values of this argument must be represented as decimal values.

Month

The Month function converts a valid date to a number from 1 to 12, representing the month for a given date. For example, Month(#5/16/1972#) would return 5.

Syntax

```
Month(ValidDate)
```

Arguments

ValidDate (required) | This is any value that can represent a valid date. In a query environment, you can use the name of a field to specify that you are evaluating all the row values of that field.

MonthName

The MonthName function converts a numeric month designation (1 to 12) to a month name. For instance, MonthName(8) would return August. Values less than 1 or greater than 12 will cause an error.

Syntax

`MonthName(NumericMonth, Abbreviated)`

Arguments

`NumericMonth` (required)

This is a number from 1 to 12 that represents a month. 1 represents January, 2 represents February, and so on.

`Abbreviated` (optional)

This specifies whether the month is abbreviated or not. If this argument is omitted, the month is not abbreviated. Enter 1 to return abbreviated months.

Now

The Now function returns today's date and time based on your PC's current system date and time. There are no required arguments for this function; to use it, simply enter Now().

NPer

The NPer function is a financial function that specifies the number of periods for an annuity based on periodic, fixed payments at a fixed interest rate. An annuity is a series of fixed cash payments normally made against a loan over a period of time.

Syntax

`NPer(Rate, PaymentAmount, PresentValue, FutureValue, Type)`

Arguments

`Rate` (required)

This is the stated interest rate per period.

`PaymentAmount` (required)

This is the payment amount, usually consisting of principal and interest.

`PresentValue` (required)

This is the present value of future payments and receipts.

`FutureValue` (optional)	This is the future value or final balance on a loan or an investment upon making the last payment. If omitted, 0 is assumed.
`Type` (optional)	This argument specifies when payments are due. A value of 0 means that payments are due at the end of the payment period, while a value of 1 means that payments are due at the beginning of the payment period. If omitted, 0 is assumed.

NPV

NPV is a financial function that calculates the net present value or the current value of a future series of payments and receipts based on serial cash flow, payments, receipts, and a discount rate.

Syntax

`NPV(DiscountRate, IncomeValues)`

Arguments

`DiscountRate` (required)	This is the discount rate received over the length of the period. The values of this argument must be represented as decimal values.
`IncomeValues` (required)	These values make up an array that represents the periodic cash flow values. Within this array, there must be at least one negative number and one positive number.

NZ

The NZ function allows you to tell Access to recognize Null values as another value, preventing your null values from propagating through an expression.

Syntax

`NZ(Variant, ValueIfNull)`

Arguments

`Variant` (required)	This is the data you are working with.
`ValueIfNull` (required in the query environment)	This is the value you want returned if the Variant is null.

Partition

Partition is a database function that identifies the particular range in which a number falls and returns a string describing that range. This function is useful when you need to create a quick and easy frequency distribution.

Syntax

`Partition(Number, Range Start, Range Stop, Interval)`

Arguments

`Number` (required)	This is the number you are evaluating. In a query environment, you typically use the name of a field to specify that you are evaluating all the row values of that field.
`Range Start` (required)	This is a whole number that is to be the start of the overall range of numbers. Note that this number cannot be less than zero.
`Range Stop` (required)	This is a whole number that is to be the end of the overall range of numbers. Note that this number cannot be equal to or less than the Range Start.
`Interval` (required)	This is a whole number that is to be the span of each range in the series from Range Start to Range Stop. Note that this number cannot be less than one.

Pmt

Pmt is a financial function that calculates the payment for an annuity based on periodic, fixed payments at a fixed interest rate. An annuity is a series of fixed cash payments normally made against a loan over a period of time.

Syntax

`Pmt(Rate, PaymentPeriods, PresentValue, FutureValue, Type)`

Arguments

`Rate` (required)	This is the average interest rate per period.
`PaymentPeriods` (required)	This is the total number of payment periods in the annuity.
`PresentValue` (required)	This is the present value of future payments and receipts.

FutureValue (optional)	This is the future value or final balance on a loan or an investment upon making the last payment. If omitted, 0 is assumed.
Type (optional)	This argument specifies when payments are due. A value of 0 means that payments are due at the end of the payment period, while a value of 1 means that payments are due at the beginning of the payment period. If omitted, 0 is assumed.

PPmt

PPmt is a financial function that allows you to calculate the principal payment for a specified period during the life of an annuity. An annuity is a series of fixed cash payments normally made against a loan over a period of time.

Syntax

PPmt(Rate, Period, PaymentPeriods, PresentValue, FutureValue, Type)

Arguments

Rate (required)	This is the average interest rate per period.
Period (required)	This is the specified payment period in question.
PaymentPeriods (required)	This is the total number of payment periods in the annuity.
PresentValue (required)	This is the present value of future payments and receipts.
FutureValue (optional)	This is the future value or final balance on a loan or an investment upon making the last payment. If omitted, 0 is assumed.
Type (optional)	This argument specifies when payments are due. A value of 0 means that payments are due at the end of the payment period, while a value of 1 means that payments are due at the beginning of the payment period. If omitted, 0 is assumed.

PV

PV is a financial function that allows you to calculate an annuity's present value. An annuity is a series of fixed cash payments normally made against a loan over a period of time.

Syntax

`PV(Rate, PaymentPeriods, PaymentAmount, FutureValue, Type)`

Arguments

`Rate` (required)	This is the average interest rate per period.
`PaymentPeriods` (required)	This is the total number of payment periods in the annuity.
`PaymentAmount` (required)	This is the payment amount, usually consisting of principal and interest.
`FutureValue` (optional)	This is the future value or final balance on a loan or an investment upon making the last payment. If omitted, 0 is assumed.
`Type` (optional)	This argument specifies when payments are due. A value of 0 means that payments are due at the end of the payment period, while a value of 1 means that payments are due at the beginning of the payment period. If omitted, 0 is assumed.

Rate

Rate is a financial function that allows you to calculate the interest rate per period for an annuity. An annuity is a series of fixed cash payments normally made against a loan over a period of time.

Syntax

`Rate(Periods, PaymentAmount, PresentValue, FutureValue, Type, Guess)`

Arguments

`Periods` (required)	This is the total number of payment periods in the annuity.
`PaymentAmount` (required)	This is the payment amount, usually consisting of principal and interest.
`PresentValue` (required)	This is the present value of future payments and receipts.

FutureValue (optional)	This is the future value or final balance on a loan or an investment upon making the last payment. If omitted, 0 is assumed.
Type (optional)	This argument specifies when payments are due. A value of 0 means that payments are due at the end of the payment period, while a value of 1 means that payments are due at the beginning of the payment period. If omitted, 0 is assumed.
Guess (optional)	This argument allows you to estimate the percent of total investment that will be returned. If this omitted, 10 percent is used.

Replace

Replace allows you to replace a specified substring with another substring. This function has the same effect as the "Find and Replace" functionality. For example, Replace("Pear", "P", "B") would return "Bear".

Syntax

Replace(String, Find, Replace, Start, Count, Compare)

Arguments

String (required)	The full string you are evaluating. In a query environment, you can use the name of a field to specify that you are evaluating all the row values of that field.
Find (required)	The substring you need to find and replace.
Replace (required)	The substring used as the replacement.
Start (optional)	The position within substring to begin the search; default is 1.
Count (optional)	Number of occurrences to replace; default is all occurrences.
Compare (optional)	The kind of comparison to use.

Additional Remarks

The Compare argument can have the following values:

-1	Performs a comparison using the setting of the Option Compare statement.

0	Performs a binary comparison
1	Performs a textual comparison
2	Microsoft Access only. Performs a comparison based on information in your database.

Right

The Right function returns a specified number of characters starting from the right most character of the string. For example, Left("Nowhere", 4) would return "here".

Syntax

```
Right(String, NumberOfCharacters)
```

Arguments

String (required)	This is the string to be evaluated. In a query environment, you can use the name of a field to specify that you are evaluating all the row values of that field.
NumberofCharacters (required)	This is the number of characters you want returned. If this argument is greater than or equal to the number of characters in string, the entire string is returned.

Rnd

Rnd is a math function that generates and returns a random number that is greater than or equal to 0 but less than 1.

Syntax

```
Rnd(number)
```

Arguments

Number (optional)	This numeric expression determines how the random number is generated.

Additional Remarks

If the Number argument is omitted from the function	The next random number in the sequence is generated.

If the Number argument is less than zero	The same number is generated every time.
If the Number argument is greater than zero	The next random number in the sequence is generated.
If the Number argument equals zero	The most recently generated number is returned.

Round

Round is a math function that allows you to round a number to a specified number of decimal places. For example, Round(456.7276) returns 457.

Syntax

```
Round(Number, DecimalPlaces)
```

Arguments

| `Number` (required) | This is the numeric expression you want to evaluate. In a query environment, you typically use the name of a field to specify that you are evaluating all the row values of that field. |
| `DecimalPlaces` (optional) | This is the number of places to the right of the decimal included in the rounding. If omitted, the Round function returns an integer with zero decimal places. |

Second

The Second function converts a valid time to a number from 0 to 59, representing the seconds of the minute. For example, Second(#9:00:35 PM#) would return 35.

Syntax

```
Second(ValidTime)
```

Arguments

| `ValidTime` (required) | This is any combination of values that can represent valid time. In a query environment, you can use the name of a field to specify that you are evaluating all the row values of that field. |

Sgn

Sgn is a math function that returns an integer code associated with the sign of a given number. If the given number is less than zero (has a negative designation), the Sgn function returns -1. If the given number equals zero, the Sgn function returns 0. If the given number is greater than zero (has a positive designation), the Sgn function returns 1.

Syntax

`Sgn(number)`

Arguments

`Number` (required)   This is the numeric expression you are evaluating.

Sin

Sin is a math function that allows you to calculate the sine of an angle.

Syntax

`Sin(Number)`

Arguments

`Number` (required)   This is any numeric expression that expresses an angle in radians.

SLN

SLN is a financial function that calculates the straight-line depreciation of an asset for one period.

Syntax

`SLN(Cost, Salvage, Life)`

Arguments

`Cost` (required)   This is the initial cost of the asset; must be a positive number.

`Salvage` (required)   This is the value of the asset at the end of its useful life; must be a positive number.

`Life` (required)   This is the length of the useful life of the asset.

Space

The Space function allows you to create a string with a specified number of spaces to a string. This function comes in handy when you need to clear data in fixed-length strings. For example, you can use the Space function within an expression such as *Space(5) & "Access"*. This would change the string "Access" to " Access" .

Syntax

Space(Number)

Arguments

Number (required)   This is the number of spaces to include in the string.

SQL Aggregate Functions

SQL aggregate functions are the most commonly used functions in Access. These functions perform either mathematical calculations or value evaluations against a given expression. These functions are typically used in a query environment where the Expression argument refers to a field in a table where you are evaluating all the row values of that field.

Syntax

Sum(Expression)   Sum calculates the total value of the all the records in the designated field or grouping. This function is typically used with the following data types: AutoNumber, Currency, Date/Time, and Number.

Avg(Expression)   Avg calculates the Average of all the records in the designated field or grouping. This function is typically used with the following data types: AutoNumber, Currency, Date/Time, and Number.

Count(Expression)   Count simply counts the number of entries within the designated field or grouping. This function works with all data types.

StDev(Expression)   StDev calculates the standard deviation across all records within the designated field or grouping. This function will only work with the following data types: AutoNumber, Currency, Date/Time, and Number.

Table continued on following page

`Var(Expression)`	Var calculates the amount by which all the values within the designated field or grouping vary from the average value of the group. This function will only work with the following data types: AutoNumber, Currency, Date/Time, and Number.
`Min(Expression)`	Min returns the value of the record with the lowest value in the in the designated field or grouping. This function will only work with the following data types: AutoNumber, Currency, Date/Time, Number, and Text.
`Max(Expression)`	Max returns the value of the record with the highest value in the in the designated field or grouping. This function will only work with the following data types: AutoNumber, Currency, Date/Time, Number, and Text.
`First(Expression)`	First returns the value of the first record in the designated field or grouping. This function works with all data types.
`Last(Expression)`	Last returns the value of the last record in the designated field or grouping. This function works with all data types.

Sqr

Sqr is a math function that calculates the square root of a given number.

Syntax

`Sqr(Number)`

Arguments

`Number` (required)	This is the numeric expression you are evaluating.

Str

Str is a conversion function that converts a numeric value into a string representation of the number. For instance, Str(2304) would return " 2304". Note that positive numbers converted with Str always have a leading space to represent the positive sign. Negative numbers have a negative sign as the leading character.

Syntax

`Str(Number)`

Arguments

`Number` (required)	This is the number you want to convert to a string. In a query environment, you can use the name of a field to specify that you are evaluating all the row values of that field.

StrConv

The StrConv function allows you to convert a string to a specified conversion setting such as uppercase, lowercase, or proper case. For example, StrConv("my text",3) would be converted to proper case, reading "My Text".

Syntax

`StrConv(String, ConversionType, LCID)`

Arguments

`String` (required)	This is the string to be converted. In a query environment, you can use the name of a field to specify that you are converting all the row values of that field.
`ConversionType` (required)	The conversion type specifies how to convert the string. The following constants identify the conversion type. ■ 1 - Converts the string to uppercase characters. ■ 2 - Converts the string to lowercase characters. ■ 3 - Converts the first letter of every word in string to uppercase. ■ 64 - Converts the string to Unicode using the default system code page. ■ 128 - Converts the string from Unicode to the default system code page.
`LCID` (optional)	This is the LocaleID you want to use. The system LocaleID is the default.

String

The String function allows you to return a character string of a certain length. For example, String(4, "0") would return "0000".

Syntax

String(LengthOfString, StringCharacter)

Arguments

LengthOfString (required)

This is the number of times you want to repeat the StringCharacter.

StringCharacter (required)

This is the character that will make up your string. If you enter a series of characters, only the first character will be used.

StrReverse

The StrReverse function returns an expression in reverse order. For instance, StrReverse("ten") returns "net". This works with numbers too; StrReverse(5432) returns 2345.

Syntax

StrReverse(Expression)

Arguments

Expression (required)

This is the expression that contains the characters you want reversed.

Switch

Switch is a program flow function that allows you to evaluate a list of expressions and return the value associated with the expression determined to be true. To use the Switch function, you must provide a minimum of one expression and one value.

Syntax

Switch(Expression, Value)

Arguments

Expression (required)

This is the expression you want to evaluate.

Value (required)

This is the value to return if the expression is true.

Additional Remarks

To evaluate multiple expressions, simply add another Expression and Value to the function. For example: Switch(Expression1, Value 1, Expression2, Value2, Expression3, Value3).

When the Switch function is executed, each expression is evaluated. If an expression evaluates to true, the value that follows that expression is returned. If more than one expression is true, the value for the first true expression is returned.

SYD

SYD is a financial function that calculates the sum-of-years' digits depreciation of an asset for a specified period.

Syntax

`SYD(Cost, Salvage, Life, Period)`

Arguments

`Cost` (required)	This is the initial cost of the asset; must be a positive number.
`Salvage` (required)	This is the value of the asset at the end of its useful life; must be a positive number.
`Life` (required)	This is the length of the useful life of the asset.
`Period` (required)	This is the period for which asset depreciation is calculated.

Tan

Tan is a math function that allows you to calculate the tangent of an angle.

Syntax

`Tan(number)`

Arguments

`Number` (required)	This is any numeric expression that expresses an angle in radians.

Time

The Time function returns today's time based on your PC's current system time. This function is ideal for time stamping transactions. There are no required arguments for this function; to use it, simply enter: Time().

TimeSerial

The TimeSerial function essentially builds a time value based on the given hour, minute, and second components. Keep in mind that this function works on a 24-hour clock, so the expression TimeSerial(18,30,0) would return 6:30:00 PM. This function is perfect for converting disparate strings that represent a time when combined, into an actual time.

Syntax

```
TimeSerial(Hour, Minute, Second)
```

Arguments

`Hour` (required)	This is any number or numeric expression that has a value between 0 and 23, inclusive. In a query environment, you can use the name of a field to specify that you are evaluating all the row values of that field; this is true for all the Syntax in this function.
`Minute` (required)	This is any number or numeric expression. If the number specified for this argument exceeds the normal range for minutes in an hour, the function increments the hour as appropriate. For instance, TimeSerial (7,90,00) would return 8:30:00 AM.
`Second` (required)	This is any number or numeric expression. If the number specified for this argument exceeds the normal range for seconds in a minute, the function increments the minutes as appropriate. For instance, TimeSerial(7,10, 75) would return 7:11:15 AM.

TimeValue

The TimeValue function converts a string representation of a time to an actual time value. For instance, TimeValue("4:20:37 PM") would return 4:20:37 PM. The function also works on a 24-hour clock.

Syntax

TimeValue(String)

Arguments

String (required)

This is any string or expression that represents a time ranging from 0:00:00 and 23:59:59. The string can be either a 12-hour clock entry, or a 24-hour clock entry. In a query environment, you can use the name of a field to specify that you are evaluating all the row values of that field.

Trim, LTrim, RTrim

The Trim function effectively removes both the leading and trailing spaces from a string. The LTrim function removes only the leading spaces, while the RTrim function removes only the trailing spaces. These functions come in handy when cleaning up data received from a mainframe source.

Syntax

Trim(String)LTrim(String)RTrim(String)

Arguments

String (required)

This is the string you are working with. In a query environment, you can use the name of a field to specify that you are evaluating all the row values of that field.

TypeName

TypeName is an inspection function that returns the type information of a variable. For instance, TypeName("Michael") would return "String".

Syntax

TypeName(Variable)

Arguments

Variable (required)

This is the variable you want to evaluate. In a query environment, you can use the name of a field to specify that you are evaluating all the row values of that field.

Table continued on following page

Additional Remarks

The string returned by the `TypeName` function can be any one of the following:

`Object type`	An object whose type is *objecttype*
`Byte`	A byte value
`Integer`	An Integer type
`Long`	A long integer type
`Single`	A single-precision floating-point number
`Double`	A double-precision floating-point number
`Currency`	A currency value
`Decimal`	A decimal value
`Date`	A date value
`String`	A string type
`Boolean`	A boolean value
`Error`	An error value
`Empty`	Variable has not been initialized
`Null`	Variable contains no valid data; a Null value
`Object`	An object
`Unknown`	An object whose type is unknown
`Nothing`	An object variable that does not refer to an object

UCase

The UCase function converts a string to uppercase letters.

Syntax

`UCase(String)`

Arguments

`String` (required)	This is the string to be converted. In a query environment, you can use the name of a field to specify that you are converting all the row values of that field.

Val

Val is a conversion function that extracts the numeric part of a string. For instance, Val("5400 Legacy Drive") would return 5400. One caveat to the Val function is that it stops reading the string as soon as it hits a textual character. Therefore, the number you are extracting needs to be at the beginning of the string.

Syntax

Val(String)

Arguments

String (required)	This is the string you want to evaluate. In a query environment, you can use the name of a field to specify that you are evaluating all the row values of that field.

VarType

VarType is an inspection function that returns the subtype code associated with a variant's character type. For instance, VarType("Michael") would return 8 because this is the subtype code for a string.

Syntax

VarType(Variant)

Arguments

Variant (required)	This is the variant you want to evaluate. In a query environment, you can use the name of a field to specify that you are evaluating all the row values of that field.

Additional Remarks

The following is a list of the subtype codes that the VarType function can return.

0	Empty (uninitialized)
1	Null (no valid data)
2	Integer
3	Long integer
4	Single-precision floating-point number

Table continued on following page

5	Double-precision floating-point number
6	Currency value
7	Date value
8	String
9	Object
10	Error value
11	Boolean value
12	Variant (used only with arrays of variants)
13	Data access object
14	Decimal value
17	Byte value
36	Variants that contain user-defined types
8192	Array

Weekday

The Weekday function returns a number from 1 to 7 representing the day of the week for a given date. 1 represents Sunday, 2 represents Monday, and so on. For example, Weekday (#12/31/1997#) will return 4.

Syntax

```
Weekday(ValidDate,FirstDayOfTheWeek)
```

Arguments

ValidDate (required)	This is any value that can represent a valid date. In a query environment, you can use the name of a field to specify that you are evaluating all the row values of that field.
FirstDayOfTheWeek (optional)	This specifies which day you want to count as the first day of the week. Enter 1 in this argument to make the first day Sunday, 2 for Monday, 3 for Tuesday, and so on. If this argument is omitted, the first day is a Sunday by default.

WeekdayName

The WeekdayName function converts a numeric weekday designation (1 to 7) to a weekday name. For instance, WeekdayName(7) would return Saturday. Values less than 1 or greater than 7 will cause an error.

Syntax

WeekdayName(WeekdayNumber, Abbreviated, FirstDayOfTheWeek)

Arguments

WeekdayNumber (required)	This is a number from 1 to 7 that represents a weekday. 1 represents Sunday, 2 represents Monday, and so on.
Abbreviated (optional)	This specifies whether the weekday is abbreviated or not. If this argument is omitted, the weekday is not abbreviated. Enter 1 for this argument to return abbreviated weekdays.
FirstDayOfTheWeek (optional)	This specifies which day you want to count as the first day of the week. Enter 1 in this argument to make the first day Sunday, 2 for Monday, 3 for Tuesday, and so on. If this argument is omitted, the first day is a Sunday by default.

Year

The Year function returns a whole number representing the year for a given date. For example, Year(#5/16/1972#) would return 1972.

Syntax

Year(ValidDate)

Arguments

ValidDate (required)	This is any value that can represent a valid date. In a query environment, you can use the name of a field to specify that you are evaluating all the row values of that field.

Index

Printed in the United States of America
ED-10-09-12